# Additional Praise for *Borrowed from Your Grandchildren: The Evolution of 100-Year Family Enterprises*

## Advance Praise from business families

*Once again, Dennis Jaffe reveals a treasure trove of stories for families and advisors that demonstrates how generations can benefit from teaching and learning from one another. Dennis shares practical examples and best practices used by family enterprises, including family councils, family offices, and family foundations, strategically designed to move the family, its business and its wealth forward—generation to generation. Whether you are just beginning your journey or have multiple generations in play, this book is filled with insights, ideas and actionable next steps to turn a family enterprise into a family legacy.*

—Dirk Junge
Retired Chairman, Pitcairn

*Owners of family businesses with a desire for multi-generational endurance face a complex and never-ending task to pursue both commercial and familial success. Dennis Jaffe and his team have scoured the world for successful exemplars whose practices have allowed them to surpass normal experience and expectations. This is an exceptionally valuable source of inspiration and guidance for family business owners and advisers who wish to pursue and refine effective multi-generational stewardship.*

—Alexander Scott
4th generation family business owner and director, FBN-International

*When I want authoritative, wise, and knowledgeable insight on family businesses, Professor Jaffe is my one-stop shopping center. The range of both knowledge and wisdom that Jaffe possesses makes him a national treasure.* Borrowed from Your Grandchildren *is a synthesis of this knowledge and wisdom.*

—Mitzi Perdue (Mrs. Frank Perdue)
speaker, business owner, author of *How to Make Your Family Business Last*

*We all need to give Dennis recognition and gratitude for his tremendous research and wisdom around how we can all lead our companies in a way that will leave the world a better place. I believe family business is the foundation of society around the world and is the best way to bring social change for the good due to its multi-generational nature. We all thank you for the work that will be recognized for generations to come and we are forever grateful.*

—Charlie Luck
President/CEO Luck Companies

*A wealth of practical insights for families and their advisors based on success factors distilled from 4th generation and older family businesses. Unique concept of the "generative family" to explain how families re-invent and adapt themselves and their businesses. Over 100 relatable and honest family stories to illustrate and reinforce the various concepts.*

—Yuelin Yang
Deputy Group MD of IMC Industrial Group (and nephew of the founder)

*No one but Dennis and his team have ever interviewed so many successful 100-year family enterprises from all over the world, and distilled their recipe for success in such an engaging and easy to read book! The real-life stories from major business families around the world, combined with the insights and best practices that Dennis brings in this well-structured book, make* Borrowed from Your Grandchildren *an invaluable resource for every family business in the world, be it small or large, 1st gen or 5th gen! I can't wait to get all my future grandchildren a copy of the book for their 18th birthday!*

—Edouard Thijssen
**CEO of Trusted Family, leading online governance platform for family businesses, 5th generation family member**

*Dennis focuses on "generative family enterprises" around the world with common attributes.* Borrowed from Your Grandchildren *is an inspiring book for our Tan family, now with four generations. It is our dream and our goal to evolve into a 100-year "generative" family enterprise. This book gives us great inspiration and references in developing legacy and stewardship of our family and business.*

—Sunny Tan
**EVP, Accessories Group, Luen Thai Holdings Ltd.**

*I have been a great follower of Dennis Jaffe's work over the past 20 years. As a 4th generation family member of a 100+-year-old business, his work has been indispensable to helping our family and many others to navigate the opportunities and challenges of surviving and thriving through five generations of ownership and beyond.* Borrowed from Your Grandchildren *is no different. Dennis clearly defines how other families have survived and thrived in a way that makes it possible for others to follow in their footsteps. I have always believed that to have a successful family business, one must have a good sense of humor and short-term memory, or as in Dennis's words, resilience. It is easy, in a family business, to focus on the business and neglect the family. Still, Dennis's research proves that one must focus on the family returns: Legacy, Social, Human, Financial, Capital. Without success in these areas, the business will not have the solid foundation it needs in the family to attract and retain the top talent required for the business to succeed for the second 100 years. Encouraged by Dennis's work, our family has evolved our thinking, cultivating and caring for the family far more than we ever have before.*

*So much of the family business research provides insights into 1st, 2nd, and 3rd generations; however, not much research has been done for 4th generation businesses and beyond. To have survived and thrived for four generations is remarkable and difficult. It is a fairly isolating experience, as there are so few peers available to share successes and potential pitfalls. Dennis's work provides a clear path and connects those families out there who are on the lonely journey of being a 5th generation family business and can pave the way for those who want to get there.*

—Meghan Juday
**Non-Executive Vice Chair, Ideal Industries**

## Advance Praise from Family Advisors

*As the world continues to become more interconnected and complex, generative families need to evolve and adapt together. Dennis Jaffe has written an informative book for the 21st century. While the core pillars of family values and family constitutions remain the same, this book highlights the importance of building a resilient culture while being able to anticipate unchartered waters and emerge even stronger.*

—Peter K. Scaturro
**former CEO of Citigroup Global Private Bank and former CEO of US Trust Company**

*In this tour de force, Dennis Jaffe debunks the myth that every business family is destined to suffer the fate of "shirtsleeves to shirtsleeves in three generations". Filled with rich and engaging interviews with members of thriving multi-generational families, Jaffe and his research team expertly identify the practical secrets of success of the many families that beat the odds and create long-lasting legacies. This book is destined to become a classic for every family - and family advisors thereto - that aspires to be become a long-lived, flourishing, generative family.*

—Tom McCullough
**Chairman and CEO, Northwood Family Office, Co-Author,** *Wealth of Wisdom: The Top 50 Questions Wealthy Families Ask*

*An amazing resource for multi-generational business families and professionals that advise them. I love the premise of the book. Rather than focusing on all the things that can go wrong, try to learn as much as you can from the families that have already succeeded for more than 100 years. And the stories – hearing them in the words of so many families from around the world – are inspiring. Each family is clearly unique. At the same time, seeing common practices and behaviors that have helped shape so many incredible family legacies is fascinating. I couldn't put the book down!*

—J. Richard Joyner
**President, Tolleson Wealth Management**

*Transgenerational success may be elusive but* Borrowed from Your Grandchildren *shines a light on the fact patterns behind those families who have achieved it. Jaffe's research-based story telling is an approachable and tangible guide for families looking to leverage the lessons learned by those who went before them.*

—Jim Coutré
**Family office and philanthropy professional**

*Discover a treasure trove of insights into what forms the essence of highly enduring and generative century-old family enterprises in yet another groundbreaking research by one of the most renowned and influential family enterprise advisors of our time.*

—Aik-Ping Ng
**Co-Head of Family Office Advisory, Family Governance and Family Enterprise Succession, Asia Pacific, HSBC Private Banking**

*Dennis Jaffe's in-depth, qualitative research on what makes family enterprises pass the test of time offers valuable and actionable insights for families and the advisors that serve them. This is a must read.*

—Arne Boudewyn, PhD
**Head of Institute for Family Culture, Abbot Downing**

*Through decades of experience and painstaking research Jaffe has created the definitive work on multi-generational wealth. In this very approachable book, both families and those who advise them will find insights and practical guidance on how to successfully manage the challenges associated with significant wealth.* Borrowed from Your Grandchildren *is an instant classic and a significant contribution for those of us who work with ultra-affluent families.*

—John Zimmerman
**President, Ascent Private Capital Management of U.S. Bank**

*Dennis Jaffe has outdone even himself. His latest book,* Borrowed from Your Grandchildren, *builds on the exhaustive interviews he has conducted during his ongoing research into what makes a successful "100 year" family-owned business. Now he turns to the families themselves: what makes a successful 100-year family? He lists and explains factors that distinguish these families. I especially liked his inclusive definition of "family". These great families were not families in the sense of being a household; they can be seen as tribes, or clans, with members dispersing but sharing common values and purpose as business and financial partners. Their definition of family is inclusive and expansive, and often extends to include their employees, key advisors, and even their home community. For anyone curious about how great families succeed this collection of family stories is an invaluable resource.*

—Barbara R Hauser
**Editor-in-Chief, International Family Offices Journal**

*A tour de force in research and narrative sociology for any professional advisor wanting to understand the DNA of successful multigenerational business families. Jaffe's work provides a colorful mosaic about how these diverse multigeneration families think about their wealth, their values and responsibilities toward their communities. Documenting in technicolor the evolution and fabric of these successful families, as Jaffe has so well done, will arm any advisor with a unique framework with how to add more value to the families we serve. The chapter on family philanthropy is both simultaneously refreshing and fascinating to read and particularly relevant today as we grapple with affluence in America – Jaffe keenly paints a clear picture, without judgment, of their understanding and moral commitment to the responsibility of giving back to society.*

    *No one has more appreciation and understanding of the complex brew that makes for a successful legacy family than Dennis Jaffe. Granted the privilege of interviewing multiple members of families that have prospered for over 100 years, Jaffe distills the fundamentals of their success. A strong sense of mission and values coupled with robust governance and concerted development of the next generation are the factors that characterize these families.* Borrowed from Your Grandchildren *is an exciting, studiously researched roadmap whether your business is just starting out or has been around for generations. An equally terrific read for those of us who work with these families. Researchers always look for patterns to help make predictions. The patterns Jaffe uncovers are worth revisiting as every generation transitions into leading the family, the business, or both.*

**—Madeline Levine, PhD**
**NYT bestselling author of** ***Ready or Not, The Price of Privilege,*** **and** ***Teach Your Children Well***

*Excellent research and review of over 100 successful family businesses to determine what makes them successful over generations; in a nonjudgmental and nonevaluative manner. Terrific guide for families who wish to beat the "shirtsleeves to shirtsleeves" curse, and professionals who assist in their journey.*

**—Pat Soldano**
**President, Family Enterprise USA**

*Families and business have been the building blocks of successful societies around the world. They have their own cultural construction, attributes, and functionalities. Dennis and his colleagues present a wealth of experiential stories forming a treasure trove of practical examples of what denotes a generative family. The key component is stewardship. These families share with us the importance and skills necessary to be great stewards of family wealth.*

    *Much has been written over the past 30 years about families, business, ownership, and wealth. This book enables the reader to learn through historical, organizational, and practical analysis the key components of successful families of wealth. Indeed, these families not only tell their own stories, but they highlight and underscore the relevance and importance of the research, its findings, and conclusions. A primer for all, a learning tool, a resource for reflection and wisdom.*

**—Laurent Roux**
**founder and CEO of Gallatin Wealth Management, and a partner in the Willow Street Group,**
**a family office and independent regulated Wyoming trust company**

*A tour de force in research and narrative sociology for any professional advisor wanting to understand the DNA of successful multigenerational business families. Jaffe's work provides a colorful mosaic about how these diverse multigeneration families think about their wealth, their values and responsibilities towards their communities. Documenting in technicolor the evolution and fabric of these successful families, as Jaffe has so well done, will arm any advisor with a unique framework with how to add more value to the families we serve. The chapter on family philanthropy is both simultaneously refreshing and fascinating to read and particularly relevant today as we grapple with affluence in America – Jaffe keenly paints a clear picture, without judgment, of their understanding and moral commitment to the responsibility of giving back to society.*

**—Roy P. Kozupsky, Esq., Rimon Law**

# Advance Praise from Family Researchers:

*The definition of opus is "a large-scale creative work"... which aptly describes* Borrowed from Your Grandchildren. *Dennis and his dedicated research team have captured a treasure trove of learnings from "the best of the best". On every page, they have highlighted the resilience, the hardiness, and the entrepreneurial mindset characteristic of these generative business. Importantly, they have included ways that families can take action. This is not only a literary opus... it is a gift to the vast and significant global enterprising family community.*

—Justin B. Craig
**Visiting Professor of Family Enterprise, Kellogg School of Management, Northwestern University**

*A landmark and a long overdue "must book" which all those working and involved with family firms should read to understand what makes family business complex and at times challenging. Introducing an innovative concept "generative family", he firmly establishes a conceptual framework for understanding the multigenerational growth and development of family companies.*

—Toshio Goto
**Research professor, Japan University of Economics**

*Dennis Jaffe has produced a classic work of great insight and relevance not only for managers and consultants of family firms but for all students interested in the breed as it progresses across the generations. In today's climate of opportunistic executives driven by quarterly returns, a long-term orientation of evolving business stewardship represents a far more promising way forward. Dr. Jaffe shows us the path with convincing arguments and superb examples. I cannot recommend this book more highly.*

—Danny Miller
**Research Professor, Co-author of** *Managing for the Long Run: Lessons in Competitive Advantage from Great Family Businesses*

*Dennis Jaffe has written a thoughtful book which is eye-opening, extremely interesting, and helpful. Using his background in sociology, he takes us into the lives of wealthy families and the challenges they face in managing succession. His real-life examples will help families build successful working relationships. Highly recommended!*

—Annette Lareau
**Professor of Sociology, University of Pennsylvania**

*From our earliest days in our own families, we learn from stories, which provide a link to our past and help us develop a vision for our future. In this book, Dennis Jaffe has curated an exceptional collection of stories to deepen knowledge of the complexities, challenges, and triumphs of multi-generational family enterprises.*

—Patricia M. Angus, Esq.
**CEO, Angus Advisory Group LLC; Adjunct Professor and founder, Family Business Program, Faculty Director, Enterprising Families Executive Education, Columbia Business School**

*Creating thriving multi-generational business families is no easy feat. This engaging book gives you practical know-how plus key insights on how to achieve this goal— backed by Dr. Dennis Jaffe interviews with business families globally in addition to his decades of advisory experience working in the field. This is a must read for anyone attempting to take on such a daunting, yet worthy goal.*

—Florence Tsai
**Author of** *Phoenix Rising—Leadership + Innovation in the New Economy and Founder of Centerprising*

# Borrowed
# from Your Grandchildren

# Borrowed
# from Your Grandchildren

## THE EVOLUTION
## OF 100-YEAR FAMILY ENTERPRISES

## Dennis T. Jaffe

**WILEY**

*Library of Congress Cataloging-in-Publication Data is Available:*

ISBN 978-1-119-57380-7 (hardback)
ISBN 978-1-119-57382-1 (ePDF)
ISBN 978-1-119-57381-4 (ePub)

Cover Design: Wiley
Cover Images: World skyline © Antikwar/Getty Images, New York skyline © bananajazz/Getty Images, Human figures image: Wiley

Printed in the United States of America

V10017551_021220

*To Cynthia, my life partner, my three sons and their life partners,
and our growing third generation, who are the future*

# Contents

# Foreword: Rice Paddy to Rice Paddy

Rice paddy to rice paddy, clogs to clogs, shirt sleeves to shirt sleeves—all in three generations. These proverbs are the ways, in various cultures, that the three-generation cycle of families' failures to prosper and their tendency to decay are described. There are many other such proverbs. Each culture I know of has one. In fact, this proverb is the only one I have ever discovered that is universal culturally. I have spent this lifetime, literally since I was four and first heard my mother state the shirtsleeves form of the proverb, asking myself two questions every day. Why should there be this sad outcome for a family? And what might a family do to avoid its dictate and flourish for at least three more generations? While I have worked hard to find answers to these conundrums, until now I had only my experiences, those of a few colleagues, and some thoughtful academic treatises to use to try to form answers.

Now with the advent of Dennis Jaffe's book, *Borrowed from Your Grandchildren: The Evolution of 100-Year Family Enterprises*, I have solid data to affirm that such long-term flourishing by a family is possible. Dennis's in-depth interviews provide the first solid evidence I know of that explains how families that stay together over one hundred years evolve to include their third, fourth, fifth, even in a very few cases their sixth generations, and continue to prosper. Dennis's willingness and that of his co-researchers to go deep into such families' evolutions is a major contribution to our field, a field of professional practice in which we seek to help families thrive, a field in which we seek to help those families, whose vision and mission, their highest intention, is to avoid the proverb's sad prediction. In practical terms, we seek to help them avoid being added to the list of families whose stories end with the outcome the proverb foretells. To say that our families and those we serve will be positively influenced by this book's findings and by the family stories it recounts is to understate the book's significance. In my opinion, this book will profoundly change a family's outcome provided the family members commit to avoiding the proverb as their highest mutual intention and utilize the practices of successful families the book describes to materialize that intention. Should a family do these two things—commit to avoiding the proverb and use the practices outlined in this book—it can substantively increase its odds of flourishing for at least another three generations. Yes, this book is that significant a contribution to a family knowing how to prosper.

This foreword is not a book review. It is rather a way for readers to connect with the salient points in the book they are about to read. It should seek to offer the reader some main points to consider that will carry him or her into its depth. Which among Dennis Jaffe's principal findings might I then bring to your attention? Which of them point toward your deeper appreciation of how your family and any family you advise might succeed in attaining its one hundredth birthday? A one hundredth birthday celebration with nearly all of its possible members still in relation with one another, still deeply committed to the family thriving, and renewing their commitment to one another to working toward helping the family achieve another one hundred years of success?

First, in my experience, a family that seeks to become a one-hundred-year flourishing family and, as Dennis's research suggests, become a generative family almost always intuits that becoming a family of affinity is its deepest spiritual purpose. While this concept has many elements, perhaps the most succinct way of describing this intuition and the ethic it engenders and enables is that its members are committed entirely to the enhancement of the individual journey of happiness of each family member over the entirety of each family member's lifetime toward the goal of the entire family prospering. This is the family's generative dream, and its practices reflect this way of knowing how to help the family system enable family flourishing. Or if you like, the family is committed to every family member's individual boat rising so that the whole family fleet becomes a powerful armada for its long-term flourishing. In this way, the family becomes a family system that can meet and endure all the storms it will face as it seeks to attain its one hundredth birthday and go on being generative by offering the same intuition for its members over the next one hundred years. Families of affinity are much too rare. But Dennis's book proves they exist and can be emulated.

A family of affinity, as Dennis describes, learns from its second generation on that to have future generations continue the family's journey to flourish, become generative, and avoid the proverb's dictate, the family must create family systems that are positively attractive. Why? Because the family knows this is the only path to assure that future generations will be attracted to join. Otherwise the family will disappear. The realization by the second-generation family members that they must create such a positively attracting family system and the actions these family members then take to make this realization actionable are the moments when Dennis's one-hundred-year families are born.

What intuition does a generative family discover and awaken in itself that in turn leads family members to dream of becoming and being a flourishing family? There are many, and the most important is the family's realization that the word "wealth," in the context of the family, means the well-being of each family member and of the whole family, not exclusively the success of the family's financial means. In this one major awakening lies so much of the family's future prosperity, its generativity. With this awareness, the family gradually comes to know that it consists of multiple capitals, the most important of which are qualitative. The family discovers that growing its qualitative capitals, supported by its quantitative capital, *never* led by it, is the key to future family flourishing. It is with this awakening and the awareness that follows that the family becomes generative and truly begins its long-term journey toward its members' and its future-generation members' happiness. The family is now on the path to becoming a family of affinity with all of its rewards for human happiness.

These qualitative capitals include the following:

*Human capital:* Are all family members thriving?

*Intellectual capital:* Is the family a learning system that is constantly growing its individual and communal learning? Are its members sharing what they are learning so the capacity of the whole family to meet the challenges it will face is enhanced?

*Social capital* (or to use Dennis's term, *relational capital*): Is the family capable of making extremely good strategic joint decisions, of governing itself? Is the family working toward cultivating a long-term ability to avoid the following:

> *Internal sequestration:* Death by poor social relations with one another and its insularity (often not leading to fission and death by heat but far more often death by inertia in the family members' relations with one another and death by cold).

> *External sequestration:* A failure to meet attacks on itself from the outside world. Are its social relationships creating fusion? That is, are family relationships leading energetically to positive growth so that 1+1=3? Are those same relationships leading to positive connections through philanthropy with nonfamily members?

*Spiritual capital:* The family's ability to form a common generative vision that seeks to enable the long-term flourishing of each individual and of itself; to do together the seven-generation generative thinking that all successful families learn to do; and to offer a vision and set of practices that are positively attracting to future family members so they will join the family's long-term journey.

As I am sure you can feel and see, it's these four qualitative capitals and their constant positive development and evolution that lie at the core of a successful family journey. They are what Dennis's research found and describes—and what my life experience affirms. The growth of these capitals is the key to these families flourishing. These capitals and their evolution will determine whether a family becomes a family of affinity.

The awakening of the second generation to this deep awareness leads to its creating and evolving a system of joint decision-making, grounded in consistently growing each of these capitals, toward each and all family members' boats rising, that will become the system that is positively attracting to the next two generations of potential family members. This awakening will enable the family to become the thriving generative family Dennis discovers and defines.

Of course, such families continue to grow, develop, and evolve their quantitative capital, their ventures, whether as businesses and/or as financial enterprises. What these families know—and what families falling to the proverb don't seem to discover—is that their efforts to grow their quantitative capital must be designed to support their having the *means* to enable them to grow their far more important long-term capitals, their qualitative capitals. By understanding this relationship between their qualitative and quantitative capitals, these families achieve what I consider the *great knowing* that leads to, and that Dennis's research shows and affirms, their generativity and flourishing, their long-term success, their growth of agile, awake, and aware human beings able to participate in the great cooperative journey to grow a flourishing family while fully becoming whoever they are meant to be as individuals.

I now turn to what these historically successful families of affinity discover as important principles to be integrated into their shared vision. The learnings these principles engender then become practices the families utilize as their journeys unfold.

First, as Nassim Nicholas Talib writes in his book *Antifragile: Things That Gain from Disorder*, they become family systems that are ever more resilient, ever more agile, all toward meeting and overcoming the internal and external sequestration events that will attack their systems. They learn how to grow their systems beyond resilience to immense capacities for endurance against all the odds.

Second, they grow stewards, family champions, and family elder wisdom keepers/way showers who lead the work of growing a family of affinity. They discover among themselves family members who espouse seven-generation visioning and awareness and enable such family members to lead their process. They seek family leaders who understand that the wealth of the family lies in the well-being of each and all of its members, leaders who seek to keep every family member's boat rising.

Third, they construct conservative generative structures that are antifragile. These structures are then able to assist in the families' endurance as they enable joint decision-making systems to develop that permit very long-term strategic planning and the tactical execution of those plans over a long-time horizon. These joint decision-making systems encourage, as Cicero tells the story, old men to plant trees so their grandchildren will have shade. These systems encourage copper beech trees, which need 150 years to mature, to be planted today, as there is no time to waste to get them started growing. Yes, these are systems that encourage metaphors and stories like these two for how families think and encourage their members to consider the family's potential in the long term and generatively imagine future generations flourishing.

Fourth, and perhaps most importantly, these families understand that if their families are to stay the course and have third-, fourth-, fifth-, and sixth-generation members join in, they must enable these future-generation members to decide to join in. What do they know that so few families seem to know, and what does this knowing require? They know that in a lifetime each of us, likely only three or four times, makes an existential decision, a decision in which our lives and our happiness are at risk, to decide to join one group instead of another. These families—especially the elders of these families—know what wise elders of human communities have always known: human beings cannot live alone. We live in communities. We are not hermits. However, communities require that we give up personal freedom to help the other members of the community in the hope they will help us. This seems clear. But how often in a lifetime do we voluntarily give up freedom? It is the rarest of moments. We know the risks of doing so, and we almost never take the plunge. Families that flourish, that are generative, know that their futures depend on their future members making a positive decision to join in, *and* they know how difficult that decision will be for them. Thus, they seek to create systems that are positively attracting to future generations to join in. They know that their families' futures depend on at least some of their rising generation members taking the existential plunge to give up freedom to join in.

Why might rising generation members take this plunge in a particular family? Because they find the invitation to join the family journey an invitation in which they perceive that the family's generative vision, the family's spiritual self, its core beliefs and virtues are all working together to offer them more personal freedom to discover and become themselves, more opportunity to bring their unique selves to life than any other group competing for them to join. These rising generation family members decide to *give up freedom to gain freedom*. Only the most positively attracting family system, one devoted to the growth and development of rising generation members, can offer such invitations with any hope of such members signing on. This great knowing and the actions to make these critical invitations real are, I believe, at the heart of why such a family is generative and long-lived and why most families aren't. Such a family knows it has succeeded when its rising generation members form new horizontal social compacts committed to these principles and committed to offering a future rising generation the same invitation their wise elders offered them. The formation of each rising generation's new horizontal social compact, committed to each of the above principles and particularly to the family system being positively attracting to new members, with its promise that giving up freedom will enable the gaining of freedom, is the evidence that the family has the continuing capacity for endurance and the ability to continue to flourish and be generative for another two generations.

So we have Dennis to thank for providing us with the research that confirms our intuitions about why a family flourishes, why it is able to be generative for many generations, and how it does this. His gift of this book offers the proof we need that the proverb's dictate need not be predictive. The stories of the families he profiles assure us that if we learn from their stories, our family need not be another family where the proverb comes true. It is my hope that your family and those you guide as their advisors will take to heart Dennis's great findings, act on them accordingly, become a family of affinity, and flourish for many generations.

May your journeys be blessed. May you and each of your family members flourish and achieve happiness. May your family flourish and be generative.

Namaste
James (Jay) Elliott Hughes, Jr.
Tahoe, August 2019

# Preface

Family businesses are among the world's most enduring and ubiquitous economic and social institutions. They are the foundation of social relations and communities; as humans evolved from hunting to agriculture, trading, and industrialization, family businesses evolved as well to make this possible. They take many forms. Our nature as human beings is expressed in how we act in our economic life, and family businesses are the most common manifestation of this. While the market view of commerce emphasizes economic behavior as individual choices and rational self-interest, this book takes the perspective that at the core of our economy are living families that seek and stand for so much more than financial profit.

This book presents the findings of a global multiyear project to understand the evolution and essence of large, global family enterprises that have succeeded over generations (a glossary of terms used in this book is at the end of Chapter 1). The research team interviewed family leaders from different generations of over one hundred large global families, each of which has thrived as a shared economic entity for more than three generations. These families are successful both as extended families and as businesses. By viewing the evolution and history of the largest and most successful global families, by looking back and looking forward, we can learn something about the nature of social evolution. We can also observe the human foundation of global commerce, which has largely been hidden from view. By hearing from families with great wealth and longevity, we can look beyond individual businesses to the positive foundations and use of economic wealth.

## Long-Lived Business Families

My purpose is to learn from the best of the best family enterprises—extended families that have been in business for more than three generations—to uncover the internal secrets of their success. Their wisdom can help families just starting on this path—those moving into a second or third generation and facing significant challenges. Their stories can also be instructive to the millions of lawyers, accountants, bankers, coaches, consultants, board members, and other trusted advisors who offer resources to families to keep them on course. While the families my research team and I interviewed own complex businesses and other assets, I see them as families first because that is what the owners are. As family members, the owners have personal relationships, and these relationships are about far more than just running a profitable business. Such a family is more than a single business, or a business alone, because the family can start, buy, and sell many businesses as it adapts and grows across generations and because the family consists of many households related to and caring about one another and their future.

I am particularly interested in long-lived family businesses because, by their nature, a family business or family enterprise is fundamentally different from a public corporation. The owners of a public corporation have nothing in common, and no relationship, other than a desire for a profitable business. In a family business, the owners know and care for one another and share values as well as a desire for profit. This makes a huge difference to the enterprise.

The family has concerns beyond profit that go beyond the business. The family's business expresses a core aspect of the soul and identity of the family. Their values, reputation, role in the community, and impact are all considered in its oversight of the business. Because the business originates from a family, it also embodies and reflects the nature and personality of the owning family. All of this creates a different form of business, arguably one that is more complex and faces more agendas. When a family enterprise lasts for several generations, its family nature is a central feature of how it operates.

The book's title comes from the observation "You don't own a family business; you borrow it from your grandchildren." When I first heard this expression, attributed to a fifth-generation family member of the Hermes family, I was blown away. Professionals spend a great deal of time helping older generations consider whom they want to "give" the business and their wealth to. This notion turns it around and views the family's enterprise and wealth as a gift from the future that current family members are able to use only with conditions. It catches the most important difference between family and nonfamily business: the awareness that current family members make decisions looking generations ahead. I have since learned that this worldview is adapted from Native American and other global indigenous cultures, who do not believe that land and natural resources can be owned by individuals; they are to be shared, valued, and preserved for the future. That mindset makes so much difference to the nature of families who have acquired large amounts of wealth, and how they see the role of their families as stewards of their family wealth.

## My Journey

This project has been a dream of mine and a labor of love. After nearly forty years of teaching, research, and practice, since the dawn of family businesses as a field of study, I have wanted to do this project. A dozen years ago, after working only inside the United States, I began to wonder how families from other cultures were similar or different. I knew that family businesses emerged in every part of the world, and I wanted to see if the practices and tools professionals were suggesting to them were applicable in other cultures. Because my experience was only with US business families, I assumed that I had only a partial picture of the nature of these foundational social institutions. For six years I have traveled and met global families, many of whom became part of this study.

In many ways, my work today, after fifty years, was formed by my youthful passions. After graduating college in the late sixties, I was a founder of a project for runaway youth. We called it *Number Nine*, after a Beatles song. We helped runaway young "street people" call their parents and set up an intergenerational conversation, in a safe and neutral place, to talk about their differences. These conversations were my first experience of how values and behavior could be so deeply contentious and hurtful in a family. I also learned that parents had to allow their children to grow in their own way but also find some common ground with the values of their elders.

Later on, my career took me into the corporate world, where I worked with the effects of deep change in corporate cultures. This field of study looked at how each business developed its own culture, usually stemming from the values and vision of the founders. As businesses grew, the culture came under strain, and the businesses had to adapt but also retain important features of the founding culture. Many of these businesses were family businesses, though at the time that fact was not really known to me.

In the early 1980s, several groups—containing organization consultants, family therapists, lawyers, accountants, financial advisors, and family business leaders—began a seminal joint conversation. Talking across professional boundaries was unusual, and it led each profession to begin to view their work differently, through the eyes of others. Across the disciplinary boundaries, these groups found a common interest in family businesses. We realized that their nature, presence, and influence were largely ignored in professional business literature and practice. Right under our noses was a deeply important field of study that we had ignored. I attended some of these meetings, and two formerly disconnected strands of my life coming together. I saw that the nature and relationships of the family were at the root of family business and that the resolution of family issues was necessary for businesses to succeed over generations.

To undertake this study, I assembled a team of talented researchers and advisors, each of whom contributed time and ideas as well as conducted interviews and gathered the data. Their biographies are included in the appendix. To launch the study, we had the support of two global family enterprise organizations: Family Office Exchange and Family Business Network. They enabled us to develop our research model and contact families that thrived over multiple generations. After publishing our first working paper, we were fortunate to gain the support of Bank of America's Merrill Center for Family Wealth, which sponsored the working papers we produced each year.

## The Research Perspective

The perspective that led to this project is somewhat different than the perspective of other family business research. It stems from practices called *action research*, research based not on discovering causal connections between family and business but upon asking how to help families in business be more successful and avoid difficulty. This research is not just for other researchers but offered to the families and their advisors to help them do a better job. The project is premised on several basic assumptions as follows.

*Study the best, not the average or most troubled.*

Management psychologist Abraham Maslow, one of my mentors, noted that you would never learn very much about healthy people if you only studied those with mental illness. Similarly, there is a limited amount one can learn from studying

family businesses that have failed, collapsing amid conflict and poor business practices. That doesn't necessarily help to see how to create a climate for success. If you
avoid failure, you don't necessarily achieve success. There's more to it.

You don't have to look too far to find an article about how to destroy a family business. Using business relationships to redress past family wrongs or to serve
endless family financial needs can undermine even the strongest business. Natural
forces of business maturing and innovation take down many more. It is much harder
to sustain thriving family enterprises across generations. How can a family increase
its chances of long-term success?

The field of management has benefited greatly from studies of the most successful businesses. There are many books by business leaders; these books are inspiring
but also a little suspect as they share only one side of their story and do so in retro-
spect. Personal success stories are a staple of business and family business literature.
They are inspiring, but a more dispassionate view is also needed.

A number of research and theory-based books have also tried to distill the wisdom of long-term business success: Thomas J. Peters and Robert H. Waterman, Jr.'s
1982 breakthrough book, *In Search of Excellence*;[1] James C. Collins and Jerry I. Porras's *Built to Last*[2] a decade later; and many follow-up works. These volumes are my
guides to a form of research that is called "appreciative" because it looks at what is
good about business and how it can be enhanced.

Appreciative inquiry, an approach designed by David L. Cooperrider and Diana
Whitney,[3] has led to some of the most useful and practical research on the nature
of successful companies. In this approach, a researcher or consultant begins with
what the business or entity is doing that works well and expands upon that, rather
than fixing problems. Families find this perspective both attractive and useful. This
is the view taken by this entire project.

The research can be labeled "narrative sociology." By presenting their stories
and experience without evaluating, I uncovered the collective experience of
long-term global generative family enterprises, those family business and financial
operations that succeed over multiple generations. Throughout the course of the
book, I present what these families actually do. This is nonjudgmental and nonevaluative. But since I am studying the families that are most successful, I cannot escape
some aspects of value judgment. By focusing on long-lived families, I necessarily
call upon reflections about what elements of their experience teach families how to
survive for the long term and help them anticipate and even avoid disaster.

*Family is the foundational unit of study, and businesses are vehicles to support family
goals and values.*

It is to be expected that business researchers look at business as their basic unit
of study. The rise and fall of a business is their focus, including the role of a family
as owners and operators. But what if the family sells the business and moves on to
other pursuits? Is this the end? In this research, I view the family as the basic unit
of study and how businesses and other assets create resources for the family on its
journey. Taking this view, I look at the people and the journey across generations,
as family members pursue different opportunities and paths and are still able to
remain together as aligned partners. With this perspective, it becomes clear that

their goals are more than just running an effective business and that these wider goals are essential to understanding these families.

*Success takes place over time and must be viewed as an evolutionary process, a journey of resilience and reinvention.*

Most research represents a "snapshot," a view of a family or business taken at one moment in time. But evolution of a family takes place over time and across generations, with the continuing challenge of preserving the legacy wisdom and also adapting and finding new paths forward. To understand families, research must look at its evolution, how the enterprise solves successive problems and overcomes challenges at different stages of development. Family enterprise is dynamic and evolutionary. Their stories are movies, not snapshots.

I present stories about the evolution of these generative families as well as their businesses and other family enterprises. My focus is on creating a picture of the diverse ways that generative families resolve the common challenges facing a family enterprise over generations. Because of the diversity of such families, I am not able to make quantitative comparisons. Instead, I report what these families do, without judgment, and try to ascertain common patterns.

My goal is more than just telling stories, however. I also want to document the evolution and nature of a unique social institution—an extended family that is joined not just by blood but also by a legacy that leads them to be owners and stewards of often large business and financial conglomerates. While their influence can be seen in their businesses, this research goes behind the business to look at how the extended families create, sustain, and influence their businesses and role in society.

*If you've seen one family business, you've seen one family business.*

Much research, unfortunately, is in a hurry to generalize and make causal connections to understand family enterprise. But I believe that the diversity of global family enterprise is so great that there is no way to speak of family business in general as a single entity. We can articulate common patterns, but we can't really get to the point where saying that one specific action "causes" success. But if we listen to enough families, we can see that if something is done by so many families that are successful, it may be a good thing to try that in an earlier-stage family as it tries to survive for one more generation.

## Overview of the Book

The book is organized to present the evolution and nature of the global generative families that my research team and I studied. There are four parts:

**Part One: The Wisdom of Generative Families** offers an overview of the long-term history of family enterprises. I suggest that the recent challenges facing family enterprises are unique and unprecedented. I introduce the concept and nature of the generative family, the focus of this research.

**Part Two: The Evolution of the Resilient Family Enterprise** looks at how the family evolves as a shared enterprise over generations. I present a "movie" of how generative families evolve over four or more generations and then focus on the business; how these families change over generations; the elements of the unique family enterprise culture that characterizes generative families; and the origin of the role of steward that emerges in families that oversee a portfolio of diverse ventures.

**Part Three: Inside the Family: Family Governance to Create a Great Family** focuses on an area of activity that is unique to a family enterprise: the organization, governance, and activity of the family separate from the business. It presents the key elements of family governance, including the family assembly, family council, owners' groups, and the board, and how they are all tied together in a family constitution, a master agreement that defines who the family is, what it does, and how it works.

**Part Four: The Rising Generation: Sustaining the Future** discusses how the family takes up the special task of preparing family leaders to sustain and move the business into new generations.

## To the Reader

This research project is intended to help families who are either beginning their journey across generations or finding themselves enveloped in increasing complexity in the form of internal family disagreement and external global change. If you look ahead to the future, the experience of generative families can help you design your own path, as you pick and choose from what other families have done.

This book is also designed to help family advisors of every professional designation take a broader view of the families they serve and, in so doing, teach and advocate for their families to adapt new practices that are designed with their future in mind.

Each chapter contains stories and narratives from the families in the study. These stories and narratives explain the many ways that generative families act, grow, change, and thrive. There are many paths, but I believe the general themes about mission, values, governance, and development of the next generation are essential building blocks of multigenerational success.

My intention is for the stories in this book to be of practical use for families that desire to move into generative territory. If you are a member of such a family, this book may help you make decisions and develop practices in earlier generations to orient your family to potentially become a long-lived generative family. To do that, at the end of each chapter, I offer a section containing tools and activities that apply the learnings that were presented. It is entitled "Taking Action in Your Own Family Enterprise." Each one suggests ways to apply practices from the chapter to your own family enterprise. The activities can also be used by advisors who are helping families.

Whether you are a member of a new family business, a successor at one that has been successful for several generations, or a family advisor or employee, learning about generative families will help you look ahead to your future. I am excited to invite you to go on this journey with me and to celebrate and learn from the most valuable, successful, and impactful family enterprises.

## Notes

1. Thomas J. Peters and Robert H. Waterman, Jr., *In Search of Excellence: Lessons from America's Best-Run Companies* (New York: HarperCollins, 1982). It is interesting to go back and reflect on the businesses featured in this book. Most of them are in fact family businesses, but this fact is not mentioned or considered important enough to document. This observation supports the notion that in the late twentieth century, the presence of family businesses and their influence was overlooked or ignored.
2. James C. Collins and Jerry I. Porras, *Built to Last: Successful Habits of Visionary Companies* (New York: HarperCollins, 1994).
3. David L. Cooperrider and Diana Whitney, *Appreciative Inquiry: A Positive Revolution in Change* (San Francisco: Berrett-Koehler Publishers, 2005).

# Borrowed
# from Your Grandchildren

# PART ONE

# The Wisdom of Generative Families

P art One introduces the concept of a generative family and describes what they are. Long-lasting family enterprises are a predictable development of any society. Today, with their vast size and complexity, they face unique and unprecedented challenges to continue to thrive. Family enterprise are complex and difficult to describe. This section sets the stage for my inquiry, defines key terms, and describes the nature and evolution of these entities, which are at the foundation of so much global wealth and social development.

These chapters look at what family enterprises are and how they emerged both historically, over eons, and then in terms of generational transitions. Chapters 1 and 2 introduce the research study, and the key concepts that will be developed throughout the book. Chapter 3 is a brief history of global family enterprise, so that we can see how the common elements and practices of generative families have developed over time.

# CHAPTER 1

# Learning from the Best

## Researching Long-Term Family Enterprises

Everywhere in the world there are family businesses. When we enter a restaurant and see parents cooking and serving and their children doing homework, when we buy clothing or cars, when we visit a resort or convenience store, we are frequently interacting with a family business. Seeing the family there, personally responsible, causes us to hold the family in special esteem, as the family commitment and visibility seem to guarantee quality and care. Families lie behind our food supply, manufactured goods, as well as service companies.

Many became huge global enterprises while others are tiny but sustainable, with several family members helping out to earn a livelihood. We look with admiration and a touch of envy at the success of long-lasting families that parlay business and financial success into a glittering life of privilege, status, and power. But we also read about families diminished by dysfunction or by displaying and using their wealth to no discernible purpose. We are sad for these families, but maybe we also experience a bit of schadenfreude about their misfortune. How did they begin with so much and end up with so little? Despite the existence of some troubled families, many of the best families sustain themselves *as families* over multiple generations and raise successful children who both enjoy their wealth and pursue philanthropic and socially responsible ventures. These families appear to be both blessed and good. We wonder that makes some families great and others dissolve into dysfunction.

When it comes to global commerce, the impact of family enterprise is inestimable. Networks of business families, many of them having grown over several generations, form the economic, social, and political infrastructure of every nation. While there are different ways of defining such enterprises, estimates in every country are that a majority of businesses, and of the economy, are family-based. In developing countries, a majority of the large businesses are owned by families. As I will show, these businesses are based on more than economic return. While some are self-centered, even corrupt, a theme of social values and responsibility echoes throughout many global business families. They want to see their businesses as contributing to the well-being of their community and nation.

All over the world, uncountable families create successful businesses that they want to see continue and benefit their successors. But few are able to sustain themselves even into their second generation with the same level of wealth and success. If such success is a marathon, how do these most successful long-term families prepare themselves for the rigors they will face? Many of these families learn from the envy and admiration of their communities; they strive to live up to their reputations. They also want to learn from successful families, how to express their values and succeed across generations. Professional advisors also want to know what these families do so that they can guide their client families along this path.

Every culture has a proverb akin to "shirtsleeves to shirtsleeves in three generations." Why is this observation so universal? Is family wealth really so ephemeral? While probably not meaning that third-generation families enter poverty, it does suggest that sustaining shared family wealth after the third generation is immensely improbable and difficult. While every new family of wealth would like to outlast this prophecy, only a few succeed. If they do, they enter largely uncharted waters.

Many wise voices propose paths these families can choose in order to avoid this fate. This study adds a new perspective. It recounts in their own words the practices and stories of more than one hundred large, global families that have successfully transitioned significant businesses or financial wealth through at least three generations over a century or more. They have lived what others have wished for or talked about. Theirs are the stories of those families that recognize the "shirtsleeves" possibility and respond "not yet."

## What Is a Family Enterprise?

It's easy to spot family businesses but harder to define what they are. In smaller family businesses, family members work together across generations as owners and operators. How do they pass skills and sensitivity to each new generation so that the inheritors can grow and sustain themselves? When families get larger, not all family members can work in the business. Over time, many family businesses turn operations over to nonfamily leaders. But the extended family, whose members have a familial relationship with one another, remain majority owners and actively engaged in the enterprise.

- The first defining quality of a family business is that they are a business where the majority owners share a personal relationship, which usually includes shared values and nonfinancial goals that are as important as making a profit. This bond among the owners makes family business very different than a public corporation where there is no personal link among shareholders.
- A second defining quality of family business is that young family members who are not yet owners are preparing to become owners. Because of their future ownership, they feel some connection to the business, which must be taken into account. The current owners are concerned about their future and take active steps to prepare the future owners for their stewardship. Owners are concerned not with today but with the future; their self-interest is to pass a "gift" to their children, and prepare them to receive it.

Over time a family may sell its initial legacy business and then choose to remain together to become a financial family entity. Or it may acquire and share ownership of multiple businesses. It may add property and a philanthropic foundation out of profits. Thus, a family with a single family business may evolve into what I call a family enterprise, containing a portfolio of jointly owned assets. In this book, I look not just at family businesses but at the multiple family-owned ventures that evolve from a single family household owning a single business to shared ownership of a growing, diversified, expanding extended family enterprise.

My focus is on the extended family moving across generations. Along its journey, such a family may come to own multiple family assets, including:

- Privately held companies
- Public companies with the family remaining in control
- New ventures started by family members or new businesses bought by the family
- A holding company for multiple family enterprises and assets
- A family office to manage and coordinate family assets and activities
- Trusts that own assets for beneficiaries
- A family foundation for charitable and philanthropic endeavors

These asset types often overlap. For example, a privately held family business might include a few nonfamily owners or investors. Stock in a public company may be held by a family trust or a family holding company. The family might own several business entities, each with their own boards but with family owners making the major decisions.

A family enterprise is characterized by shared, collective leadership by a related family that wants to continue into the next generation. Along with its ownership, the family exercises discretion and control over the use and development of a variety of assets.

Family enterprises form the majority of businesses large and small in every country in the world. Since they involve related family members, they need to be understood as more than just businesses in isolation but as an expression of the intention, identity, and legacy of the families that own and operate them. They are disciplined businesses, and they are also families that care about each other. What is the nature of this complex hybrid?

The impact of the enterprise on the family can be positive or negative. The family enterprise can offer a lifetime livelihood for generations or can be fought over and cause permanent family rifts. The family enterprise can be an icon of high quality and offer employment and status to villages and nations, but the enterprise can also exploit people and destroy the environment. A family enterprise doesn't run on its own forever; it needs regular rebuilding and renewing. By their action or inaction, next-generation family members can add significantly to the family enterprise's success or destroy it.

Successful family enterprises are incredible engines for generating wealth and expressing the owning family's values about people, business, and the community.

These values are the basis for the quality of their goods and services, for their relationships with employees, other businesses, and the entire community, and for their philanthropic work.

But only a small fraction of the families that create businesses sustain them for more than a single generation. The few surviving enterprises are huge and have a powerful impact on the community, global commerce, and the environment. They also have a strong influence on family members and all those touched by the family's various operations. Much can be learned from them.

Successful family enterprises can be long-lived. Among the 750 largest global family businesses,[1] 230 are older than one hundred years, and another one hundred or so are older than seventy-five years. Ninety of the 230 are public companies, with majority ownership or control by a family. They are spread over every country, though some countries, like Japan, Germany, and the Scandinavian countries, contain a larger proportion. In every country, it is estimated that the combined net worth of family enterprises contains a large majority of the country's economic wealth. Successful long-term family enterprises are thus large, profitable, and influential.

## Beyond the Fourth Generation

The family business literature and its key models describe generations one, two, and three, but descriptions stop there. Whither the fourth generation? Is it just more of the same? Or are there just too few of them to bother to study? We know they exist, and they are large and important. But to my knowledge this is the first time there has been a study of who they are and what they do. The study of long-lived families and their business and financial ventures is important because this is the goal of many families who have not reached that milestone. What awaits them if they reach one hundred years? Another opportunity in such research is that the long-lived family can look back on its first three generations and report on what they did that was helpful and not.

And the fourth generation differs from third and earlier generation families. When a business family reaches the third generation, internal and external forces threaten the family's ability to continue as partners. A family reaching this milestone faces a choice point: Should we continue together as a financial or business entity or just distribute what we have and let each household move forward in its own way? A few courageous families make a conscious decision to continue united. By sharing the experience of families that have successfully crashed through this barrier, I offer a roadmap of the hard work and expansive outcomes that result.

### From Small Business to Family Conglomerate

I begin with a story, the first of many stories that will be shared in each chapter. These stories feature the exact words of family leaders, which will be indicated by italics. Unlike the stories to follow, the family in this first story is a composite, created to introduce the key themes and developmental model that will be featured throughout

(continued)

the book. This story shows how each generation of a family enterprise becomes larger and more complex and how the family must evolve through internal and external challenges:

> *Great-grandfather Albert started a factory, which had the good fortune to manufacture a patented building element that everyone needed. At the beginning of the twentieth century, the business expanded along with the new skyscrapers that formed the new industrial cities. Albert had a son, Claude, and a daughter, Sophie. Following tradition, Claude, barely thirty, began to work in the business.*
>
> *Albert used his wealth to buy a ranch, and Sophie and her new husband, Raymond, lived there and managed it. Everything was incredible until the patriarch died suddenly just before his fiftieth birthday. Claude discovered that Albert's finances were a mess and that the business was threatened by his loose management practices.*
>
> *Claude, Sophie, and Raymond struggled but were able to make both businesses profitable, especially the manufacturer. Claude and Sophie each had a pair of children and shared ownership in the manufacturer and the ranch.*
>
> *The third generation grew up with great wealth but, absorbing the lessons of their parents, developed a positive work ethic. The whole family got together regularly at their huge vacation home on the ranch.*
>
> *As the third generation grew to adulthood, a series of changes swept the family and its businesses. First, Claude and Raymond began to buy real estate in their home city. Raymond and Sophie's son joined them after he finished business school. Claude received an incredible offer from a huge conglomerate and sold the manufacturing business. In addition to buying more downtown real estate, Claude's son located a cross-country shipping company for sale and persuaded the family to buy it. After a difficult transition, this new venture—like their other ventures—began to grow. After the sale, Raymond and Sophie's daughter married a fellow she met while traveling, and they moved to Australia. They wanted to take their share of the funds from the business sale to begin their new life overseas. And finally, given their Christian values about tithing, the family began a foundation, to which it contributed 4% of its profits each year.*
>
> *As the members of the fourth generation began to grow up, they were part of a huge and complex set of family ventures that offered them incredible possibilities for their lives. But do they want to remain together as business partners? What will their wealth be used for? How will things be organized in the new generation? Who will be in charge of each business and the embryonic family office, which manages the family's real estate and other investments? How can the next generation prepare to be part of all this?*

## Generative Families: Continual Cross-Generational Value Creation

Threats and crises naturally emerge as a family enterprise extends across generations. Success soon leads to emerging new challenges that lie beyond the experience of prior generations. In this book, I look at how a business family deals with success and moves across generations. I will present these families not at a single moment in time but through their ups and downs, changes and renewals, across generations. While only a relatively few families are able to survive and thrive across many generations, the wisdom and activities of the members of these successful families are objects of fascination, as they are role models and inspirations for each new family business that dreams of generations to come.

I call such families *generative* because of their creative achievement in sustaining a sense of family connection and a profitable, vital family business or group of family operations. They uphold their coherence, partnership, and family connection against the tides of dispersion and separation. I estimate that fewer than 1 percent of family enterprises become generative in these ways. But their impact is great in that these families together own a large proportion of global wealth and perform great service to their communities.

Generative families are rare, unique, and important. In a time when the lifespan of businesses is declining, these family enterprises represent a rare species that sustains consistent control over a long period of time. In fact, if a business is still operating over the course of two generations, it is very likely to be family owned. These companies are important because, unlike so many business ventures that focus only on current profits, they endure long term with values that transcend profitability. They stand for something, offering lessons that can be learned not just by family businesses in their first generation but also by nonfamily ventures that want to operate with values beyond the bottom line.

Generative families are a special and unique family/business hybrid. They are a small subset of the huge number of family businesses, but they are incredibly significant in their social and economic impact. They form the bedrock of socioeconomic activity of every country. This project looks at how they become what they are and are able to combine family and business to have such impact. As I will show, these families share features of ancient structures that have been with us since the dawn of civilization. In the modern, industrial world, they have grown and expanded, taking on modern features. As we examine successful models for enterprise that look to the future and whose family owners act as responsible stewards, the generative family is a prime model of how business success can benefit society.

Given that so few families survive with both financial fortunes and family relationships intact, I wanted to learn how this wonderful achievement occurs. While these families began with a legacy business, I view them here as evolving *families*, not just businesses, sharing a changing portfolio of assets and business ventures.

This book celebrates the resiliency and hardiness of generative families. They are generative because rather than depleting or consuming resources, they add to and amplify the various forms of family wealth. Such a family uses its resources not just to sustain what it has but also to create something new. It extends its legacy—the family members' values and practices—in new directions that add not just to the family's financial wealth but also to its human, social, relationship, and spiritual "capital."

As I will show, one of the essences of their success is balance. They are able to balance what seem to be opposing polarities, business and family, legacy values and innovative practices, and individualism and collaborative teamwork. In Chapter 6, I present the concept of the generative alliance as a model for balancing voices and constituencies to build a successful generative family enterprise.

These families are more than the businesses they own; they also share a family *culture* of relationships, values, traditions, respect, and learning that underlie their business capabilities. Their family culture is the foundation of their business acumen. Such families dominate the economies of many countries because they are able to innovate and pursue opportunities with sustained commitment and resources. Beyond their business activities, these great families have a powerful impact on the social fabric of their countries.

When family business was first conceived as a field of study, in the 1980s, the family was viewed as inseparable from its legacy business. The assumption was that, without the business, a family lost not just its livelihood but its identity. The experience of one-hundred-year families, however, is quite different. These family businesses are not single businesses owned by a family so much as ever-changing business partnerships. These partnerships share a business legacy, values, and culture as they navigate through a turbulent environment. A single successful business may provide the initial thrust, but sustaining and growing family wealth demands skills exercised over many lifetimes. This is not an easy task, as can be seen in stories of family wealth squandered by heirs and successors. Passing on the dedication, creativity, vitality, and innovation of the founding generation across new generations is a challenge of the highest order. How that happens is more about the nature of the extended family as a family than about wealth creation by any particular business.

The ability to adapt, renew, and reinvent in response to challenge and adversity while sustaining a consistent culture and set of values is the essence of generativity. After creating success in a legacy business, each successive generation builds on this legacy, adding value through innovation, new ventures, and inspiring visions for family and business success. Business families do this by encouraging and developing the creative energy of each new generation.

My bookshelf includes more than forty volumes of histories of families from this study. These books highlight inspiring origin stories. A founding patriarch rises from humble roots and sees an opportunity. Powerful matriarchs help build the businesses and are teachers and role models for family values with their children. Dedicated and passionate family members and employees create transformational products and services. The books feature family pictures of stern couples and playful children and show how each new generation contributes to the enterprise. Businesses are sold or expand globally, bringing the family's values and vision into an ever-wider playing field. No matter how disciplined and professional the business becomes, however, it still expresses the family's spirit and values in its business practices.

Generativity is both a public and a private activity. A business family's public achievement cannot be sustained without the private and personal project of building a great family. A great extended family contains many households organized into several branches that are aligned to steward a portfolio of shared assets such as a family business, family office, or family foundation. These legacy families affirm shared values and an active commitment to inspire, develop, educate, and pass on leadership at an opportune time to each new generation of capable and committed young people. They use their resources to develop their capability and commitment.

This study looks at families, not individual businesses. Through the book's focus on the expanding extended family over generations, I show how business is a path to creating value for the family, its business or businesses, its community, and its society. But the business is a creation of the family with its values, vision, and commitment. Creating wealth is not an end in itself. Sometimes it seems more like a useful by-product rather than the central intention. Many of our families have sold their legacy business, but they continue as partners, sometimes sharing other resources. The business is a vehicle for family success. Family culture and identity are sustained across the family's many ventures.

It is hard to listen to these families' stories and not admire and respect what they have done. In a time when there is much concern about the concentration of wealth in the hands of "the one percent," this study, showing how these families make use of their wealth, is an important addition to the dialogue. While this study should not be taken as an apologia for wealth concentration, it does offer a positive narrative about how great wealth is used. The successful one-hundred-year family is not necessarily a selfish group of consumers of excessive luxury goods. Instead, it can become a socially responsible entity, using its vast resources responsibly to make a difference in the world. When we compare activities of a family enterprise with those of a public corporation, we see the special nature of a family that shares not just resources but a values-based connection that can be of great benefit as a new generation faces harrowing global challenges.

## What My Research Team and I Did

My research team and I located global family enterprises that succeeded over more than three generations and that were able to align goals and create positive family relations in what can be a huge family of owners. These we defined as generative families. How did we define and select the "best" family enterprises? In the absence of good data on outcomes and our desire to look beyond financial results, we proposed three objective criteria for successful long-term family enterprises:

- **Business/financial success.** These families created a successful business, or set of family-owned ventures, with current annual revenues of more than $250 million[2] (with the average family's net worth being much greater). Half the families had sold their legacy business and had transitioned to become a family office, often including a family foundation.
- **Adaptability over generations.** These families successfully navigated at least two generational transitions of shared ownership, with control being passed to the third generation or beyond.
- **Shared family identity.** These families retained shared connection and identity, with practices and processes that sustained their values and personal relationships as an extended family.

How did we find these families and persuade them to talk with us? Initially, we recruited them through the sponsorship and support of two leading global networks for such families: Family Business Network and Family Office Exchange. Each gave us access to family members who fit our three criteria. We reached out to them and offered them anonymity in exchange for sharing their experiences and history. The book recounts their direct words from these interviews, without revealing their exact locations or identity.

The 100-Year Family Enterprise Research Project has so far interviewed family leaders of older and younger generations of just over one hundred such families, from more than twenty countries. Our ongoing research project[3] opens the curtain on the private worlds of the longest-lasting and most successful global family enterprises. This study turns to these families as *teachers,* helping other successful families learn how to sustain success and connection across generations.

The people we interviewed talked candidly about how they went about building a great family with sustained wealth and active, responsible, engaged, and effective successors. Because of the isolation great financial wealth often causes, learning "straight from the source" is a rare and valuable opportunity. Their personal accounts allowed us as a research team to part the curtain and learn about the family dynamics and activities behind their public success.

The research team and I interviewed a family leader from each family at length and in depth. (We interviewed two family members from different generations in about 20 percent of the families.) We asked them to describe their evolution over generations and tell illustrative stories that describe not just what they did but how they were able to do it. Among the families in our study are renowned families from different countries, many of them household names.

To honor the privacy of families whose names are well known and iconic, none of the families or companies are identified. I disguised details of their families and businesses without changing the spirit or meaning of what they said. Because I use their own words, the reader can see not just what they did but how they see their actions and account for them.[4]

The interviews focused on generational transitions, including such questions as:

- How does the family influence and interact with its business and financial assets?
- How do you remain unified and connect as a family over generations?
- How do family owners manage their business and financial relationships?
- How does the family teach and prepare their next generation?
- How did these practices evolve?
- How do you as a family define success?

Throughout the book, I share the stories of these families primarily by direct quotes from the interviews. These are indicated throughout the book in italics. I also present many longer narrative case studies, or stories. Their stories and direct words illustrate how they have thrived not just as a loving and connected family but what they did to produce new generations of committed, active innovators, adding capability, complexity, and new directions to the expanding extended family. Since those interviewed are leaders in the third or later generations, they can look back with some distance and perspective on what was successful in earlier generations. I believe this will help families that have achieved public business success to succeed as well at the second, less visible, task: to develop and empower their rising generation.

Although they are a diverse global group, these families have many commonalities in how they organized themselves as extended families and in the time and energy they devoted to this task.[5] I present their stories to inspire, guide, and focus those who want to follow them and share their insights that illustrate how they have thrived as loving, connected families and vital businesses. The stories also demonstrate their activities to produce new generations of committed, active innovators who add capability, complexity, and new directions to the expanding extended family.

While these generative families are all moving past their third generation, their stories are relevant to the much greater number of families now moving into the second generation. The conditions for the success of these families were set early on, when they made the first decision to create a disciplined and values-based business culture and to develop the capability and interest of their rising generation. Choices made by the second generation set the family on a generative path. Their activities for defining purpose and values, adapting to major change, holding annual family meetings, educating and preparing the young members of their third generation for leadership, and giving back to their communities can all help position first- or second-generation business families for transition to the third generation.

## Describing the Families in This Study

The families in this study range from the third to the fourteenth generation of shared family enterprises. Each of these families takes on a new form almost every generation. The families represent every sector of the world (see Figure 1.1), with 62% of them from North America (US and Canada).

More than 80 percent of the families still own their legacy businesses, though many of them have shifted from family to nonfamily leadership, gone public, or acquired or bought into additional businesses. Most of the businesses are approaching the centennial mark. They are huge, with the average net worth being well above $1 billion. Most of them remain privately held. These legacy businesses form the foundation for developing the family enterprise, in which the family develops or

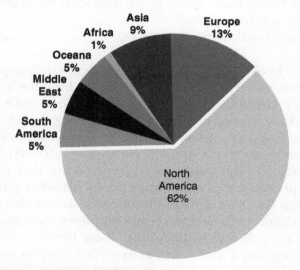

**Figure 1.1  Global representation of families.**

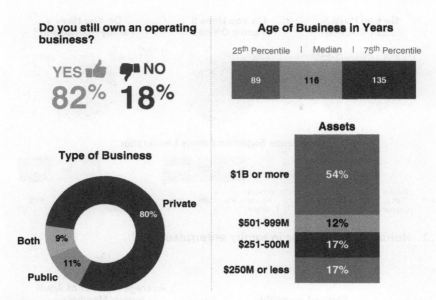

**Figure 1.2   Business ownership.**

diversifies into other ventures, like a foundation, a family office, property, or other investments. (See Figure 1.2.)

The legacy family businesses represent just about every category of business, manufacturing, resort, financial, food service, engineering, transportation, media, forestry, farming, and service companies. Many families own more than one business or a business that has expanded into several areas. The families also have family real estate, investments of all kinds, family banks, venture capital funds, family offices, and charitable foundations. Whatever kind of commerce is possible, the families in this study are in it.

These are not just business families but family enterprises. They commonly develop a family council, where the family conducts what I call "the business of the family," activities that develop relationships and engage and develop each new generation. I will have a lot to say about family councils in later chapters. As the family adds to its wealth, by selling its business or harvesting profits, it often forms a family office. And the family places great value in giving to its community by creating a family foundation or other vehicle for philanthropy. Figure 1.3 shows how each of these new entities is very common to generative families, and in fact, by the fourth generation, generative families tend to have all three of these.

I labeled each generation of the family in relation to the business founding generation, which is G1. In this study, 62 percent of the families have control and leadership in the fourth or later generation and 31 percent in G3. The families are large and growing. In the third generation there are an average of forty family members while in the fourth or later generations the number rises to an average of 130. The rising number of family members, I will show, is one of the triggers to implementing family and business governance. (See Figure 1.4.)

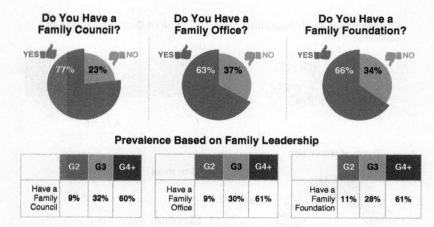

**Figure 1.3   Nonbusiness entities in family enterprises.**

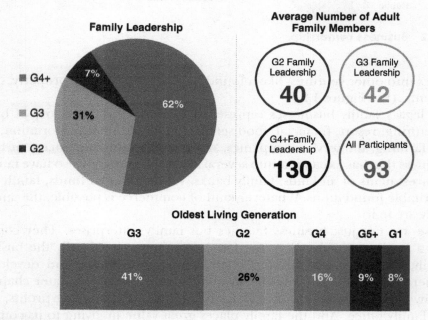

**Figure 1.4   About the family.**

My focus is on the transitions and development of these families across generations. The greatest number of families in this study are transitioning from G3 to G4. Based on these families' longevity, the respondents in this study reported on over 250 generational transitions! My research team and I interviewed active and influential members of the emerging, or rising, generation, who recently entered or were preparing to take responsible leadership roles.

The research focused on common qualities of generative families across the world. However, it should be noted that there are some interesting differences when comparing the 58 families from North America with the 37 families from other parts of the world. The sample, unfortunately, is not large enough or random enough to draw any conclusions, other than to point them out.

Families outside North America are larger and older, with more family members. Of the world families, 82 percent have a value of more than $1 billion, compared to 37 percent in North America; 88 percent of North American legacy businesses are private while only 69 percent of the others are; 77 percent of the global families have family offices compared with 54 percent from North America. Global families are older, but fewer of them have family councils or boards with independent directors. I suspect that this is due to sampling rather than regional differences, but there is also an impression that North America is a forerunner in applying the governance mechanisms described here.

## Glossary: Definitions of Key Terms

This glossary contains the terms and key concepts that you will encounter in each chapter. Since there is no agreed-upon terminology for referring to the concepts and practices of long-term family enterprises, I offer these definitions to refer to as you read each chapter. Other work about such families may use slightly different terms:

> **Board of directors:** A formal group, legally representing the owners of a family company or asset, that oversees the performance of the family ventures, hires and fires the CEO, and guides the family company through challenges and crises. It can contain some family owners and also independent nonfamily directors.

> **Dynastic family:** Long-lived extended families with a strong sense of family connection and commitment but not necessarily linked by values other than wealth. Only some of them can be called "generative."

> **Exit policy:** An agreement that defines how a family owner can request the other owners to buy his or her ownership shares and how those shares are valued.

> **Familiness:** The qualities and resources that come from the personal relationships and family network that add value to the family enterprise.

> **Family:** The extended family of descendants and married-in relatives of a wealth creator who started a successful business and whose ownership and control was passed on to succeeding family generations.

> **Family assembly:** A multipurpose gathering of all family members, usually held yearly, which combines business reporting, education, family issues, and fun.

> **Family constitution:** A formal family agreement that integrates and expands upon legal agreements and expresses what the family stands for, its values, and how various family entities and structures operate and interact. The constitution contains the rules of the road that guide the family, often containing personal information about the purpose and goals of the family enterprise.

> **Family council:** A working group, usually elected, that represents the family members to coordinate and carry out family activities, to manage communication within the family, to resolve differences, to report to the business board of directors, and to manage family assets and resources.

**Family enterprise (sometimes referred to as an enterprising family or business family):** A family that shares ownership and control over various assets, which can include a legacy business, new businesses, a family office, vacation and investment property, and a family foundation. By the third generation, the enterprise has many elements that may or may not include the original "legacy business," the source of family wealth.

**Family of affinity:** A family that contains only the family members who share a particular set of values or vision for their investments. A family of affinity arises when some blood family members decide not to remain part of the family enterprise and ask for their ownership to be bought out.

**Generative alliance:** How a generative family balances three cultural orientations that unite to enable the resilience of such a family enterprise: the **legacy values and culture** of the family, **professional business expertise and organization** that develop a strong and effective business, and **opportunistic innovation** that allows the family to continually seek new avenues for the family enterprise and allows the family to continually reinvent itself across generations.

**Generative (or legacy) family:** The whole extended family that has created a thriving family enterprise, with the intention of having family involvement across generations and with continuity of values and family commitment. A generative family consists of multiple, individual "households," which also identify as part of one of several family branches, stemming from their connection to siblings of the second generation.

**Governance:** The agreements, skills, and structures that enable the growing family to define values, mission, and policies; maintain connections; oversee the business and the family participation in it; and distribute consistently and fairly financial and other rewards.

**Household:** A nuclear family living under one roof, with parents and children.

**Legacy business:** The original business started by the family.

**Next, or rising, generation:** As each generation grows up, I call them, somewhat interchangeably, the rising,[6] emerging, next, or successive generation. Their growing children are "heirs" or "successors," depending on whether I am referring to their role as inheritors or their role as emerging family and business leaders.

**Nonowning family members:** Family members who are not owners or shareholders in the family enterprise. These are young people who may expect to inherit ownership in the future or married-in members whose spouses may or may not be current owners.

**Numbering and identifying generations:** By convention, the financial wealth creators form the founding generation, or G1. Each successive generation has a new number: G2, G3, G4, and so on.

**Owner-to-be (or owner-in-waiting):** A family member who does not share current ownership of family wealth or assets, but who, by virtue of his or her family role, expects to inherit ownership in the future.

**Owners' council:** The family members who have some degree of ownership of the family enterprise and who meet to select the board members, give input to the board and family enterprise about their goals and wishes, and make sure that the family members have overcome business disagreements and achieved alignment.

**Steward:** A family owner in a family enterprise who looks responsibly at the use of family assets with a concern for sustaining them for the benefit of later generations.

**Ventures:** Individual businesses and financial entities that are owned or created by the family enterprise.

## Notes

1. PWC Family Capital 750, 2019. Available at familycapital.com.
2. Here and throughout the remainder of the book, monetary amounts refer to US dollars, unless specified otherwise.
3. The first working paper, "Three Pathways to Evolutionary Survival: Best Practices of Successful, Global, Multi-generational Family Enterprises" (2012), presented survey data from 200 families. The second paper, "Good Fortune: Building a Hundred-year Family Enterprise" (2013), offers an overview of the evolution of these families over generations. Subsequent papers were "Releasing the Potential of the Rising Generation: How Long-Lasting Family Enterprises Prepare Their Successors" (2016); "Governing the Family Enterprise: The Evolution of Family Councils, Assemblies, and Constitutions" (2017); "Resilience of 100-year Family Enterprises" (2018); and "Social Impact in 100-Year Family Enterprises" (2019). They are all available on Amazon, in print and electronic versions.
4. I have slightly shortened and edited their stories and direct quotations to be more readable.
5. There were not enough families from different areas to make meaningful comparisons of differences across various parts of the world. In another book, *Cross Cultures: How Global Families Negotiate Change Across Generations* (Northfield, MA: FamilyWealth Consulting, 2016), James Grubman and I compared the cultural styles of family businesses around the world.
6. This term comes from James E. Hughes, Jr., Susan E. Massenzio, and Keith Whitaker, *The Voice of the Rising Generation: Family Wealth and Wisdom* (Hoboken, NJ: John Wiley & Sons, 2014).

2

# Creating a Great Family

## The Virtuous Circle of Family and Business

The generative family is a unique institution. It represents the successful interconnection of two different social systems—a family and a business. And both institutions, family and business, are in continual motion, as they expand and become more complex over generations. Almost all family enterprises stumble as they seek to remain together as family and business. They fragment as parts of the family go their own ways and as businesses rise and fall. The generative family is able to ride these waves and remain together over generations while so many of its peers are not.

Generative families enjoy great financial resources (the median in this study was $700 million). Collectively, they control resources well in excess of $100 billion—or roughly the annual GDP of a small country. But they have come to view their true wealth more broadly than simply financial.

This study probes the nature of their success. That success consists of developing the ability to take the positive aspects of family—personal relationships looking to their long-term future—and melding them to create effective business and family wealth. The generative family is a complex and multifaceted organization that builds and sustains both a huge family *and* a huge business/financial entity. Both family and business must be designed for different purposes but also to interact and work together. The generative family enterprise has built an organization that can sustain both a family and its businesses.

Many features of this achievement are of interest to aspiring families and advisors of these families. Generative families are masters at blending the best features of business and family. The family nature of generative families exerts a beneficial influence on their business and financial realms. It influences the values and the culture of business to take a longer-term and broader view of its purpose and policies. The business in turn influences the many family members, not only by providing wealth but also by offering opportunities to take on roles in society that aim at the greater good. In generative families, there is a virtuous circle of family and business influence.

This chapter introduces the core elements of generativity that will be developed further later in the book. The generative family avoids the three-generation "curse"—and instead thrives across multiple generations—by developing a culture that carries its benefits to generations of successors. I will show that keeping a family enterprise together is not simply a matter of good intentions and good fortune. Generative families are able to succeed because they set up a complex set of entities that work together to sustain a family vision that adapts to social and economic change.

Wealth alone does not ensure success. It stems from how the family views its wealth and uses that wealth to develop its family enterprise. Generative families not only build a strong business or financial enterprise but also a strong, vibrant, and connected family that uses its wealth in many ways to have positive impacts on the family, its business, and its community.

## A Great Family Is the Core of Family Enterprise

The research made a central discovery about generative families: after a family creates great wealth and prepares to enter the third generation, the focus shifts from creating wealth to considering how the wealth will be used. *These families invested some of their wealth to create a strong, supportive, creative, "generative" family.* This investment is not seen as a means toward a more effective business; the family wants to invest in building the extended family because that is what it wants to do with its wealth, in line with its core values.

Business success makes it possible for the generative family to do many things; what it chooses to do is invest in its current and future family. Becoming a great family is greatly different from managing a family enterprise. It is a personal process, growing out of positive, trusting relationships among family members reestablished in each generation. The family develops a vision, culture, and set of values that reflect a deep sense of purpose for its wealth. The family has a great deal of wealth, and it then defines clearly what it wants that wealth to do.

A nuclear family household lives together and is a hierarchy of parents at the top with siblings arranged by age. Family households often experience divorce, and become blended families that are more complex, but the ordinary family is a small network of deeply connected people. A successful family shares a desire for everyone to grow and thrive, enjoys spending time together, cares about each other, and shares wealth and resources.

In recent years, the composition of nuclear households is growing smaller. One- or two-person households are common, as children leave home, and single, divorced, and unmarried households proliferate.

Our generative families are a very different type of family. They are in some ways a throwback to earlier times, and in other ways a new type of family, born out of the new possibilities offered by their affluence and business and financial interconnection.

The word "family" takes on a broad and uncommon meaning in the third generation of a family sharing a business or other financial assets. Such a family is no longer a single household growing up together. A third-generation "family" enterprise is an extended family of several households, growing at an exponential rate. I define this family type as the *extended family of descendants and married-in relatives of a wealth creator* who started a successful business and whose ownership and control was passed on to succeeding family generations.

By the third generation, a single founding family contains several branches, usually associated with each G2 (second generation of family wealth) sibling. While respecting and identifying with the founder's values and goals, each branch takes on its own cultural personality. Differences emerge. Because the emerging extended family alliance shares ownership of what can be huge businesses and investments, it must create a process for aligning diverse agendas and goals, sharing resources, making decisions, and finding appropriate roles for the increasing members of the rising generations. In addition, beneficiaries may not want to live their lives in partnership with their relatives, so the family must offer an equitable path to parting ways.

The family business is the tool and creation of an extended family of owners who share a family heritage. These family owners constitute both a business and a family. Their challenge is how to create deep, personal, caring family bonds within this larger community that may be dispersed into several locations. Other than sharing business and wealth, what do they want to do together as a family? What do they share in common? What is their family identity?

The presence of family wealth offers opportunities and challenges to the rising generation of family members, opportunities and challenges that are not available to less fortunate people. They have the option of becoming involved in the family enterprise in many different roles, not just as employees. This is an opportunity and a responsibility. Each new family member can also decide to become a passive owner and not be further involved in the family business. These family members frequently accept a buyout and sell their shares in the family enterprise. They are now family members but no longer owners. They have exited the family enterprise.

Those who choose to remain in the family enterprise are owners, *and* they are a family. Generative families see ownership not just as an entitlement but also as an opportunity to serve their successors and society. This long-term and service perspective is called *stewardship*, a particular philosophy of ownership. To become good stewards, family owners must develop skills, define their vision and values and put them into action, and work together to continually adapt and add to their enterprises. While members of these families are able to enjoy their wealth, they also want their wealth to make a difference.

## Family and Business: Divergent Social Systems

To many people, family and business are different realms, places where different standards and values hold sway. Family and business can be defined as follows:

- The family is about providing care and love, raising dependent children to adulthood, and offering unconditional support. You are always part of your family, and your family shares everything. Family is about who you are.

*(continued)*

*(Continued)*

- Business is transactional, and people are accountable to one another. They are paid for their service, and service can be terminated at any time. Business is about what you do. If you don't like it, you can choose to exit. Personal relationships are beside the point.

But a closer look shows that the boundaries between family and business are not as fixed as we might at first think. Workplaces are networks of personal relationships, and some of them are deep and enduring. Families can become transactional, and love can turn to conflict and resentment.

A family business represents an attempt to merge the positive aspects of family into a business. When it is a family business, some of the family values and virtues of care and support are transferred to the more conditional expectation of performance and economic return.

As we will see in later chapters, a core challenge for a generative family is being able to separate family from business issues. In early generations, they are often fused. Over time, the family must learn that if they have a number of large, complex family ventures that they care about, they will have to be able to separate one from the other.

This fourth-generation European family learned this lesson when they began family meetings after the last member of G3 passed away:

*We have business meetings every month. That's different than having an intended meeting to talk about, "These are my personal issues, and this is what I want to bring up." Sometimes they crisscross. Somebody can say, "My personal issue is that my income comes in from my real estate. But now my income is not coming because your team is not doing their job to promote my property or to make sure it's taken care off." So sometimes, business and family merge. It's a fuzzy line.*

*We needed to separate from meeting every day to talk about all sorts of things, to set up a meeting related to business, different than family, and to have family time that has nothing to do with business or family issues. Just to have a regular lunch, which was always the case for the last twenty-five years. We meet every Friday for lunch. Whoever was born afterwards just grew up with that. This is how it gets done.*

Blending family and business elements can also cause conflict. The family role, or unconditional support, can be in conflict with the need to perform and help the business get its job done. Personal relationships cannot be transferred wholesale into the business because business talent and capability does not always follow family lines and hierarchy.

Many of the challenges and dysfunctional elements of family business stem from family behavior and rules overriding business needs or from the business being run for the personal benefit of current family members, without adequate consideration of business responsibility and the future. There comes a point where the family has to decide if its priority is immediate family consumption or sustained business effectiveness. To best serve the growing family, the family must run the business in line with good business practices and not use it as an employment agency, playground, or funding source for family members. At some time, in the first or a later generation, the family has to make a choice to transition from family-first to business-first orientation. That shift sets in motion many of the changes that are seen in the development of long-lasting, successful multigenerational family enterprises. These can be seen clearly in the experience of generative families.

## The Hybrid Family/Business Social System

Family enterprise is a complex social system. Within a family enterprise, family members are both *relatives* and business *partners*. Some family members may also be *employees* of the enterprise. Over generations, the "family" becomes an ever-enlarging group of household families, in many ways a tribe, united by inheritance of shared ownership in various family enterprises.

The family benefits from the enterprise in many ways, but shared ownership by more and more family members also leads to challenges and stresses that can only be managed by creating a family organization. Using the term "family enterprise" rather than "family business" emphasizes that a family enterprise involves much more than financial or business resources.

A successful multigenerational family enterprise rests on the foundation of two significant achievements—one visible and public, the other private and personal:

- Public: The family enterprise is a community icon. The founders are lauded as creative social leaders while their children are scrutinized for how they use their privilege.
- Private: The hidden success that comes with building a great family with trusting relationships that prepares a "rising" generation ready, willing, and able to shoulder the emerging challenges.

A business family's public achievement cannot be sustained without the private and personal project of building a great family. While we see their public face, rarely are we invited into the intimate worlds of the personal relationships, private conversations, and disputes that form the foundation for their success. The anonymous interviewees in this study provided access to this private world so that others can learn how these types of families are created and involved to achieve their public success.

A great extended family contains many households organized into several family branches aligned to steward a portfolio of shared assets such as a family business, family office, or family foundation. These generative families affirm shared values and an active commitment to inspire, develop, educate, and pass leadership to each new generation of capable and committed young people. We will see how they continue to renew this alignment over generations and sustain their identity as a family.

The one-hundred-year family enterprise is never a bystander to its family wealth. While the enterprise begins with a huge financial success, that was not the end point but rather the starting point for the successful families highlighted in this study. After the first-generation success, the one-hundred-year families in this study decided to use their material success to create a second successful entity: a connected family with shared values, a family dedicated to making the highest and best use of the special resources and opportunities that have been given to it. These family members decide to create a conscious family, a group of people who are personally tied to each other through a legacy and a commitment to becoming stewards for their own and future generations. These family members move from being a family of inheritance to a *family of affinity* that shares a vision, a set of values, and a commitment to actively build something together.

These families expect many family members to make a commitment to becoming engaged in the stewardship activities of the family enterprise. Some family members may work in the business, but the stewardship role goes far beyond employment. It often includes paid and unpaid work as a board or community member creating shared family activities. Over generations, generative families offer many opportunities to become engaged, and a number of members of each generation must choose to become active leaders in various family activities.

## Sustaining and Renewing Shared Purpose and Values

Generative families discover that having family wealth is only the beginning of a long and complex journey. Each successive generation must answer the question: *What do we want to do with the family wealth?* Each generation develops its own shared purpose that motivates family members to become more than passive, disinterested consumers of the family wealth. The members of each generation find ways to become engaged and committed to planning, making decisions about, and sustaining the resources of the family. They get together to consider and plan for how they will use their wealth to develop the next generation, to provide for each other and the community, and to have a positive impact on the family, the community, and often the world. This special family-building task is not for everyone. The generative family differentiates itself from the blood family by allowing family members in each generation to freely choose to be part of the family enterprise or remove their portion of the family wealth.

Each emerging generation of owners has to affirm that they want to continue. They may be constrained by trusts and entities that make it difficult or impossible for them to leave. But each family has to reaffirm and redefine its purpose for being together and the values and policies by which it will make decisions about its business and wealth. These are not just business decisions. They also involve the family and what the family members want to achieve together. The possibilities and opportunities of shared wealth are often more extensive and exciting than what each person can achieve on his or her own, so each generation can discover a reason to stay together. But to do something important and difficult together, the family needs policies and agreements about how it will work together. Each family enterprise must define its purpose and practices, its mission, values, and governance. To achieve this goal, family members create a parallel process and a structure that sits alongside their business. Just as the family owners need governance for their legacy company and other investments, so, too, they create a governance system to organize and manage family activities. As the family expands into an extended family "tribe," family governance becomes more and more visible and important.

Because these families recognize their true wealth in the human and social capital they accumulate, they have taken active steps to cultivate and grow that capital through communication, education, and clear decision-making or governance. With ever greater insistence across generations, they consistently elevate their focus away from amassing more financial capital. Their attention is almost wholly qualitative rather than quantitative.

Generative families offer lessons to others, lessons that have been tested in the crucible of experience:

- All of the families created a great business first and subsequently decided to **become a great family**. The latter accomplishment took longer with much more collective effort.
- These families are always aware of and working toward a **shared core purpose**, based on a commitment renewed by each new generation.
- These families respect their legacy and core values, but they continually **adapt, innovate, and change** as they face new realities inside the family and in the business environment.
- After starting as hands-on owner/operators, the families have adopted an **owners' mindset,** in which the family enterprise may offer special opportunities to family members but in which the family is united as responsible owners who operate the business professionally to create family wealth within the parameters of its values.
- These families value the development of their **human capital**, which includes the lives, experiences, skills, and knowledge of generations to come. Human capital also includes the legacy of positive impact these families have had on employees, customers, and communities.
- These families act as **values-based,** socially responsible entities, using their vast resources to make a positive difference in their communities. Their philanthropic commitments grow out of and in turn deepen their focus on human capital.

## Six Core Qualities of Generative Family Enterprise

My research team and I asked each family to share the most important factor in their success. Despite the diversity of families and their enterprises, six common factors emerged (arranged in order of their stated importance to the families; see Figure 2.1). Each of these core qualities is featured in different parts of the book.

1. **Shared values and core purpose** (all chapters). The most common factor was the family's shared values, which applied to the family's business, its conduct as a family, and its conduct toward its community. The family's legacy from earlier generations came from a framework of values that were taught, shared, and used in all of the family's dealings. These values were about the use of the family's wealth.
2. **Cross-generational engagement and support** (Chapters 4 and 8). The extended families talked about building closeness, respect, trust, and connection across the generations. They spent time and listened to the members of each succeeding generation. Since the individual households were often dispersed, these families were active in setting up a community that convened regularly and engaged all generations in shared learning.

*(continued)*

*(Continued)*

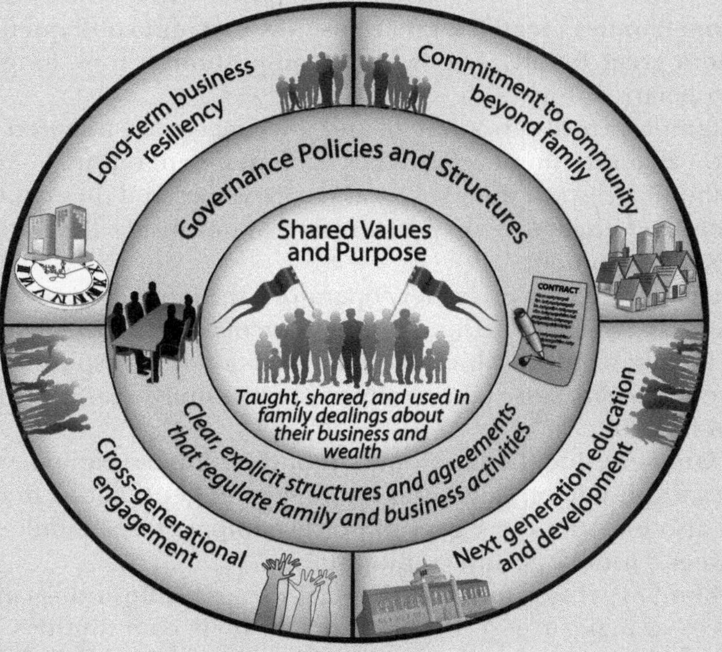

**Figure 2.1    Six qualities of generative families.**

3. **Long-term business resiliency, growth, and development** (Chapters 5 and 6). These families held a long-term view of their businesses and saw their enterprises as a foundation for their other activities. With a long-term view of their businesses, these families were continually redefining and renewing every one of their ventures. Because their business success made them special and offered unique opportunities, their attention to a strong, growing portfolio of enterprises was shared by everyone in the family.

4. **Governance policies and structures to guide development and decisions as a family and business** (Chapters 8 through 12). In order to achieve their values and sustain their success with emerging generations, the families developed clear, explicit, and often complex structures to regulate family and business activities. Many family members were active in governance, and they shared information throughout the family. They developed the following tools: family councils to manage family alignment, education, and development; boards to oversee their business and financial enterprises; and family agreements (in the form of constitutions, protocols, and shareholder agreements) to organize their engagement, interactions, and decisions with clear roles and boundaries.

5. **Education of the rising generation about responsibility, stewardship, and values** (Chapters 13 through 15). These families saw their new generations as the human capital to continue and build upon their success. The next generation was a resource and their goal, and they had to live and breathe the goals and commitment to the family enterprise. From the time the members of the next

*(continued)*

> generation were children, these families invested in the education and development of each new generation of their extended family.
>
> 6. **Commitment to community beyond family** (Chapter 7 and 15). The wealth of these families was a gift shared with nonfamily employees, suppliers, and customers and with their community. Each family applied its values to develop philanthropy and social policies supporting long-term commitment to its employees and community, and development of environmental sustainability.

## Family Capital: Fulfilling the Promise of Family Wealth

To develop a purposeful community, the generative family must design meaningful and impactful activities that concretely advance their shared purpose. These values and goals concern more than making profit. The family wants to add value to one another and beyond the business to the world. The family feels a wider social responsibility because of its huge success in business.

What special activities and achievements are possible for a generative family that has already created a large and successful business and extensive family wealth? One way to look at this is through the lens of different types of "capital," sources of value a family can develop together to justify its actions. These added sources of capital enable new family members to want to commit their time and energy to each other and shared projects instead of going their own way.

While we think of capital as primarily referring to money, in fact there are many nonfinancial sources of value. Generative families all use family governance to expand family capital in the broadest meaning of the term. Generative families focus on creating five types of capital.[1] (See Figure 2.2.)

### TYPES OF FAMILY CAPITAL

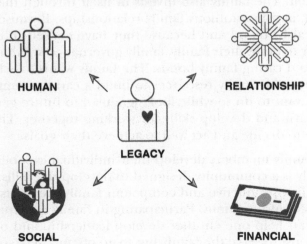

**Figure 2.2  Types of family capital.**

**Legacy capital.** Legacy (sometimes called "spiritual") capital arises when the family celebrates and renews the values and inspiration that created its family wealth and allows the family to inspire new activities. The family also expresses its values and relates them to an overall vision and mission for the family. When a family develops governance, one of the first activities is to share and teach the younger generations the story of the family. Generative families have done something special in creating their wealth, and those in charge of family governance gather materials, artifacts, pictures, and stories about the family's history and legacy. There are family videos, museums, picture books, histories, and memorials to the founding generation. These inspire the emerging generations to pursue their own paths that build on this legacy by using family resources to take the family in new directions. Young family members often take the lead in interviewing and learning their family history from their parents and grandparents. Related to this are the values and message espoused by the family pioneers, values that they connect to their success. If the elders are alive, they can share their story in person. Family governance often begins by defining the family legacy and then having the successors ask how they can further this. Inspired by their grandparents, they ask, *What will we do to fulfill our responsibility for wise and thoughtful use of what they have given us?*

**Financial capital.** The second form of capital concerns nurturing and caring for the financial and business resources of the family—*financial stewardship*. Family financial capital is about teaching the new generations of the family how to practice oversight to protect and preserve the family resources. This begins with making sure that the business reflects the family's values, intentions, and goals. The family does this by creating policies and practices so that family members who are engaged in the business are aligned with and working for the agenda of the whole family. There are family guidelines and policies for family employment and participation in other roles, such as being on the family board of directors. Finally, the family must sustain its financial resources by limiting and setting rules for distribution of family wealth while reinvesting in the business to develop future wealth. These policies must be understood, agreed upon, and experienced as fair to all. This can be a challenge.

**Relationship capital.** The family also invests in itself through the development of active, caring, fair, and harmonious family relationships. Because family members are not just related by blood and because they have chosen to continue to meet and work together to build their family, family governance activities include ways to develop positive and caring family bonds. The family wants to achieve the best for everyone and to use the family resources to build a caring community within the family—and they want to do so while looking ahead to future generations. Family members must learn and develop skills for working together. Through unity and trust they are able to decide and act well to achieve their goals.

**Human capital.** Family members develop their individual capabilities in each generation. The family is a community designed to develop the skills and character of every family member. Productive and competent family members can oversee and add to the resources of the family. Participating in family governance is a way that family members can help one another develop leadership and offer one another opportunities not just to serve the family but to go off and make other sorts of contribution to the world, which is the focus of Chapters 13 and 14.

**Social capital.** Finally, social capital refers to how the family's mission is expressed in the wider community. Family governance creates policies and goals for family innovation in ways that encourage family members to help the family enterprise enter new types of business and wealth creation. It also involves giving back to the community through philanthropy and social investment. As part of its governance, a family can create a "family bank," where family members can apply for funds and support for new ventures. Some of these are for-profit, but others represent ways that the family can use its wealth to make a difference in its community and the future of the planet, as will be seen in Chapters 7 and 15.

**Table 2.1  Five types of Family Capital.**

| Capital | Definition | Expressed As |
|---|---|---|
| Legacy | Mission, values, core purpose, and shared meaning, all of which forms the foundation of the family, its approach to wealth, and family members' relationships to each other | • Understanding the deeper meaning and purpose of family wealth<br>• Establishing a family mission and values statement<br>• Telling the family story to the next generation<br>• Talking together about values and what is really important |
| Financial | Resources to reinvest and support a comfortable lifestyle and ability to make decisions, manage, and sustain investments productively | • Creating clear and realistic expectations among the heirs<br>• Teaching values and responsibility about managing wealth<br>• Generating a sense of responsibility and capability to support the long-term strategy<br>• Developing competent oversight for family resources |
| Human | Development of the character, skills, and identity of each heir to understand how to manage wealth, find important work, and live in a complex, difficult, demanding global environment | • Having age-appropriate discussions about money with heirs<br>• Building self-esteem and identity, independent of having money<br>• Helping heirs develop a sense of purpose for their lives<br>• Developing skills and capability to help heirs make their way independently |
| Relationship | Ability to stay connected within the family and to compromise and work together, to create caring, positive, and productive relationships, and to develop structures to make decisions and manage family capital | • Generating respect and trust through regular communication<br>• Developing family social networks<br>• Writing a family constitution<br>• Holding regular meetings of family councils and boards<br>• Having accountability to and clear communication with beneficiaries<br>• Listening and learning from each other |
| Social | Commitment and respect, compassion and connection to suffering and concerns of others, responsibility of a place of service within the community, and use of resources to support the future of the planet | • Expressing the family's values in the community through action<br>• Involving all family members in service and philanthropy |

## Two Parallel Organizations of Generative Family Enterprise

Each generation creates a new story and forges a new path, not only continuing what came before but also opening a new chapter with new directions. Innovation and entrepreneurship do not end with the initial wealth creator; instead, each generation takes different paths to reach new milestones. Each new initiative provides a foundation for the next stage of the family enterprise.

By the third generation, most generative families shift from having a single legacy *family business*—one in which family needs and dynamics are primary—to becoming a family *enterprise* that stewards strong professional business and financial ventures that run on clear, firm, and effective business principles. To accomplish this, the family has to step back from active management and adhere to a new sort of discipline. This disengagement may surface difficulties. For example, how should the family deal with family members accustomed to perks and entitlements? How can the family maintain the values that it stands for—the spirit of the family enterprise—as the business becomes more impersonal and professional?

As a family enters the third generation, its future is problematic. Family members and their advisors must help the family look at what is ahead and what is possible and forge a plan and alliance to make it happen. The challenges that face the family cause it to outgrow its existing organization, where family and business activities are intertwined and conducted by largely the same people. By G3, the family has already begun to differentiate business and family activities and create different entities to manage them. The family enterprise divides into two "pillars": a family organization and a business/financial one. Each is important, and each one must influence and intersect with the other, creating a challenge of maintaining alignment and cooperation across the boundaries between family and business.

Each pillar creates working groups and operating principles to organize itself. The business has a board and some sort of owners' council, both of which oversee the leadership and operations of each business and financial entity. They form the family's business oversight and governance. In addition, an entirely separate organizational structure emerges for the family. To remain together as an extended family, the family itself must meet and define its mission and purpose to capture the allegiance of each new generation. The family creates a family assembly, which brings the whole family together to build a shared culture and define the family's values and interests. A family council coordinates and organizes the family as a community and looks after its interests. Within the family community, the family sets up activities to develop the human capital of the rising generation, the family's relationship capital, and the family's social capital in its community and the planet. These two "pillars" each offer roles, activities, responsibilities, and interaction defined by a comprehensive family agreement, called a *family constitution* or charter.

*Governance* is thus the platform the family creates to fulfill its promise and potential. It organizes the family and its commitment to doing something useful and important with its wealth by attracting and focusing the energy, creativity, and commitment of talented family members in successive generations. It is *conservative*, in that it is designed to preserve legacy values and culture, but also *generative*, in that it creates and develops what are only possibilities as the family grows.

The visions of third- and later-generation family enterprises are about much more than money. These emerging family visions specify *values* about how the family's businesses will operate and how they will treat employees, customers, and suppliers—in short, how the family will embody values-based business. Generative families choose to reinvest profits in their businesses and invest in social ventures by creating family foundations and philanthropic initiatives. They also make an investment in themselves—developing the human resources of family members to be thoughtful, responsible, and productive. Family governance is how the family organizes its resources to best achieve its values and invest in human, social, and family "capital."

*Family governance* is the pillar of governance that includes the agreements and shared activities that organize the growing family to remain aligned and collaborative and to sustain its multiple ventures and investments as it crosses generations. Family governance is more than a defensive measure. It is *aspirational*, reaching toward a vision of great things that are possible for such a privileged family. The extended family realizes that its wealth offers infinite possibilities for the next generation. To decide to work together rather than divide up its wealth, the collective family must create its own vision, a dream of what it wants to become and what it wants to do. The family members realize that together they can do things they could not do as individuals.

But if the collective family wishes to remain together, each individual must give up some personal power and autonomy to the family confederation. Some family members choose to leave while others enter by birth or marriage. In each generation, the family members must therefore renew their commitment to each other. The extended family creates a family organization to realize its shared vision; this is its governance structure. The family council, assembly, and constitution work together to organize and make explicit the family's shared agenda and how the extended family relates to its businesses and wealth.

In the third or fourth generation, the shared wealth and number of household shareholders may be immense. What was done informally, often by a single family leader, is now done by many. Members of this "confederation" must learn, or invent, systems for working with the thicket of investments, businesses, real estate holdings, and family foundations. The family may be dispersed and live in many places. Young cousins may barely know their relatives who are also their business partners and may even resent them because the younger cousins have different levels of ownership. There are many activities to organize and many decisions to be made. How does all of this happen?

Developing family governance demands not just good intentions and investment but also a lot of work together as a family. Family members must show up and agree to work together. It is often difficult, and conflict arises. While the public hears that certain "families" control many of our largest global corporations, the reality is that a "family" is a group of households and shareholders who have difficulty even agreeing when and where to hold a meeting, let alone how to align their different agendas. To fulfill their promise, these families need a shared identity and strategy for achieving desired results.

When young people look ahead to ownership in a three-generation family enterprise, there is a lot to master. They face a blend of legacy legal agreements as well as leaders and working groups that create order (and some rigidity) in family financial relationships. Trusts shift ownership and decision-making from family members into the hands of professionals.[2] There are also corporations with nonfamily owners having their own shareholders' agreements and structures. The family then finds itself negotiating with an institutional third party. Heirs in a family enterprise discover that they are not only partnering with parents, siblings, and cousins, but that they must also understand their role in working with professional advisors.

## Challenging Five Prevalent Myths About Family Business

One of the objectives of this book is to challenge certain dysfunctional myths that have grown up about family business. Although the study of family enterprise only began in the mid-1980s, it has since become a sizable global activity in itself. Several common misconceptions limit researchers' perspectives. The actual experience of generative families—those that have succeeded both as businesses and as families beyond the third generation—challenges these myths.

Myth 1. Family business faces a predestined decline across three generations.

**Reality**: As they repeat the observation "shirtsleeves to shirtsleeves" and observe data that few family businesses reach the third generation, many business families have internalized a belief that business growth occurs only in the first generation. Then, the myth continues, there is decline or stagnation in the second generation if the business does not evolve into a traditionally managed business with minimal family involvement. The role of the third-generation cousins is simply to step back and allow professionals to run things. This study shows, however, that the picture of generative families is not a path of linear and front-loaded development followed by decline. Rather, generative families follow a cycle of continual change and reinvention across generations.

Myth 2. Wealth creation takes place largely through the achievement of a single entrepreneur in the first generation.

**Reality**: While the founders clearly make an incredible contribution, in many of the families interviewed for this book, the founders were only the first of a series of wealth creators. The founders may begin their enterprise with a sibling or cousin whom they can trust and who shares their drive and vision. Several founders, for example, developed small unremarkable businesses that became supercharged with the addition of a son or daughter who led expansion and growth. A generative family enterprise often has several different wealth creators in successive generations.

*(continued)*

Myth 3. Wealth creation mostly results from founding one successful business.

**Reality:** Family business success includes several seminal activities. Initial success must be followed by additional, less newsworthy activities to sustain the business. A good local manufacturing business may move across national borders or create new products under the leadership of second- or third-generation family leaders. War, social upheaval, or technological shifts might force a successful business to reinvent itself. A mature business produces capital to move into new areas, and each successive event spearheads further wealth creation.

Myth 4. Sale of the legacy business marks the end of the family enterprise.

**Reality:** While the sale of the legacy business is a huge transition for an extended family, generative families make an explicit commitment to renew the family and reorganize as a business family. The sale does not dissolve the business but marks a choice point where the family members must decide that they want to remain together as business or investment partners. Some family members may decide to exit at this time.

Myth 5. Business success occurs because the family moves away from involvement and influence.[3]

**Reality:** The most demeaning myth about family business is that family businesses are "lesser" businesses that have to evolve into professional enterprises by removing the emotional bonds of the family. The reality of the generative families in this study is that the business is built on a deep foundation of family culture and values about how to do business. This family culture sets values about trust, respect for employees and customers, a professional work ethic, long-term vision, and innovation. These qualities sustain the vitality of the business over generations. Professional businesses that lack these cultural values may have great difficulty sustaining innovation and growth, just as nonfamily businesses with similar values may tend to be more successful. The presence of the family as owners (even if they include nonfamily owners as well) is the generative engine for the business. While family values and practices can certainly undermine the business in some cases, generative families minimize the ways that the family drains the business while optimizing the positive qualities added by the family.

## Taking Action in Your Own Family Enterprise

At the end of each chapter, there will be a section with specific suggestions about how to apply the learning in that chapter to your own family. Many readers choose this book with an eye to learning how to use the wisdom of generative families to advance their own family as it grows and evolves. You can do these activities on your own or together with members of your family as a shared learning activity. It is always better to do them together with other family members, especially with members of other generations. Advisors also can use them with their client families to open up discussion of the material presented in each chapter.

## Family Capital Assessment

Every family can expand its family capital. But a generative family has many options as it considers what is possible and what it might do together, whether it wants to continue to work together, and what it wants to do together. The family can conduct a family capital assessment using this worksheet.

| Consider below some of the key forms of "capital" you and your family could develop in each area. For each type, estimate the current status of your bank account in that area, whether low (L), medium (M), or high (H). | | | |
|---|---|---|---|
| Capital | Degree L/M/H | What Your Family Does Now | How Your Family Could Raise Capital |
| Legacy | | | |
| Financial | | | |
| Human | | | |
| Relationship | | | |
| Social | | | |

## Notes

1. This is an important concept, and practitioners have proposed several taxonomies of nonfinancial family capital. They have a great deal of overlap, and this model is one that combines elements from several of these.
2. Almost all the family wealth was held in trusts, a legal entity where the control of an asset is separated from the benefits. The influence of this separation has many consequences for new family members, and this study has not looked at how the trust structure and governance interacts with the forms of governance that are explored here.
3. The research for this book builds upon the pioneering work of Danny Miller and Isabel Le Breton-Miller, whose book *Managing for the Long Run: Lessons In Competitive Advantage from Great Family Businesses* (Boston, MA: Harvard Business School Press, 2005) pointed out the positive nature of the family culture in successful family enterprises.

# 3

# The Social History of Family Dynasties

Family business, or more broadly, family enterprise, has always been at the core of human society. Their form and nature shifted as society evolved from villages and agriculture to global trade and commerce. Millennia ago, nomadic families began to ally to form clans, villages, communities, and then states. The engine of social and economic development was always the family. At its core, a community is a network of interconnected enterprising families that help and care about one another. Society is made up of connected families, not isolated individuals. Families form the bridge between, on the one hand, intimate life and livelihood and, on the other, communities, nations, and trading networks.

While much is new and unique about how generative families function in our postindustrial world, many continuities arise from the sociobiological heritage of families as the building block of society. This chapter contains a brief, impressionistic journey through social evolution, with snapshots from several stages of emergence of global family enterprise:

- Prehistory of Extended Family Formation
- Asian Origins of Thousand-Year Family Enterprises
- Traders and Financiers: Accumulating and Sustaining Vast Family Fortunes
- Paternalistic Industrialization: The Company Town
- The Gilded Age in the New World
- Managerial Capitalism: The Rise of the Modern Corporation and the Eclipse of Family Business
- Hidden Champions: Family Business Quietly Enters the Modern Era
- "Refamiliazation": Family Advantages Reemerge in a Wired but Short-Term World

This history highlights what it is about family presence and ownership that gives family-owned businesses a competitive advantage. While much can be learned from previous generations of dynastic families, forces of digitalization, globalization, and fast change make the contemporary situation facing families fundamentally different. To sustain themselves, the adaptive capabilities that arise from their nature as family enterprises are needed more than ever.

## Prehistory of Extended Family Formation

The history of family business is the story of human civilization. A family is the social and economic unit of species survival. In order to nurture, protect, and launch children, the family had to provide security and a livelihood as well as teach children to survive into adulthood. Part of that teaching was sharing the parents' work experience—how to hunt or farm and how to develop skills to produce something valuable toward trade. Every family was also a family business, in that livelihood was a family activity. Every family was a business by necessity.

Following eons of nomadic tribes, the emergence of agriculture allowed human groups to cluster together and help and support each other. Villages were formed. Trade built social connection and community prosperity. Individual family units became extended families, which in turn became clans, that is, groups of intermarried, interdependent families. Several clans made a tribe, which built alliances that led to the creation of a kingdom or state. Families learned that they could thrive if they practiced trust and cooperation. Through marriage and building and defending communities, the circle of who was to be trusted and relied upon became larger. Land was held by a family; families allied through marriage were able to add to their holdings, leading to the rise of different levels of family wealth. But there was always a clear boundary between the family, where safe refuge, cooperation, and trust existed, and outside the family, where suspicion and competition resided.

A young person had little choice but to follow the path of his or her parents. The home was also a family workshop, whether the families were farmers, hunters, craftsmen, or traders. Families often took the name of their profession, identifying themselves as weavers, smiths, cooks, farmers, coopers, or tailors. The family passed its knowledge and resources to its children.

Clans, communities of related families, arose when families intermarried. Living closely and exchanging goods and services built interdependence, trust, security, more wealth, and a better life. While each family's business was important, the core was the family—its values and resources as well as the people who emerged in each generation to move it forward. Tribes selected leaders, and families became more or less wealthy. Children found mates from nearby families, enabling families to share and accumulate resources, and create alliances, by marriage. The social roots of inequality rested in the differentiation of families and their inherent drive to succeed and provide a better life for their offspring.

In a dangerous world, extended family communities became safe refuges. They built walls and weapons to defend their homes. Inside, they limited competition for resources, emphasizing sharing and caring as being more adaptive. Trading resources and mutual aid gave rise to what anthropologist Marcel Mauss calls "the gift economy," in which people develop obligations to one another.[1] By giving and receiving gifts, people have an obligation to repay, which can take different forms. If these social obligations didn't exist, Mauss suggests, there would be a state of war between families. Gifting also offers an opportunity for people to socialize and develop emotional bonds across families. The gift exchange is reciprocal altruism and develops trust within a community. Even today, societies exchange gifts on holidays, and large extended families like the DuPonts stay connected via a family ritual of exchanging holiday gifts and visits.

Every family was also a commercial entity. Differences in the amount of wealth began to emerge as some families were better at what they did, more fortunate in family alliances, or talented enough to do something that was highly valued. A successful family expanded not only by offering employment and livelihood to its children but also by having so much work that it began to employ nonfamily members. When a family accumulated land, wealth, and expertise, it became a wealthy family dynasty.

The drive for advancement of offspring and relatives is an essential element of social structure. If parents do not invest in their children's future, motivation and drive to succeed will be blunted. Children are their future, and because of children, families began to practice altruism and develop trust as they built with the future in mind. Abstract motivation for everyone to work hard or help others was not yet a part of human nature. Social bonds and relationships led people to care for one another and their children. Nepotism grew naturally as a reason for the family to exist. The extended family was a reservoir for shared purpose and values, a drive to build and create, and an engine for social innovation, altruism, and long-term outcomes. In his book *In Praise of Nepotism: A Natural History*, Adam Bellow defines nepotism not just as "undue preference for kin" but more so as "doing things with kinship."[2] He goes on to say, "In each of these great families, success was a multi-generational project. The question is: How did they do it?"[3] In short, Bellow argues, "Nepotism, properly understood, is an aspect of what anthropologists call the gift economy—the system of noncommercial exchanges that serves to regulate moral relations between individuals, families, and groups in a prestate society."[4]

These elements of society led family businesses to become the fundamental social institution. Practices like education of children, intermarriage, family alliances based on social networks, and social trust through exchange are the reason we have successful human societies. The family business and wealth could be passed down across many generations.

## Asian Origins of Thousand-Year Family Enterprises

Family businesses can last not just for generations but for centuries, particularly if culture and social conditions are stable. Some of the oldest known families that have owned and managed business are in Japan. Toshio Goto has written about the origins of family enterprise in Japan hundreds of years ago.[5] The families espoused a value system of Confucianism, a social-religious philosophy that prescribed family cooperation with established roles and respect for elders. The Confucian ethic is comparable to the Protestant ethic, which emerged a millennium later, prescribing principles and values for ethical family relations and social enterprise.

Goto views the nature of these effective families in the development of management skills, organization, accumulation of "reserves" to cover periods of difficulty, separation of ownership and management, state-of-the art bookkeeping and personnel management, and adherence to philosophical principles families pass on to their children. These factors prefigure the ideas of managerial capitalism that would arise in the twentieth century. Japanese families used the term *House* for the extended family, which could reach out by marriage, adoption of unrelated children, and alliances to include talented nonfamily members. The perpetuation of the House and its enterprise was the central purpose, a social process that has since taken root in many cultures.

The principles and practices of these ancient Japanese businesses, following Goto, prefigure common practices that this study has found in long-lived families today:

> *While Confucianism itself as an ethical philosophy and a prescription for family and business relationships is recognized as having made a unique contribution to the longevity of Japanese family firms, it can also be said that the specifics of its teachings and the business ethics it incorporated are factors that have similarly contributed to the longevity of family firms worldwide. These are family unity, a commitment to continuing the family legacy as the bedrock of survival, a product catering to basic human needs, allowing the business, rather than the family, to come first, an obligation to community and customer service, conflict arrangement and a system of governance.*[6]

Offering a credo for the next generation, employees, and the public is a common activity in dynastic families that continues today. In Asia, family enterprise embodied a cultural style that we call *collective harmony*.[7] In this style, the individual gains significance by being part of a family and the social fabric. An individual does not exist without being a part of a family. One adheres to the wisdom of society, which has developed over many generations and which is represented by the tradition of one's parents and ancestors. One's purpose in life is to fulfill the dreams of one's family. Society is made up of networks of harmonious extended family relations.

The founder/patriarch wants to pass on acquired wisdom to each new generation; this is often expressed in a family values statement. One ancient family, the Mogi, now approaching its twentieth generation of food manufacturing (Kikkoman soy sauce), codified its family rules for living hundreds of years ago. This set of family rules was meant to teach and direct the behavior of the family's successors. Reading them is remarkably similar to reading modern family constitutions and codes of conduct that arise in today's generative families. They read as follows:

- Make strong morals your foundation and focus on money last.
- Don't forget your foundation.
- Strive for harmony in your family.
- Avoid luxury: a simple life is a virtuous life.
- Do the job that you were born to do, and only that job.
- Treat a loss and a big gain the same.
- Competition can help you get ahead, but do not compete unfairly or to an extreme.
- Make your main meal boiled rice and barley and one bowl of miso soup.
- Eat the same food as your servants.
- Be strict with yourself but be kind to your servants.

- Keep your personal expenses low.
- Use the rest of your money for the good of the community to a level in keeping with your circumstances.
- Keep track of your finances and save money for the unexpected.
- Have a family reunion twice a year. At these reunions, don't judge your family members based on their income, but rather on their character.[8]

One of the oldest continuously existing family businesses is Kongō Gumi, which has been building temples (and now apartments and high-rise buildings) continuously in Japan since the sixth century. The family was commissioned by Prince Shōtoku to bring its expertise from Korea and build the first Buddhist temple to celebrate the adoption of this philosophy by the region. The craft of temple building was passed down by the family. Through the centuries, leadership passed to the oldest son, if he was capable.[9]

In addition to passing craftsmanship across generations, like other successful families, Kongō Gumi also transmitted traditions and values. The family expressed these in a statement of family values, codified first by the thirty-second "master" of the family enterprise. Like other ancient family values statements, this one is surprisingly relevant even today:

- Always use common sense.
- Do not drink too much, use obscene words, or harbor vicious will toward others.
- Master reading and calculating with the abacus, and practice [your craft] all the time.
- Give each task your full attention.
- Don't diversify; concentrate on your core business.
- Be well mannered and humble, and respect status.
- Respect others and listen to what they say, but don't be overly influenced by their words.
- Treat employees with a warm heart and kind words. Make them feel comfortable and work with them heart-to-heart but create an atmosphere that reinforces your role as the boss.
- Once you accept a job, do not fight with other people about it—especially clients.[10]

This statement anticipates many elements seen now in generative families, such as a personal philosophy of ethics and high performance, dedication, respect for employees and clients, and good business and management principles. These values were taught to successors in each generation. There is a philosophy of dedication, focus, discipline, and commitment that is about business importance rather than personal wealth and enjoyment.

Japan was a closed society with relatively little contact with the outside world until the arrival of Commodore Perry in 1853, which led to the opening of Japan and a path of growth, modernization, and Western influence that was taking place everywhere. For Kongō Gumi, the modern era ushered in a time of great social and economic change and a need to evolve. The family faced crises. The thirty-seventh master passed away, leaving three daughters—a challenge to male succession. His wife, Toshie, made the decision to become the thirty-eighth master, and she led the business for many years. She in turn passed the business to her youngest daughter, whose husband took the family name and was adopted into the company as the thirty-ninth master. During his tenure, there was a world war, and the family had to adapt to many societal changes. While the core of its business remains temple building, the family diversified into apartments and commercial buildings in order to keep its business afloat and take care of its employees, who expected lifetime employment. The emerging fortieth generation has been educated in the West and has adopted modern business technology and practices while respecting and continuing the family's legacy values and traditions. These traditions, as the remainder of this chapter will show, are remarkably similar around the world, which suggests that there is something biologically hardwired into humanity to develop family-based economic entities.

## Traders and Financiers: Accumulating and Sustaining Vast Family Fortunes

With the Renaissance, aristocratic commercial families emerged in the West, taking advantage of the rise of global trade. These families formed global alliances, facilitated trade and commerce, and also supported the arts and philanthropy. They often feature courageous, visionary, and colorful founders who forged a family enterprise out of modest roots. They spotted opportunities for making products, providing services, and producing goods that could be transported into wider and wider geographies. They helped found and support governments and also financed the development of cities, wars of conquest, and wars of commercial opportunity. They even had family offices, led by a nonfamily leader or majordomo. These were wildly successful families, but too often they were also tragedies, as the family then declined and fell apart in later generations.

The most famous example of a great house was the Medici family, which ruled the Republic of Florence through economic, political, and religious dominance during the thirteenth to fifteenth centuries. Beginning as a family textile business, the Medicis then created a bank, which became one of the largest in the world. Out of their economic power, the Medicis accumulated aristocratic titles and political power. Several family members became popes. Marriages cemented alliances with other powerful families, so their influence was felt throughout Europe. The Medicis are remembered as art patrons, sponsoring the building of cathedrals like St. Peter's as well as centers for art, music, and drama. Their support led to the development of opera and the invention of the piano. Their family used personal relationships to build and sustain vast power that touched every element of society. Their values led to the support of art and religious institutions that lasted well beyond their own century of influence.

But as they accumulated fame and political power, the Medicis neglected the economic engine of their success—the bank. It declined, setting the stage for the family's loss of social and political power. The incredible wealth and influence of prominent families frequently leads to their decline. Over multiple generations, a wealthy family tends to become deeply integrated into the social leadership and consumption of their wealth and, like the Medicis, begins to lose its focus as a shared enterprise. More and more Medici family members joined the aristocracy and leisure class, and the business and wealth-producing focus was lost.

This is the fate of most dynastic families in their third and later generations: the fruits of success lead to their downfall. Thomas Mann's classic novel *Buddenbrooks* tells the story of this gradual decline of family will and talent, as the great family succumbs to temptation. Generative, successful family enterprises find active ways to counteract this tendency, but it is always a seductive option to family members. The allure of assimilation frequently overcomes the discipline and shared effort that goes into sustaining a business empire.

The Medicis are an example of a cultural style we call the "honor culture," which is characterized by strong unquestioned family leadership and patronage. Medici family members were extremely loyal, needing protection from enemies. While reaching out to other families to create alliances, they were also constantly jockeying for power against them. Their rise, their hegemony, and their downfall were all the result of winning and then losing, often through violent power struggles. This style differs from the Asian "harmony culture," as the Medicis' honor culture style stemmed not from trust and connection to a cultural heritage but from suspicion and self-preservation within a larger community of warfare and conflict. Honor cultures are more volatile and emotional and less constrained by duty and obligation.

In the Medicis' time, family fortunes, once built, were sustained through mechanisms of success rooted in kinship systems. Primogeniture allowed landholding to remain with a single family. Marriage was another practice to keep wealth within the family. Families intermarried, cementing alliances and connecting families and thus allowing huge fortunes to grow. Today, when marriage is a personal choice rather than a family transaction, the use of prenuptial agreements serves this function for family wealth.

## The "House" of Rothschild

The archetypal family enterprise began in Europe in the dawn of the era of creating nations and then continued through urbanization and industrialization. The heirs of Mayer Amschel Rothschild were able to capitalize on these changes and even have a hand in hastening their adoption. Looking at their history over seven generations, it is not surprising to see many features that today are common in the generative families in the research my team and I conducted.

Mayer grew up in the Jewish ghetto of Frankfurt in the mid-eighteenth century. As a Jew, his career choices were limited, the most appealing being that of money lender and trader. He prospered by demonstrating high intelligence, dependability, and accountability and by cultivating patrons. He also groomed five of his sons for their future roles in the family business. He called them his "five arrows." The oldest, Nathan, was sent to England and was a second-generation entrepreneur, creating a huge new business there. In the early 1800s, Mayer's other sons developed businesses in other countries.

*(continued)*

*(Continued)*

Mayer's vision extended to the values and shared practices of his heirs. He instilled a set of values and practices of cooperation, trust of family, a mindset of secrecy outside the family, rules of excellence and accountability, and an emphasis on anticipating and adapting to new sociopolitical events. This was, after all, the age of revolutions and the emergence of nation-states as well as a time of wars and economic disruption. The family was also able to adapt to the evils of the day—bribery, secret intelligence gathering, war profiteering, and opportunistic alliances. Inside the Rothschild family, however, the rules of trust, fairness, cooperation, altruism, and development of the next generation held sway. Four years after Mayer's death in 1812, the brothers developed a clear cooperative business agreement containing their values and practices, similar in many ways to the modern business family constitution. They agreed not to allow lawsuits among themselves and developed a system of apprenticeships and advancement for the numerous members of the third generation. Their ability to cooperate and work together allowed them to innovate quickly and adapt to new situations much more quickly than traders or businesses based in one place.

The third generation faced additional challenges. No longer outsiders, the members of this generation were tempted to display their affluence and assimilate into their nation's wealthy elites. They were seduced by their wealth, which threatened their cooperation and internal meritocracy. As they became public figures, competitors emerged in new banks and institutions. But the Rothschilds' rules and traditions were strong enough to keep them united and able to adapt even in the face of success. They were able to continue to develop talented sons in their now five separate, interlinked, national family enterprises. They were adaptive to social upheaval, helping one another in financial crises, and were able to thrive into the fourth and later generations. Now into their seventh generation, male and female heirs lead varied family enterprises, from banks to land, wineries, venture capital, and investments.

The Rothschilds originated several features that continue to characterize generative families. They followed clear legacy values and rules laid down by the founder and his sons. In their case, they spread out and created independent banks in different countries, tied together by high trust for family, constant communication (using the secret language of the ghetto), co-ownership, cooperation with the business first, strict discipline, mutual accountability, internal secrecy, patient reinvestment of capital, marriage into other families, modest lifestyles that do not overly display wealth, grooming of members of the next generation with a sense of obligation for their roles, selection of heirs by merit, and family relationships. Elements like arranged marriages to suitable mates and exclusion of women (and in-laws) from the business have changed more recently following the developments in the rest of society.

Comparing the Rothschilds to a similar family, the Bleichröders, which did not survive, it is evident that clear values, consistently applied and adapted by each new generation, is instrumental to the Rothschilds' intergenerational generativity. Historian David S. Landes writes:

> *The two dynasties represent a kind of dualism: rootlessness vs. roots; anxiety vs. assurance; haughtiness vs. pride; outer vs. inner-directedness. The heart of continuity, I submit, is the question of identity and self. The Rothschilds knew who they were and where they came from, and therefore, where they were going; by the third generation, the Bleichroeders had changed their minds about who they were, or at least who they wanted to be, and had lost their way.*[11]

Dynastic families prioritized the family enterprise over individuals and house-holds. The family name, reputation, and wealth were viewed as a unit called, as we have seen, the *House*. The house was the wealth-creating and -sustaining part of the family. Clear leadership and control were centralized into a single family leader or into a group of directors, as with the Rothschild family. This is the honor culture.

The new economic dynasties were based on networks of families that could sustain trust, cooperation, and communication across boundaries. While communication was difficult, it was possible to move money across boundaries, share information, and reduce risk. The value of a family network and the advantages of shared family values, policies, and trust enabled family dynasties to sustain their wealth and postpone decline.

The Rothschild model of family solidarity, internal trust and cooperation, and external adaptation and business development is a common pattern in many countries as they transition to modern industrial states. Families are able to provide the capital, the organization, and the sustained effort to modernize societies. The Wallenberg family grew in Sweden over five generations of entrepreneurs. They invested in many businesses and are among the very wealthiest families in the world.

Over several centuries, European families have developed both great family enterprises and huge businesses. Another example is the French Wendel family, whose fortune began with iron ore on the border of Germany. This family has grown despite social revolutions and warfare. The French Revolution, two world wars, and also family strife and conflict have greatly challenged this family. But through the perseverance of family matriarchs, development of successive generations of family entrepreneurs, many children marrying well and adopting professions that added to their network and prominence, and the ability to adapt in business, the family continues to thrive. After being split into two parts by the First World War, the family used its sterling credit to borrow and invest in modernizing their plants in order to provide higher grades of steel better able to compete with British and other European competitors. Like many such families, by 1977 they had sold most of their factories and have now become a financial family, with a family office and diversified investments.

Traditions in India and China and in Jewish communities of families wandering into new territory account for some of their strength as generative families. These families didn't have land, so they had to make their living through trade. Their wan-derings made them families with the goods and resources of different places, and they could draw on family networks to buy, sell, and transport. They couldn't depend on anyone else but their extended family networks. So they taught and valued trust, cooperation, and partnership over individualism. They also used marriage to cement alliances and sustain and expand wealth. Before the twentieth century, marriage in most societies was not based on personal relationships but was an economic trans-action initiated by the family leader.

A global group of families that have been in business for more than 200 years, with family in ownership and direct management, the Hénokiens Association offers some insights into the factors that promote longevity. These forty-eight families shared histories of businesses that in Europe average nearly 300 years and that in Japan have existed for many more centuries than that. The member families include Hōshi Ryokan, a Japanese inn founded in 718, and the Italian Beretta family, a gun manufacturer over five hundred years old. These families cite five factors that they connect with their longevity: leveraging family assets, overcoming roadblocks, planning succession, promoting professionalization, and valuing adaptation and innovation. As I will show, especially in Chapter 6 on family culture, my study of contemporary family enterprise uncovered similar strengths.

## Paternalistic Industrialization: The Company Town

As they move into the modern, global, industrial era, family enterprises began to give up some of the practices and trappings of medieval family enterprise; this allowed them to become more adaptive and flexible. Skill and capability as well as loyalty to the family values and practices became more important than seniority in birth order to maintain the family's commercial success and impact. The role of primogeniture, passing the family resources to the oldest son, became less important than it had been to sustain the family territory. In some families, the hidden role of women came to the fore, as widows and daughters showed that they had the talent and demanded participation. The choice of whom to marry began to pass from the family to the individual. The perks of landed gentry and aristocracy gave way to the ascent of economic power in the dawn of the industrial age.

Family businesses developed new industrial ventures following the model of family landholders. Large, long-lived industrial families were frequently associated with their communities, and they felt a strong responsibility for the well-being of their employees and their families. This paternalistic view of taking care of employees has developed into today's value-based concern for the social, economic, and environmental impact of their work.

### The Cadbury Family and the Emergence of Social Responsibility[12]

From their origins as founders of a grocery store in Birmingham, England, during the first industrial revolution, Britain's Cadbury family has built a strong reputation as one of the country's leading family in business, social entrepreneurship, and philanthropy. They have been driven by a clear sense of purpose and priorities articulated and built around their Quaker identity. Eighteenth-century Quaker entrepreneurs in Britain and America adhered to a Puritan set of values and lifestyles, a clear set of principles that contributed to their business success: simplicity, frugality (they reinvested most of the profits in the business for long-term growth and innovation), solidarity, and social equity. They were willing to invest in the business success of their fellow Quakers by providing finance, business advice, and access to community business networks, with a strong belief in access to opportunities and social justice. The Cadburys are the archetypal example of these Quaker entrepreneurs. Their religious community was a sort of extended family.

John Cadbury opened his first grocery store in 1824 and soon identified a business opportunity in the mass production of chocolate drinks. He opened his first factory in 1831. From the very beginning, business and values were intrinsically linked: John,

*(continued)*

a devout Quaker, believed chocolate to be a healthy alternative to drinking alcohol and set about to democratize chocolate consumption, thereby aligning profit and the social good. One of his first products was even named "Churchman's chocolate." In 1866, the medium-sized business invested in a new technology developed by the Dutch van Houten family, and their gamble paid off, unleashing an era of fast growth and market domination.

In the 1880s, the Cadburys made business and social goals come together through the creation of a new community, Bournville, built around their new factory. "Why would an industrial area be squalid and depressing," wrote George, second generation co-owner of the family business. "No man ought to be condemned to live in a place where a rose cannot grow."[13] George and his brother found a greenfield site and set out to build a new factory surrounded by a model community. The latter was designed as a for-profit venture and expected "to operate on an ordinary commercial basis," according to an early commercial pamphlet.[14] By 1900, George Cadbury had built 300 houses on the greenfield site, hoping that the village might become a model where industry would produce well-planned, village-like communities, with good but cheap homes of all sizes, and green space to be enjoyed by all. Quaker ethics informed their emphasis on shared green spaces for recreation driven by the core religious values of creating "healthy," alcohol-free communities. By doing so, they pioneered the concept of low-cost plus low-density plus green working-class communities. They proved it could be profitable to private developers and governments and served as inspiration for future Quaker-built garden communities.

Faced with the unprecedented challenge of managing explosive growth during the first industrial revolution, and of finding solutions to overcrowding and societal shifts from a mostly agricultural to an industrial society, they brought "innovative ideas to scale by investing their time and energy"; they did not "just write checks"; they used their business skills to build modern industrial communities with a sense of purpose, reinventing for the urban era the integration of work, housing, and leisure that had existed in rural England. John Cadbury was instrumental in infusing the community's business model, social interactions, and aesthetics with his Quaker values that encouraged and rewarded the pursuit of wealth and saw risk taking by entrepreneurs as valuable expression of stewardship.[15] Bishop and Green themselves point to the parallels between modern and ancient philanthropy.[16]

From the 1930s, Western government policy took over urban planning and social policy, with the creation of the 'Welfare State." As Britain and most of Europe embraced a US model of growth that favored large publicly traded companies with a clear separation of ownership and management, the stakeholder model of financial, social, and environmental goals preferred by family businesses lost momentum; family businesses themselves opened their capital to outsiders, hired non-family CEOs, and refocused mostly on financial goals. Business schools and leading consulting firms drilled the importance of shareholder value, and Milton Friedman's economic ideas reigned supreme.

The Cadburys adapted by turning to new societal challenges where institutions were failing to provide early answers. In 1992, Sir Adrian Cadbury turned his attention to corporate governance. The unexpected collapse of two leading UK firms (Coloroll and Polly Peck), soon followed by the default of two other titans, BCCI (a bank) and Robert Maxwell's media empire, triggered major investigations, and a loss of faith in

(continued)

*(Continued)*

existing corporate governance and regulatory bodies. What became known as "the Cadbury Report," written by a committee led by Sir Adrian, sought to restore faith in large corporations and set the tone for British corporate governance for decades. It recommended the professionalization and increased independence of the board of directors, a voluntary code of conduct, and more transparency, with companies expected to "comply [with the code] or explain [why they deviated]." On the later evolution of Cadbury's governance and identity under new owner Kraft, Sir Adrian was scathing: "a bidder can buy a business. What they cannot acquire is legitimacy over the character, values, experience and traditions on which that business was founded and flourished."[17] By tackling the issue of governance, the Cadburys tried to reinfuse business with a sense of social purpose, and to protect the workers whose company pensions had disappeared, and the small investors who were the last to learn of the impending failures.

## The Gilded Age in the New World

As trading and manufacturing opportunities in Europe allowed families that created unique goods through their craftsmanship to develop businesses, new family fortunes arose in the fledgling United States. The Civil War marked the downfall of the landed aristocracy of the Southern states and the rise of the industrialists in the North. Larger enterprises grew up in the early stages of industrialization. These ventures, and trade in commodities from the rich natural resources of the New World, led to the fast accumulation of enormous fortunes. Industrialization and new technology created the opportunity to develop immense wealth and employ vast numbers of people. Without regulation, the power of the land or factory owner made employees almost serfs.

The Asian harmony culture and the European honor culture were the original models of family business, with the honor culture spreading to other continents by colonial transmission. But with the industrial age and the rise of cities and social migration, a new cultural style emerged. In this "individualist" cultural style, the individual is recognized as the basic building block, as individual initiative becomes more important than inherited social norms. Individualists are culture creators and build new fortunes without links to previous generations or the benefit of inherited social aristocracy. This type of industry created whole new family dynasties. This style is exemplified by the behavior of the business leaders of the emerging industrial age in the United States.

Many of the embryonic US family businesses at the dawn of industrialization were more notorious than beloved. The entrepreneurs who founded them were often viewed as greedy, immoral "robber barons" whose pursuit of profit was at the expense of workers and society. They attained great wealth and expected to pass it on to their families, but as a group, they were not good stewards. Next-generation siblings of many hugely wealthy families were quick to dissipate the wealth, mismanage the businesses, and fragment and disperse. They were the exemplars of the "shirtsleeves to shirtsleeves" mythology, and their behavior merited it.

Along with the rise of family fortunes came the creation of legal structures that enabled continuity of the family's wealth across generations. Sociologist George Marcus has spent a lifetime observing the dynamics of these "dynastic" families that accumulated vast intergenerational wealth. He observes:

> This country is now old enough to have accumulated a large number of great fami-
> lies. Though we have insisted for two hundred years in viewing ourselves as a society
> of striving individuals, the constructive contributions of these families are too obvi-
> ous to deny any longer. Americans admire the Adamses, Roosevelts, and Kennedys
> not just for their unity—a value that is becoming increasingly difficult to preserve in
> our mobile society—but for their sense of common purpose and the spirit of public
> service that they cultivate.

Families developed estate plans and trusts to retain their fortunes across generations, creating vast new family dynasties. Marcus writes:

> A legally devised plan to transfer and conserve patrimonial capital in one generation
> becomes in the next generation an organizational framework for extended family
> relations—actually a formal model or surrogate of the family, with law rather than
> the founding entrepreneurial patriarch as its source of authority. Law overlays, and
> to a degree, complicates kin relations by giving a more formal organization to the
> extended family clan than that of most middle-class families.

These entities—trusts, foundations, and family offices—create the institutional
structure by which the family can sustain its wealth and institute rules and policies
that regulate the tendency to fight and struggle for power and authority. The hiring of neutral family advisors to manage these entities allows families to find ways
to regulate themselves and keep their values and connections alive. Long after the
founder has passed away, the family legal organization can help manage the growing
network of family relationships. Marcus continues:

> In generational aging and transition, a family must create a transcendent, control-
> ling version of itself in the organization of its property to achieve a coherence of
> organization that can preserve the mystique of its name and ensure its continuing
> exercise of patrician functions in its social environment.

Thus, even if a wealth creator shows little talent or interest in the family future,
the trust or family office can oversee the family's wealth and business. The family
structure and governance, my study shows, reinforces the family's desire to instill
and pass on a distinct culture and values in each generation.

Gilded Age wealth creators were not very attuned to preparing their children
for wealth or training them for their role. They had no idea that this was important
or that it was a role that needed preparation. They were self-made and self-oriented
and did not look to the future. They often worked at cross-purposes: they showered
their children with the trappings of affluence to show their power and importance
while at the same time expecting their children to make it on their own.

## Managerial Capitalism: The Rise of the Modern Corporation and the Eclipse of Family Business

Industrialization and the Gilded Age produced highly centralized family wealth that, after the passing of the founder, was difficult to operate and sustain. With the growth of the large businesses—railroads, real estate, stores, manufacturers, raw materials, hotels, and cars—the challenge of running them successfully led to the adoption of a new business model, one based on mechanical and bureaucratic rationality. As these businesses grew, traditional family governance models could not manage the huge task of sustaining the family along with disciplined oversight of huge businesses. Enter the public corporation and the rationalization of management and leadership.

The modern era of business is identified with Alfred Chandler's model of the corporation, embodied in the structure and operations of General Motors. As industrialism spread, large businesses needed to rationalize their operations and create machine-like organizations that operated by principles of mechanization and bureaucracy. There was no place for the personal management of companies and less need for the secrecy, alliances, and communication networks of the family. Family enterprises did not disappear, but the pressure to rationalize and separate ownership from control in order to raise capital and form public companies put family businesses on the defensive.

The large bureaucratic corporation is run by managers for large groups of shareholders who have no personal connection with one another or any shared goals or values, other than the desire to share profits. In this model, direct control by families was replaced by a group of professional managers who used rational principles to create effective organizations. Business research defined the problems of "agency" as the distinction between the different goals and agendas of the professional managers, who were compensated for being loyal to the owners, and the goals and agendas of the owners, but who had to be watched closely. Over time, the company leadership became tied to these leaders, who were hired and fired for their performance.

At the turn of the twentieth century, there were dozens of car companies, using artisans to turn out costly but beautiful and creative models. Two huge companies emerged. Henry Ford created the modern assembly line for manufacturing and pioneered the mass-produced car. He created a loyal labor force by raising wages significantly and by creating the "company town," which was a feudal, company-owned community that offered housing much as the system overseen by a medieval lord. But this was motivated not so much by caring but by the economic need to have a dedicated and dependent labor force. Ford had a team of social workers who enforced rules for his employees' family behavior in a highly coercive manner. At its worst, he created a kind of private police state among the workers. Alongside his giant achievement as an industrial pioneer, there was an oppressive approach to labor relations that became counterproductive, leading to the rise of labor unions to challenge these practices. The caring community-based industrialism of the Cadbury model was replaced by a more predatory, less benevolent attitude toward workers. Family enterprises adopted either of these models, but the values-based Cadbury model offered clear advantages over the long-term.

Ford was a giant as an industrialist but not very effective in inspiring loyalty or innovating in his own model. After developing the affordable Model T and doubling the wages of his employees, his success was so great that he appeared to stop learning and innovating. He resisted suggestions that he offer cars in colors other than black, that he upgrade and develop different models for different economic and social groups, or that he actively advertise and market his cars. In his mind, his creation was all that people needed. Period. He was unable to change, let go of power, and listen to or trust others, including his son, Edsel, who tried to dutifully follow his example. Henry never let him lead, despite his capability. Edsel died very early, and Henry reemerged as the sole leader once again.

The company declined, and the beneficiary was Chandler's General Motors, which was one of the first huge modern companies, with many shareholders and no family behind it. In fact, they bought up family car companies to develop their life-cycle model of brands and consumer marketing. It was only after World War II that Henry's grandson, Henry Ford II, brought in a business-disciplined group of "whiz kids" from the US Department of Defense to organize the company. While the Ford family retains ultimate control to this day, the company was able to develop by delegating management to a succession of nonfamily leaders. They have rekindled their family values and legacy along a new path.

The Chandler model was popularized in the emerging business schools, which focused exclusively on the business, not on the owners. Under this model, there was no reason to understand or even look at the families that had founded these companies. The business could be studied as an entity in itself. If everyone was concerned with rational self-interest, it should make no difference if the owners were a family or a bunch of disinterested strangers. Family business was seen as archaic, needing to adopt a rational business structure and delegate leadership to nonfamily managers. If there were stories about family business, they were about how family leadership in the second or third generation caused the business to lose value or self-destruct. The emerging field of family business began to counter this trend, but the prevailing assumption that the highest form of business was the rational, managerial enterprise has kept the study of the family aspects of family enterprise from being fully integrated into business schools and research.

Since the business was the only focus, the role of the family in defining the business's values or culture was below the radar. Family oversight over the culture and over the role of nonfamily operating managers was hidden from public view. The rational model of family enterprise did not clearly recognize the difference between the Cadbury or the Ford approach by families. The presence of family influence was not always obvious and tended to remain hidden, and this reinforced the focus on the management of the business. But given the huge footprint and success of public corporations, the focus of the media and business education was on nonfamily managers and not on the governance or control exercised by the family. Since the focus of business education was on the business alone, when the business was sold, went public, or merged with another, this was seen as the end of the family enterprise. However, as this book shows, if we look at the evolution of the business as a unit of enterprise, over time families buy, own, and sell multiple businesses and exercise oversight via ownership control. When the family is looked at as the core rather than an individual business, a different view of enterprise emerges.

## Hidden Champions: Family Business Quietly Enters the Modern Era

The rise of managerial capitalism did not lead to the demise of family enterprises, but for a while their prevalence and role was hidden and largely unheralded. Without much public attention, family businesses were thriving all over the world. Media would publicize family feuds and conflicts, which were colorful and offered a look at the private worlds of family owners. The media presented family wealth as a morality tale, where the rapacious owners who did not deserve their wealth were given their comeuppance. Negative press about business families became the norm; family feuds and dysfunction sold many newspapers, many of them owned and operated by families themselves.

In the twenty-first century, there have been significant difficulties in public companies that do not practice focused oversight and long-term focus. Professional managers are agents for the dispersed owners, and rather than subordinate their personal self-interest, they want to earn their salaries and bonuses by producing short-term profit, if necessary, abandoning legacy values in this quest. Business leaders can be awarded significant ownership and compensation to the detriment of smaller shareholders and the long-term value of the company. Pressure from shareholders who want immediate returns can also damage the long-term prospects of a company. The pursuit of immediate gains and profitability can make a rational company very risk averse and unwilling or unable to invest in new ideas, innovations, and long-term projects with higher risk but potential reward.

But when a family business is successful as a large public company, family control and ownership actually can add qualities that are in limited supply in managerial companies. During the rise of huge companies, the cases and theories studied in business schools focused on these larger public companies. But there was another layer of business development, one in which family companies are the major players. These are small- and medium-sized enterprises (SMEs), mostly privately owned by a family, that succeed under the radar, applying an approach to business that is hugely effective but differs from the bureaucratic impersonalism of large public companies. These have been labeled "hidden champions"[18] because, while highly successful, they largely exist with quiet leaders and do not seek publicity. While they are found all over the world, they proliferate in German-speaking and Scandinavian countries, which have a long tradition of a stakeholder view of enterprise.

They are profitable companies with unique products that inspire customer loyalty and market leadership. They reinvest in innovation and development and are expanding globally and in new products, with a clear focus on a core technology or product. They have long-term leaders, originally from the founding family and then from successful internal leaders who have a great loyalty to the company. They also have a clear set of values about the quality of their product and their loyalty to customers, suppliers, and employees as well as a long-term vision and plan. As later chapters will show, this model is common to generative family enterprise.

Two recent books[19] compare the evolution of key families that avoid this decline. They profile families that were early models of generativity. The accounts describe qualities of family enterprise that, when carefully and thoughtfully applied to commerce, are adaptive rather than dysfunctional.

The qualities of hidden champions apply to family enterprises in general. In 2005, Danny and Isabelle Le Breton-Miller studied high-performing and long-lived global family businesses.[20] Their research contains many case examples of how these families had clear and inspirational values that were attached to their products and brands and how they created businesses that were about alignment regarding core purpose, adherence to cultural values and long-term sustainability, closeness to customers and suppliers, creation of a strong and dedicated company culture, and ability to make quick and adaptive decisions. Unlike other family businesses, the more successful ones were more transparent, were based on sharing information within the company, were loyal, trusting, and respectful to others, and were collaborative. They were able to extend power and authority within the company while having the courage and willingness to make quick decisions and changes when needed.

## Are Family Enterprises More Effective and Profitable Than Nonfamily-Controlled Public Corporations?

A lot of research has been done to determine whether a family business is better or worse than a nonfamily business. Some studies have shown that family businesses, especially those led by the early generations, perform better while others find the opposite. Looking deeper, we see that family businesses have different functions in societies in the early stages of commercial development, when there is the lack of infrastructure of laws and practices to guide and regulate business development. We also see that the definition of family business is difficult. A family can exercise control not only by owning the company or a majority of the shares but also by different types of stock, cross-ownership, and use of family trusts, all of which allow continued family control over key functions of the business. With this view, many public companies continue to have family control, even as they appear to be public, managerial corporations. How many businesses are noted as family-controlled makes it difficult to gauge their performance vis-à-vis nonfamily enterprise. So mixed results are found when the questions asked are overly general and do not differentiate between different types or stages of family enterprise.

Family enterprises began to change in the era of managerial corporations. They distinguished themselves by continuing to adhere to their family values, and in successive generations, they sometimes even challenged the corporations they shared ownership of to respect them. The families also began to shift their focus from accumulating wealth to defining and upholding the purpose of their wealth. New generations pursued social missions that diverged from those of the corporations. A Gilded Age family that pioneered this new direction of family enterprise was the Rockefeller family, which overcame the exploitiveness of its family wealth creator to move the family in new directions.

## Rockefeller Family: Philanthropy and Values-Based Enterprise

In the United States, the archetypal family enterprise is that of the Rockefeller family. This family began by recognizing and creating the oil monopoly in the beginning of the industrial age and evolved into multiple philanthropic and socially responsible family financial offices and entities. As it enters its fifth generation, the family continues to have an identity in philanthropy and also as a series of family enterprises that organized into what is called a "family office" and have continued to bring financial value to the extended family.

This is a sharp contrast to other families that have sold or moved beyond their initial legacy business. After selling their businesses, many families fragment and divide their wealth, losing their shared identity. The contemporaries of the Rockefellers in the new industrial age—such as the Vanderbilts or the DuPonts—may have continued to offer wealth to family members in successive generations, but the shared impact, identity, and ability to conduct shared ventures has ended for these families. They are wealthy but can no longer be considered family enterprises, with a shared vision and a reach across generations. The Rockefellers sustained their values and shared identity and preserved their wealth across six generations, nearly a century after they lost control of their family business.

Rockefeller wealth grew rather quickly, with the founder, John D. Rockefeller, creating the oil cartel and exploratively unifying hundreds of smaller companies at the dawn of the industrial revolution in the late nineteenth and early twentieth centuries. Although Rockefeller was reviled at the time, leading to a landmark breakup of his empire, he still emerged as the wealthiest person of his generation. His wealth passed to his son, John D. Rockefeller, Jr. (known as Junior), whose life project was to change the perception of his family and to use the wealth for social good. He pursued a lifetime of philanthropy, as an entrepreneurial pioneer of the activist philanthropist. Like his contemporary Andrew Carnegie, JDR Jr. looked at the future of the family and saw its mission and purpose as the service of society due to his deep religious beliefs. While his business behavior has been challenged, his deep commitment to his religious-based approach to philanthropy has continued to define his family's legacy for four succeeding generations. The Rockefellers' example offers a model of how generational succession in family wealth builds upon a foundation of values and principles that the family upholds as new generations and new ventures arise.

With the coming of the third generation of the vast wealth of the Rockefeller family, the emergence of five strong-willed male heirs had the potential for working at cross-purposes or developing severe conflict. To forestall this, early in their adult lives, after

*(continued)*

they returned from the war and began their careers, the brothers crafted the following family agreement:

> We, the undersigned, being brothers and having interests and objectives in common, have joined together in our desire to continue the tradition of public service and fearless leadership established by our grandfather and carried forward and extended by our parents. In uniting our efforts and coordinating our activities, we hope to be more effective in aiding in the preservation and development of the republic form of government and the private enterprise system which in our opinion have been fundamental factors in making the United States a powerful nation of free people . . . .
>
> In line with those convictions, we are prepared to subordinate personal or individual interests as and when necessary for the sake of accomplishing our broader objectives. We propose to use our individual abilities and those material resources which are at our disposal to further these objectives. By acting together with a common purpose, we will be in a stronger position not only to promote our common interests, but also to foster and effectuate our individual interests. We will be free to pursue independent and varied interests, at the same time taking full advantage of our diverse interests in the attainment of common objectives. Accordingly, we hereby form a partnership, the objective of which shall be to carry out the foregoing objectives.[21]

The family exited active management of its oil companies generations ago and embarked on a path of investment and philanthropy. The family created one of the first "family offices" to manage these entities and the affairs of the five brothers and their sister and their growing families. Like the Rothschild brothers, the Rockefeller brothers agreed to subordinate competition for the greater good of the whole. Their resources were vast and diverse. The family office hired outstanding nonfamily advisors to lead their different activities, including investment in their social missions, their many vacation and wilderness real estate holdings, investments in many forms, and the interests of growing members of the fourth generation.

The more unique and notable innovations by the overall family were the steps taken by the individual families to develop their values and personal relationships. The overall family met regularly at one of the family's large estates, and vocal members of the fourth generation challenged family values and the philanthropic mission of the family. As a group, the members of the fourth generation brainstormed the values they shared for promoting the common good, as individuals and in collaboration with others. These values are:

> Nurture family through the generations, provide safe environments for open dialogue, respect diversity, consider every topic within a larger context, think long-term, serve effectively within your communities, support the value of leadership and public service, and do not take yourself so seriously.[22]

These values underlie the interactions of family members and the projects they undertake as a philanthropic family.

The family was also notable for investing in the development of and commitment to the next generation. The family was always reframing and challenging the family to live according to its values. The fifth generation even entered into a lawsuit against its former family business, now Exxon, that challenged Exxon's environmental record.

Each generation has worked as a community not only to follow the family values but also to define its own philanthropic approach. Eileen Rockefeller Growald,[23] one of

(continued)

*(Continued)*

the youngest members of the fourth generation, which created the Rockefeller Family Fund, recalls how her generation developed its own approach to the family legacy. This generation created several family rituals. One, a ceremony called "Passages," involves new adult family members and spouses being formally presented and welcomed into the family. A second ritual is called "Intergenerational Dialogue" and was introduced by a G4 couple who had formed a group that held "Public Conversations." These dialogues helped older generations share and teach the work each generation was doing in its public service. The family met regularly at large family gatherings, where there would also be many smaller group project teams and meetings. Each generation would meet as a community and also form smaller project teams that dealt with shared areas of interest. For example, Growald helped found an organization called the Collaborative for Academic, Social, and Emotional Learning, and through this group, she brought emotional intelligence skills and training to other family members.

Melissa A. Berman, the president and CEO of Rockefeller Philanthropy Advisors, notes:

> [T]he Rockefellers must have a special governance gene. A great deal of thought goes into the structures of their family organizations, their councils, their meetings, and their various committees. That careful planning has made family members very astute, from an early age, about the difference between governing and managing. It also makes them astoundingly good board members, and it continues to foment their interest in founding new institutions.[24]

## "Refamiliazation": Family Advantages Reemerge in a Wired but Short-Term World

After a period of huge growth in public companies and the rise of a rational, bureaucratic model of organization, we have begun to experience the downside of these huge public companies. They are plagued with investors who want to see short-term profits and who do not have the patience to invest in long-term success. Their leadership turns over quickly, and they find it difficult to maintain a consistent culture or sustain core values that take into account the needs of nonowners, such as employees, suppliers, or their community. Viewing these deficiencies of public companies, we have begun to rediscover and turn attention to the family enterprises that developed largely outside of public attention as the economic foundation of most countries. We have begun to see that their virtues as business entities with a long-term focus, patient capital, and trusting relationships enable them to sustain long-term consistency in leadership and a culture that adheres to stated core values.

As we enter a new century of global business, characterized by uncertainty, unpredictability, high risk, and dramatic technological innovation, the public company managerial model may no longer be the most adaptive form of business. All over the world, business is discovering advantages of long-term family ownership and control. Family enterprises are not new. They have always been there. But instead of being hidden, they are now emerging from the shadows. Their model of personal capitalism is more suited to a period of social and economic volatility. In an impersonal world, they can sustain trust in personal relationships extending from the family. They have patient capital, which can withstand reverses and lack of immediate return.

In the twenty-first century, the family business has come to center stage once more but in a different form. When a family firm is able to overcome emerging challenges in each generation and continue to grow and expand, it can become a portfolio of family ventures, united by family control, values, and oversight. Writing about the Benetton family, historian Andrea Colli writes, "The family seems to have been able to coexist with professional management by building up an organizational structure where the virtues of family involvement are associated with the advantages derived from the delegation of responsibility into a multi-subsidiary structure."[25]

There has also been a shift in how the family is viewed. Earlier, the focus was on the family as owner of a legacy business. In the twenty-first century, families have begun to differentiate themselves from their roots in a large legacy business. Many generative families continue in the form of family offices, as family holding companies for a portfolio of enterprises, or through identification with a foundation or various family philanthropic vehicles. The basic unit is no longer a family business but the evolving family as a values-creating cross-generational group. The family enterprise is more than just a business.

The emergence of new models for family enterprise was made necessary by the vast societal changes taking place in the twenty-first century where the special advantages of family enterprise were sources of competitive advantage. The sweeping changes are all part of a new information-based industrial revolution:

- Rise of digital platforms and technology in communication and manufacturing
- Globalization: diminishing cost of moving goods, rising connectedness
- Sale of family business, leading to family ownership of huge amounts of capital, and reorganization of families as diversified family offices

Indeed, as this book will show, these changes offered capabilities that public nonfamily companies found it hard to duplicate. They created a need for companies that can assemble information and adapt quickly. The huge corporate behemoths were at a disadvantage while family businesses were not. The newer view of the family enterprise can be considered a response to the mechanistic assumptions of managerial capitalism. As Colli writes, "The family firm ... presented a human dimension where 'people mattered.' It also held out the prospect of a new production mode—one much more creative and less impersonal, molded by elements like friendship and kinship."[26] By working within a framework of trust established within a family, with a long-term commitment and set of values about people and business, and with an ability to try out new ideas, the family enterprise presented an antidote to certain consequences of industrial corporations. By keeping identity and power as a family, the family owners could also exercise leadership in communities, commerce, and society. Rather than seeing the business as a commodity that can be bought and sold, a family enterprise is viewed by the family as a community to which they have certain obligations and values.

This study of one-hundred-year generative family enterprises enables us to look more closely at the potential embodied in these family enterprises. This book looks at their evolution as families that share business and financial assets and shows how the presence of family stewards as owners drives them to act and operate with values and relationships at their core. With their ancient roots as the foundation of society, maybe it is time to learn more from their example as we look to create business and financial structures that support the good of everyone as well as the well-being and vision of wealthy families.

## Notes

1. Marcel Mauss, *The Gift: Forms and Functions of Exchange in Archaic Societies* (New York: Norton, 1967).
2. Adam Bellow, *In Praise of Nepotism: A Natural History* (New York: Doubleday/Random House, 2003), 465.
3. Ibid.
4. Ibid.
5. Toshio Goto, "Longevity of Japanese Family Firms," in *Handbook of Research on Family Business*, eds. Panikkos Zata Poutziouris, Kosmas X. Smyrnios, and Sabine B. Klein (Northampton, MA: Edward Elgar Publishing, 2006), 517–534.
6. Goto, 517.
7. The model of three global family business cultures is presented in Dennis Jaffe and James Grubman, *Cross Cultures: How Global Families Negotiate Change Across Generations* (Family Wealth Consulting, 2016).
8. Quoted in William Shurtleff and Akiko Aoyagi, *Early History of Soybeans and Soyfoods Worldwide (1024 BCE to 1899): Extensively Annotated Bibliography and Sourcebook* (Lafayette, CA: Soyinfo Center, 2014), 237.
9. This account of the history of Kongō Gumi was taken primarily from William T. O'Hara, *Centuries of Success: Lessons from the World's Most Enduring Family Businesses* (Avon, MA: Adams Media, 2004), 1–15.
10. Quoted in O'Hara, 7.
11. David S. Landes, "Bleichröders and Rothschilds: The Problem of Continuity in the Family Firm," *Family Business Review* 6, no. 1 (1993): 96.
12. This history was contributed by Isabelle Lescent-Giles.
13. https://www.cadbury.co.uk/about-bournville.
14. Outka, E. 2009. *Consuming Traditions: Modernity, Modernism, and the Commodified Authentic* (Oxford: Oxford University Press), 33.
15. A. R. Bailey, "A Quaker Experiment in Town Planning: George Cadbury and the Construction of Bournville Model Village," *Quaker Studies* 11, no. 1 (2007): 89–114; also B. Hilton, *The Age of Atonement: The Influence of Evangelicalism on Social and Economic Thought, 1785–1865* (Oxford: Oxford University Press, 1986).
16. http://philanthrocapitalism.net/bonus-chapters/ancient-giving/.
17. https://www.ft.com/content/2f99b24a-5328-11e5-8642-453585f2cfcd.
18. Hermann Simon, *Hidden Champions of the Twenty-first Century: The Success Strategies of Unknown World Market Leaders* (New York: Springer, 2009).
19. O'Hara's *Centuries of Success* goes back over a thousand years to profile Japan's Kongō Gumi, arguably the first multigenerational family enterprise, and the Hōshi Ryokan, a resort that still exists today in almost its original form. It then moves into Europe to tell of the oldest and most successful European dynasties. In *Dynasties: Fortunes and Misfortunes of the World's Great Family Businesses* (New York: Viking/Penguin, 2006), Harvard

economic historian David S. Landes profiles a dozen families from Europe and the United States who pioneered industries.

20. Danny Miller and Isabelle Le Breton-Miller, *Managing for the Long Run: Lessons in Competitive Advantage from Great Family Businesses* (Boston: Harvard Business School Press, 2005).

21. Quoted in Peter Collier and David Horowitz, *The Rockefellers: An American Dynasty* (New York: Holt, Rinehart & Winston, 1976), 244.

22. *An Entrepreneurial Spirit: Three Centuries of Rockefeller Family Philanthropy*, ed. Donzelina A. Barroso (New York: Rockefeller Philanthropy Associates, 2005), 21.

23. The history of the family's values and philanthropy, according to family members from the fourth and fifth generations, is recounted in Barroso, *An Entrepreneurial Spirit.*

24. Melissa A. Berman, "Foreword," in *An Entrepreneurial Spirit*, 3.

25. Andrea Colli, *The History of Family Business, 1850–2000* (Cambridge, UK: Cambridge University Press, 2003), 64.

26. Ibid., 23.

# PART TWO

# The Evolution of the Resilient Family Enterprise

This section looks at the journey of families as they evolve as a shared enterprise. I present a "movie" of how what I call "generative" families evolve over four or more generations. The next chapters then focus on the family's business; how it changes over generations, the elements of the unique family enterprise culture that characterizes generative families, and origin of the role of steward that emerges in the family that oversees a portfolio of enterprises.

Chapter 4 takes a broad view of the evolution of the embryonic family enterprise in its first four generations. We then see, in Chapter 5, how the family evolves from a legacy business to a portfolio of family ventures that make up the family enterprise. Chapter 6 presents the unique elements of a family culture that embodies the family enterprise, and how they together make up what is known as the "generative alliance." Chapter 7 looks at how the value of social responsibility impacts family ventures and creates a social vision that families follow. And finally, Chapter 8 shows how by the third generation, the role of family owners shifts from owner/operator to steward, and how the family governance creates a board to oversee the enterprise.

# PART

# The Evolution of the Resilient Family Enterprise

# CHAPTER 4

# The First Four Generations

Every great family enterprise begins with a family psychodrama. The family has an origin myth about an obsessed, visionary patriarch (only three of our families were started by women, none of them from the United States) who overcomes limited means and creates a thriving business. His wife is a pillar of quiet strength as she raises the next generation, and maybe pursues a less high-profile career. Following this great business achievement, the second generation faces even greater challenges: sustaining the business, dealing with diverging family interests, creating a shared vision of the future, and balancing family justice and fairness with business reality.

By the third generation, a business family faces questions about how to use its wealth, whether family members want to continue to work together, and if so, what they want to do. After a generation or two, the legacy business usually gives way to a diversified portfolio with multiple family assets and entities, including trusts, investments, real estate, a foundation, and even the sale, renewal, or expansion of the original. While the effects of this evolution are readily seen in the family's business and financial activities, the key actions that make this possible take place within the family itself. This reality is often hidden from the public. This chapter outlines the developmental path described by the generative families interviewed for this study, which will be further amplified in the remainder of the book.

Generative families evolve into complex extended families, moving from a single wealth-creator couple to successors often loosely connected to each other, their legacy, and their shared business and financial interests. The members of the first generation are also parents, who want their children to inherit ownership and responsibility. Each sibling forms a new household, and these siblings' children become the third generation. To sustain the enterprise, second- and third-generation family members must follow the founder's wishes but work together in relative harmony. This is easier expected than accomplished. Their collaboration is deeply tied to their sibling relationships and history together, although they often have to overcome different interpretation of the founder's vision or about how to proceed.

The successor households and family branches decide whether and how to continue the legacy. If they succeed, the extended family becomes a dynastic family with a shared heritage but increasingly loose connection and identification as a family. The inheritors may take steps to build shared identity, connection, and partnership capability. When they do, they become more than just wealthy dynasties; they become generative families.

Becoming a generative family is a multigenerational endeavor involving many family members. It is not a decision or event; it is much more. Challenges continually emerge, and family members' choices can endanger the family's future survival. To endure beyond G3, the family has to evolve and transform itself over and over again. Recollections by later-generation family members provide a glimpse into the huge impact of business origin stories and key decisions. But they are not enough to insure survival. Several common actions in G2 and G3 set the stage for continued success.

## G1: Legacy of the Wealth Creator

Business founders all over the world exhibit certain qualities that appear to account for their business success. These founders usually come from humble origins and do not create the business with the conscious intention to become rich. They have a dream as well as capability, grit, and persistence to realize that dream. They are confident as they recover and learn from setbacks and failures. Because of the immensity of their challenge, they are often highly controlling and work twenty-four hours a day. They are never satisfied, always striving for new achievements. The business is their life, and family members are clearly second. These characteristics are seen in business founders all over the world. While being born into different cultures, wealth creators appear more similar to one another than to others in their home communities.

The entrepreneur is not alone; the matriarch is the mother of the children and usually takes on the role of maintaining the household and creating the family culture. She is often the liaison between the two generations, a hidden partner and confidant, perhaps the only person who can challenge the patriarch and resolve conflict. Responsible for the care and development of the next generation, the matriarch takes a leading role in the choice to begin to create a family enterprise and, if so, setting the groundwork for making it happen. She often acts as their advocate as well.

While the wealth creator can have the intention of setting up a family enterprise, it is often the matriarch who develops the human capital to sustain it. Second- and third-generation family members acknowledge this pivotal role, but there is a tendency for the family to ignore or minimize her contribution. It is most visible, however, in a situation where the wealth creator dies and the matriarch receives business ownership and control and has to set up the structure and process for installing the next generation of leadership.

Here is one third-generation family leader's description of his mother's role as a translator and mediator after his father passed away. Many matriarchs emerge after having a private role with the business leader, visibly helping the next generation take over:

*My mom stepped up. She was always with my dad. A lot of people would ask, Was she a housewife? She was a professional, but she was not involved in day-to-day operation of the business. On the strategic, board side, she would be an active leader in meetings. She was able to manage the family dynamics on both sides as it related to the business.*

*She was very aware of the steps for all the last 50 years and the history before that. She was able to fill in a lot of the gaps of things that we didn't know because the know-how was gone. We had just put the structure to translate some of the know-how into the organization.*

*After my father passed away we had constant regular meetings between all the family members. We talked about family issues, but also about the business. For the first six months, we were meeting every single day because the situation was that there was this bombardment. We were blindsided.*

My colleague James Grubman describes first-generation wealth creators as "immigrants" to wealth.[1] By that he means that they did not come from wealth and that their wealth creation brings them into a new cultural group—people with significant wealth. These wealth creators take their legacy values and habits into this new world, and their children, who are raised as "natives" in the world of wealth, have a mindset, concerns, and even values that are very different from those of their parents. The immigrant parents may revert back to middle-class values they were raised with and train up their children to "make it on their own" as they did. They do not understand the need also to teach them skills for working together and how to prepare them to be wealth inheritors. Part of the common disconnect between the first and second generations stems from these divergent perspectives and histories.

Added to their perspective as immigrants, wealth creators have a common entrepreneurial self-made style that makes them great at creating wealth but not as well suited to pass on what they know. Their drive, instinctual wisdom, controlling nature, and the immediacy of the challenges they face mean that they are noteworthy for *not* planning the future and not attending to their families. While my research team and I didn't interview any founders, in speaking to third- or later-generation successors, our team saw awe and respect for the business creator, without the ambivalence and emotional pain of G2, mixed with awareness of the limits of the wealth creator's engagement and preparation of their families. The wealth creator did not *intend* to become wealthy, and he is often not prepared for the challenges and demands of great family wealth.

Second-generation children, unlike those of third- and later-generation family members, grow up in the household of the wealth creator and are acutely aware of their parents' shortcomings. They can feel neglected and compete for attention. They may be fortunate to have a mother not involved in the business who anticipates their needs, teaches, holds them accountable for values and responsible behavior, and prepares them for their inheritance. But the second-generation successors find themselves reacting to their elders, and the members of the third generation, more distant from the influence of the founder, often become innovators taking the family enterprise in new directions.

Looking back to their founders, the family members we interviewed recalled several possible starting points in the legacy plans of first-generation wealth creators:

- **Modest small business success.** The wealth creator starts a modest local business and remains successful until he passes it on to his children. Building on this initial success, second- (and occasionally third-) generation successors build them into huge businesses.

- **A king who never lets go.** The wealth creator leads the business until he dies or is incapacitated. The heirs are left to clean up the mess or learn to work together, often with significant competition and rivalry. The wealth creator has often avoided or neglected planning for the future.
- **Control from the grave.** Seeking to maintain control over his heirs as a way to sustain his values and success, he creates a constraining structure to continue the business, with minor roles for his children as decision-makers. To succeed, these children often have to rebel.
- **A matriarch who oversees orderly family succession.** The unexpected passing of the founder before completing a plan or developing next-generation leadership allows the hidden partner to demonstrate her capability and leadership.
- **Sale of the business.** The business is sold or divested before or upon the wealth creator's death, distributing money to the next generation, which has to choose whether to continue or to create a trust that holds succeeding generations together.
- **Dispersal via individual paths.** This is the process of dividing inheritance to allow each person to go in his or her own direction. Unless the successors decide to remain partners, this signals the end of the shared family enterprise.

Each of these outcomes poses a different challenge to the G2 heirs. But the central question for G2 is to decide to commit to shared family enterprise together as partners and then determine how to do this, whether by continuing the business, diversifying, or pursuing a combination of both. But whatever the path, the G2 heirs need to make the commitment to work together and confront the new challenges facing their shared enterprise.

While the founder clearly wanted the business to continue in the next generation, his preparation and planning were often incomplete. It is left to members of the second generation to decide to continue the business and learn to work together. While the wealth creator made a great achievement, it is others—the spouse of the founder or new leaders from the second or third generation—who make the crucial decisions to undertake the developmental tasks that create a generative family. They make the decision to invest in the family and do what is needed to develop the capability, commitment, and family and business organization to allow the business to grow.

## G2: Collaborating Siblings

In the most successful families, G2 siblings inherit not only wealth but also the legacy values, reputation, and constraints placed on the resources by their parents. They may be educated and prepared for the challenge ahead, but that is not common. While their options are limited, members of the second generation view their legacy as a challenge, which they intend to respect by taking the enterprise in new directions, responding to opportunities, and enriching them with their own knowledge, values, and preferences.

After growing up as a single family in one household, the second generation separates into multiple families with different spouses, roles, perspectives, and concerns about the jointly owned enterprise. Several family members likely work in the business, but almost everyone expects to inherit some of it, and has ideas about what should be done. For the family enterprise to succeed, the siblings must develop the ability to communicate, work out differences, and be fair to all.

My research team and I learned about the transition from G1 to G2 from family members already in G3 or G4. From this retrospective view the first transition looked uncomplicated. One commonly cited success factor was that only one member of G2 seemed interested in managing the family's business or finances and that the other siblings were comfortable with this arrangement. In most of the families interviewed, the transition took place decades ago when traditional practices reigned: women and younger siblings deferred to the oldest son. This result suggests that contemporary practices—in which all siblings are often encouraged to take an interest in the family enterprise and in which traditional notions of inheritance are weaker—hold the potential both for more conflict as well as for a more informed transition from G1 to G2.

G2 siblings face a new playing field the founder could not anticipate. The emergence of a global, digital world poses business challenges that can affect any business. Innovation and competition are always happening. New family members have different expectations, ideas, and needs, which have to be considered. And they are a "sandwich" generation, living between their parents and their own adult or soon-to-be adult children who also want to be part of the enterprise. How can they please everyone? They have to do a lot of balancing if they are to survive, and much of this cannot be anticipated or planned for. In fact, the estate plan of the founder can be an obstacle and a problem.

The transition from G1 to G2 demands dedicated and creative work. G2 siblings must accept the huge but narrow success of the wealth creator and build a structure within which the growing family can sustain and develop its legacy. They cannot coast and just keep things going. Many of the families interviewed for this study recalled that working together as a collaborative sibling group was deeply meaningful for the family, themselves and their children. They came to know each other in a different way. In many cases, as the new generation realized the extent of its wealth (financial and human), the discussion moved to how to serve the rest of the community, the positive uses for their gift. But they also acknowledged that their task was far from easy.

Several typical challenges complicate the transition of the G2 siblings:

- **A legacy of paternalism:** Nearly all of the family enterprises my research team and I studied were founded by a man. These founders by their nature do not share much information and control with the rest of the family. In many cases, the G1 father took care of everything, and the members of the next generation, sometimes very suddenly, had to discover what the family enterprise contained and decide what they were going to do with it, how to run it, and how they would identify their ultimate goals. They had to learn to be empowered and take responsibility on their own.

- **Developing trust:** Sibling rivalry arises in all cultures. In a family enterprise, the risk is that childhood rivalries overpower collaboration and shared purpose, leading to conflict that undermines business success and family harmony. In many of the cases in this study, a member of G2 (often the oldest son) was named expected successor. The presence of a designated successor does not guarantee a smooth transition, however. Members of G2 must develop new ways to communicate and make decisions together in the absence of the authority of G1, and they must work with respect and trust with the other members of their generation.

- **Increasing transparency:** Members of G2 usually grow up with very little information from the business founder, who was accustomed to keeping his own counsel. Yet for the members of the next generation to learn to work together and feel they are being treated fairly, they *all* need basic information about the business and finances. Several of the families interviewed for this study made clear that along with sharing relevant business, financial, and legal information, there is a need to learn "what it all means." Most G2 members find themselves living with trusts. In such cases, they must learn their roles, rights, and responsibilities within this complex structure. It's not everyday knowledge.

In the face of these challenges, the interviews conducted for this book underscore three particular practices that contribute to successful transitions from G1 to G2. They are necessary because a group of siblings, who have a complex emotional history and who grew up with family wealth, face a different context and set of challenges than their parents.[2] These three practices are:

1. **Affirming shared purpose:** A family enterprise cannot easily remain unified and connected over generations if the members do not share an emotionally and personally meaningful purpose and set of values. Several G2 families in the study reported that they did not see any reason for staying together and were moving to separate. This outcome should not be seen as failure but rather as an affirmation of individual freedom. If siblings do not have a reason for remaining partners, they should not be counted as failures if they decide to manage their financial assets on their own. The transition from G1 to G2 thus represents the first time that G2 siblings face the question "Do we want to be partners in a family enterprise?" Bound up with this question is often another related question: "Do we want to sell or keep the business?" The decision to sell does not necessarily lead to family dissolution, as the family can decide to remain together as financial partners or can take the family in a new direction, rather than dissolve.

2. **Learning cooperation and collaboration:** Many of the families interviewed for this book enjoyed a long period of cross-generational apprenticeship between G1 and G2. This apprenticeship usually started when one or more G2 members started working with their father. The role of the G1 wife

"homemaker" should also not be underestimated. In many of these cases, the G1 mother was an active participant in preparing members of G2 to work together. Siblings have to get beyond their competition and rivalry to identify their shared interests and different skills, interests, and abilities. This does not happen by chance but entails a commitment to work together and learn the skills of collaboration and teamwork, which are not natural to siblings. If the founding generation presents this ethic strongly, clearly, and by example, there is less chance of disabling conflict. Who will lead and what is to be done must be decided together, not assumed.

One G2 sibling returned to his family after the death of his father, hoping to help the family create a family office. He began to propose governance policies and make changes. His siblings didn't seem to understand what he was proposing or want to get involved. He felt like an unappreciated servant. This family didn't remain together very long.

For a more successful family of G2 sibling leaders, the shift from their G1 father's way to a team approach was profound. With a dozen family employees (both G2 and G3) and a medium-sized business, they began to communicate and work together much more closely. One of their G2 leaders notes:

> *When my father ran the business, it wasn't transparent. The family was not informed about two major acquisitions. We were asked to sign documents without even reading them. . . . We all see that now in our generation, so we're moving into this more transparently. I'm bringing transparency because I'm CFO. I'm presenting numbers that nobody ever got to see before. It's all generating more communication. . . . We're starting to see ourselves differently as not just fighting between each other as business people but as shareholders of a company that has value.*

3. **Initiating governance:** After being informed and learning to work together, G2 siblings need to set policies and make decisions. This is often when governance enters the family's life in a conscious form. *Governance* refers to the agreements, skills, and structures that enable the growing family to define values, mission, and policies; maintain connections; oversee the business and the family participation in it; and distribute consistently and fairly the financial and other rewards. Governance had little meaning in the founding generation; the founder usually had little idea of what this is or why it might be important to his children. The chapters that follow present the evolution of governance practices.

Setting up governance is a new experience, and siblings may run into unexpected conflict as they uncover divergent values, needs, and future agendas. It may not be clear who is supposed to take charge of this or how it should be done. Governance evolves out of circumstances, as the sibling group confronts challenges and decides they need to develop policies and practices to work together to resolve them.

A family "champion" must emerge to reach out and call the family together. This person is not necessarily the designated family business leader. Some of the families in this study have a self-appointed family leader who initiates a process of engagement and collaboration, frequently amid skepticism or disinterest from other family members.

One G2 interviewee reported that his family started a new manufacturing business after his father sold a business that he inherited from his father. G1 and the three members of G2 became the "owners' council" of the new business. Over time, G2 spouses joined their meetings, and they began to call this group their "family council." The business grew far beyond expectations, and the family faced a variety of new challenges: pressure from competitors; the demand to become more global; the task of recruiting seasoned nonfamily executives (including a CEO as G1 retired) and independent directors to its board; the management of an active family foundation; the investment of other assets; and, not least, the introduction of the maturing members of G3 to the business and the council. The time G2 invested in governance was well repaid as G3 took initiative, assumed control, and met these challenges over many years.

Another family only initiated formal governance after the sale of the business caused several family members in the business to lose their jobs. The sale revealed that members of G1 and G2 had conflicting attitudes about the use of the proceeds. G1 had struggled to develop the business while G2 grew up as the family lifestyle became more comfortable. Still, nobody was prepared for the fortune that came from the sale: they had to step back and consider what it would do to their family and what they wanted. While still active, G1 wanted to begin to pass authority to G2 as the siblings demonstrated their capability for leadership. Members of G2 were raising their own families and living in different areas; they wanted the members of G3 (their children) to get to know one another. This led the family to decide to hold a meeting. Both G1 and G2 had a chance to express their intentions and desires. The family then created two values statements: one focused on the legacy values, and the other articulated the values the family wanted in G2 and G3. Over time, this meeting led to regular family meetings and the creation of a family council. The family describes its own trajectory as evolving from a family business to a family office.

## G3: A Community of Related Households

The first reality of the members of G3 is that, as a family, they are no longer the offspring of a single household but rather have become an extended family community consisting of many households. Succeeding thus far, they are the beginning of a family dynasty. What ties them together in a special way is that they are all partners and beneficiaries in family wealth and responsibilities that force them to work together. In order to keep the family enterprise alive, they have to work together and act responsibly to sustain it. This does not happen naturally because a working group of a large number of loosely related family members is a difficult entity to maintain. That is why so few of them persist.

The transition to an extended family of G3 cousins brings with it many new complexities:

- The number of family members increases exponentially. Siblings usually grow up in one household. Cousins belong to several family entities: their nuclear family, their "branch," and the larger extended family.
- While they may have met the wealth creator, they are not emotionally impaired by his presence or deeply connected to him as a person. He is more of an idea and an abstract example.
- Members of G3 grow up in separate households, each containing a new family member, an in-law, who is a stranger to the family. The families are often geographically dispersed as well. G3 households thus develop different values, styles, and expectations about money. Although a trust or business structure may connect the family as owners or beneficiaries, individuals may not feel "on the same page" personally.
- Cousins naturally begin to orient to the values and interests of their individual family of origin or branch. As the branches spread, the family enterprise faces the challenge of keeping cousins aligned and connected.
- Cousins may not be sure why they are connected to the family enterprise; they need to make a new commitment to it and, as such, move from being a blood family to a family of affinity, a family by choice.
- G2 siblings differ in their ages by only a few years. G3 cousins may differ by decades.

In general, if a family enterprise wishes to stay together from G2 to G3, it must build personal relationships *across* family branches and develop shared extended family identity that motivates members to *want* to do the work to remain partners. This does not happen naturally, and the generative family must actively initiate practices to develop them.

In family after family, these questions emerged:

- Why are we together as partners?
- Is there anything special about our partnership that we want to continue?
- How much income does each new household expect from the financial assets?
- Is it time to sell the business?
- Who is best able to lead the diversification and development of the family enterprise?

These questions arise from a common set of conditions:

- By the time G3 matures, G1 has likely departed the stage and become the memory of a larger-than-life figure.
- A G3 family can no longer be considered "new wealth." G3 members have likely grown up in a family with the trappings of success, and they usually expect continued success.

- G3 members probably do not all have the same information about the family's business or finances. They have heard different stories and have different expectations about what the business will provide them. Some members have likely been closer to the business and expect to become leaders while others are more distant from it. The "insiders" see the challenges while "outsiders" may expect rewards, impatient of sacrifice.

At some time, most often in the third generation, the culture of the family enterprise must shift from the directive leadership of a single individual to shared leadership by a family group that must develop a process for working together. The chapters that follow describe how the family culture shifts to a collaborative team and how governance is needed to manage its operation. (See Figure 4.1.)

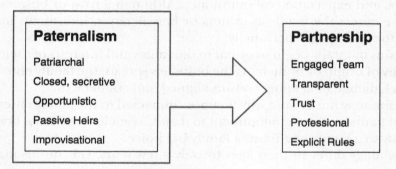

| **Paternalism** | **Partnership** |
|---|---|
| Patriarchal | Engaged Team |
| Closed, secretive | Transparent |
| Opportunistic | Trust |
| Passive Heirs | Professional |
| Improvisational | Explicit Rules |

**Figure 4.1   Paternalism versus partnership.**

Many families recalled that the business provided G1 and G2 plenty of money or work for everyone. This abundance, along with the strong personality of G1, precluded much of the need for explicit policies in G1 or G2 about governance. But even the family enterprise built on the most abundant business or forceful founding personality faces strains by G3. If the enterprise is to remain together, G3 members must agree on a common path.

### Adapting to Change

Meeting the challenge of finding core purpose and commitment to continue as a family enterprise for another generation also depends on the successful family's ability to *anticipate* the difficulties and *adapt* itself to them. Third-generation family enterprises cannot rest on the preexisting policies or practices that have gotten them this far. They may even have to reevaluate or shift a previous policy that now must be challenged.

For example, after his G2 father died, a G3 family leader found that several of his cousins expected to join the board to direct the family real estate company. However, he realized that some of them were not ready for the job and appointed some of their more qualified spouses to the board instead—a move that previous generations would likely not have made. Because of his position in G3, he knew that he had to defend these choices to the family. He thus convened sessions to educate the rest of the family about the challenges facing the business and about the role and responsibility of the board. Despite bruised feelings, his siblings and cousins grew to accept his decision. He also reached out to involve G4 members in these sessions. This shift from actions that serve the family to those that serve the long-term needs of the business can be upsetting to family members who have grown up expecting automatic membership in certain roles.

Successors fortunately have the ability to question family activities and initiate new ones. Generative families seem to be unusually open to new ideas and, as later chapters will show, to the initiative of these younger generations to create timely change. They can sometimes push the older generations to make changes that they find difficult or even avoid.

Successful entry into G3 seems to require several changes in how the family operates, which add responsibility and take away perks from the successors. For example, members of G3 must redefine their behavior to affirm the following:

- Commitment to what is needed to sustain the business or family portfolio of assets.
- Development of an owners' mindset, where decisions are made for the long-term support of the business.
- Creation of policies and agreements that define and support clear and orderly decisions being made by the diverse family owners.
- Active plans to develop capability within the rising generations of family owners.

How do members of G3 anticipate and manage the challenge of reconciling so many divergent individual agendas? As we will see later in Chapter 11, developing an active *family council* is a key element of the response. One G3 family that owns two large businesses—a farm and a bank that is a public company (with the family a majority owner)—took a proactive view of the family business as it entered its second half-century. The five G3 family branches, with nearly twenty members and a thirty-five-year age span, realized that they didn't know much about one another.

They had begun to meet regularly to consider their future, as a family council composed of two members of G2 and seven of G3. The first question they faced was whether they saw themselves as one extended family or five. After much discussion, they decided that they wanted to be one unified family but realized that doing so would take a commitment to one another and the next generation. To get to know one another as partners and develop commitment to each other, they decided that the whole council would be involved in every decision for a period of time. While they saw this could become unwieldy, it was also necessary for them all to learn to work together and get on the same page. They wanted to learn how to practice collaborative leadership across all five branches. They elected a paid family chair to help them learn to work together rather than do the work for them.

The family designed some governance processes in G2, but the new council agreed to be reviewed by members of G3, as they began to see themselves as family leaders. They defined the council as a "Board of Boards" to oversee the boards of their individual businesses and their family foundation. While the chair of each of their businesses would be a family member, they began to search for "the best nonfamily CEO we can find" for each one. In the bank as well as the farm, the family owners made it clear that the family was committed to the multiple entities as long-term owners.

As this family demonstrates, since the members of G3 grow up apart and may not know each other well, they must develop activities to get to know each other and develop personal bonds. A family member from another family said:

> *I knew some of my cousins growing up but since we all lived in different locations, we really weren't very close. These meetings helped us get to know each other again and to interact and find out who we all are. So far that has been very helpful to get that family connection going as opposed to just the business connection.*

In addition to a family council, most families in this study regularly gather all family members, including spouses, in a *family assembly*. This gathering is necessary because, given the dispersal of households, development of personal relationships does not occur naturally. To sustain family identity and connection, it's necessary to set aside time, effort, and organization. Many families do not see the need or have the desire for this, so they do not build generative families.

This assembly may include fun activities like a family summer camp for kids or shared vacations, which help family members bond. But it is more than a social gathering. It is organized to share information, communicate, and make decisions. This group is also often called upon to ratify the agreements and policies proposed by the family council. And it may offer educational activities, which help G4 members create development plans for their future. These plans give G4 members a chance to think about whether they want to become involved in one of the family ventures or even to propose new entrepreneurial ventures.

## G3 Members Define Their Own Direction

One group of G3 members defined their own path in a small-town manufacturing business, where the two G2 brothers and their families grew up as they worked in the business with their G1 father. The brothers were rivals, and there was always conflict between them as they took over the business and each raised a large family. The G3 cousins grew up together, hugely influenced by their grandparents. Some began to work in the business while others moved away. While G1 and G2 developed the business, which was very successful, G3 pondered the family's future:

> *Originally most of the founder's family, second and third generation, grew up in the same small town. There was a culture of close relationships, especially between the third generation .... The second generation did a pretty good job of not letting the business relationships overflow into affecting family relationships. The cousins grew up spending time with each other and at social events and became really close to each other. [We have] similar spiritual and core social values.*
>
> *There was conflict within the second generation that stemmed from conflicts in the first generation ..., and there was a branch mentality to an extent of both shareholder ownership and roles in the company or roles on different ownership councils .... But we think we've gotten through most of that now with the transition of [a G3 member] to chairman of the board.*

*(continued)*

The G3 members of this family struggled to overcome their rivalry and competition for the "slots" they inherited. They began to meet separately and told G2 they were comfortable with a leadership transition that would be fair to both family branches. They made it clear they trusted one another and were working well together. Each family had its own family council that "provided a voice for the family members whether they are shareholders or not." They added an ownership council, which brought together the two separate family councils. The ownership council created family events such as regular teleconferences, an annual "family camp," and learning forums and webinars for the next generation.

They also created a shareholder agreement governing work in the business. The business had a board of directors composed of equal numbers of independent directors and family members. They created a formal role for G3 members to become "board observers," where they would attend board meetings and go through a process to apply for formal board membership. These activities developed a firm foundation for family connection and participation in a huge business. They agreed that in five years, the third generation would take control of the board.

This example reminds us that even though they grow up in different households, it may be precisely G3 members who look beyond the "branch mentality" and the historical differences that underlie that mentality to anticipate the possibilities of family togetherness and adapt new ways of working together to actualize those possibilities.

Generative families all face these challenges. One of the main avenues into doing so is through *reevaluation* of the legacy business. Sometimes difficult changes are in order. In one family, following the death of the G2 family leader, his brother ran the company for more than a decade. When G3 members became owners, they learned the business was barely breaking even. They created a board of directors with some independent directors and G3 family members. The board in turn forced out the G2 family leader and hired a nonfamily CEO. While the business quickly became much more profitable, the branch whose father was pushed out was very upset.

The shift in G3 to revitalize the business, while necessary for business reasons, can lead to deeply hurt feelings and cause family feuds or rifts. Because they are an extended family as well as shareholders, the family cannot ignore these reactions. If they do, they risk one branch wanting to exit and divide the business. By the time it reaches G3, every family enterprise has faced a request by some family members to sell their ownership. Generative families are able to agree and allow family members, and sometimes whole branches, to separate. See Table 4.1 for more on the characteristics of each generation in a family enterprise.

## G4: Business Renewal and Family Reengagement

A G4 family enterprise looks back upon more than a half century of success. But success gives rise to new challenges, which lead the new G4 leaders to question and redefine many paths the family has followed. As they disperse and diverge, family members grow less connected, to the point where cousins may not know each other well, despite their shared ownership of family assets.

**Table 4.1  Generational characteristics in family enterprises.**

| G1 to G2 | G2 to G3 | G3 to G4 | Beyond G4 |
|---|---|---|---|
| **Collaborating Siblings** | **Emergence of Cousins' Community** | **Business Renewal: Family Reengagement** | **Business Independence: "Tribal" Extended Family** |
| Sibling partners | Branches of cousins | First and second cousins | Many relatives; independence of family and business |
| Commitment to stay together | Dual allegiance—branch and extended family | Diverse members aligned to shared mission, looking beyond branch mentality | Active, professional board with family involvement |
| Learning of ways to work together and respect differences | Acceptance of diversity of needs, values, and perspectives | Familiarization with each other across many locations and families | Many types of relationships guided by family policies |
| Development of communication about differences | Renewed commitment to family enterprise | Renewed legacy business or decision to diversify | Whole family gatherings to build community of shared legacy and purpose |
| Employment open to interested family members | Limited space in business; employment policies | Exit policy for those who do not share commitment to the enterprise | Limits of wealth to support families; focus on human, family, and social capital |
| Development of transparency and collaborative decisions | Definition of purpose for family to remain partners | Development of family policies and meetings to balance family and business | Family council and independent board |
| Family gifts to community | Develop shared philanthropic focus | Preparation of next generation for stewardship | Next-generation education program |

The fourth generation continues family ownership, but the family now has gone on so long and has so many members that it is far more than a single family. It is a family dynasty, publicly known for its wealth, influence, and impact, with family members who may not have to work and who are unsure of what the family enterprise is or how it works. If relatives are to work together and sustain leadership, the family has to create a complex and multifaceted organization. It has to organize the family, separate from the business, and also clarify the family's relation to each separate business. Family members may not be involved or may take on a variety of important roles in governance or operations.

Entry into G4 is a sign the family has successfully developed the ability to adapt continually to new circumstances. These G4 members are an extended family by blood, but more and more they have also become a voluntary *family of affinity*, so defined because some family members choose to drop out of the enterprise aspect of the group while a core group actively chooses to remain together. In a sense, rather than considering this type of family as an extended family because of its commitment to its family enterprise and its shared values, goals, and activities, a family of affinity can best be considered a clan or tribe of families sharing a common heritage.

The families in our study that are thriving beyond G4 evolved over a century or more to consist of two types of large, intertwined, but increasingly independent entities:

- **A "tribal" family/community of engaged owners:** The many far-flung cousins develop close connections not only because of their legacy but because they share activities. Together they make decisions, educate each new generation, and perform community service. They like to be together, and they share far more than a business. As a group of strongly connected individual families, united by blood, economics, a legacy and culture, and shared commitments, they can be thought of as a modern-day tribe. Their legacy and values are incorporated into a shared culture for their enterprise, as they change and adapt to new realities.
- **Professionally run, diversified enterprises, which might contain a large legacy company, several companies, investments, real estate, a family office, and/or a holding company:** The business is clearly differentiated and distinguished from the family, management from ownership. Management is professional. Many of these businesses employ thousands of people, who are attracted to the special culture and values that long-term family ownership brings. Six of the sixteen "beyond G4" families in our study retain significant family involvement in management. While half the families have brought in a nonfamily CEO, they remain open to having a family leader if a qualified leader emerges from the family.

Families at this point in their evolution have several common qualities:

- **Explicit values** about policies for how they use their money and run their businesses
- A rich **history** they celebrate together
- Extensive **family organization** overseeing their decisions, finances, leadership, and control of the enterprise
- Activities devoted to **growing human capital**, including regular family meetings, next-generation development activities, and philanthropic and community activities

Despite these valuable assets, the key to understanding the success of G4+ families is to see that these assets comprise only the opportunity; the family itself must adapt and change in order to continue as a unified and clearly defined working group. A family with two G3 branches had a thriving business. But by G4, one family member reported:

> There was a sense of family in gatherings and interaction, but it was more ritual and duty-based than with any kind of clear compelling family purpose and direction, and there wasn't much authenticity.... There wasn't openness, trust, and communication... not much sharing and

*respectful family history and legacy. . . . I think the mission and purpose was to make money
and be successful, get some social status, but I think I was disappointed by the spiritual poverty
of this.*

When this G4 son returned to lead the enterprise, he found a great deal of disorder and felt he had to "save the business." However, he did not have the support of
his siblings or cousins. When another member of his generation was forced out by
a G3 owner, there was mayhem, and the G3 generation decided to put the business
up for sale, as the family could find no compelling reason to stay together.

A common experience of the fourth generation is the decline of the connected
family. To sustain connection, it must be renewed, and practices and cultural policies must be developed to reinforce it. Relationships don't just happen; they must be
encouraged and engineered. Recognizing a shared legacy and sustaining an extensive family organization are points of engagement for G4+ family members. To continue as an entity, such families must develop a delicate, multilevel mindset vis-à-vis
the business and each other:

- The family must see the business as *independent* of the family. The family is
  increasingly seen as an outside force, a benevolent parent to the business,
  which it treats like an adult child: allow it to grow on its own.
- The family members must clarify their role as *owners*, not necessarily business
  managers or operators. The family must shift from being an owner-operator,
  which often characterizes the business in G1 and G2, to becoming an ownership group.
- The family members must have personal relationships, share values, and have
  a commitment to do the work needed to sustain a unified, productive family
  enterprise that can face and overcome differences between relatives.

The business has also likely been transformed:

- It is now either a large legacy business, or it has been sold and become a series
  of assets that may include real estate, a family office, ownership of one or more
  companies, and a family foundation.
- A cadre of professional nonfamily managers has emerged, and the family faces
  pressure to professionalize its operations, talent management, and policies for
  family involvement.
- The enterprise has also likely reached into new ventures to develop new
  wealth.
- In almost all cases, the "trust wave"[3] has swept the family's assets into trusts and
  turned family members into beneficiaries and perhaps trustees. They must
  follow the rules and their authority is limited.

As a key element of the family council and assembly, almost all families transitioning from G3 to G4 take on the task of actively *developing the human capital
and relationships of G4* and beyond. Since the family members often live far from
their original community, they have to work to develop connections in their new

generation. One such family, which owns a farm and food business with an extensive tradition and reputation in the community, has eleven G3 and more than twenty G4 members. Every blood relative is a shareholder, and several G4s work in the business. They feel both a deep emotional and financial commitment to the company. One family member said:

> When I go to these [shareholder] meetings, I just want to be a good ambassador. I know that I'm an owner, but I don't know how to run the company. I'm just really proud that we're doing what we're doing, and I want my kids to be the best people and the best ambassadors that they can for our name because this is a small town and people would go, "Oh, you're that person." I think that's what we all have instilled in our kids.

Many shared activities are emerging in this family. They initiated a strategic planning process at the board level to look at their business future and a parallel process for the family by the family council. The family council began as "a liaison between the family and the business so that we would be the family voice to the board, so the family knew they had a voice with the board. . . . But now the family council has become about relationships."

The council is creating a next-generation education program to develop the skills and capability of G4, whether or not they decide to enter the business. From an initially limited role, the council is becoming more active to include and engage the more than fifty family members. They have a number of council positions and have even created the role of "communication manager." The business cards of the G4 members title them "Ambassadors" so that they can visit stores and places owned by the family and meet the employees. The family culture has a strong spirit of commitment to the business and to supporting each other's growth and development.

The following example speaks even more forcefully to the growing importance of attending to family relationships. This family had an intensely private G2 leader who built a diversified series of businesses, including a family office, which he passed on to his two G3 sons. The older son ran it, selling a large business and further diversifying, and then by agreement he retired, and his brother took over.

The family began to meet under the leadership of a trusted family advisor and set up a foundation and other activities for the growing G4. The impetus for these activities came largely from the women in the family, who wanted to exert influence in this male-dominated milieu. Family legacy also played a role. The G3 member interviewed for this study remembers that the family initially did not know much about G2's business dealings. They gradually learned more through family briefings, including the fact that their business was celebrated as dedicated to their employees and social causes. They now wanted to apply these values to themselves. G4 became active, especially in the family foundation.

G4 contained eleven cousins, with complex relationships that included multiple divorces and blended families. As a family, they confronted the family legacy of failed marriages and the effects on their children. As the G3 respondent explained:

> My generation has been very sensitive to broken families and appropriate spousal choices. . . .
> We're much more relationship concerned. There's been an evolution of being very aware of

*disharmony in previous generations and a real commitment by ours to find more harmony in our partners and in our families and our real commitment to being with our children. Our parents were so busy working, not that we were afterthoughts but on some level that is kind of what it was.*

Notwithstanding such powerful practices and focus, the transition from G3 to G4 is often a time of family fission. Indeed, one way a family enterprise can remain united is by giving family members the *freedom* to leave and receive a fair price for their ownership from the rest of the family. Because it is a family business, members usually cannot sell their shares to anyone but another family member. So a G3 family needs a clear policy for internal sales and the ability for family members to leave a partnership that does not serve their interests.

However, it is also important to recognize that family disconnection is not irreversible. Some of our families had a period of disconnection before a new generation decided to reinitiate connection in the growing new generation. A family enterprise with a 150-year history and more than 135 adult members from G4, G5, and G6 is working on transition to G4 leadership. This family has held annual family meetings for more than fifty years. A G3 respondent recalls her first meetings forty years ago when she was in the sixth grade: *"I remember meeting with the outside board members and being so impressed with the adults who took their time to meet with those of us in our age group."*

Fast forward thirty years, when a new family CEO became concerned about diminishing family attendance at these meetings. He initiated a process of reengagement. The family had a legacy of male leadership in a family largely consisting of women, who felt disenfranchised. The new CEO saw that the business needed focus to become more professional and profitable but also that the family was not involved. His first step was to call for volunteers from G4 to work on a task force on family employment policies. They developed family internships and ways to teach the family about the business.

The task force then evolved into a nine-member family council, elected by the whole family. The council initiated a more active format for annual family meetings, where family members could learn about the business. The council created an interactive agenda for each meeting, with special events and programs for younger members. Over the past decade, they have created or revived a family video, trips, and a family education program. The family created four ongoing task forces: communication, governance, education, and family meetings. With active engagement of the family council, they passed leadership to a new G4 family CEO.

The family council, family assembly, and focus on G4 are all means to the same end: the cultivation and strengthening of family relationships. Sometimes by the third generation, those relationships have weakened to the point that the best thing the family can do is to acknowledge reality and dissolve the legal or business structures that tie them together. But if they want to transition from G3 to G4 as a family enterprise, then continuing to foster those relationships will be their true work. As will be seen in the next section, the focus of the family enterprise after G3 rests on twin pillars: the family and the enterprise, separate and interdependent.

## Business Renewal

About 40 percent of the families in this study follow what might be called a "classic" cross-generational developmental arc, from entrepreneur to a generation that grows and professionalizes the business and then to a point in the third or fourth generation where the increasing numbers of family members have to decide the nature of their engagement in the business. A family develops governance mechanisms in order to enable it to evolve and adapt, both within the family and in the business environment.

Following are two examples in which the family moved to clarify the *boundaries* between the business and the family. A third example shows that, despite the importance of family and business independence at this stage, a G4 family found it necessary to *reengage* with the business.

### A Renewal Task Force

In this family, the long-term G3 family leader had done the work of recruiting a non-family CEO successor and developing a board that contained members of G3 and G4 as well as a majority of independent members. But by G4, there were nearly fifty family members from three branches with a history of conflict. Despite that history and despite barely knowing each other, the G4 began to meet as a group, trying to resolve conflicts around dividends and to discover whether they had any further commitment to each other. To deal with these issues, they formed four task forces on governance, next-generation development, dividend policy, and philanthropy. As they met, their branch identity gave way to a new identity as a generational cohort. Since the business had embarked on an ambitious ten-year plan, the family created one as well. The family formed a family council of twelve members, with a full-time paid family chair to lead the efforts.

The task forces allowed the family not only to create policy to resolve conflict but also to learn to work together. As one family member said:

> Through the task forces process, we were able to build working relationships and then from these working relationships we were actually able to develop friendships.... Ten years ago, our annual family meeting was fraught with conflict and stress, and I think it was seen as a burden. Someone saw it like they were giving up their weekend to come and be with the family business, and now I think that the family feels excited about coming to the family meetings. It's fun, and it's exciting, and people are happy to see one another.

The family made a substantial commitment to the development of the next generation. It allocates 2 percent of the family distribution to fund a personal and leadership development program. The family member continued:

> We've really tried to develop this human capital element of the next generation as well. At our annual family meeting, we have an educator come and work with that next generation to try to make the experience of being with the family and being with the business as positive and fulfilling as possible.

*(continued)*

*(Continued)*

> *We have this person working on team building and leadership training and problem solving, and we spend several hours during our annual meeting with the next-generation activity. We get the adults to come work with the kids at the kids' level. So we're not asking the kids to come to our meeting—we're going and meeting them in the context of building relationships in ways that work for that age group.*

## Managing the Family–Business Boundary

A non-US family business started by two brothers, with a history of four generations of talented and dedicated family CEOs, now controls a large public company and several other ventures. The family numbers 450 members, spanning the globe, who meet for a large family reunion every two years. They are deeply involved in the business.

Ten years ago, as the G4 leaders began to retire at the prescribed age of sixty-five, issues arose concerning succession as well as employment policies for next-generation family members, the inclusion of women in the business, and the management of the family's large and ambitious foundation. They realized that the family reunion was not the best place to address these issues, nor was the business board, with its blend of family and independent directors.

In response, G4 and G5 created a family council to manage the family's engagement in the business and other nonbusiness activities. The council created guidelines for entry, advancement, and succession in the business. One of the unique features of this process is its requirement that any family member employee who wishes to enter senior management receives an extensive assessment and pursues a one-year project in social entrepreneurship outside the company. The latter requirement reflects the family's deep commitment to its community.

As mentioned, it is crucial for G4+ families to develop both independent businesses and independent families. At the same time, in a number of families, the need arises for the family to reengage in a period of profound decision.

## Coming Back Together

For many years, a visionary G2 leader led a large, public, family-controlled company. The enterprise included a family office and other ventures, and the G2 leader fostered a strong tradition of independence in other family members to pursue their own professions.

The identified G3 successor died unexpectedly. His brother reluctantly took the reins. The G2 leader had wisely created a strong board of talented independent directors. As the G3 leader began to transition to G4, the choice arose to sell the business. One family member said:

> *That was the crisis when a generation, my own fourth generation, who haven't really had to spend much time talking to each other, suddenly had to enter into dialogue and say, What do we do?*

*(continued)*

> *We were going to crystallize the wealth that was created over ninety years. Do we want to stay in business together? We had come to the exit decision as part of the strategic review . . . . It wasn't that we weren't functioning effectively. It was that we'd recognized that the rewards were unlikely to warrant the risks. At that stage, we had to look each other in the eye and say, "Do we want to stay in business together?"' And the response was yes.*
>
> *We went through a process of consultation with everybody, developing a strategy. "This is what we are going to do and if you don't want to do it, here's the exit and please, the exit is there. If you want to go, let's do it with your head held high, and let's keep friendly and happy, and there is no compunction, no pressure on you." Some of us think that it's a good idea to keep the family capital together because we think we've got a better chance of allowing it to endure. And nearly all of us said let's keep going, "This cash has fallen into our laps. We didn't create it so what's the responsible solution?" And that is how we've continued to operate since then. Suddenly we became a collaborative group, so my generation needs to work out what we are going to do.*

The family developed an ethic of independence, so the challenge facing G4 was to shift that focus to shared engagement. The respondent in this study, a G4 family leader, recalls that his father cautioned against too much family involvement. He held that a family business *"can impose a dreadful servitude on people, but nevertheless, he had this sense of duty [to the family]."* They also had to face the reality that the next generation would be wealthy but not rich. The respondent said:

> *So we're managing preservation. They see what we are and where we've come from merely as a background to who they will become, that there is no sense of entitlement to either position in the business or income or anything else other than they see it as part of their roots, something they are pleased about. And they'll give a little bit of time and bandwidth to become effective shareholders and owners.*

## Large Legacy Companies

A large legacy company creates special conditions for a G4+ family. As long-term shareholders, family members want the business to remain strong and profitable. They also want the family to live the values embodied in the business. They often see the business as a public trust. They feel a connection to their employees, their products, and their communities. Finally, they usually want members of future generations to serve on the board and potentially work in the business.

G4+ families with large legacy companies make use of all the practices discussed in the preceding pages. What makes them different is that they often find themselves deploying many of these practices at once.

This G4 family captures elements seen in many generative families. They contain six hundred members, of whom 250 are owners. There are living members of five family generations, and twenty-six family members work for various entities in this conglomerate. This family has always had a policy of encouraging family members to work in the business, but it underwent a major business and family reorganization nearly a decade ago as the family began to see that even as revenues in its business empire grew, its profits did not. One family member said:

> *About eight years ago, we said, "You know, we need to be a little more intentional, because this family is getting bigger, it's getting more spread out . . . ." That's when we decided to say family is family and business is business, and we started to go through a transition, moving*

*from a family business to a business family, and that was a critical step for us to make that move. Because when you have a family business, employment becomes a birthright, and we were getting too many family members into the business that weren't qualified and performance was suffering . . . .*

*The difference between the two is that a family business's first and foremost primary goal is to maintain family harmony, and profits are secondary. And the business family focuses on business first; profits are respected and performance first. It's about the right people in the right spot, so they're qualified throughout the business. We went from focusing on business harmony to business performance. It was a real hard thing for us to do, and we did that. And we've been on track ever since we were in the tremendous turnaround in the performance of our business.*

The transition was stressful. The board, made up only of family members, had to remove some nonperforming family members who were large shareholders. They created what they called an *owners' council* and downsized the board to contain three family members and four independent directors, plus the family CEO. They made these decisions unanimously but also created a clear policy by which family members can sell their shares.

The family got clearer about its values as a family, defining its family mission, vision, and values in an explicit family constitution. In addition to the owners' council, which represented the 250 family owners, they created a *family council*, representing all six hundred family members, and a *philanthropy committee*, with four G4 members and two from G5, to oversee the family's commitment to give away 10 percent of its profits. The family appointed a full-time family chairman, who was responsible for maintaining family harmony by policing the boundaries between family and business, mediating conflicts that arose, and facilitating the development of family members so that they could be qualified and productive when they served the business. The family chair was the key to establishing and sustaining the business-first orientation without discouraging family members from working in the business.

The policy of business first has not kept family members from working in the business. The business actively recruits the most talented family members. But it has created an active, multifaceted program of education and personal development to prepare members of the emerging generation for entry and leadership in the business. It begins when the children are young and continues as they grow up:

*The parents need to make sure they're talking about the vision and values around the dinner table. Once they get older and they become inquisitive, we have a whole set of things that we do with the family, starting with the younger kids . . . . We actually start at the age of twelve and categorize them from age twelve to age twenty, and that's a wide group, but it's wide on purpose because we want some of the twenty-year-olds to be the mentors to some of the twelve- or thirteen-year-olds. So you have them together as a group. We take that age bracket, and we do functions with them; two to three times a year they'll do different events. And we call it "cousin-palooza . . . ." We'll do fun events throughout the year, and one of those will be some type of learning as well. Education doesn't revolve around what we do; it revolves around who we are because you get these kids together and introduce them, and like, "Hey, I know you; you sit next to me in science class. I didn't know we are related."*

The family has many social events, as well as a website and Facebook page, so family members can get to know each other in their early years. As these young people get older, the family provides information about the business and about internships, summer jobs, mentoring, and career development. The family offers an extensive leadership program and other opportunities to learn and grow together. As they learn, growing family members come to understand that working in the business is not an entitlement—it is a responsibility. But the family is active in recruiting family members into the business: it seeks out talented family members working outside and tries to interest them in coming on board. Every year, all family members working in the business (currently twenty-six) have a weekend together with each other and their spouses to talk about their special experience together.

## Both Family and Business

This G7 family has a similar tradition of a family business, which has evolved into a diversified conglomerate of businesses that are run for both profit and values. For several generations, the family was run by a succession of paternalistic patriarchs, but over that time they slowly evolved an active governance structure bringing the family together. They have had annual family meetings for over one hundred years and developed a family council as well as next-generation education programs more than a generation ago. The dispersed family has always been active and inclusive. From the beginning, spouses were welcomed into the business as shareholders. As the next generation grows to over one thousand, they have developed an exit policy that allows family members to go their own way. With blended families, divorces, and stepchildren, the definition of who is family is increasingly complex.

In the 1960s, the fifth generation faced a choice. As this generation was huge, the question was whether the family really wanted to be involved in the increasingly elaborate business ventures. The answer from the family was yes, and family members began to build upon the regular family meetings they had already held for many years. They developed an active structure that included oversight of the business, family meetings, and a foundation. These moves necessitated developing an elaborate family organization independent of the business. That organization contains a family council of ten people elected by the family. A full-time family president elected for a five-year term (with a three-term limit) leads the council, which manages family activities and governance. There have been several accomplished and dedicated family presidents. My research team and I interviewed the current president, who compared her role with that of the leader of a complex nonprofit organization.

The annual family meeting is a special event, paid for by the family, where many social, educational, governance, and service activities take place. At the last annual family retreat, two-thirds of the nearly five hundred family members attended. One family member said:

*What encourages people to come is that our children are now making relationships with their cousins, and we have this program that's built around the zero- to thirteen-year-olds that is so important that we find that they just beg their parents to go. Sometimes we hear back that the parents don't really want to go, but the kids are very anxious to engage with their cousins. All of that is wonderful because of the experience they're getting. Not only are they getting parents to come who*

*(continued)*

*(Continued)*

*might be on the edge, but they're creating a relationship with each other so that by the time they get into the boardroom or the family council, they have relationships and they know each other.*

*So I think the next-generation program is inspiring the next generation to kind of pick up the flag and keep marching forward. The biggest challenge is that we can't do any of this without having a business. We can't pay for summits or pay for people to participate in family councils or [become] family presidents if we're not making money.*

The family board includes three independent directors, the nonfamily CEO, and nine family directors. The shareholders conduct a strategic planning process for the business and the family every ten years. There is also a foundation, focused in four areas, that provides roles for many family members. A recent survey asked family members what was more important to them, the family activities or the business, and the responses were divided fifty/fifty. The family is about both family and business.

This chapter introduced a ten-thousand-foot overview of the evolution of generative families over four generations. As we proceed, we will look at each of the elements that are common to generative families who have entered or moved through their fourth generation of wealth. We will first look at how the family develops resilient, adaptive business and financial entities, and the family culture that arises from their legacy and emerging leadership in each generation. We explore the family's role as stewards and how they oversee and set the tone as business owners. Then, we shift to the most unusual and unique aspects of family enterprise—their development of family governance structures such as a family assembly and family council that guides the family development alongside their business and financial assets. Finally, we look at how generative families invest and engage their rising generations of young people to commit to and steward their enterprises into a new generation.

## Taking Action in Your Own Family Enterprise

### Telling the Story of the Family Journey

Every family has its own journey across generations. Generative families find many ways to share the stories of their family and business. By the time a family enters G3, new family members may not know the founder or the story of the origin of the family. To inspire the next generation and teach the values of the family, the older generations must create opportunities to share the family story with their successors. This is important because without a conscious effort to tell the story, negative stories, distortions, and hearsay may be shared and believed. The family should take steps to share and talk about its story in a positive way but without forgetting or denying difficulties and even conflicts. Young people are hungry for this knowledge, and unless the family actively shares it, the youth are susceptible to negative stories and misinformation.

Families tell the story in various ways:

- Grandparents can spend time with their grandchildren and teach them about the family. Parents can do this as well.
- The family can collect and save artifacts and treasures and show them to the children.
- The younger generation, using video, can interview elders about their recollections and memories. Family members can collect stories not just from each other but also from employees, advisors, friends, and customers.
- Older family members can take younger family members to visit the business and other special places, teaching and sharing what they are about.

## Notes

1. James Grubman, *Strangers in Paradise: How Families Adapt to Wealth Across Generations* (Northfield, MA: Family Wealth Consulting, 2013).
2. The different realities of the first and second generation are described as emerging from different cultures. There are acquirers and inheritors. For accounts of the transition between first and second generation in family wealth, see Dennis T. Jaffe and James A. Grubman, "Acquirers' and Inheritors' Dilemma: Discovering Life Purpose and Building Personal Identity in the Presence of Wealth," *Journal of Wealth Management* 10, no. 2 (2007), and Grubman's *Strangers in Paradise*.
3. "Trust wave" is a term from James E. Hughes, Jr., Susan E. Massenzio, and Keith Whitaker, *The Cycle of the Gift: Family Wealth and Wisdom* (Hoboken, NJ: John Wiley & Sons, 2013).

# Business Resiliency

## Common Transformations Along the Path

While previous generations of dynastic multigenerational families might have faced an environment of stability and continuity, the journeys described by our contemporary generative families were far more complex and eventful. By the third generation, no contemporary family enterprise remains as it was a generation before. The business expands into new markets and products. It may go public or add other shareholders. Or perhaps the legacy business is sold and the family diversifies. New family members are born, grow up, or marry into the family, and they bring different values, skills, and interests. One constant hallmark of the generative family is its resilience, the ability to adapt and change, in response to either success or adversity.

Over nearly one hundred years, each family in this study has been through major transformations. Some have become diversified, migrating into other areas by modifying or expanding their portfolio of products and services. A business that old has faced multiple setbacks and crises; some even faced bankruptcy. In an enduring family enterprise, crises lead to adaptation, rethinking of how they work and exploration of new paths ahead.

The social, business, and cultural environment is changing, as a new global, digital world unfolds. The extent of change posed by new communication technology, globalization, environmental destruction, and instability of global commerce threatens the survival of even the most successful enterprises. Each new generation exhibits diverging expectations, needs, and dreams as their family creatively responds to the predictable crises that arise.

In each generation, the business is endangered. It can fail or be sold, and the family can choose to disperse into separate households. Generative families keep deciding again and again that they want to take up the deep challenges to stay together and adapt. To succeed, they must question traditions and challenge long-standing cultural traditions to sustain family closeness in an increasingly impersonal world.

This chapter outlines the evolutionary path of generative families. It introduces the common challenges of family and business growth and development emerging in each generation and looks at how generative families manage the increasing complexity of creating a strong family connected to a thriving family enterprise.

## Surviving a Crisis

After a generation or more of success, every business faces crises: new technology, business recessions, increasing competition, or the need for reinvestment capital can challenge the business. Here are two examples:

- After surviving a world war and occupation, one family found itself once again in a country where it was unwelcome. Three G3 cousins pooled their considerable skills in international trade, and each moved to a different country. Like the Rothschilds, these cousins ended up creating three new businesses, all of which grew and thrived far beyond the scope of their original business.
- After three generations of success with an iconic product, another family business saw that new technology was making its product obsolete. But the company had tremendous recognition and affection. After business school and apprenticeship at a consulting firm, a third-generation family leader was asked to come aboard and redefine the business. After exploring people's perceptions of the company and its products, the family came up with a new mission that led it in new directions but with a continued focus on consumer goods. Its reputation gave it visibility while the new leader moved manufacturing offshore and created a new generation of products. He helped employees displaced by the transition find new jobs and rebuilt the obsolete factory as a product development center. The company successfully leveraged its legacy of brand recognition to a new generation of customers and products.

Internal and external challenges trigger the need for the family enterprise to adapt and change, sometimes in major ways. Common "triggers" that lead the family to reevaluate and transform business policies and practices include the following:

- A sudden death highlights lack of a qualified successor inside or outside the family.
- New technology leads to new competitors and need to reinvest.
- With more shareholders and a maturing business, a sudden or gradual decline in profit moves the family to pay attention.
- If the business is doing well, the family faces offers to buy it.
- As the business generates profits, the family extends and diversifies into other investments or business ventures.
- Generational transitions bring more shareholders to the table and sometimes add new professionals who challenge the management of a break-even business.
- Inevitably some family members want to sell their shares, and the other shareholders must face the questions of whether to buy them out and how to value the company.

In our globally connected world, deep changes occur ever more rapidly. One seventh-generation family leader observed that for six generations, things were predictable and orderly. The business passed from first son to first son, with the business operating in the same way with skilled craftsmen and laborers. During the past twenty years, however, the family experienced more change than all previous generations combined. The business environment became global, technology transformed, and competition emerged everywhere. Internally, the family decided that all family members—sons and daughters, younger and older—were eligible for leadership positions, not just the number-1 son.

Families, however, are designed to strongly *resist* change. They strive toward providing security, predictability, and stability. Many business founders and leaders want things simply to continue unchanged because they have known nothing but success. They avoid and deny anything that suggests their old ways have to change. Many business families fail because they are unable to retain the spark of creativity that could create value for the new generation. In these cases, businesses may become stale and vulnerable. Conflict may erupt, calling the direction and leadership into question. Family members worry about how they can avoid decline.

As business elders live longer, they want to enjoy their success and grow weary of having to reinvent themselves. Indeed, a core aspect of the ability to change is skill in deciding when to "harvest" the value of a family asset by its sale. This can free the family to pursue new opportunities as new generations, with different perspectives, emerge. It can also free the family so that the second generation can "rescue" the family by taking it in a new direction. Each generation has the opportunity to reinvent the family enterprise. This chapter presents the most common transformations experienced by generative families and how they actively prepare for them.

## Continual Reinvention

What does it take to sustain continual business innovation and adaptation? Resilient businesses approach a turbulent environment by anticipating and adapting rather than reacting.

A common model for the growth and development of a business is the S-curve. A founder with limited resources struggles to build a successful business, and the business then takes off in a spurt of exponential growth. But growth cannot continue forever. The curve eventually levels off or declines as products mature, competition emerges, or technology and tastes change. The business now faces a crisis and must

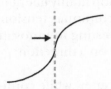

**Figure 5.1  An S-curve.**

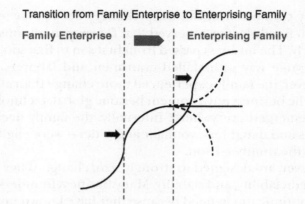

Figure 5.2   Addition of a new S-curve.

find a new pathway to growth or face decline. A family enterprise experiences periods of exponential growth, but its continued success rides on the family's ability to renew itself when growth slows or crisis strikes. (See Figure 5.1.)

A generative family seeks opportunities to create new S-curves or extend current ones. It jumps from a maturing or declining effort into the development of new products or markets or a new venture or investment. Prospects for change depend on where you are on the S-curve; this is not always apparent. When the family undertakes a deep transformation in its business, the family potentially enters a new S-curve. (See Figure 5.2.)

Few generations begin and end with the same business in the same place. Enterprises face *external* threats like social media, global competition for core products, new brands, aftermath of war and political threats, or maturing and obsolete products. Businesses can't wait too long; they have to anticipate and respond to challenges. If the family's only asset is a single business, the threat is especially severe. The old leaders are mortal; they must find innovators within the family who have the will and the skill not just to sustain their vision but to adapt and change.

Our research allows us to look back on the journey over three or more generations of each generative family. We can envision a timeline outlining the twists and turns of such a family's journey across generations. A family can create a personal version of Figure 5.3 to remember and connect the sequence of key events in their history. This is one way that the family educates and inspires the younger generation about the family story.

Innovation and entrepreneurship are not the sole province of the founding generation. Generative families develop family talent to redefine themselves in each new generation. They experience a continual tension between maintaining the status quo, "harvesting" wealth, and investing in innovation for the long term. The family has to deal with dissent and agree on a direction; generative families accomplish this successfully.

They buy, sell, innovate, and renew while continually redesigning their business. As Chapter 6 will show, they can do this as "craftsmen" by innovating their core

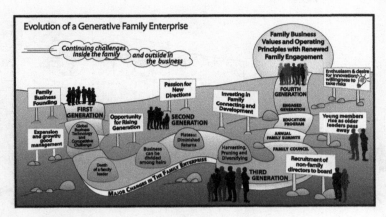

**Figure 5.3  Timeline of key events in the family journey.**

product or technology or as "opportunists" by seeking out new business directions or ventures.

The change capability of generative families is often due to the initiative of their rising generation. The young successors are not satisfied with accepting the status quo, as lucrative as that may be. They are anxious to prove themselves and excited about new directions. Their global education has taught them new ideas and possibilities, but to put their skills and knowledge to the service of the family, they need support from their elders. The rising generation needs to listen and learn from the elders' wisdom and experience before charging off in a new direction.

## Turning Points: Four Major Transformations of Generative Families

A majority of the generative families interviewed for this study move along a path punctuated by four huge milestone transformations:

- **Harvesting** the legacy business by a sale or other event that accesses liquidity
- **Pruning** the family tree by buying out some family members, leaving only those committed to business ownership
- **Diversifying** by buying other businesses and making other investments, thus creating a business portfolio
- **Grounding** by creating a family office to centralize and oversee the multiple business entities and operations, and continue the family identity.

Each of these transformations deeply changes the nature of the family. The generative family emerges from each of these major transformations with a new focus that continues its legacy values and builds upon family strengths. The family works actively through the resilience cycle to anticipate, redefine itself, and work through changes. While families do not go through these milestones in strict

**Figure 5.4   Evolution of the family enterprise.**

order, the progression from single-family business with a few owners to a portfolio of enterprises with a family office and a pruned (but still sizable) set of family owners defines the path of most of the generative families featured in this book. (See Figure 5.4.)

### "Harvesting" the Legacy Business: Liquidity Offers New Opportunities[1]

When a wealth creator tells future generations, "Never sell the family business," the heirs are wise to take this admonition with a grain of salt. No business can last forever. A business-owning family should not wait for its business to fail. Instead, it looks ahead and periodically asks:

- Does this business make sense for us now?
- Can we remain competitive in the face of new technology, globalization, and social change?
- Can we handle and operate the business as it should be managed?
- Do we have the resources to invest in sustaining excellence?

Most families wanted to hold onto their legacy businesses. But sometimes, even a strong and vibrant business can be threatened by external factors like social changes or new technology. One family, reluctantly and with great reservations, decided to sell its legacy business. A senior member of the family related:

*Nobody wanted to sell the company, but because we were offered a premium that was 67 percent higher than the day before, we felt we had to take the offer. We realized that if we turned down the offer, we'd have to allocate significant resources to rebuild the company, and this would involve major changes in leadership. We weren't sure whether we could persevere through the turmoil this would cause, so we ultimately decided to sell.*

Some studies imply that the sale of the legacy business means the end of the family as an organized entity. Our research found, however, that this is far from the case. The sale of the legacy business is a major transformation—a watershed event—but it leads generative families to a new beginning. Selling a business means transferring value for money and leaving the business behind. The term "harvest" refers to a family's departure from majority ownership of its legacy business because, for the family, the event is not an end. In agriculture, a harvest allows the field to regenerate and then be replanted. A family that harvests decides to take resources from a single business to nurture and develop other opportunities. The sale of assets can occur more than once; a few families report that they harvest a major asset every generation to offer some family members the chance to go out on their own and take on new challenges. The new reality can also be traumatic for a generative family. It can mean the loss of family identity that was embodied in the business and its place in the community, and entry into unfamiliar territory.

Half of the families in this study "harvested" their legacy business. This has two transformative effects on the family:

- It allows some family members to cash out and leave the family partnership. Other family members choose to support their lives and individual family needs by remaining in the family partnership. Selling an asset is like letting pressure out of a pump; it allows the family to continue to operate while reducing pressure for continual returns on their invested assets.
- It allows the new generation to develop new ventures that employ their skills and meet the family's need for new sources of wealth. Several families had more than one major family business. By selling one of their assets that either needed new capital or was bringing slower and less predictable returns, they were able to refocus on new efforts and investments.

As a result of the harvest, the families in this study commonly develop several sources of wealth—a holding company, family office, or perhaps a private trust company that combines the benefits of a family office with that of a trust. Any of these arrangements enable them to buy and sell investments.

Even though the family may value its legacy business highly, there may be good reasons to harvest. While the business performed well in the past, it may be maturing, producing lower returns, or needing a significant infusion of capital. The enterprise may have grown to enormous proportions but attracted few family members to manage it. In cases like these, a family often feels comfortable detaching its identity from the business. Even though there may be sentimental ties to the business, the family may decide to move on, to find a new source of identity and outlet for its energy.

Who makes this decision, and how is it made? In most family businesses, the decision is made by only a few family members at the ownership or board level. They may not share an offer within the family because of confidentiality, or they may not feel the need to inform the family at all. We see a different process of decision-making in generative families. Board members or key shareholders might make informed decisions, but they understand that due to the emotional significance of the proposed sale and the values of the family, nonowning family members should be consulted, too. Members of the younger generation, who stand to become owners in the future, are especially important. Do they understand and agree with the values and challenges that are being considered in the sale? They are the ones who will lose an opportunity because of the sale. The generative family finds a way to engage the whole family in the conversation about the possible sale and solicits opinions before taking action.

Sometimes, upon listening to the voices of its members, a family may decide against a sale. Instead, it recommits the family's energy and resources to renewing the business. Here are three examples:

1. *The challenge at this point was to bring in a nonfamily CEO. But we questioned whether he or she would be able to maintain the culture and the values that we have established. We have a very strong culture that is part of the fabric of our company. Part of our sadness about selling the business came from the feeling that we might lose this wonderful legacy and culture we've developed.*

2. *There has always been a strong commitment to the long-term ownership of the business. We've been approached countless times, even monthly, by venture capitalists or competitors who want to buy the business, but we've never even discussed these offers at the board level because the family has made our policy clear. We simply say, "We're not interested," and move along. We have a commitment to maintaining the business for future generations.*

3. *If all the assets of the business were liquidated, everyone would have a bunch of money in their pockets. But we would just feel sick, like we let down our ancestors who built the business and never thought of selling it.*

## Deciding to Sell

Despite the central role of the legacy business in sustaining family connection and identity, there may be business reasons to consider a sale, as this G3 leader observed:

*By the time the question came up about whether to sell the business, the family members were pretty distanced from the business. Most of them have professions, so the business is always in the background. That represented the culture of the family when we decided to sell. That decision was actually initiated by nonfamily, nonexecutive directors who said, "You've had an amazing ninety-year run, but now you're running a lot of risk. We're worried about the risk you're carrying as a family."*

If they are not committed to the business, minority family owners can force a sale.

*They had an empire—all the land around the city center. But ultimately, they had to sell because the small shareholders wanted to sell. Often the small shareholders are unhappy and turn sour. And when someone turns sour, they start to act badly.*

If the family does not have the will, skills, or resources to address emerging business needs, it can preempt a later crisis by a strategic choice to sell and diversify. For example, one family controlled a large but poorly performing public company. Content with their considerable dividends, they did not demand change until performance worsened and threatened the dividend. The family was approached by a buyer who wanted to take the company in a different direction than the family wanted. Nevertheless, given the decline that had not been addressed, the family felt it had to sell. Because it was a public company, the deal was much in the news, and this made the very private family uncomfortable. Family members were glad to descend back under the radar after the sale was consummated.

It's important to note that family advisors may become a separate interest group of their own and that their own self-interest may further complicate, or even undermine, the situation. The following family eventually sold because it lost connection to and trust in the business:

> We had limited input to a trustee office that organized things for us. We should have learned twenty years before that we needed a more robust structure. Our advisors told us that they could provide that structure, but this didn't build family leadership because we weren't a part of that structure. Communication within the family wasn't robust and there wasn't a clear way of pulling it together. When the possibility of a sale came up, there was an attempt to improve communication and empower the family. But the advisors felt that their power was threatened by the sale. They were always worried about what was going to happen to them instead of working for the best interests of the family.

A sale transports the family in a new direction that it must address and adjust to:

> For a long time, our family got together because we were all connected to the company. We would meet with our advisors four times a year and meet with the company twice a year. Family board members met monthly with the board, and we had a lot of family meetings around that. We would also attend reunions, weddings, and funerals. We saw a lot of the family collectively. After the sale, we realized how important the business had been in holding us together. We try to meet quarterly, but we don't have that same glue that holds us together. It's very difficult to create new things for our meetings.

As the following sections will show, after the harvest there is a critical period to rebuild family partnership and reconsider whether the family will recommit to new shared investments or enterprises. For many families, the business sale does mark the end of the family as an organized, shared enterprise. For the generative family, it marks a turning point to a more diverse and creative future together.

## G4 Redefines Its Identity After Sale of the Legacy Business

A family crisis sometimes occurs after a major event like the sale or a public optioning of a legacy business. After this experience, the family may not feel the same identity and purpose as a family. Governance offers the family a platform to chart a path to reengage

*(continued)*

*(Continued)*

and renew the identity and vitality of the extended family. A hundred-year European business faced a core choice when it was acquired and went public, being absorbed into a large conglomerate. The retiring G4 family leaders described the transition and the uncertainty about future success as a united business family:

> *If it's the right thing to separate from the business, did we still want to remain together as a business family? As the young guy and business leader at thirty-four, I asked myself, "What are you going to do next?" My job became to work out the appropriate solution for our family. We began with a process of total inclusion. In other words, consultation with everybody to develop a strategy. There was no barrier to leaving; if you want to go, do it with your head held high and let's keep it friendly and happy. But some of us think it's a good idea to develop the family capital. We realized that together we've got a better chance of allowing it to endure. Nearly all of us wanted to keep going. We sat down and said, "This cash has fallen into our laps. We didn't create it so what is the responsible solution?" And that is how we've continued to operate since then.*
>
> *We recognized that we didn't have a process of family governance, collective activities as a family. The business was there. It was successful. There was no need for governance before. It was driven by a handful of people. Suddenly we become a collaborative group, so my fourth generation needed to work out what we were going to do. We formed a family council. After a few years, we wrote a family protocol. We put governance in place because we recognize that in my generation there are fourteen of us and we produced thirty-seven children, so the family will get anarchic without it. We've been lucky, and let's see if we can put some structures around us that enable the next generation to continue.*
>
> *One is family gatherings. Every two years, we invite every descendant of the original founder to a huge event. We've probably done six or seven of them now. We have become much more interested in community connection as a family than in adding to business knowledge because I think that's very complicated. Now we're an investment fund. But what is much more important, selfishly for my children, is that the next generation become a coherent group who know each other as individuals, like each other, spend time with each other, and when you can go and talk to each other and don't bring out their lawyers. How can they continue to have a dialogue as our generation did? So we facilitate these off-site weekends. We pay for them. The family just turn up. They're all to do with team building, intergenerational games, activities, making music, dancing. This is pretty extraordinary stuff, and it was quite slow to get going. As one cousin said to his wife as he left a couple of years ago, "My goodness, I just wish we could bottle that spirit." We're just getting together and recognizing there is a process to go through to enable us to function as a coherent group. But it doesn't get any further than that.*
>
> *Now we're beginning to introduce a bit of business education. What I worry about, more than anything, is lack of engagement. When you have a service business, it's hard for people to identify with it because if we don't have a product, we don't have a presence in the marketplace. I was talking to a high-profile entrepreneur in the UK recently about this. He's saying, "I've created all this money, and my family aren't engaging."*
>
> *They trust you and all you can do is go through the motions and put the structures in place and try to spend as much time as you can to ensure that they work, but you're not going to know whether they actually do it until you're not there. I'm fortunate that I work for my family shareholders, who clearly trust me. The downside of that is it's hard to get them to engage over and above a superficial level because they're busy people with busy lives. We represent all sorts of professions, doctors, researchers, farmers, bankers, you name it. So this is just part of who they are. We go through the process; the difficulty is engagement.*

### *"Pruning" the Family Tree: Becoming a Family of Affinity*

As new members enter the family by birth and marriage, the challenge of sustaining commitment to long-term goals while sacrificing shorter-term profit distributions reemerges as each new shareholder seeks a good return from his or her asset.

These changes do not come without pain. Often, families have to reinvest profits, which cuts down on the short-term returns to family members, who may not be patient or supportive. As a result, all the families in this study have faced the choice of **pruning** the family tree by buying out a branch or member who does not want to reinvest. Each family has a "liquidity event," buy-out process, or distribution, whereby members have the opportunity to redecide whether or not to remain partners.

If a family member lives far away, does not feel excited to be part of a community of second and third cousins, or wants access to capital to spend or invest in a different direction, he or she may choose to leave.

Remaining entails responsibilities that some family members do not want to take on:

- *Commitment of time and energy* to governance—both oversight of the business and participation in shared family activities
- *Spending time and working with other family members*
- *Willingness to forgo short-term profits* and income for long-term investments

As the number of family owners increases, each shareholder holds a smaller share, making it more difficult to achieve alignment and shared goals. The families in this study adopted redemption policies that allow smaller family owners to sell their shares either back to the company or to other family members. All the families in this study have adopted *exit policies* as part of their family shareholder agreements; these policies are necessary safety valves to avoid tension around differences and destructive conflict.

Different branches develop divergent interests. Some look at their business portfolio and decide to separate a long-term business with moderate risk from riskier entrepreneurial ventures. To others, owning a larger part of a smaller business can be more attractive than a small share of a larger one. Such horse trading occurs in most of the families in this study; the development of a fair and clearly defined internal family marketplace for shareholders can sustain family ownership while allowing individuation.

It makes a big difference if the parting is natural and friendly rather than the result of conflict and disagreement. Many generative families report natural events where the family divides in a way that does not disrupt their family relationships:

> When the family broke up in generation two and generation three, it wasn't a breakup. It was an amicable, "Let's live together but not have a marriage certificate." You know, "Let's get along with our cousins or our uncles" or whatever it is, "and have a very good relationship in the family" because family is first.

In the third or fourth generation, some families divide their partnership by branches. When a family is so hugely successful that it owns multiple businesses or reaches a size where integration or synergy is a challenge, it may be adaptive for the family to separate branches. Several large families have gone in that direction; one member stated that it was the "village tradition" to go in separate directions as they split into several loosely connected branch portfolios. In some family traditions, the parents divide resources into separate packages for each of their children.[2] While they may miss the chance to build on a greater scale, they have their own forms of success as each family member is able to create his or her own unique destiny.

However, such arrangements need to be carefully planned. By allowing owners to exit, the family postpones the geometric rise in number and dilution of share ownership. That is why many generative businesses have a relatively small number of shareholders. Those who remain are willing to forestall current profits for longer-term goals.

Upon the sale of a legacy asset—a liquidity event—each family member has a *choice*. One option is to go his or her own way with the new liquid capital. Alternatively, some family members might continue to invest together by forming an investment group or family office. For example, after the sale of their huge legacy business, the largest of three family branches chose to continue as an investment group:

> The decision to separate into three branches was organic. We'd been talking about it for a long time. The sale moved us in that direction without needing a referendum. We took a good amount of time to figure it all out. We talked to other families who have gone through similar stuff and to a lot of advisors about our options.
>
> After the sale, family members could decide to go off on their own. This was complicated, however, because the ownership was in the trust. Ultimately, we decided to continue the trust together with new advisors and trustees. Family members had the choice to place their assets in our investment partnership.
>
> At this point, family members began to have access to stock. We have redemption policies and ways to access liquid cash. However, we want to make sure that they think through any withdrawals carefully, so we offer them resources like lawyers and accountants.

## Maintaining the Vision by Choice

Family members committed to the business do not want pressures for immediate dividends to trigger a sale of the business. They feel removing capital deprives future generations of the benefits of their legacy ownership. Instead, to deal with the pressures from those who want immediate returns, a generative family offers a path for individuals or a branch to sell their shares. By the fourth generation, *not one of the generative families in this study contained all of the blood family members as shareholders*. Instead, each family offered a choice for family members to opt out of the family enterprise. (Some family trusts, however, do not allow this option.) Generative families become, as my colleague James Hughes, Jr., observes, *families of affinity*.[3] When an exit path is offered, each family member must voluntarily decide to remain in the collective. In this way, they remain a family by choice, not blood.

This shift is especially important because family enterprises tend to limit the profit distribution to owners, preferring to reinvest in the company for the benefit of future family owners. Those who want immediate liquidity are encouraged to sell as in this example:

> *In our family, this reconsolidation allows family members who are not interested in the business to cash out. These members don't understand the business; they just want the highest dividends. Now they can sell their nonvoting shares and do what they want with the money, leaving the few who are truly committed to the business to reinvest in it. This worked well for the second and third generation. In fact, this method has been a sustainable competitive advantage for family businesses. Instead of dealing with disputes over high dividends versus reinvestment, they're able to take all that energy and focus on customers and associates.*

A fifth-generation Asian family had this process for reducing the number of shareholders:

> *If we continue letting the family tree just grow without any thought of pruning, the dilution will become too great, and we may not be able to maintain the original vision of the business. It started with my uncle, then my father had four sons, and although my father gave me a bit more of his shares, the dilution really continued. If I continue to share with my children, then each branch of the tree will become very small as we move on.*
>
> *I shared my idea about tree pruning with another second-generation family business leader. I suggested to the second-generation business leader that we needed to find a way for those who want to exit the family enterprise to sell their shares. We can't turn away family members, but we can trim the number of shareholders by allowing them to cash in their shares. Then only those who are more passionate about the business will remain as the shareholders. As we move to the fifth generation, we may have to do another pruning.*

Some business families face another kind of liquidity event: the dissolution of a trust.[4] Most trusts have an ending date, but when they are set up, the ending date may be generations away, so there is little consideration of what the date means. However, when that date actually approaches, the beneficiaries of the trust need to make a choice about how the trust's assets will be held in the future. They must decide whether they want to remain together and, if they do, how to invest the money. Here's how one family dealt with this issue:

> *Each branch had significant assets and trusts. Eventually those trusts would break, so the question was: How do we keep people engaged together? What happens when people have the freedom to leave? In 1995, the sixth generation gathered for the first time. Three of us fifth-generation leaders asked them to help develop a strategic plan for the trust company. We began to anticipate what would happen next.*

## "Diversifying" from Single Business to Portfolio

The evolution from owner/managers of a legacy business to managing a portfolio of businesses often arises when a new generation of young leaders begins to take over. This generation arrives with new energy, top-notch business educations, apprenticeships, and commitment to the family. These new leaders may see challenges ahead for the legacy business and investigate possible ways to renew it, reinvest, expand, or take on other investors. For example, liquidity from ESOPS (employee stock ownership programs) might allow some family members to cash out while the family continues to own and control the business. Conversely, offering stock to key family executives or advisors might enable them to continue to contribute to the company. Family owners may then seek opportunities to buy another business or pursue new investments within a family office or private trust company. These families discover many opportunities. They may be large enough to create an internal economy in which different family members can invest in certain projects, each with different degrees of cross-family ownership.

After harvesting, the family comes to own not one but several assets. Harvesting profits or selling a business may allow them to begin an investment fund or even buy new businesses. They often accumulate real estate, lovely family homes, land they lease to their business, and other investment buildings. They may form a family philanthropic foundation, which can involve family members. With several ventures and accumulating capital, the family needs to define its goals and policies and allocate resources to each asset. Even if they have managers for each individual entity, the oversight of the whole portfolio of ventures, balancing priorities, allocation and harvesting of funds, and new directions, some group of family owners must make decisions across assets. These decisions must take into account what family members in current and future generations want from the family wealth. Some will look for new ventures and others will pursue a social or philanthropic path.

After selling the legacy business, a business family has a rare opportunity to regroup and redefine itself. This opens the door to new entrepreneurial ventures by the family. Here's how one family created a new enterprise:

> Today we don't have a fancy public family business. We have a tightly run, profitable business that provides investment opportunities available nowhere else. Our real estate department operates at a 99 percent occupancy rate. We have malls, apartment buildings, and offices. The trust management looks after the partners of a private capital fund with nine different managers across a variety of disciplines, including venture capital. All this provides opportunities for each generation. Although we don't have a visible business any more, we don't want to lose these opportunities for future generations. We hope for new entrepreneurialism and new invention.

While the older generation and professional managers may tend toward a conservative approach and risk avoidance, the emergence of a rising generation with a desire for innovation can move the family in a more entrepreneurial direction. The entrepreneurial energy of the new generation can challenge and balance the conservatism of the older generation and the professional business leaders. The family needs to engage these talented young people after they have developed capability and credibility but before they are fully established outside the family orbit. The family also has to initiate checks and balances on investments and new ideas so the enthusiasm and desire for risk by the younger generation is balanced by prudence. However, the older generation cannot be too conservative. One family missed the opportunity to invest early on in one of the Internet pioneers. The younger generation presented the idea passionately and thoughtfully, but the family was not willing to take the risk.

A European manufacturing business went through this evolution. As described below, two generations had to work through their differences:

> *The company rose from our single operating family business into a financial holding company with a family office. We needed to diversify and shift our focus beyond our industry in Europe. There were a number of issues that were hotly debated between the third and fourth generations. Should we sell the business? If we sold, how should we invest the proceeds? Should we invest in more diverse holdings, or should we distribute the proceeds to the shareholders?*
>
> *Financing had become more difficult. If we went to the bank, we were offered higher rates, so we decided to separate the export activities in Africa from the core company and set up a holding company at the top. Some noninvolved family members were allowed to separate themselves from the core activities. This was a positive thing because it allowed the managers to make decisions without needing to get input from these members.*

This Middle Eastern conglomerate typifies the organization of non-US family ventures that have diversified into many parts:

> *The family holding company used to be comprised exclusively of family shareholders: these shareholders held either 100 percent or a majority stake in all of our businesses. But last year, for the first time, we took a minority stake in one of our own SBUs because it required such a heavy investment (it was a supermarket chain). Outside investors put in money; now we're 49 percent, and they're 51 percent.*

A family enterprise can contain both public and private business entities. They may be combined into a family holding company, as was done by this fifth-generation European conglomerate:

> *On the private side, we have a holding company, which is the original company. This now amounts to about 50 percent of the public company. The public company has four economic drivers: a power utility, a commercial bank, a consumer goods company, and real estate. All of these are public, but the private holding company holds a big chunk of the public company. We now have a market cap of about seven billion dollars.*

A family with a legacy business dating back more than a century started a family partnership outside its public company. This partnership had a family advisory board and two family member executives who joined the business after working for venture capital and financial firms. Their venture capital investments fit the interests of their rising generation and were supported by the capability of experienced family and nonfamily leaders.

The transition to a portfolio of shared assets represents a deep transformation of the family, as this European company learned when it crossed generations:

> *In 2009, we had a liquidity event: we sold part of the farming company. This enabled us to buy out my grandfather, so he could retire in peace. We also had funds to buy out the generation*

*of my father and my uncle. However, this raised a lot of disagreements. Some people wanted to sell the company while others were absolutely against it. It was a very difficult time involving many arduous and heated discussions.*

*Eventually, the majority of the family agreed to sell the company. This was a momentous decision because it was our core business. Next, we reached an agreement with the older generation about a generational transition. Ultimately, we were able to buy out the elders, and we ended 2009 with my generation in control of the family council.*

Moving to a portfolio of businesses and other shared assets also allows for differences in the type of family leadership. Instead of a single leader, the family might select multiple leaders with different skills who manage different types of assets. Some families, especially those outside the United States, allow family members to acquire and manage different businesses. However, the portfolio needs a central holding company or board of directors that can manage the interaction of all of the assets together. The legacy company may have had a single family leader in the previous generation; the shift to a portfolio opens the door for shared leadership by family members who can oversee different areas. A designated next-generation leader can never have the authority of the original business founder, as he or she answers to many other family owners. Accompanying a designated leader, there is usually a board, investment committee, or special task force to diversify the family investments.

## Adopting an Entrepreneurial Mindset for the Family Portfolio

In generative families, taking prudent risks and adopting new directions often win over the more conservative elements of the family. As an example, after selling the legacy business, this rising generation found the opportunity to influence the new family direction:

*At the beginning, of course, we were just one single operating unit. Later, when the operation started generating enough cash, we began to diversify. We created our own diverse portfolio to have as a security blanket if something happened to the core business. This has been a continuous strategy; it's never been set aside or forgotten. And we've always continued to increase our portfolio.*

*After a time, we felt uneasy because we were doing so many things at the same time without a strategy to tie them all together. We were missing opportunities. Now that we've moved to a holding company, we have an overview of all the businesses, and we can interrelate each business. This enables us to prepare strategies for sales, production, and growth for each business. We can also create synergies among the various businesses.*

*The goal of the holding company is to continue to purchase more companies and create more opportunities, always with a clear strategy. Two months from now, we're going to have the first consolidated statement for the entire group.*

*We all have an entrepreneurial mindset, an excitement about creating new business opportunities. It's challenging and exciting and a lot of fun. This spirit comes from the family mission, our way of looking at life. We're never satisfied with the status quo. The lessons we learned from our upbringing have made us reach for continuous movement and change.*

*We sometimes feel the need to settle what we have before we look for new things. But every time we say that, something new comes along, and everybody gets very excited. There's always somebody looking for something. We have a very solid liquid investment portfolio, and that makes for peace of mind as we move ahead.*

## "Grounding": Family Offices as Centers for Governance and Family Identity

All over the world, we see a dramatic growth in the number of entities called *family offices*. After the success of a family business, the family might begin to accumulate wealth from other assets. A "liquidity" event like a business sale or accumulation of capital from profits creates the need for the family to manage assets and investments outside the business. At first, if the business is privately held, the other assets can be managed from within the business. But if there are other shareholders or the business is sold or goes public, the financial affairs of the extended family will need to be managed separately.

A family office provides new services to a family, including tax filing and legal compliance, financial advising, wealth portfolio management, support for family lifestyles, administration of trusts, and estate planning. The office also supports family meetings, governance activities, and family education. It lies between the extended family, its business, and its financial and business entities. Having new focus and new "center" means that the family often has to alter its identity and how it sees itself and operates.

The location of these services outside the legacy business creates what is called a family office. If the family has a large amount of capital or multiple assets, the office can be quite large and contain a large professional staff. In effect, it becomes another business owned by the family that must be governed. Forming a family office after the sale of a legacy business creates a new center for the identity and shared engagement of the family apart from its business. A family has to decide whether it wants its own office or whether it wants to join with other families and receive these services through a multifamily office, trust company, or financial firm.

Nearly two-thirds—63 percent—of the generative families in this study have a family office. (See Figure 5.5.) With each new generation, the likelihood of having a family office increases. (See Figure 5.6.)

In the third generation, only a third of our families had a family office. By the fourth generation, 61 percent of our families had one. Forming a family office is often not a clear decision at a single point in time but may evolve as the family requires attention to taxes, investments, personal expenses, philanthropy, and shared family activities outside the business. While this makes the governance more complex, a family office enables the family to remain together as an organized, value-creating entity.

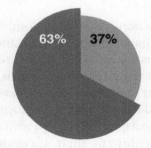

**Figure 5.5  Percentage of generative families with family offices.**

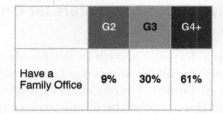

**Figure 5.6   Increasing percentages of family offices over generations.**

A family office may be created after the sale of a large business as described here:

*We have an investment management committee that recommends certain investments—and we do a bit of our own research. We also have a family office with a very small staff. We have experts in investments, legal matters, philanthropy, and tax preparation. For some things, like tax prep, we might pay a little bit more, but we feel that we're getting the latest and greatest strategies.*

It is not unusual for a G4+ family to sell its legacy business and diversify. The maturing business may not offer the returns that could be realized in other ventures. As the family grows, some family members of the geometrically expanding family want to exit the family enterprise. The family must design and implement clear policies to govern the trading of their shares. Upon such a sale, many families create or expand family offices to manage the proceeds for family members who choose to reinvest and to take advantage of opportunities not available to individual investors.

The families studied here see themselves as much more than family investment groups. They see the family office as *multidimensional*: it helps them manage not just their money but also the family's many familial, social, and philanthropic connections. It is the center for family governance and educational activities. In these cases, as the following two examples reveal, the sale of the business is not an end but a new beginning.

One G4 family divided into branches eighteen years ago after an IPO led to the sale of its business and creation of several family offices. One branch with forty family members came together to redefine how the members wanted to work together. They felt deeply connected to the tradition and values of the family, but now, as members of a financial family, they developed governance appropriate to their financial future.

Every two years, they hold a family assembly, combining fun, strategic review, and shared learning. They already had a family council, and they developed a family constitution. It included provisions for a shareholders meeting twice a year and a foundation that met several times a year. They have begun to convene a next-generation group and are developing clear guidelines about access to money and distributions. When an issue arises, they deal with it within the appropriate group.

Another family office began a generation ago with the sale of the family's remaining interest in a large public company their ancestors founded at the turn of the twentieth century. The sale enabled members of the three large family branches to decide whether they wanted to be part of the new family office. A majority signed on, and they have continued to create financial wealth. The board contains members from each of the three branches and from three generations. Members of G4 have moved onto the board and management of the family office. One hundred family members travel to the annual shareholders meetings, though the family would like to have even wider participation from its seven hundred family members.

The family has not been without conflicts and tensions. In order to resolve them, they have committed deeply to values of transparency, trust, and engagement. They exercise this commitment through the election of thirteen family members to the family council, which holds open meetings:

> *You foster trust through being open and through communication. If you don't have these things, communication and openness, you can't really have trust in any kind of relationships, professional or personal. If people don't feel that, they don't add to the connectedness of the family. . . . So the role of the family council is trying to straighten out some of the ill feelings over the years. People have left the business because they didn't feel trust.*

This family has a deep tradition of values about family connection, not only in regard to governance but also as a way to enhance the well-being and development of each family member. The family has used its resources to support, for example, a family member who is an accomplished artist and to encourage other family members to "follow their dreams." The family has frequent family gatherings. There is a family website that contains a growing library of family stories and interviews with elders who are videotaped at family gatherings. The family has developed a seminar series for younger family members on topics like tax, budget, investing, and insurance; these seminars are attended by thirty to fifty young family members. Since 1980, there has been an auxiliary—or "junior"—board for family members who want to learn about finances and become involved in governance. This group has graduated family members to join the official board, which includes nine family and four nonfamily members.

As with other types of family business, the family exercises control over its assets. The family has values about investments, and the family members want to sustain their identity as a family. Moving away from a single legacy business, the family office becomes the heart and soul of the family, the place where the family efforts are centered. If there is a family council, a board, family activity for education, a family vacation home, or support for individual households, the family office is where all these things are coordinated. Providing these family-related services is seen as worth the extra cost.

The family office oversees and administers assets beyond the legacy business. Acquiring additional assets allows the family to diversify; this lessens the risk of owning just a single huge asset. The diversified family office might include a trust, a holding company, an LLP, a private trust company, or other forms of partnership. It is governed by a board or trustees separate from the board of the legacy company. Family members can be board members, owners, staff, or CEO of these entities. They make the "business" pillar of family governance a sort of double pillar as the family office grows alongside the legacy business. Family conglomerates have complex structures that may own several large investments and companies. The goals of the family office are to preserve and grow assets, build a diverse array of businesses, and act as a center for other family activities.

Why do generative families often prefer single-family offices rather than being part of a shared multifamily office (a less expensive alternative)? This is because in addition to the financial services, the family office acts as a clubhouse and community center for the extended family. If the family is not widely dispersed, the family office has even more value to the family. In visiting family offices, one often finds a museum of family artifacts and long-serving staff who are close to family members and are available to assist them with issues and concerns. Members can get help not only with tax and financial issues but also with relationship and personal issues that arise in the family. Family office staff can help negotiate prenuptial agreements and divorces, assist in buying houses, boats, planes, and art, and attend to safety and security. There are places for family meetings to be held and places to store and keep family records. The office embodies the family's identity and commitments.

To allow the family to act as its own trustee for a family trust, a complex, highly regulated bank-like entity called a *private trust company* can be created. For example, a family that owned and controlled a large public company began to diversify by selling stock in the business. The family needed a home for these new investments, and it wanted to consolidate the investments that were held in various institutions and trusts. The family could justify the expense of setting up a private trust company because it wanted to be actively involved in investment decisions using the wisdom of its talented fourth generation.

As a family accumulates wealth, it often wants to invest as a family according to its legacy values. The family sees opportunities to combine its values with its investments. However, some family members may not share these values or want to invest in other ways. The solution to this conflict lies in allowing family members to cash out. Many families report that when they set up their family office, they offer family branches and members the option to exit and take their money out and also an opportunity to initiate a new period of growth or redefine their business and investment values.

Larger families have more complex and varied needs for their family offices. They may have farming, ranch, and vacation properties that need active oversight and other natural resources with complex regulations and tax implications. In addition, they may have venture capital arms with active or passive investments, concerns about impact and social responsibility, philanthropic arms that oversee foundation assets and the foundation itself, and other personal investments by family members. The family office might manage investments and personal affairs of many individual households. For example, when it sold its legacy business, a four-branch family split the proceeds. The largest branch formed a family office and moved into new investment areas, but this new family office served only sixteen of the sixty-four family members.

Some family offices might oversee the initiation of *ad hoc* family task groups. One such task group might be an investment committee to manage the family investments. Other families might have small internal offices and outsource the investment management to other financial advisors. The emerging functions of the family office allow the expression of innovation and entrepreneurial impulses as the enterprise moves in new directions.

### The Structure of Resilience

Generative families are characterized by how they handle planned and unplanned transitions—the degree to which they anticipate and respond to emerging challenges. Behind the family's success there is often a struggle inside the family, first about whether to change and then about how to accomplish that change. After each transition, the family develops increasingly complex business and governance structures to manage its growing enterprise and family. The existence of these structures enables the family to discover their new path and resolve their differences.

Family enterprises, even generative ones, make mistakes. One new family leader initiated the purchase of a competitor, telling the family he would make it work. It didn't. As a result, the family learned to be more involved in such decisions. Another enterprise was not performing well when the new generation took over. The members of the new generation didn't want to sell, so instead they cut costs and reduced family perks in order to turn the business around. After this wrenching change, they had to rebuild family relationships. The overreaction was forgivable; in fact their continued success stems from their willingness to forgive and move on.

Unanticipated changes, like the early death of a key family leader or the emergence of new technologies, can tear a business apart. Generative families, however, act decisively in response to each challenge. At best, the family anticipates a crisis or at least sees an early warning sign.

We see a three-phase resilience cycle in how generative families respond to change:

1. **Prepare/anticipate:** Even when they are not preparing for a specific change, the family expects and anticipates broad general changes such as the need to develop a new generation of family members or prepare for a shift in customers or products. They notice early warning signs and face their import.
2. **Engage/decide:** As a change approaches, generative families gather to consider what it means. They engage multiple family members and listen to differing points of view before they take action.
3. **Redefine/renew:** After the change, generative families do not go back to the way things were. They find a new path and work to implement it. While they respect tradition, they are able to let go of anything that is obsolete.

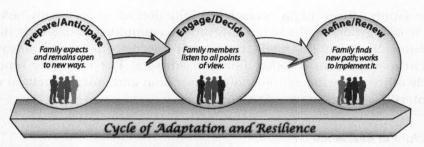

**Figure 5.7   Cycle of adaptation and resilience.**

Another way of viewing resiliency is as a *learning mindset*. Rather than trying to dominate and impose their will, family leaders are open to new ideas from inside and outside the family. Businesses that exhibit resilience in the face of continual change have been characterized as *learning organizations*. The ability to question old ways and experiment with new ones is an aspect of resiliency, especially important to counteract the conservative tendency of the family owners. Without learning, there cannot be real change.

### Dealing with Pitfalls

In spite of a family's best efforts, however, many pitfalls can derail the enterprise. It can overexpand or become too focused on family politics while neglecting the external challenges. A business family might think too highly of itself and overvalue its business. A family may idealize its values to the extent that it ignores signs that the family is not living up to the values. In order to bring such tendencies to the surface, one family decided, *"We should have an advisor as an ombudsman for family members who don't feel comfortable coming directly to another family member with a complaint or suggestion. We depend on her for content at the family meetings."*

By facing challenges or issues that may be buried or ignored, the family becomes aware of the impending need for change. The initiative for a major transformation often arises when a new generation comes into power. When a rising generation takes control, it's important that its members take stock of what they have inherited and consider what is needed to sustain that inheritance. As one family member put it, *"The third generation received the reins of the business about ten to twelve years ago, though, at that time, they were no longer young. One of their bravest decisions was to remove themselves from operations. Everyone that worked in the business left their executive positions, and they created new regulations among themselves to allow new leadership to emerge."*

Because generative families pay attention to warning signs, they quickly become aware of upcoming difficulties and latent signs of discord. According to one family member, *"It's easy when the company is doing well, but it all changes in a difficult business climate. You need to build shareholder relationships to prepare for tougher business times—for unforeseen economic or global transitions."* Another younger family member noted, *"We looked at our whole organization all the way down and made changes to fit our generation. We realized that our dynamic and needs were completely different from the older generation. The structures we had in place were obsolete. We worked for a year reevaluating our whole structure."*

Generative families are clear that the purpose of family enterprise is for sustaining enduring values as much as profit. Generative families view values and success as connected; articulation of clear values supports long-term business continuity. Poor business results can be a sign that the culture has not been attended to—or sometimes, good business results can divert attention from a company's culture and values. In the excerpt below, a third-generation leader tells of losing his way and the measures taken by the leaders to regain the company's values:

*Another transition led us toward value-based leadership. From the early nineties to the 2000s, the company tripled in sales and increased approximately by a factor of nine. However, we lost our way relative to values, and I lost my way as the leader. I was terribly focused on acquisitions and new products growth, but I lost the* how, *the cultural part. We began focusing on the executive chain, working eight days a year on leadership development and value clarity. When we rolled this out to the company, employees started taking this stuff on and asking for more. We began to embody values-based leadership; in fact, these systems and processes are in place today. That was a single pivot point around culture in the history of the company.*

Family conflicts about business issues can be difficult for a family to resolve, but generative families are characterized by making tough decisions and carrying them out. Here's how one family handled conflict:

*It's hard to work with your family members. Specifically, my father and one of his brothers have had a lot of differences; they hardly ever agree. One is extremely conservative, and the other is more progressive, and this has caused a lot of issues over the years. For example, they argue a lot during the board of directors meeting. When the consultant came in, he said, "My goodness, this needs to be settled. You have to resolve your differences." He had some strong conversations with them and tried to teach them conflict resolution skills. It helped, but they still have their ups and downs.*

Members of the first and second generation of a generative family build a foundation of culture and values that leads them to be adaptive and resilient. We present the common elements of this culture in the next chapter. As families and as businesses, they are open and transparent and able to learn and grow in their interactions. They fight the tendency to avoid or deny the need to change. They listen to the new voices of each generation, seek new ways of doing business, and learn from external resources and teachers. They develop capabilities that are reflected in their family business culture and in their governance mechanisms.

## Taking Action in Your Own Family Enterprise

This chapter presented a view of the family enterprise as an evolving social system that must develop the capability to be open to continual change. As you look at your family across generations, here are some activities that you can do to reflect upon your own resiliency and changeability.

### Facing Transitions

Every multigenerational family enterprise has experienced major transformations like the Big Four (harvesting, pruning, diversifying, and grounding). In addition, each family can look ahead and anticipate the need for any of these transformations in the future. Success in your family journey depends upon how well prepared you are when the event occurs and how well you realign and redefine your family in response to it.

As you think about each of your family's major transformations, reflect on when it took place within your family. For each one, consider how you approached each of the three stages of preparing for change. You can start by answering these questions:

- Has your family gone through any of these major shifts?
- Do you anticipate the need for any of them in the coming years?

You might then conduct an assessment of how you managed the transformations that your family has experienced. This assessment can be done from the perspective of preserving family connection and business adaptability as well as what you might have done to improve your handling of the changes.

|                        | HARVESTING | PRUNING | DIVERSIFYING | GROUNDING |
|------------------------|-----------|---------|--------------|-----------|
| **Prepare Anticipate** |           |         |              |           |
| **Engage Decide**      |           |         |              |           |
| **Define Renew**       |           |         |              |           |

It's never too late to set in motion positive measures to make your family change-ready in the future. Toward that end, you might want to look ahead at possible major changes and consider how your family is anticipating and preparing for them.

### Family Enterprise Timeline

As you learn about and explore the history of your family enterprise, you can see it as a journey that you can record on a timeline. This will be used to develop your family enterprise history. At the bottom of the paper, you should make a dateline showing the years. You can begin on the left with the date of the founding of the legacy enterprise (or another meaningful date, such as the birthdate of the founder). Divide up the length of the paper with the years.

Next, fill in the date of the founding of the legacy business on the left, and about four-fifths of the way to the right side, make a line designated **Now**. Beyond this line, you can speculate and anticipate events that may happen in the future.

Now, begin to fill in the key events for the business and the family. You might divide the paper vertically into a top and bottom half. The top might portray business events and the bottom events related to the family. Some families construct a timeline together by placing a large sheet of butcher paper, several feet long, on the wall. You can then fill in dates and events using marker pens. Other methods include large sticky notes that can be moved around and family pictures related to major events. Whatever method you choose, in the end you will have a timeline of the key positive and negative events in your family and business history.

If you are building this timeline with other family members, start with the memories of the elders and then the recollections of the younger generations. Also, ask different people to recall the same event, because people are likely to remember important events differently.

**Family Enterprise Time Line/Journey**

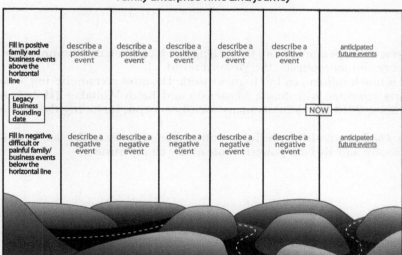

### Resiliency

You, your family, and its various business enterprises have experienced many changes and turning points. Now, with the help of the timeline you constructed, consider how well you anticipated or responded to unexpected events as well as those that were caused by your own actions. You can focus on each important positive and negative event, its consequences, and its impact.

As you reflect on each event, discuss what you did to prepare for or anticipate it. Then consider what was done afterward to build on the new situation and take the family and family enterprise forward. You can talk about each of the three phases of change that were described: Preparing/Anticipating, Engaging/Deciding, and Redefining/Renewing. How did your family experience each stage? After you have looked at what was actually done, you might discuss how you could have approached and recovered from that event more effectively.

*Future Casting*

- Look ahead to the future and the changes you can prepare for and anticipate.
- Select a time in the short or medium future that makes sense to you such as the next five years—or a longer period like ten or twenty years. Alternatively, you might select an important date, such as the time a trust ends or when a family member plans to retire.
- Mark that event and imagine together what it will look like if you prepare for and respond to that change in a resilient, positive, successful manner. Generate a picture of what success will look like.
- Next, consider the most effective things that you as a family can do to prepare for and anticipate that event.
- Finally, consider what specific steps you and your family can take right now to begin to prepare for that event.

## Notes

1. The harvest concept comes from James Hughes, Jr., personal communication.
2. This is more common outside the Western world.
3. My work is much influenced by Hughes's work. His most recent offering, *Complete Family Wealth*, was cowritten with Susan Massenzio and Keith Whitaker (Hoboken, NJ: John Wiley & Sons, 2018). It presents many useful concepts, including that of the family of affinity.
4. The film *The Descendents* wonderfully captures the ferment in the family when a trust is due to dissolve and also the powerful role of the family trustee.

# CHAPTER 6

# The Generative Alliance

## Building and Sustaining a Values-Based Culture

When you enter a family business, you experience a distinctive *culture*, a collective personality that arises from the values and legacy of the founding family. Culture refers to the look and feel of the environment, the rituals, stories, common activities, and traditions of a group. You see pictures, charts of achievements, events, and inspirational quotes. There is also the style of meetings, how the space is arranged and feels, how people are addressed and recognized, and what personal achievements are acknowledged.

Culture shapes the unique identity of a business. It is not what the business does but how it does it, what it values, and how the members of the business relate to each other. A family enterprise is strongly identified with its founding family and traditions; therefore, it tends to have a strong and well-defined culture. At the foundation of the culture, there are values about product quality and reliability, relationships among employees, how people are treated, compensated, and promoted, and what sorts of behavior are allowable. This chapter looks the elements found in the cultures of family enterprises that seem to be linked to their adaptability and long-term success.

The culture of a family enterprise begins with the business style and financial values of the founder that are then sustained and expressed by each successive generation. They achieve this while also remaining a close, connected, and consistent family, sharing and teaching values and skills to each new generation that moves into leadership. Consistencies in the culture around core values and practices are sustained even when there are major upheavals and transformations (as presented in Chapter 5).

Unlike the culture of many public businesses, the culture of a multigenerational family business is enduring and consistent. A strong, well-defined culture defines in a predictable way what the family stands for: its values, practices, and ways of doing things. This creates trust between family and nonfamily stakeholders as well as with customers, suppliers, and the entire community in which it does business. It makes public and explicit how the family owners stand for more than short-term profit. This commitment is usually clearly and publicly stated, so if there is a breach or even a perceived breach, it can be challenged.

Culture reflects the customs, traditions, habits, policies, and unwritten rules, including the core values, that are embodied in the activities of the people involved in the enterprise. It has been observed that people are loyal to the culture, rather than the strategy, of the company. A study of the culture of business using a common culture measurement tool found that on four key cultural traits—adaptability, mission, consistency, and involvement—family businesses scored higher than nonfamily businesses.[1]

A distinctive family culture does not emerge all at once. It begins with the legacy values and actions of the business/family founders, then evolves as the family renews and develops itself in each new generation. While each family's culture is distinctive, with a different personal style and flavor based on its personal origins, there are consistencies across generative cultures. Culture forms the major pathway for the expression of the adaptive capability of the family. Culture has consistencies across generations, but each new generation also renews the family commitment and often adopts or revises elements of the culture.

A generative family builds a resilient business culture able to anticipate and overcome crises as they emerge while becoming stronger in the process. Adaptation is a challenge for any business, but when a family is involved, the task is even more difficult. This is because families have a tendency to be conservative and uphold the status quo; the tradition of parental authority, for example, can limit their ability to change. By contrast, to our surprise, my research team and I found that the wisdom of the generative family enterprise lies in its resiliency in the face of change.

Despite all of the diversity in family enterprises, common cultural themes such as collaboration, inclusiveness, transparency, fairness, and adaptability are associated with their long-term survival. I have coined the term *generative alliance* to refer to the balance of three cultural orientations that unite to enable the resilience of such a family enterprise:

- The legacy values and culture of the family
- Professional business expertise and organization that develop a strong and effective business
- Opportunistic innovation that allows the family to continually seek new avenues for the family enterprise and allows the family to continually reinvent itself across generations

This chapter offers a model for how common cultural practices connect to each orientation.

## Crossroads Commerce: The Development Arc of a Generative Family

This one-hundred-year, six-generation family has been punctuated by periods of fast growth, plateaus, and innovation and change. Each period ushered in major changes in the enterprises or how the family realigned to include a new generation. The story of Crossroads Commerce (a pseudonym) illustrates how aspects of a generative alliance anticipate and initiate change at each transition point that sustains family resiliency.

*(continued)*

Crossroads Commerce was founded in 1880. The founder moved to a newly thriving farming community. Seeing opportunity, he bought a general store and began to buy farmland with federal homestead assistance. His brother and sister moved to the community and joined him, and both the farm and the store prospered. The founding brother had two sons and a daughter, all of whom entered the business.

**G2**: Tragedy struck when the founder died in an accident while still in his prime. His oldest son took over and ably ran the business. His brother helped on the farm and his sister helped out in the store. Ownership passed equally to the three G2 siblings, forming three family ownership branches. They bought more farmland and stores in other communities, and both the stores and the farms benefited from their attentive, patient management. They also clearly defined the values that the family shared and brought to their business.

**G3**: There were early cross-generation transitions. The three G2 siblings passed away when relatively young, pushing young members of the third generation into leadership roles. By the third generation, the now-dozen family owners divided their enterprise into two divisions: farming and commercial. The G2 sister's children moved to another city and sold some of their shares to the remaining branches but remained part of the family as minority owners. The businesses prospered but stayed on a long plateau with little innovation.

After a year of marriage, when his father-in-law died suddenly, a young lawyer who had married a third-generation daughter was asked to join the board of directors. His mother-in-law was overwhelmed by the demands of being on the board of directors and saw him as a promising resource. He eventually became CEO and chair of the board; at that time, the board consisted of two family members from each branch. He was trusted by all and was able to mediate between the interests and personalities of the three branches. He added huge value to the business by developing a strong culture of performance and business results in each business, and he recruited talented, ethical, loyal executives to work in each one.

These young third-generation family leaders also began to innovate and change. After many years, they were seeing diminished returns at a time when they had to meet the needs of more than fifty family members. The family had many loyal employees who respected their stewardship, but family members no longer worked in the business. The board, however, was active and hands-on. Family board members "ran" each division—farms and retail. Their business faced no competition for many years, but now they needed innovation and renewal in both businesses.

**G4**: They entered a new rapid-growth phase, adopting what I will call the Opportunist orientation. The family recruited experienced nonfamily independent directors to the board. These independent directors added further expertise to the nonfamily managers on the farms and in the stores. The members of the family's fourth generation initiated a flurry of innovations in the business. They recruited two more directors with experience in new technology for farming and retailing. The independent directors helped them develop a growth plan, as the fourth generation expressed a desire to take greater risks. Their aim was to expand both businesses, especially the commercial division, which had the capacity to grow rapidly.

The fourth generation's enthusiasm and desire for innovation challenged the complacency of their parents, who nonetheless allowed them the opportunity to put their

*(continued)*

*(Continued)*

ideas to work. However, many members of G4 had grown up detached from the business and did not feel connected or informed. So, with the support of the aging third generation, the family affirmed its core values as it educated and reached out to the children.

As it focused on recruiting outside talent for the board and in management, the family also began an active process of engaging the emerging fourth generation. The family created a family council as the board became more professional and independent, and the focus of learning and innovative energy shifted to this council. The council began holding family summits each year and began an active educational program to teach business and financial literacy skills to young family owners. The family sought new business ideas and opportunities and was able to make quick decisions to support promising ventures. This was exciting and challenging to the well-educated and capable G4s. The result was that the fourth generation became not just interested but also engaged and informed about the business.

The council actively supported the board in investing in new ideas and developing a plan for growth and innovation. The council also perceived that the two businesses were very interdependent and feared that a downturn could hurt both businesses at once. The council initiated a search to acquire a third operating business that would diversify the family. At the same time, the family sold some of its farmland to generate capital for an acquisition. Currently, the fourth generation has taken over the family board positions in addition to leadership on the family council, and the members of the fifth generation are benefiting from the renewed family engagement developed by their parents.

Looking over the development of this family enterprise over four generations, each aspect of the "generative alliance" can be seen. First, there was the focus on the legacy values of the founder and his son. In the second and third generation, the business prospered as the family adopted a business-first, Craftsman focus, which will be described in the next section. Business development was guided by a core of family values that emphasized a long-term business culture of commitment to excellence. To foster innovation and change, the third generation added an Opportunist orientation, which will also be described in the next section. In order to make all of these elements work together, each generation developed a more complex and increasingly professional system of governance that fostered both family connection and business excellence.

## Craftsmen and Opportunists: Two Business Success Strategies

Major transformations in the family enterprise challenge the practices and traditions of long-standing employees and leaders. One of the dynamics my research team and I saw is that these families had to find a balance between disciplined, professional business and the need and desire of family members to innovate. These two tendencies often seem to be opposites, so the resilient family enterprise must find ways to respect each one and develop avenues of expression for each.

### Professionalization

The G4+ families with operating businesses all report a point in time when the family made a choice to professionalize the business, even if it meant challenging the current family leaders. The family had to recruit people with greater professional skills than existing family leaders to advise and work for the family. Families report this as a shift from family first to business first in their focus. Professional management must be empowered to challenge and change traditions that are no longer functional. Sometimes professional managers or frustrated family members remove an ineffective family leader; other times the need for change emerged when a new generation took control. This shift is always stressful for the family.

## Innovation

A well-run business does not run forever. A business or product matures, and the emergence of disruption from new industries and technologies is well known. Generative families are able to add a constituency for innovation and entrepreneurship through the engagement of their next generation of young people, whose education, values, and social environment lead them to get excited by new ideas and, because the family has resources, to push for their consideration. They often cite the example of "great-grandfather" as their model.

Families pursue these two broad strategies of business development across generations. First, they develop the drive to discipline and quality of the "Craftsman," who builds a product or competency better than anyone else, enabling the business to defend itself and thrive within its niche. Second, families draw on the initiative of the "Opportunist," whose curiosity, adaptability, intelligence, and willingness to risk leads to success in many diverse areas.

## Craftsman

The Craftsman develops the special capability of *doing something better than anyone else.* The Craftsman extends and develops within a single S-curve. Many of the families in this study created a product or a technology that served a need, and they competed with larger entities by producing great products and being exceptionally responsive to customers. They created a disciplined, productive, cost-efficient, professional business. And as they kept creating better products, they moved to supply larger and larger markets. Whether these products were industrial supplies, books, shipping, consumer goods, or food products, they often created strong brands that became global or focused on a technology that was hard to duplicate. Companies like these become market leaders in specialized areas that other companies find it hard to enter. They often create the technology early, continually reinvest in new products, and expand into new markets with their core capability. This path is exemplified by the German Mittelstand[2] companies that succeed with patient and focused effort, develop brands known for quality, and build effective and disciplined businesses.

## Opportunist

The Opportunist adapts by *seeking out and seizing upon new opportunities.* Like traders, the Opportunist is always looking for good deals. The Opportunist takes the family onto a new S-curve (presented in the previous chapter), developing diversity by cultivating different strengths in family and nonfamily leaders. For instance, while on their annual drive to market in the cities, one family in the cattle business noticed that certain spots were becoming centers for grazing and commerce. The family bought land and acquired companies in these areas. Families like this one develop a portfolio of assets and are not sentimental about selling those assets that no longer produce. They are entrepreneurial and continually pursue innovation and new ideas.

While either of these strategies is important on its own, many of our generative families are able to adopt both, pursuing them together or at different stages of their evolution. These families develop effective professional businesses that are also opportunistic in seeking and moving in new directions. Sometimes different generations or unusual situations require a particular focus on one style, but the alternative remains important as well. The two styles represent different capabilities exhibited by the family at different times. Generative families are not undermined by conflict between Craftsmen and Opportunists but appreciate that there is a time and a place for each one and that they must coexist. At different times, one or the other may be in ascendance.

## The Generative Alliance of Stakeholder Groups and Interconnected Paths

Creating a single, aligned, disciplined business that is adaptive and vital in a changing global business environment is a wonderful achievement. But it is not enough! A disciplined professional business can easily become stale and lose its vitality to a competitor or new technology or simply lose its drive or focus. To counter this tendency, a family enterprise must also remain entrepreneurial, opportunistic, and open to discovering new paths with new ventures. This requires a different mindset and skills, as the enterprise rediscovers some features of the higher-risk, more improvisational style of the business founder.

*Generative families have the capacity to act as both Craftsmen and Opportunists by drawing on the talent and energy of different stakeholders.* Business leaders recruited from outside the family are joined by entrepreneurial, innovative members of new rising family generations. Generative family enterprises exhibit a unique ability to blend these two kinds of energy—energies that are not usually present together in nonfamily ventures. They are able to do this because they also have consistent values and culture. They develop governance activities that blend the voices of these two groups of stakeholders.

This combination of business discipline, entrepreneurial expansiveness, and legacy values forms the "generative alliance." The emergence of this alliance is a key element in achieving success across multiple generations. It refers to the ways that the different stakeholder groups in the family enterprise combine and balance their special capabilities and concerns to benefit a greater whole. (See Table 6.1.)

The first element of this alliance is *legacy,* the contribution of the founders. As they develop a successful and fast-growing business, the founders articulate and

**Table 6.1   The Generative Alliance.**

|  | Core Value | Definition | Stakeholders |
|---|---|---|---|
| **Legacy**<br>*Foundational<br>Culture* | **Tradition**<br>Trust, Fairness,<br>Respect,<br>Stewardship, Integrity | Enduring business values,<br>policies, and traditions of<br>prior generations | Elders, founding<br>generation |
| **Craftsmen**<br>*Business<br>Discipline* | **Excellence**<br>Quality, Continuous<br>improvement | Creating a great<br>business by doing<br>something better than<br>everybody else | Family business<br>operators, nonfamily<br>executives |
| **Opportunists**<br>*Entrepreneurship* | **Innovation**<br>Creativity, Discovery,<br>Pioneering | Anticipating change and<br>seeking new, innovative<br>opportunities | New-generation family<br>members with education<br>and experience in new<br>areas |

maintain a foundation of legacy values, policies, and practices that they pass on to family members in the next generation. This foundation forms an enduring organizational culture that family and nonfamily members can depend upon. The knowledge that the family is committed to these principles over the long term creates a safe and comfortable environment for collaboration and trust. This commitment creates a culture where family members, employees, and the outside community all know what the business and the family stand for, where everyone is invited to contribute in an appropriate way.

Building upon this foundation of values and culture, the family develops a strong business that continues to do something really well—the *Craftsman* path. After its initial success, the family invests in building a business structure, culture, and discipline that will enable the further development of the enterprise. It continues to create new products and expand into different markets. It moves from an improvisational, founder-oriented style of operation to one where capable and talented people with business skills are in charge. These managers include nonfamily members who support and augment the talents of family leaders.

My research team and I saw a common pattern in the second or third generation, as Craftsmanship leads to a more disciplined, professional business. Many rising-generation family members take on redefined roles as owners who do not directly manage business operations. The family partners with nonfamily leaders who share their values and vision and add new skills the family does not have. There is also a shift from a single legacy business to owning a portfolio of ventures. Family members no longer expect to be business operators; they are now *owners* looking to add to and sustain family wealth.

But a family enterprise cannot succeed long term simply as a good Craftsman with a single business. New challenges emerge, and the family enterprise must develop and transform itself in major ways. The family enterprise has to be open to finding new directions and employing the talents and interests of new family members who are growing to maturity. In addition to being craftsmen, these family enterprises also have to develop, or remain, *Opportunists*. This is the third element in the generative stakeholder alliance. (See Figure 6.1.)

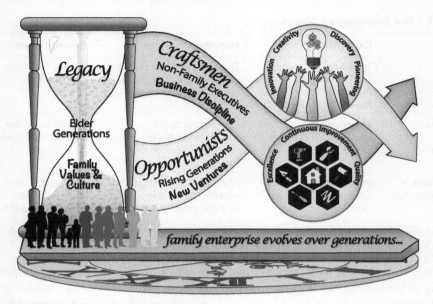

**Figure 6.1   The Generative Alliance.**

Three contributing groups of stakeholders blend their skills and perspectives to create this alliance:

1. **Elders** from the founding generations who pass on their deep lifetime commitment to family values to the business and their family heirs
2. **Professional nonfamily leaders**, **advisors**, **and executives** who share the family values and contribute their business expertise and diverse skills
3. **Rising generation family members** who, through their education and outside experience, value innovation and then challenge the other two groups to take risks and find new opportunities

A generative family continually develops, sustains, extends, and redefines itself as it passes through the major transformations described in Chapter 5. But there is always a consistent and enduring core: the legacy values and ways of doing business that make up its identity as a business family. While each family is unique, several broad but consistent patterns make up the cultural DNA of the generative family. These patterns enable the family to develop disciplined, professional businesses while retaining the ability to adapt and renew. The unique generative family culture this study uncovered combines and blends the developmental paths of both the Craftsman and the Opportunist.

The generative alliance is the product of an open and fluid business and family system, where ideas and pathways flow between the business and the family, even when there are clear policies and practices that define decision-making and roles in each area. The family's adaptiveness rests in its ability to listen and develop new paths based on responsible and thoughtful input from different areas—such as the new energy and ideas of the rising generation or the wise counsel of business advisors or nonfamily leaders.

Family enterprises run into trouble when one part of the alliance takes precedence over the others. If the legacy values predominate, the business cannot grow or innovate. If the Craftsmen are preeminent, the business runs well, but may forget its founding values or neglect to adapt and innovate. If the Opportunists reign, impulse can overcome good judgment and sound business practices. The successful family is able to respect each orientation and balance them in practice.

## How the Generative Alliance Creates a Distinctive Family Enterprise Culture

Six cultural themes are common to almost all the families in this study. Taken together, their presence differentiates generative families from enduring but less successful family enterprises. Because family owners also have a history, legacy, and personal relationship to one another and their business, it follows that their values, goals, and operating principles are more extensive than those of owners who simply desire a good financial return.

Researchers view this family-based culture as a competitive advantage held by family enterprises over public companies that do not have family oversight.[3] It has been defined as "familiness," referring to the family-based resources and qualities arising from family control and ownership. These six themes are clearly linked to aspects of the generative alliance.

The older the family enterprise, the more pronounced are each of these qualities. These six cultural qualities, common across different countries, appear to differentiate generative families from less successful business families, are represented in Figure 6.2:

- Long-term commitment and patience to achieve goals
- Extension of family values to business
- Disciplined, focused, professional business
- Deepening the talent pool through collaboration with nonfamily leaders to recruit the best
- Professionalization of family leaders to be responsible stewards
- Entrepreneurial attitude and new ideas encouraged in each new generation

## Legacy Elements: Long-Term Commitment and Extension of Family Values into the Business

Two practices allow the family enterprise to respect and preserve its legacy: (1) a long-term perspective about results and (2) active sharing and affirming of family values for the business.

### Long-Term Commitment

Generative family enterprises are not looking primarily for immediate profit or short-term gains; they are there for the long term. As stewards, they look more than

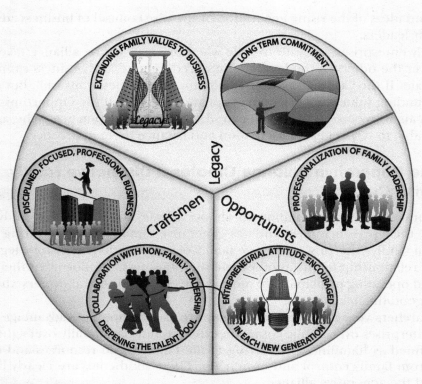

**Figure 6.2    Elements of family culture supporting family enterprise.**

a generation ahead for the benefit of their children. They caution current family owners not to come to depend on an annual income from the enterprise (though in every family some family members ignore this, sometimes to their detriment). This perspective engenders patience as they develop the values, skills, and resources of each new generation to contribute to the growth and development of the enterprises. Without such patience and thoughtful preparation, success would be hard to sustain.

Time fuels the drive of generative families across generations. Their attention is always focused ahead—on future generations and the future of their business. They make significant investments in the business and look ahead for opportunities. They exercise what has been termed "patient capital" for return on their investments. As a European family elder observes:

> By definition, if you are thinking about the next generation, not just the next quarter, that's another twenty-five years. You want the story to continue; that's deeply rooted in all family businesses. That long-term perspective is very, very important. This is reflected in the HR policies of the company; the employees know that you are in for a lot more than just making money.

Long-term commitment has many advantages, the most common being freedom to take on major, often risky, projects, without worrying about short-term costs or disaffected shareholders. These families are able to exercise patience to see results. This attitude extends from the family into the values of the business culture, as these three families observe:

1.  *Our single biggest advantage is the long-term horizon. I don't worry about the month or the quarter or the year; I worry about whether everything we do is going to help us to be in business for another hundred years. That's what I like about being here.*

2.  *It's an advantage being private because you can make long-term decisions and be very diverse. For example, we have recently gone into two of the huge mines—a high-risk investment. If we were a listed company, the shareholders would say, "What the hell are you doing?" But we can diversify into industries we like. We're also quite counter-cyclical. If the property market's completely dead, we'll double down. If the property market's heated, we'll start selling.*

3.  *Some companies that aren't family businesses are too focused on financial quarterly decisions. We believe a long-term view or lifetime decisions are made even though the short-term outcome of some of these decisions may be more painful. We've tried to define guiding principles relative to the business; we've tried to anticipate by looking at other family businesses that have hit obstacles and then developed written policies to guide them as opposed to just following past precedents.*

Commitment comes from the entire family, as a member of one such family expresses: "*The family has a very strong sense of pride and ownership of the company, so there is a reluctance to sell any shares or liquidate their interests. Their sense is, 'I want to pass this down to my children and grandchildren and let them be part of what our grandfathers created.'*"

A long-term vision allows the family to be patient and not act impulsively if there is a setback. The family is willing to reinvest its profits and forgo immediate distribution to fund and support initiatives that take a while to implement. This commitment is not to a single business but to a shared cross-generational partnership and values reflected in everything the family does.

This is not a one-time choice but must be affirmed regularly by the family members because it demands so much of them. With every generation, each family must answer the question: *Do we want to stay together?* Sometimes the family decides that "the business would have a better future without the family, and we would have a better future without the business." Unless the family is willing to make a substantial commitment to overseeing the enterprise, it is not to their advantage to remain owners.

Going into its seventh generation, a natural resources business evolved into a family conglomerate with dozens of operating businesses. These had been acquired with the engagement, encouragement, and oversight of an entire family assembly as an advisory voice. The family CEO of this group observes:

> *The challenge is making sure that we're renewing our wealth, so we can continue to support a growing family. Some of our recent business decisions focused on how we are going to get to 2030. How can we build a business that can provide us with the income we need to fund family programs and annual meetings? That's very different from the way most businesses would look at such things; it's really looking long term versus short term. At the same time, you have to put money into the shareholders' pockets, so you're obligated to provide liquidity on an annual basis. It's a huge challenge to create liquidity in a private company.*

Long-term commitment also represents a dependable personal commitment to respect loyal service to the family. One European conglomerate has several family managing directors who oversee the various enterprises. They say that family members who work in the business "*die with their boots on.*" No one has ever left. When the current family CEO took the job, he did so understanding that it would be his last job. He's most proud of the fact that the family members in the business live no differently than their one thousand employees. He's proud of the loyalty and mutual respect that they've cultivated both with employees and with hundreds of family owners.

### Extension of Family Values into the Business

The business founder has learned some things through the initial success of the business, and he wants to share these with his successors. These often take the form of values and practices that serve not only good business but also ethical personal behavior. These expected behaviors also form the heritage that inspires not just the family but employees and the public as well to respect the family's work.

Nepotism is an expression of this value, offering preference to family members and loyal employees, as this family leader observes:

> *Nepotism has an extremely bad name; it has a negative connotation. But we've found it to be extremely positive because of all the brothers, sisters, uncles, and cousins of our nonfamily employees that bring their families into the business. We have families that have more than two hundred years of service over four generations of uncles, sisters, and brothers. The family culture has expanded to all employees, and we have just about zero turnover. We have a guy in our electronic department that has sixty-eight years of service. In the twenty-five years I've been here, we've had eight people retire with fifty years of service or more.*

The sense of "family" in a family enterprise extends beyond blood family to include employees, suppliers, customers, and the community. The extended family consists of more than just blood family members. This explains their ability to engender commitment and inspire performance and shared purpose. Facilitative values about how family owners do business have been instilled in the culture from day one. They continue because, even as business leadership passes outside the family, the culture reflects, reinforces, and stands for these values. As the family becomes a *family of affinity,* long-time employees and advisors take on quasi-family roles and status. This fifth-generation leader recalls how his father viewed the family's legacy values:

> *You don't need to focus on furniture, table, office, or a fancy-schmancy thing. It's about what you bring to the table, how you engage with people, how you communicate with your family, your values, with your organization, with the community that you're in.*

Employees are important, respected, and have equal standing to family employees and the owners. When a family clearly states its values, it creates trust that people outside the family depend on. Of course, these expressed values must be backed by policies and action that are congruent with them. In generative family cultures, talk and action are clearly connected, as this third-generation family member with a profitable business notes:

> *Our culture is that employees are treated like family. We created an ESOP [Employee Stock Ownership Plan] so employees could share in the profits. Family owners receive very small dividends. The message is that key employees who actively produce value for the business take precedence over family financial rewards. If family members want to convert their ownership to cash, they can redeem stock every year. But selling stock is a costly and consequential decision that family members do not take lightly.*

The family extends its personal stamp upon the business because, as owners, the family stands for more than just business. One family member describes this:

> *We keep our focus on the question: Why we have done this? You have your four goals of growth, risk, liquidity, and profitability, but as a family shareholder, what is the nonfinancial reason that you care about this company, that you care about being an owner of this company, because if it is just owning a bank, there are a lot of banks out there that you can buy stock in. What makes the difference in owning our bank? Part of it is the family's values and cultures are instilled into the company. A nice thing about being the majority shareholder and the only shareholder for a long time is that we developed the values and culture to represent the family's values and culture. But the answer that the family members give to us is what it does for our communities. We are a community bank in fifty locations. We give a lot of money back and a lot of time and effort and encourage our employees to give back to their communities. So as the family members look around, they see what our bank means and giving money in some cases but also what our employees and its officers are doing in those communities to make those better places.*
>
> *The family needs to understand the culture and values of the company. I have a meeting with a family coming up in two weeks, and I don't think the family clearly sees the corporate values and corporate culture. They see one part of it, and that is the giving back to the communities, but they don't see the part about the being the best bank that we can be out there and being where we are in the top banks in the country and recognized for this and all those other things that we do to make sure that our employees feel great, comfortable about who they are working for, and our communities feel very comfortable about us being in their communities. We have the products and services that they need, and they want to be with these customers.*

This family created a family protocol that clearly defines its values, how those values apply to the operating business, and how the values can be applied in practice. As happened in the following family, the protocol often emerges after a family conflict. In the best cases, such a conflict is resolved in a positive way. The family member says:

*The most important part of our family enterprise is shared values. Family values form your business values. For future generations, the person that comes in to the business first must work a few years outside the family. Everybody must have a bachelor's and a master's degree in some relevant topic before going to work in the family business. We agree that family comes before business. That's another protocol. We have a list that's about fifteen items. We started with a family protocol, and then it shifted more to business. Then it shifted with a painful lawsuit. Now that we have this holding company, it's shifted again to the business and it's more professional. But it always comes back to family. The family topic is always in the agenda. The other process is a career path. My dad was very clear about a career path.*

The following statement by a nonfamily CEO defines the necessary qualities for a professionally run, values-based family enterprise, qualities that give the family enterprise a competitive advantage over a public company:

*As managers, executives, employees, and staff, the number one focus is always on family, whether it's the client's family or the employees' families. We make sure that employees are able to care for their own families. If you've got things happening at your kid's school in the middle of the day, whether you are a file clerk or an accountant, you should be able to be there without having to take time off. Allowing people to be at their family events conveys the importance of family. Because they're aware of the attention given to their families, everyone here wants to work hard. People are generally here for a very long time. Most of our employees give over twenty years of service.*

*I can't say enough positive things about the family I work with. In 2008, when the world was falling apart financially, many family offices were deciding, "No raises or bonuses this year. It's a bad year, so we can't really do this." For us, the discussion that took place with employees was: Are you telling me that even though this has happened, the family that we represent is not going to feel the impact of this? It's not going to change their life in any way. So what about all the families that work for you? They're absolutely affected by this. If you're only being great leaders at times when things are solid and strong, what does this say? The reality is we should look at our employees and say, "You need a bigger increase than normal to help you get through this downturn." We made sure everybody received the equivalent to help them through the financial strife. That showed true strength in their leadership and why the idea of family is at the core of everything.*

One family has a strong values statement passed down by the founder that is taught to each employee. The values are emphasized in hiring, and each employee is expected to adhere to them. When this family acquired a much larger division of a public company with a very different culture and values, the family made a clear offer to employees of that division: "*You are welcome to join us, but we expect that you will adhere to our values.*" To the family's surprise, most employees of the acquired company chose to stay.

Family values about employees are particularly important when the company is challenged by a crisis. When the pressure is on, employees want to know where they stand and whether the family will continue to honor its values. One family was on the verge of selling its three-generation family manufacturing business. It was deeply rooted in its community but was facing cost pressures to move manufacturing overseas. A private capital firm approached to buy the company. They were close to the sale when the family realized that there was deep resistance on the part of its employees and customers. Ultimately, the family decided to not sell and instead hired a nonfamily CEO. A family spokesperson stated:

> The customers were not happy that we were selling the business, nor were our employees. They saw the value of the family's policies in pricing, product quality, and timeliness of delivery. Although it's never been explicitly stated, this is why all of these things work so well and pricing is competitive. They could pick up the phone and call my dad if something went wrong.
>
> There's the high touch factor in a family business that is important to customers. We're exploring this with our new CEO. How do we use that factor to our advantage, now that we've decided to remain family-owned for the next generation? How do we use that and create a story around it? The story is that we're a professionally run family business, but we have strong family values and want to hold onto our very special culture.

Another view of the extent of this commitment to employees and community is expressed by a fifth-generation family leader. This view—known as the "stakeholder" view—holds that the family has a moral obligation to serve different communities. This stakeholder philosophy stands in marked contrast to the view that the only responsibility of a business is to generate profit for shareholders (the next chapter adds to this discussion). In recent years, many public companies have learned from the example of family enterprise by adopting this view of their corporate responsibility. As this quote illustrates, in this view families see their obligations as owners much more broadly:

> Responsibility to the company sometimes lies above the shareholders. Especially in this small town, where we are one of the major employers, the success of this company is all-important. Our commitment to our employees makes for a kind of shared value and a dedication to make the company a success. If we focused only on our shareholders, that would be the death of the business.

## Craftsman Elements: A Disciplined, Professional Business and a Deepening of the Talent Pool

To succeed, a family must establish a business culture that selects, aims for, and emphasizes good business practices. Because the business has grown so quickly and so huge, the family must support a culture where the business does what is best as a business. It has to look beyond its own members to recruit, promote, and reward experienced businesspeople and allow them to use what they know. This means that family members, who are the owners, have to step back sometimes out of respect for the skills and knowledge of others. The business culture respects good business practices, and it selects and values nonfamily talent to do what the family desires but cannot do on its own. The business culture in some ways moves beyond the family, leading family members to learn new roles as stewards rather than as operators.

### A Disciplined, Professional Business

Whatever values are held by a family, each family business is intended to be profitable. The family's values and entrepreneurial attitudes have to be housed within a sustainable, professional, disciplined, focused, and competent business. The first-generation business founder may have been an improvisational leader, often operating without a design or plan, moving forward on opportunities, taking risks, and making gut decisions. As successive generations enter leadership, however, they face the challenge of adding efficient business practices and discipline. They cannot continue to run on improvisational family leadership; they have to recruit and develop skilled nonfamily leaders who share the family's values and long-term commitment. This in itself can bring about a profound transformation of the business, but each of our generative families was able to accomplish this while sustaining the family's personal identity and values. This was a major developmental hurdle for them.

Somewhere between the second and fourth generations, family leadership transitions to a professional, business-first orientation. The leaders must exercise the skills of the **Craftsman** to develop business discipline, professional operations, and accountability. This is a critical transition for a generative family as it attempts to deal with the following questions:

- Can our vision and culture be extended beyond the family?
- What must change about our company and the way we do business?
- How do we attract managers and leaders whose competence extends beyond that of the family?
- Will our oversight as owners embody and demand professional standards and practices?

For the family, this transition involves coming to terms with the reality that the business needs come before family perks and preferences. The family must look outside itself, to the strength and viability of the business, before it attends to its own needs. Rather than see business as an arena for meeting family needs, the family now views the business as a delicate resource that needs professional care to be sustained. This means moving from improvisational, informal practices toward creating a business culture that focuses on recruiting talent and organizing an excellent business. The care and perfectionism of the Craftsman replaces the family's natural tendency to see the business as its playground.

Since this shift involves less skilled and less professional family members giving up jobs, perks, and influence, it almost never takes place without stress, conflict, and drama. There can be a painful family rift as a dedicated but less professional family leader is asked to leave and as the family learns to respect and defer to nonfamily leaders on operational issues.

While this transition is necessary, it also causes significant stress and conflict for the family, as this European family enterprise remembers:

*For the first few generations, power was handed over from father to son, from strong character to the next strong character. It was the responsibility of the people in place to nurture and select the next leaders. In my father's generation, several family members were involved in executive management positions.*

*There was friction when appointed family leaders had to be removed; this was a painful exercise. This is one of the reasons why we said that in the next generation, we would no longer allow family involvement in management. We wanted to give our professional managers the opportunity to rise to the highest executive levels. This meant that family members would no longer be first in line for leadership positions.*

Professionalizing the business is often accompanied by diversification. This can provide the opportunity for family members to redefine their individual ventures. Some households or branches may decide they want to go off in their own directions, as in this Asian family:

*My family has one third-generation family business and my own first-generation company. I started thinking that I should play my part in moving the family business toward professional management. We needed to transform from a business family to an investment family. I decided to build an investment portfolio, so my children could leverage on my own family business. I believe that each generation should create their own wealth instead of depending on the ancestors' business. I expect my children to have different interests; I don't believe in forcing them to pick up my grandfather's business or even my business. I would like my children to be good shareholders in my grandfather's business and in my own business, but I would also like them to create their own sole ventures. I envision each child having his own enterprise that emerges from his own vision.*

Sometimes the impetus to change comes from the marketplace. When it moved to Europe, this Middle Eastern business family had to adapt to external change and redefine its very personal, hands-on business, as described in the next three paragraphs:

*The 1970s to early 1990s in Europe were the heydays of the luxury business; there were lots of Middle Eastern families coming to Europe. The family was good at negotiating with them because we ourselves were from the Middle East. We knew their mindset and cultural mores and adapted very well to their needs and attitudes. But the growth was chaotic. The family never bothered to clarify how they would organize the business.*

*The business model was essentially a trading model: buy cheap, sell expensive. This was successful until the early nineties, but at that time two things happened. One was the first Gulf War when the key customer base stopped buying. The second was competition; the luxury business started attracting a lot of competition because margins were high. Large luxury groups entered our sector. At this point, we had to become more professional and competent in management, but we didn't know how to do that. The family couldn't imagine getting competent outsiders to help us out. They couldn't even imagine how to clarify their own functioning or make compromises about their prerogatives and powers.*

> *When I joined the management team eight years ago, my very first job was to write contracts and job descriptions for everybody. It was tough for the family to accept these contracts. Even the employees resisted—they were used to oral commands. Nobody wanted things formalized; they didn't want to take the time to write things out.*

When a business transitions to nonfamily leadership, the family is often unsure about its role. When this European family conglomerate shifted to professional management, it had to learn a new role for family leadership:

> *When we adopted professional management, the biggest challenge facing the fourth generation was discovering new ways for the family to lead. They were being overshadowed by the experienced professionals on the executive team, but after three years they are finally on the case and contributing. One thing G4 accomplished was to begin to formulate strategic superordinate goals to present to the group board for discussion. For example, one goal is to see 25 percent of income come from the housing market. We wanted a balanced business with strong values, but we had to learn to spell out these values definitively—to move the input from the family into the business strategy.*

Business discipline can entail challenging nonperforming family leaders. Easing out nonperforming leaders is a challenge for any business but more so for a business family, as this account illustrates:

> *My uncle and my dad will always remember when they opened a new department led by an older uncle. There was a big emotional aspect there. This business had losses for many, many years; it finally got so bad that we had to close it. But the decision created a lot of conflict because my uncle's identity was so wrapped up in it. It was hard to tell him that he had to leave.*
>
> *This situation led the family to decide to professionalize management. Everybody agreed to shift to a formal, objective selection process for anyone in the family who wanted to work in the family business. This led us in turn to move toward governance structures that diversified the risk and to create a holding system that managed family cash flow. In addition, we had to establish shareholder agreements. We had a large minority group that wanted more transparency, feasibility, and objectivity with professional management and independent directors on the board. All this led us to our current structure.*

Another European beverage business, many generations old, made a similar shift in its sixth generation:

> *When I was on the board, we made a big change eight years ago. The company needed to be professionalized and shift to a more global outlook. This process was not easy, but we are proud that we did it in a safe, gentle way. How do things get handled when jealousy emerges because some family members get certain privileges that others don't have? Even though these may not be huge privileges, they still upset other members of the family. To avoid these conflicts, we decided that only four family members will work in the company.*

Sometimes the transition to nonfamily leadership arises when the family doesn't have a candidate for leadership:

> *The shift away from operating ownership wasn't a conscious decision. Nobody in the family wanted to do it. My son was in there for a while, and he got out. My nephew was in there, and he got out, but there wasn't another family member to take the spot. So that's when the shift to leaders outside the family happened. Some very able people came along in the next generation, however, and I'm having regrets that no family member is in the operations now.*

Having a culture of business accountability reassures employees that family needs and practices will not push aside performance, respect for employee professionalism, and appropriate rewards. Long-term business success overrides immediate family needs. Generative families usually experience a transition where the long-term orientation of the family is applied to reviewing business policies and raising expectations for the business not just to do what the family wants but also to conduct itself in accordance with principles of quality, accountability, and fair policies that are characteristic of "excellent" companies.

When a next-generation leader transforms the business into a disciplined, professional entity, the rest of the family may feel sidelined, even though they enjoy the financial benefits. A challenge arises when there isn't a clear successor and the family faces a major transition:

> *In the years my [third-generation] father was CEO, a lot of wonderful things were accomplished. Before this, our ad hoc governance process had some holes, limits, and tensions arising as changes took place, so in the late nineties, we decided to reorganize governance. When my father took over the company, he needed to get the business in shape, so he focused on strengthening the company and making it more productive. By the end of the nineties, he had strengthened the company and made some pretty major changes. We went from a corporation to a limited partnership, but these changes made some members feel alienated. He realized he needed to strengthen the family ties to the business. That's when he helped start our family council.*

Conflict can erupt when transforming a culture as family members lose status and roles. One member was given the role of shareholder relations manager; her task was to oversee the involvement of family members in the business. She reports:

> *My position was created to work with the family. Some family members were asked to leave the business with the expectation that they would go outside, gain experience, and then return. Some did, but some did not. A few older-generation senior leaders were asked to leave or placed in different positions. Several family members were taken off the board and offered a slot on the owners' advisory council. That softened the blow, but at the end of the day, it was still really hard. But because profits rose to new highs, the increased stock dividends made those wounds heal quicker.*

*The owners' advisory council represents all the family owners. Their vision is to promote harmony among the shareholder families and to enable them to speak with one voice. They set business goals, financial metrics, and risk management stewardship projects; then they work with the board to come to agreements on them. We don't want the owners' group to set hopes and expectations by talking to management—that's not their role. It's the board's job to hold management accountable, not the family. The other mission of the owner's advisory council is to help select and vote for board members.*

When a family enterprise "professionalizes," it recruits experienced outside advisors, independent directors, trustees, and nonfamily executives. The family respects them and their expertise and draws upon it to the family's benefit. However, because of the competence and firepower of these advisors, the family might step back and lose involvement with the business. This can set up a cycle of family passivity and lack of development:

*We have an outside advisor who is very, very—I'd say overly—involved. This is a real challenge for us. What should we do as a family, and what should we look for from outside people? The more somebody from the outside does it, the less the family has to do, and this sets up a negative cycle. I'd really like to see our family take more initiative to do the things that we're paying someone else to do. It makes me very uncomfortable.*

Deepening the skills of Craftsmanship with disciplined, professional business practices entails a corresponding shift of roles and awareness by family members. This process requires high involvement from both the family and the business board as each learns new roles and interactions. In the next two paragraphs, a member of a South American fourth-generation family describes it this way:

*We're a very hands-on family, and we've transitioned into being a professional family business. But how do we engage with professionals? How do we let the CEO do his job while letting the board do their job? Since we separated our board from the family council, we sometimes step on each other's toes because the family council is used to acting as the board and being involved in everything. We've had to retrain ourselves to step back and be engaged but not interfere with the boards and our new CEO.*

*We now face the challenge of buying a new core business and how we can, as cousins, work on that project together. The other challenge is that we have cousins who expect higher remuneration from their work in the business. How are we going to handle that, because we definitely want family members engaged? We want to be responsible shareholders and to be engaged in the business. But to be engaged, you have to know the business, and to know the business, you have to participate somehow. The younger members especially need the hands-on experience. But if there is a position, how do we match the job with their skill set? And how much are we going to pay them? This shift to a more professional business has become a huge challenge.*

As stewards, active owners shift their mindset from protecting their own interests to looking ahead to everyone's best interest. This can be a challenge, as this account illustrates:

*We needed to start thinking as one family instead of five branches. When you have several enterprises and a few foundations, you think, "I worry about my branch, I worry about my family, and I want what is best for them." Every family does that. But to throw that out the window and say that we believe that a one-family approach is the right thing to do is a major challenge. Yes, we understand that this is going to happen at the fourth generation anyway, but we're doing it at the second-generation level. It's hard to develop that kind of trust with my brother and sister and say, "I may not have the ability to put my kids in a position of authority, but I can trust that you are going to have your kids in a position of authority to speak for all of us—to speak on behalf of the family." I think that was probably the biggest leap of trust. But in the end, we understood that we had to go through this and that it was a very difficult process. We struggled with it.*

A trust structure with a trustee in charge can also cause family beneficiaries to feel disconnected and disenfranchised from the business. As a consequence, they may disengage and become passive spectators rather than active stewards. If this disengagement begins to take root, it must be reversed. Here is a family that took steps to engage family members within such a structure and had positive results:

*I joined the Young Presidents Organization. In my first meeting, I described how we held stock in trust and that I'm the managing trustee. So I control the company. But one of my friends said, "You're in big trouble. You don't have shareholders. You have coupon clippers, and they're not paying any attention to what you're doing." That woke me up. We decided that the best shareholders are educated shareholders, so we launched a yearly family reunion and whole-day business meeting to engage everybody, rekindle enthusiasm, and generate a sense of ownership. It's been extremely positive for the entire family to have this glue. We get great questions and reengagement and we return the next year and start all over. As a result, we're starting to get more continuity.*

Giving beneficiaries a voice by treating them as owners despite the existence of trustees who are the legal owners is a way to retain their active involvement.

### Deepening the Talent Pool by Collaborating with Nonfamily Leaders

After one or two generations in which family owners are also hands-on business operators, the family reaches a point where its talent pool cannot encompass all the needs of the family's various operations. At this point, the family must consider where it will find next-generation business leaders. Family members might continue to work in the business, but employment is no longer linked to eventual business leadership. Family oversight moves to the board and governance entities that oversee the businesses.

At this point, family members can no longer assume that their businesses are potential places of employment where they can come and go as they please. Individual family members, or a whole branch, may then choose to give up their ownership and are bought out. The new professional enterprise now has a different relationship with the family. At this time, family members may set up other business, financial, and philanthropic ventures and begin to exercise family governance. Some family members take on the opportunistic path while others support the Craftsmanship orientation.

The family increasingly looks to recruit and collaborate with nonfamily leaders who share the family's values and support its unique culture but add further skills and capability. As nonfamily leaders enter the family's businesses, family office, investments, and foundations, they work closely with emerging family leaders not in operations, especially the rising generation. The shift away from being family owner/operators while still sustaining the family culture and values is a critical transition for the generative family.

Business founders are notoriously secretive. They often don't trust their employees and are reluctant to share financial data even with family members. However, to build a culture of accountability and professional practice, the family must overcome its habit of not sharing information. As new generations emerge in generative families, the cultural value of openness and transparency overcomes the founder's tendency to restrict information and distrust of others. As this account illustrates, transparency can evolve in the culture of the business:

> *Up to the early seventies, accounting was done in a dark room where the numbers were kept away from everyone. But starting with my father's generation, we began to rely on computers, data, and formal statements and began the process of professionalizing the ERP. Now that factual data is shared with managers, we all know how we're doing. At board meetings, we go through everything in great detail. When we went public, it was easy for us to make a transition because we were already there.*

When the business faces pressures, the family feels an obligation to explain impending changes. This is part of its commitment to transparency. The family explains what it is doing and why with the employees, and this creates an alignment and a shared purpose. Here's how one business accomplishes this:

> *We also are doing a roadshow this year. The CEO and I [the chairman] are going to all the sites around the world to talk about what the family is doing in terms of the transition. Everyone knows that the CEO is reaching retirement, and we want to make sure that we're closing the circle in terms of communication.*

As they age, members of the older generation experience a diminished ability to lead the business. They lose energy and access to new ideas and opportunities. They get stale, but they are often the last to see this. Sometimes that task is taken up by members of the new generation; they may need to confront the existing powers in order to sustain the business. A fourth-generation daughter observes:

> *I feel a very strong divide between the third and the fourth generations. The third generation is much less open to change. The only way change can happen is by a buyout of the third generation's moral symbolic stake in the business. This can happen by their leaving the business either by dying, retiring, or going to Norway to fish salmon. There has to be agreement among successors and the incumbent generation about what is being done, where the business is going, and what kind of changes the previous generation might be open to.*

How does agreement that change is needed evolve? In this family, the daughter's father was pressed into service when his father died suddenly at an early age. He was unprepared and wanted to ensure that this never happened to his children. Early on, his daughter demonstrated skills that complemented those of the next generation's successor from the other side of the family. After consultation with her father and siblings, she asked for a leadership position alongside her cousin. They created a timeline and a training process that involved graduate school, work in other businesses, and finally entry into the business with increasingly demanding tasks. Her father looks forward to his retirement and her succession.

A gap between intention and reality may have to be worked out, as happened in this fourth-generation family conglomerate:

> *The third generation learned from past history. Even though members of the third generation were sitting on the boards and ready to start making decisions, the second generation remained very much involved behind the scenes, second-guessing decisions officially made by the board. But now that the fourth generation is coming to power, the third-generation board members are stepping away from leadership—and not interfering with decision-making.*

### Diverse Pathways to Professional Management

The transition to professional management takes different forms in different cultures around the world.[4] Sometimes becoming a disciplined business means confronting traditional cultural values about business, family, and leadership. Following are four family examples.

A third-generation family member from an Asian conglomerate observed how the influence of Confucian values adds additional complexity to the professionalization process. The strict confidentiality of the elder leaders coupled with the need to respect their rule kept the younger generation from making needed input. In this case, the patriarch is ninety while two highly educated and competent generations wait for their turns. In the meantime, necessary changes are delayed.

In another Asian family, all three brothers worked in the business that was their father's dream. They worked collaboratively, but as the next generation grew up, the family members decided that to remain connected, they wanted to have more fun together and engage in more nonbusiness activities. To do so, they had to modify their traditional work ethic to be less restrictive and demanding.

When members of the third generation came into power in another diversified business, they inherited assets that were conservatively managed by trustees. But they were more entrepreneurial and initiated a process of revision that took over fifteen years. They added a holding company and board, with branch membership and active family governance by good professional managers.

In a final example, a nineteenth-century patriarch passed ownership to his daughter. She immediately fired him and began to develop professional management. He was surprised and a little hurt but accepted her decision. As members of the third generation came to power, they wanted to remain unified and avoid conflict, so they created a ten-year voting trust. After a generation of professional management, a family CEO was selected from the next generation.

When the family was engaged early, several families reported that the next-generation leadership team was prepared and ready to take over leadership when its time arrived. There was a clear timetable for the retirement of the older generation. Such anticipation and preparation is certainly not the norm in family enterprises, but in our generative family group, it happened more often than not in an orderly, predetermined path.

One family had a clear business challenge on its horizon. It saw the digital age coming and needed a visionary leader to help navigate it. But at the same time, the family was satisfied with its distribution and was not willing to look for such a leader. The business didn't evolve, and the family finally had to sell it. In another family, the fourth generation wanted to appoint a nephew as chair while others felt he wasn't quite up to the job. The fourth generation appointed him, changed its mind, then selected another family member who is now chair. If the family members hadn't been deeply engaged with one another, this process would have dissolved in conflict.

Another family appointed an interim nonfamily CEO to mentor the G5s. As described below, these family members then recruited a permanent, nonfamily CEO:

> *We want to maintain our values in how we approach people. I am confident now that this will happen with our new CEO. When he first came on three years ago, he didn't understand how important our values were. Now he sees that they are part of our DNA, and they have become part of his language and awareness.*

Unexpected tragedy can strike at any time. In one business, a designated successor died in war. His younger brother reluctantly took over out of a sense of duty to the family. He was confident but unhappy. Nevertheless, he made things ready for the next generation and prepared for a transition to professional management. His successor was from outside the family.

Such crisis can lead to the shift to nonfamily leadership. Another family had a tradition of keeping a majority of independent directors on its board. After the unexpected death of the heir apparent, the family looked for a new family leader. The best candidate was from a minority-owning family branch. Another family with a majority of independent directors on its board was negotiating a sale. When the sale fell through, the family appointed a nonfamily CEO and asked him to professionalize the business. He had a private equity background and was expected to look for acquisitions and bring them to the family.

Several families in this study initially handled succession by seniority. In one business, a brother ran things for a while, then his brother took over for the next ten years. Models like this often break down due to unexpected events or difficulties with the next candidate in line. Other families sustain a long-term, two-generation partnership; this allows the new leader to develop over time.

Family members can face conflicts of interest between their branch of the family and the whole business. Ownership is often apportioned by branches; one branch may have more ownership or even a majority. In this situation, family members need to ask: "*Am I acting in the best interests of my branch or the whole business?*" As an example, members of one third-generation group observed a jockeying for succession in their parents' generation. They confronted their parents directly and said,

*"We know you are not comfortable, but you need to trust us to be fair and not interfere."* The third generation then recruited a nonfamily leader. Yet another path is to have each sibling lead his or her own business while a holding company oversees their results and keeps them accountable.

## Troubled Transitions

The examples discussed above were successful transitions. Other families were not so lucky. Several families appointed seemingly competent and experienced nonfamily CEOs who ultimately did not fit the family culture. One CEO who was used to having his own power and authority could not work with the family owners or the key executives. He was eventually forced out. Different variations of this scenario have taken place in other families in transition. One family proudly proclaimed that the third candidate that held the job was finally a fit.

Another family appointed a nonfamily CEO to turn around its deteriorating business. He was successful in rescuing the business, but the family had not installed family governance and oversight. This led to what family members called a "power vacuum" in which the family was unable to make key ownership decisions. Because of this, the business was not able to innovate or move in new directions even though it was operationally successful.

In another family, a brother was asked to take the role of CEO. He was confident but ineffective, so the family asked him to step down. He was very upset at this and began to tell his son bad things about the family. Since then, there has been continual tension that the fourth-generation leaders have had to struggle to overcome.

Sometimes, the business outgrows family capability. Several families have a family and nonfamily CEO team working together; sometimes the roles are differentiated as family chairman and nonfamily CEO. This can be a challenging but rewarding partnership if both individuals are able to be open and candid while respecting each other's authority. Facing a large number of cousins in the next generation causes some families to decide to sell the company and cash out. Other families create financial partnerships allowing individuals more flexibility about their level of participation.

## Opportunistic Elements: Professional Family Leaders and Entrepreneurial Focus for Each Generation

As the business culture develops and sometimes outgrows the family, what is the family's role in the generative culture? It oversees each business and financial entity, making sure the cultural values are maintained and the business thrives, but it also has to keep watch over change, adaptability, and new directions. Family members who take this view are Opportunists, encouraging new generations to take the family enterprise into new paths. That has a cultural consequence; the family has to embrace a different type of professional—a professional steward, who is both keeper of the flame and also a pioneer—and then allow the stewards in the family to scout for new possibilities.

## *Professionalization of New Family Leaders*

Parallel to the support of nonfamily leadership, family members also need to upgrade their own business knowledge and skills. As they grow up, members of each new generation have the option of working in one of the family's ventures and perhaps advancing to a leadership position. But as the business grows and the family's ventures become more complex, opportunity comes with conditions. The family now clearly defines the responsibilities of working in the family business. Family employees must be capable, open to collaboration with nonfamily employees, and have the accountability and discipline that befits a business professional.

When young family members become owners, they are not necessarily expected to become operational business leaders. By the third generation, if the family continues to own its legacy business, family members usually transition from family operator/leaders to board and governance roles. Family members might also be employed but ascending to business leadership is not assured. In the new business culture, family members do not come first. Instead, the family extends its values about accountability, transparency, and long-term development to include nonfamily leaders as true partners. Professionalism and accountability within the family sends an important message to nonfamily leaders: you don't have to worry that family members will limit your horizons.

When younger family members are in their school-age years, most families encourage internships or summer job programs that introduce them to the family legacy. After these initial programs, family employment may diminish as young family members attend college and, often, graduate school. They may travel or perform some sort of service work as they pursue early stages of their career outside the family orbit. Most families have a policy of requiring younger members to work several years in another business before they can be considered for a position in the family business or family office. To reenter, a family member seeking a career has to exhibit professional business skills comparable to his or her nonfamily peers. In each succeeding generation, the desired or expected level of professionalism rises. By the fourth generation, emerging family leaders tend to seek roles in governance rather than operations.

If young family members seek an executive leadership or governance role, there is inquiry, assessment, and mutual dialogue about entry. By the third generation, there may be many family and nonfamily candidates; at this point, favoritism for close family members can become an issue. To counter the tendency to promote its own children, the family makes the selection process explicit, transparent, and fair. When they apply for a job, family candidates usually must go through a parallel family vetting process since, as potential owners, they have a privileged role and will be seen differently.

Several issues are considered in family vetting, including the following:

- First, the family must assess the capability and suitability of the candidate for the position.
- Second, there needs be awareness of the effect on other employees of placing a family member in a particular role. What message will the employees take

from this? Will they be concerned about the impact on their prospects for advancement?

- Third, there may be competition within the family; another family member may expect to be chosen for the position. Cases like these must be mediated, lest the dispute spills over into the business.

As a third-generation family leader noted, family involvement should be modulated to an appropriate level:

*When I was growing up, the employees worried that there were too many family members working in the business. My generation wasn't really encouraged to work in the business, so this situation changed. Now we hear employees are concerned that the family doesn't have enough family members working in the business; they worry about the family's commitment. So now we're trying really hard to recruit family members to work in the business. It seems like things will flip again.*

Another member reported on the need to create a fair balance of capability and opportunity:

*We have employment policies about working in the family businesses. We say that you need to have the same entry qualifications as an outsider or better. There are two angles to that. My personal opinion is that if you become too prescriptive, it pushes family members away. They say it's too bureaucratic and it seems like you don't want us in the business. I think it has to be balanced.*

To develop competent leadership, many families create a long-term leadership development plan. This can be very traditional. For example, a fifth-generation European manufacturing firm has established a clear process for succession. Co-CEOs are appointed each generation to represent the two owning branches. A daughter, who is in line to become the successor from her family branch, recounted how the process began with her appointment when she was in university and the years of preparation that she needed before she could take up her role. While this is a risky choice, the family benefits because it is predictable and makes the process clear to each member of the new generation.

Most of the families in this study require family members to work outside the family business before applying, as in this example:

*We've had several fourth-generation family members hired over the last five to seven years who secured jobs appropriate to their skill sets after outside employment. In fact, we've only had one family member who didn't have outside experience, and this didn't go as well.*

The message that attracts a family member to the business is important. Sometimes, a feeling of obligation brings him or her in. One leader was recruited to "save" the business. Because he was concerned about its decline and was an experienced businessman, he felt he had to intervene. The most talented family members clearly have other options. Often, they are entrepreneurs themselves and want to forge their own paths. Nevertheless, the family might call and make them an offer. A father called his son when he was twenty-five and asked if he was interested. The son noted that this call "*planted a seed*," and a few years later, he was ready for the offer. He and his family moved from the city where he worked for a bank to the small town where he grew up.

Some families want family employees to start at the bottom, but when this happens, most families fast-track young leaders up the ladder:

> *When I joined the business, I started on the shop floor, then went from manufacturing to sales, and then slowly, slowly, took a long time to get to where I am today. It was a long, very drawn-out process. I'm sure they have some kind of a process in place today but not like what it used to be. Generally, you don't need to work outside just to join the business. But I know a few who worked outside first. The company has something called the fast track to a higher position. So you can work outside and then come in at a vice president level and advance further.*

As his family enterprise was undergoing a major transformation from products to business services, a young family member in another family saw an opportunity to make a major contribution to this effort. He was attracted to the challenge, not the opportunity for secure employment, but he demonstrated his capability for this role from prior experience. As an engineer, he was eager to put his experience to work developing sustainable factory practices; this would be a new expectation for this company. He asked if he could develop a project where family initiative would implement sustainability in its manufacturing operations. As a young person, however, he quickly became aware how hard it was to develop credibility and get the employees to adopt his plan. Still, after a longer period than he had imagined, he completed the project. He was then promoted to manufacturing operations where he was able to work collaboratively with nonfamily executives who shared his values and commitment and respected his capability.

If a family encourages many family members to enter the business, as a minority of our families do, it sets up mechanisms for evaluation, career guidance, and promotion to leadership designed specifically for family employees. Because of the number involved and the possibility of conflict about a sensitive issue, the family develops clear policies about employment—policies clearly differentiated from governance roles. One large family has a "family relationship manager" whose job is to support and assess the competence of family members. Several families require family employees to undergo a special assessment as they approach leadership level.

Others have active programs in which a young family member is given a trusted nonfamily leader as a mentor. This builds bonds between family and nonfamily management and helps family members see that their authority and skill as a family member must defer to and respect the outside leadership. Collaboration and meritocracy are helpful when filling key posts as they become open. Will it be a family member or not? Increasingly, family members are given less preference.

In another situation, two family members wanted to rise in the business. This presented both a family and a business challenge, as seen in the following three paragraphs:

> *In the third generation, a position came up, and a few family members applied. One of the family members who applied had worked in the business for about twenty years. Another person*

*who applied hadn't worked in the business that long at all. He was just a college student who went away for his education. He got his outside grants, then came back and applied for this supplemental position. But this younger guy actually got the position instead of the one who had the experience. So that created an issue, both on a business level and a family level.*

*I saw this firsthand because both individuals were in my branch of the family. It definitely damaged relationships. Things have gotten a lot better, but I know these two individuals will struggle with hard feelings for a long time. But the decision was made, and a lot of things went into it, and I personally feel it was the right decision. The right person got the position. In spite of this, you can see how the individual who had years of experience in the business would think "I should be the most qualified" even though in reality he wasn't.*

*One problem with this event was that too much personal information was shared with too many people. This was not professional. The leaders learned that personal things, especially about performance, shouldn't be shared so openly.*

As the business culture shifts, family engagement by a generative family is not swept aside in favor of professional leadership. Rather, as accountability for business results increases, family members from the current and the rising generations realize that they must add to their level of professional skills in order to serve. The family initiates an active process to set standards and to develop skills, commitment, and value-adding roles for rising generation family members who are new owners and owners-in-waiting. Part Four reports the steps to develop the rising generation by such families.

Activities that develop "professional" family members include:

- Setting clear expectations for consideration of hiring by the business
- Encouraging outside learning (university, business programs)
- Requiring candidates to work for a certain number of years for other businesses
- Carefully crafting messages about family hiring for both family and nonfamily staff
- Designating a "family relationship manager" to support family education and development
- Making evaluation of family transparent and separate from filial lines
- Keeping individual personnel decisions private and professional
- Regularly communicating about how the system is working and about willingness to make changes

### Entrepreneurial Focus for Each New Generation

In order to succeed over several generations, generative families have discovered that it is not enough to have a professional, disciplined family company. Growth and expansion of a legacy company cannot continue at a geometric pace, even though the family is growing geometrically. The family must find ways to be innovative and opportunistic. The Craftsman path must be supplemented by Opportunists.

A stale, predictable business, even if such a thing could survive today, does not greatly interest the most talented members of the next generation. These young people often have attractive outside options, so the family enterprise must compete for their attention. A disciplined, professional business may be profitable but not innovative or opportunistic. The challenge for every family is to develop the entrepreneurial mindset and requisite skills in key members of each generation. Here's a report from a fourth-generation business:

> *One of the big challenges for a fourth-generation business, rare as they are, is how to keep the entrepreneurial spirit alive. We need to keep the business innovative and productive, and we have to create an entrepreneurial mindset in the governance of the business. The company has to make sure that the businesses are growing, entrepreneurial, creative, and innovative. I hope we have the right people in place to ensure that.*
>
> *There's a new dimension that we're beginning to play with. We ask, "If you're part of this family clan, what does it mean to you as an individual? You're wealthier than your neighbor, but is this enough or is there something else?" One European business family I admire a lot said, "Well, in fact, you have more opportunities to develop yourself as a person when you're part of such a clan. You also have a good chance to become outstanding in terms of entrepreneurship." I very much like this vision, and I'm trying to promote it.*

While the business develops core competencies over generations, the rising generation frequently wants to see the family move into new areas. A fourth-generation family leader, in a business that started in farming and forest products and then expanded into newer areas like media and entertainment, observes:

> *We're trying to promote entrepreneurship among the young generation. I wish I could learn what interests them most about coming into the company. I wonder what's going on in the company that they don't want to be involved in and what strategies they do want to pursue. We haven't been very successful at pulling this out of them, but they're young, and it takes a lot of thought to come up with answers to those questions.*
>
> *Being in the venture capital business has been interesting for our family members because we've been opportunistic even if we don't have a well-defined group of industries or businesses we've been investing in. We take the view that we can identify technologies or businesses that are truly disruptive and have huge global sales potential, provided we can understand enough about what the business is actually doing. Flexibility is what we're good at.*
>
> *We've been in commodity businesses, so we know how to judge different kinds of risk. Having a multitude of businesses really does limit risk. We stay away from popular trends. But if the focus of the opportunity is related to any process we know about, like processing water or materials or anything that has to do with agriculture, then we take an interest. It turns out there's a pretty broad range of things we know a lot about, and we can apply the lessons we've learned to our new acquisitions. So we're able to bring things to the party that make us an attractive investor. For instance, we've connected small companies with engineering expertise that would have taken them forever to find.*

A family wants the most talented and capable family members to be *"in the business, not starting their own business on the outside,"* notes one fifth-generation family leader. While preparing to retire, he was selecting the next generation of leadership for his family's holding company.

The entrepreneurial focus takes divergent, creative forms. It builds on long-term commitment, family values, and business discipline while adding elements of risk and seeking out new ventures. One family has two fourth-generation co-leaders. They recruited a team of nonfamily leaders and began acquiring new businesses, all within the framework of their family's values. Another very old European business expects all of its young people to go their own way, either operating one of the family's current businesses or starting their own under the family name. There are clear paths and support for family members to start new ventures and clear accountability for results.

An innovation perspective is not just the province of family members. Wise family leaders extend the opportunity to innovate to nonfamily employees, as does this European fourth-generation family that owns multiple businesses. Their family leader notes that this cultural value was part of their legacy:

> My father was very keen on saying, "We should diversify but we should do it in a careful fashion because you need to have the right tools" and the right, what he called "talented people." And he always believed that talent can be grown from inside, not only from outside.
>
> And that was really helpful for our generation four because we believe that nonfamily members who work with you for 30–40 years become like family. Those who were not blood-related are going to be given every possible chance. For example, my father's driver had his own company that sold mobile phones. Another person in the organization was given the chance to open up cafeterias for our labor camps. My father believed that everybody is entrepreneurial in nature. If somebody was really good, then he should be able to encourage them.
>
> We now have an investment and innovation fund here for everybody to have their voice heard. We added to this a platform in the organization where everybody in the organization (because we subscribed to the idea that, "Who knows your business more than your people") could share new ideas as well. So, anybody from the least educated, who can't even write and read, has a chance to introduce their ideas of what they think could be.
>
> A sort of competition happens every quarter. A committee comes in from these people and they pick the best ideas. We reward these people and we let them be part of the initiative that comes in to change in the organization. This helps in retention of people, and gives us an improvement that's continuous, subscribing to my father's view that you can cultivate from inside. We are also able to get all the new knowledge and maintain it in one location. So, we're not left with what happened when my father passed away when some of this information was lost.

Another European family business had a successful publicly traded clothing company under the leadership of a third-generation family member. One of his cousins with a background in high tech asked to join the family business and be funded to set up new businesses. They were hugely successful. Eventually, his branch separated from the other branch associated with the public clothing company.

A question that often arises is whether entrepreneurship and new business is a continuation of the family enterprise or the start of a new enterprise, as it was in this Asian family, described in the next three paragraphs:

> The business leaders must learn to let go of their power and allow the next generation their own dreams and visions. They must be entrepreneurial enough to start up their own businesses and not just rely on the family enterprise.

*I will show my children that if they have the vision to build their own businesses, we will invest in their businesses, so we can move them to a different level. But my investment will not be majority ownership; I will be an angel investor. I would like my children to be entrepreneurs with their own passion and vision.*

*When we do that, however, will it still be the business founded by our ancestors? I would say that the wealth was given to the younger generation by the ancestors, but they created the new enterprises in the portfolio. In Asia, families have traditionally made money because of opportunity, not passion. But now, when the successors invest their money, they are passionate about changing the world. This is totally different from the way the business started. We have to give credit to these young entrepreneurs who have transformed the company and brought it into the modern world.*

## Growth versus Preservation

As each generation ascends, there is rarely unanimity in the dialogue between entrepreneurialism and conservatism. As this account shows, conflict between these competing views can tie up the business:

*When our family started, our business was like a beautiful, exquisite, massive diamond. We took that diamond and put it in a safe. A couple of times a year, we take it out and look at it and then put it back. Now, a hundred years later, the same diamond sits in the safe. Nothing else has happened really. Now there are more people who want to take it out and look at it, but it can't survive long term like that. I don't know if all of my generation feels the same way about it. Generation four has split into two camps over the issue of growth versus preservation. One camp says, "Let's just hold onto what we have." The other says, "Let's get creative and grow and make some money!" And because it's family and we have representative governance, nothing ever happens. We have to find a way to solve this conflict and move ahead.*

Reconciling these opposites is a characteristic of a well-functioning generative alliance. The family is able to act on both sides of an opportunity rather than being stuck in following one or the other.

Members of the older generation may want the enterprise to continue, but as they age and the new generation matures, they may avoid or delay real change until they get the support of the rising generation. This report illustrates this dilemma:

*We are now a holding company with print media, television, real estate, forestry, venture capital, and insurance. My dad and uncle postponed a lot of big decisions because we were not doing well in the eighties and they wondered if the family was going to be interested in continuing the business into the next generation. Now, because they postponed a lot of investment decisions, my generation has to decide whether to continue the business and how to set things in motion again.*

## The Entrepreneurial Mindset

If a family has a talented and capable family team entering the third or fourth generation, it can create a family investment group. The group described below was organized by a family with two large unrelated legacy businesses and a passion for growth and entrepreneurship in its new generation:

> *The way the G3 cousins take on new businesses evolved over the years. In the early stages of our career path, we didn't have a process, but everybody took an interest. Everybody wanted to look at new opportunities, so we formed a company among the five of us. It was informal at first. We just got together and started saying, "Look, I found this business" or "I've got this idea." From there, we started to grow a portfolio. Every year we allocate a certain amount of money to that investment portfolio. Now we have what we call the family bank. We do some research and find some promising stocks to buy. Then we bring them back to Dad, and he says, "This isn't the time to expand." But we just keep pushing and pushing until he finally comes around. These ideas have all come from our club; we bring the ideas, and then we finance them.*

Many generative families explicitly encourage family members to invest in new areas. A handful of families have experimented with a family bank or a family venture fund where family members can find funding for new ventures. For example, one respondent says, *"Our family bank allows members to find funding for projects they believe will bring either a financial return or a return in terms of human capital."* The family allows individuals to pursue their own new ventures, but the benefits and risks are also shared by the family as investors.

A large global family enterprise—owning more than one hundred businesses—describes how it has institutionalized entrepreneurship in each generation:

> *Each business operates as an independent unit with a board and a strategy committee composed of family and nonfamily members. We are an entrepreneurial family, and we want to stay that way. We've encouraged younger members to prove themselves by setting up businesses. If younger members are passionate about something, we help them to set up a business around it. They can make mistakes without criticism or reprimands. Somebody might want to set up a business in IT, somebody else wants to start a theme park, and a third person wants to do a retail business. They're all encouraged to go ahead. This is an ongoing effort—and this is why we have so many businesses.*

A fourth-generation family created a seven-member growth committee:

> *We base membership on their careers and experience, not on their family branch. They get together a few times a year to discuss how to grow the business. It's a great idea in theory, but nothing seems to come from it. The members of this growth committee put a lot of time and effort into developing ideas and suggestions. Then, when they take them to the board of directors, the board supports them, but we don't see any results. Hopefully, it will turn into something more than just talking about ideas.*

At first, there may not be a connection between the family's entrepreneurial mindset and entrepreneurialism in the business. In one large family business, nonfamily leaders were moving forward with many innovations. The family leader asked if they wanted to have the family review what they were doing. The nonfamily leaders said it wasn't necessary, but the family leader said, *"Are you willing to take all this risk and be responsible if it doesn't work out, or do you want the family to sign off on it?"* The business leaders then educated the family and got their informal buy-in and commitment.

Another family leader observes:

> *Each generation of our family respects the business they've received from the generation above them, but then they begin to change it and grow it in their own way. Nobody comes into the business and assumes that he or she is just going to ride it out. Everybody comes with an idea of continual entrepreneurship and growth.*

Another family, entering its fourteenth generation as a business family, long ago moved from one legacy family business to many ventures and investments. They proudly note their focus on individual entrepreneurship while it continues to pool its investments as an extended family:

> *Our own children worked together for about ten years in the same business. At that point, they decided to move on, and they all started their own businesses. They took a big portion of the money and put it into a common pool that they will look at in another five years. They've all invested in each other's companies, and they all sit on each other's boards. It's a strange way of continuing an enterprise, but in this family the entrepreneurial drive is too strong to focus on only one business. We view all our children as G1 in the business, even though they're fourteenth generation from the standpoint of the family.*

To release opportunistic innovation, a generative family must link attitudes and encouragement with concrete actions, by setting aside family funds to support innovation, new ventures, and various forms of social entrepreneurship by the rising generation of family members. As they call upon the family to reconsider the meaning of its values and apply them in practice, they ask the family to allocate funding and investments for such ventures. The family rightfully asks for accountability, but the active process of looking at new values-based ventures in generative families combines intention with clear pathways to action.

An example of how a young family member can develop entrepreneurial talent comes from a young third-generation member of an Asian family, who ultimately became a family enterprise CEO:

> *In 1972, I was 18, and the Vietnam War was just ending. A lot of things were moving to the Pacific because there was a huge military presence there. I noticed a Chinese Kung Fu picture was doing very, very well in the theatre. I remembered during my schooldays in Hong Kong, once or twice a year my dad would bring back some free tickets for a movie. He would tell us how he invested some money with a few of his friends in producing this film.*
>
> *I wrote to my dad: "Chinese karate pictures are doing well. Can you send me some of those from home? Maybe I can make some money on them." So he sent me some posters, and I knocked on the door of the local theatre and asked for an appointment with the manager. I showed him the posters and said, "These are great movies; can we do some business?" He says, "Yeah, bring the movies in, and we'll play them in the theatre. If one of them grosses more than $15,000, you'll get 35%. If it's less than that, you'll get 25% of the gross box office." I sent him the*

*movies, they played them, and in a week, I think it grossed over $20,000. I got $7,000. The owner of the film told my dad, "Tell your son whatever revenue he can get, he'll keep 50% and give 50% back to the company."*

*So as a college student, I made $3,500 in one week. That was a huge amount of money then. At that time, it cost just $1,800 to buy a car. So I started to grow that business with a few films my dad's friends had and then came to Hong Kong to buy more. We took them to the Pacific Islands. We built a little big business by the time I graduated from college.*

Outside the United States, especially in developing countries, generative families find their businesses are often under threat. Their country can undercut their wealth and influence by nationalizing their business or forcing them to leave. Business cannot be divorced from politics, and they can be seen as not reliably supporting the government. They react to adversity by relocating, often becoming refugees who are far poorer than they were before. The skills that make them generative kick into action, and while they have few financial resources, the retain their reputation, status among other families from their nation, networks of contacts, and their own drive and skills. Some generative families report losing most of their wealth and then starting new ventures that become as big or bigger than their previous efforts. This is more than luck. Their refugee status leads them to develop opportunistic and entrepreneurial skills as a family. Here is one of several stories from such a family.

## The Innovation Fund

This five-generation family originated in the Middle East and became very successful with a local business. Early in the twentieth century, social upheaval led their second generation to pick up and move to South America, where they remained for thirty years. They were part of an enclave of other refugees from their country and thrived in their new country. But they wanted to return "home" and relocated again after World War II. Social upheaval followed them, and they found their land seized by the government, and fled again, this time to Africa. After starting more businesses, they relocated again back to their home country, and then to a more stable part of the region. At several points, the family split as different branches dispersed to different places or started new ventures.

The fourth generation of the largest branch of the family recently experienced the passing of their revered and effective patriarch, who had developed their enterprise through several relocations and reconstructions. They contain an active and engaged G3 matriarch, three business-savvy siblings in middle life, covering a wide range of ages, and many young G5 adults. By adopting two innovative practices—a venture fund to support new ventures and investments and developing a family constitution and governance to focus their business development and accountability—they have continued to flourish. The oldest son, who is their new chair, relates:

*We grew up with the idea that home is the place where you're bonding and you're building a business—sort of like an Italian family. We wondered, "Okay, so what do we do with this bond between us?" My father said, "We're going to create a family fund, an innovation fund. And this*

*(continued)*

(Continued)

*fund is going to be funded from the existing businesses. We're going to isolate some money, not a huge amount at the beginning, and put it in a fund and we're going to ask these four [G4] family members to operate it. There was an age gap between the eldest, me and the youngest, of 20 years.*

*Our parents said, "Let's make this fund and the only condition is that you guys have to agree by consensus. Whatever you want to do, we encourage you to do it away from the existing business we're doing. The fund is to build something that will diversify the business somewhere else.*

*It was a huge challenge for us. We spent about a year and a half trying to improve our communication and to learn how to compromise. Then we started to apply that in the proposals coming to us based on solid financial reviews and we started applying. That led us into health care, F&B, a whole slew of investments in the tech space where we actually did something different than we were doing before. We had some short-term and long-term successes. Some are still in motion. Because they're going into IPO, they're solid. We became geographically diversified and we got closer together as a result of that.*

*At the same time, my mom and my dad said, "We need to make a family constitution." It was driven by the fact that there was this age gap and you could see that our interests were different. They know that all of us are going to get into the business, and they have policies about how many years they're going to work outside based on a merit basis. "You come into the organization. There's not going to be four of you who may be the chairman or CEO of all companies. Maybe none of you will be because it doesn't have to be blood." We went through this process and we were very lucky because they were willing to put this on the table.*

*We went down a long road, which took us eight years. Some were so young that we needed to wait until they were able to have the voice and be heard. Our journey from the previous generation was with a structure that we didn't have before.*

While there are many variations in the expression of family culture, and each family is unique, these common orientations and practices seem to arise in generative families all over the world.

## Taking Action in Your Own Family Enterprise

### *Culture Assessment*

The foundation for the generative alliance is developing a culture that expresses the long-term goals, values, and intentions of the family owners. This chapter has described each element of successful long-term family enterprise culture.

After reading the stories in this chapter, you might take the opportunity to assess your own family enterprise culture. Considering the six elements described in this chapter, apply them to the culture and practices in your own family enterprise. You can use the table below as a template to conduct your assessment.

For each element, consider the following questions:

- To what degree have you have implemented this?
- What do you do in this area that strengthens your family enterprise?
- What challenges or warning signs of strain are you facing in this area?
- What future steps might you take to develop this further?

| Element | Degree Used | Strengths for You | Challenges for You | Future Steps |
|---|---|---|---|---|
| Long-Term Commitment | | | | |
| Disciplined Professional Business | | | | |
| Extend Family Values to Business | | | | |
| Collaboration with Nonfamily Leadership | | | | |
| Professional Family Members | | | | |
| Entrepreneurial Focus | | | | |

### Implementing Culture Change

Obviously, these are very subjective and systemic issues, and it makes very little sense to fill this out alone. The best way to work on this sort of assessment is by naming a family task force. This can consist of the family leaders or a representative group of family owners and engaged members. Or it might be made up of a cross-generational group that also contains some nonfamily leaders. The point is not just to complete the task but to open up each area of culture for discussion. The discussion should lead to some sort of action plan in which the leadership looks to further develop the openness, adaptability, accountability, and innovative spirit of all the family enterprises.

## Notes

1. Daniel Denison, Colleen Lief, and John L. Ward, "Culture in Family-owned Enterprises: Recognizing and Leveraging Unique Strengths," *Family Business Review* 17, no. 1 (2004), 61–70, compared twenty family businesses with 389 nonfamily businesses using the Denison Organizational Culture Survey.
2. Hermann Simon, *Hidden Champions of the 21st Century: The Success Strategies of Unknown World Market Leaders* (New York: Springer, 2009). He defines Mittelstand companies as a group of mostly privately held, high-growth companies that are skilled and focused on a clearly defined area. Two-thirds of them are family-controlled, a detail that he does not focus on. He does note that, of this group, half of them have moved into a phase of nonfamily leadership. His findings mirror what my research team and I found.
3. The insight that the resources developed by positive family relationships, values, skills, and shared purpose can be a source of competitive advantage and account in a positive way for the success of special families like the ones in this study over many generations has been developed by researchers Danny Miller and Isabelle Le Breton-Miller in *Managing for the Long Run: Lessons in Competitive Advantage from Great Family Businesses* (Boston: Harvard Business Publishing, 2005), and Timothy G. Habbershon and Mary L. Williams, "A Resource-based Framework for Assessing the Strategic Advantage of Family Firms," *Family Business Review* 12, no. 1 (1999), 1–25. These researchers present the view that my research team and I have validated in this study: while family relationships can surely be destructive of a business, when aligned and used wisely they can add significant value to the success and adaptability of an enterprise.
4. James Grubman and I have written about this in the book *Cross Cultures: How Global Families Negotiate Change Across Generations* (Northfield, MA: Family Wealth Consulting, 2016). We present three cultural styles and show how family culture is influenced by each one as well as the results of family members being affected by their exposure to the other styles.

# CHAPTER 7

# Corporate Social Responsibility

## Changing the World from Local to Global[1]

*Cowritten with Isabelle Lescent-Giles, PhD,*
*and Jamie Traeger-Muney, PhD*

"We are a family company," statements and advertisements from business families proudly announce. They highlight this because they know that business families are known for their values of customer service, integrity, fairness, dependability, quality, and social responsibility. The accounts of generative families in this book support the reality of this assertion. The description of family business culture in Chapter 6 notes loyalty to and caring for customers, employees, and the community. This chapter continues that discussion by describing how generative families dedicate their companies to values beyond profit, as they assume responsibility for their employees, members of their community, social problems, and the fate of the environment.

By the third generation, family members have often created some distance from their legacy business. Even when the family delegates operational leadership to non-family leaders, there is one area where family remains deeply involved: defining values about social responsibility in their company, in other investments, and in the community. The family initiates projects, activities, and visible commitments to these social values.

Sustainability and social responsibility are a reflection of owners' values and their commitment to a long-term future, even if they may sacrifice some immediate returns. One owner notes, "*Their concern for the future leads them to consider the impact of their actions on family, employees, suppliers, customers, the environment, and community at large.*"

Generative families are acutely aware of the social and environmental impact of their decisions. They live in the community, shop and pray there, and send their children to school there, so they are sensitive to their reputation and how their practices impact others. They care about the community, and as leading citizens, they feel responsible to help the community thrive. Both short- and long-term consequences need to be evaluated when making decisions. They view business, society, and the environment as interdependent by nature.

While family values remain constant, their interpretation, application, and relevance changes over time. As heirs to the company, the younger generations may question current practices, asking questions that were not asked before: Is what we do harmful to the environment? Are our employees treated fairly, and do they benefit from our prosperity? How do we deal with adversity? Do we punish our employees or are we loyal to them?

Their emerging concern about social responsibility and environmental sustainability, as well as gendered norms about the role of women in the business, cause them to ask about and even challenge existing practices. As owners or owners-to-be, they feel they can raise these issues even if they are not directly engaged in company management.

A cross-generational dialogue often emerges about company practices and products. In some wineries, for example, next-generation winemakers question how the focus on tradition and quality creates wasteful water practices. They want to refocus on the experiential aspects of wine appreciation, rather than the more formal approach to ranking and tasting that the older generation grew up with. They want to engage millennial customers in new, more playful or authentic interactions.

## Corporate Mission and Social Values

Noted economic theorist Milton Friedman's definition of social responsibility does not resonate very well with the large family businesses in this study, precisely because his perspective explicitly splits the identity of business leaders between their roles as business executives and their roles as community citizens. Friedman explains that a corporate leader "may have many other responsibilities that he recognizes or assumes voluntarily—to his family, his conscience, his feelings of charity, his church, his clubs, his city, his country. We refer to these as social responsibilities. But in these respects, he is acting as a principal, not an agent; he should be spending his own money or time or energy, not the money of his employers."[2]

However, there is little separation between owners and their appointed agents in owner-managed family businesses: the family spends *its own money* when pursuing social and environmental goals alongside financial goals without leaving "its conscience" and "its city" at the door. The successful multigenerational family businesses in this study pursue growth with a systemic mindset. Their activities as investors, business leaders, and agents of social change build off of each other. Furthermore, they are driven by a strong sense of identity, framed around a shared history and a sense of purpose driven by core values and competencies.

To generative families, the business and the community it inhabits are deeply interconnected. One family says, "*We believe that growth is right. We are proud to be part of the big infrastructure projects that make the country grow. To grow, we need the trust of our customers.*" Each new business venture is creating value for the family while paving the way for a more prosperous community, with better roads, bridges, industrial facilities, and also better internet infrastructure.

As owners, generative families are seen as having great influence and wealth (even if the community assumes they are wealthier than they are). The community judges them by what they do with this. Ostentatious consumption is frowned upon while simplicity and discretion are appreciated as signs that they remain "one of us," even when there are obvious discrepancies in income and agency. One family, rising from lower-middle-class origins, built a huge house that the community branded "The Castle." Their children experienced the backlash more than their parents. As they grew up, they took the values of the family and started to give back in major ways, creating both a corporate and a family foundation, to balance out their parents' exuberance with their newfound wealth. Another young family member working in the company was reluctant to invite coworkers to his house for fear of their resenting his lifestyle.

The extent of family responsibility can be conceptualized as a series of concentric circles that define how far the concerns of the business and its owners extend. The Friedman model extends responsibility only to an inner circle of owners and their profits. The stakeholder view, held by most family enterprises, is that they are also accountable to employees, customers, suppliers, and the community they live in. Many family companies extend the family metaphor to include these other stakeholders, and they are respected for that commitment.

This view is ascendant in the twenty-first century. Much has been made of millennials' appetite for meaningful work. They love social enterprises like Patagonia, which are also social ventures because they put social or environmental impact at the core of "why we exist" and "how we do business." Patagonia's mission statement ("We are in business to save our home planet") drives business strategy from materials to branding and is looked up to as a model and a pioneer of socially and environmentally conscious business. Family owners are particularly responsive to views of BlackRock's CEO Larry Fink:

> *Purpose is not the sole pursuit of profits but the animating force for achieving them. Profits are in no way inconsistent with purpose—in fact, profits and purpose are inextricably linked.... Companies that fulfill their purpose and responsibilities to stakeholders reap rewards over the long-term. Companies that ignore them stumble and fail. This dynamic is becoming increasingly apparent as the public holds companies to more exacting standards. And it will continue to accelerate as millennials—who today represent 35 percent of the workforce—express new expectations of the companies they work for, buy from, and invest in.[3]*

In 1987, the United Nations' Brundtland Commission created a global compact articulating environmental, social, and governance practices for companies. These principles and practices are incorporated into values held by many generative families. (See Figure 7.1.)

Family philanthropists Sharna Goldseker and Michael Moody[4] note the young family givers' insistence on going beyond signing checks to also contributing time and skills and working more collaboratively on projects. This insistence stems in part from concerns about preserving the dignity of the employees and local community

**Figure 7.1** **United Nations' Brundtland Commission: Sustainable development goals.**

members they grew up with. These rising-generation donors recognize that skills and leadership, not just money, are at the heart of long-term business success. While contributing valuable resources beyond money is not new, it is particularly important to the rising generation and often drives their commitment to the family enterprise.

US companies view corporate social responsibility (CSR) as akin to philanthropy (i.e., giving outside the business) and tend to focus more narrowly on carbon footprint and sustainability in the narrow sense of environmental impact. On the other hand, European companies tend to approach CSR as part of their core strategy and business operations, with a stronger focus on social, as well as environmental, disclosure and programs. While the term "corporate social responsibility" is widely used in the business community and among families, it is controversial because it has become synonymous in certain circles with corporate communications and "spin." "Corporate sustainability" is becoming a more comprehensive term to indicate actions and behaviors in the business that address social and environmental impact. Generative families understand sustainability as a long-term view and a focus on stewardship across generations that encompasses profit, people, and the planet.

Researchers have suggested abandoning a "one-solution-fits-all" definition for CSR because definitions vary widely based on context and culture. Instead, companies act on a range of definitions matching the development, awareness, and ambition levels of organizations. Despite varying definitions, CSR initiatives share some common traits. According to Caserio and Napoli, CSR "affects sustainability, local community and society"; it plays a critical role "in preserving the environment, in respecting and promoting human rights and job satisfaction and in developing and supporting ethical and moral values inside the company." As a result, "CSR affects the image and reputation of companies and thus its financial and economic performances."[5] Stakeholders increasingly push for CSR to extend to product ingredients and raw materials, and behavior of companies in their supply chain.

The families in this study evaluate the consequences of their business decisions through a set of criteria articulated around the family values and incorporating social and environmental concerns. For some families, religious faith is the primary glue that binds the family, the business, and the community together and defines its core values. One Latin American family, for example, proclaims the importance of faith, specifically Catholicism, in the family's life and describes how it shapes the family's contribution to society. Another family puts the biblical principle of "Do unto others as you would have them do unto you" at the core of its community agenda.

For example, now in its fourth century, Rothschild and Co. (profiled in Chapter 3) defines itself as "a global and family-controlled group" that provides "M&A, strategy and financing advice, as well as investment and wealth management solutions to large institutions, families, individuals and governments, worldwide." The company defines its core competency as a "combination of scale, local knowledge and intellectual capital that allows [it] to provide a distinct perspective and effective long-term solutions for [its] partners." Rothschild's CSR centers on community investment and environmental action aligned on the UN's sustainability development goals (see Figure 7.1). The Rothschild family also practices philanthropy as an entire family (e.g., a network of retirement homes for the elderly members of the Jewish community) and some philanthropy as family branches (e.g., support for the Rothschild hospital in Paris, famous for its excellence in the treatment of eye diseases, as a result of one ancestor's history of eye trauma in the French branch of the family). Other family members focus on causes tied to their home cities and, at each generation, add causes that are meaningful to their immediate family.

## The Polaris Project

For a decade, the Family Business Network (FBN), a global network of long-standing family businesses, has looked at how family business can remain profitable while respecting people's values, product quality, integrity, and the environment. FBN's Polaris project, which began around the time this research project began (and which served as one of the initial sponsors of this research), has collected stories and examples of how CSR principles entered the family enterprise. This project in turn has led FBN to develop protocols for assessment and development of such practices in other businesses.

FBN's mission statement affirms the 1987 UN Brundtland Commission's goals for sustainable development, goals that "meet the needs of the present without compromising the ability of future generations to meet their own needs." The Polaris initiative shares this vision of interdependence between business, social, and environmental goals. A recent Polaris report defined sustainability as how family businesses adapt to changing business environment and build for the future. This includes business and also social and environmental goals. The FBN pledged that it was working for "a sustainable future for people, communities, environment, and future generations." To achieve this, the project advised members to start by exploring family values (how they

*(continued)*

*(Continued)*

are articulated, communicated, and used for decision-making) and what sustainability means to the family, the business, family investments, and the community. Polaris encourages all generations to participate, and this approach, together with philanthropy, is often an easy entry point for cross-generational discussion, transmission, and collaboration.

Polaris's case studies contain several common characteristics of projects and commitments to sustainability by families. They are:

- Personal, reflecting the interests of the family
- Related to business goals and mission
- Focused, with clearly defined outcomes
- Ongoing, including long-term support by family owners

Polaris is not about research, it's about action. It developed materials for family businesses to create sustainability "conversations" of the companies, and their family owners, to define their sustainability goals and set goals and practices for the future. Polaris's conversations are intended to engage groups of family members and business leaders to develop sustainability policies and practices for their business. Polaris begins with an assessment of what the business is currently doing and then goes on to help the family define some clear goals and practices in areas where the company operates. Each year, more FBN members begin this evaluation and transformation project.

## CSR: Building Block for Sustainable Success and Long-Term Growth

Long-term sustainability is in the DNA of generative family businesses because their top priority is to pass on the business to the next generation. As a result, these family businesses prioritize long-term over short-term goals. This leads to an appreciation that industries have a life cycle, that sustainability means change, and that there is a need to embrace new industries, new technologies and new practices with each new generation.

Sustainability is not just environmental. It reflects the long-term values of the family and its focus on growing without losing sight of the social and environmental effects of the business. Each family defines this slightly differently, as its history, legacy, and type of business leads it to emphasize different elements.

A family member explained it this way:

*You have to decide what and how we're going to create added value for humanity, for people. Then we come back to responsibility—if the family decides you have to maximize making money, that's easy and then you can do anything. My grandmother always told me: never do it for money because you will never be successful or have enough. You have to create added value for the people around you. If you do that well and better than anybody else, then you will make money.*

*Money is a consequence; it cannot be a target—maximizing shareholders' value to me, the whole free market economy. We have to rethink this whole issue. That's why I'm working on this Polaris project on sustainability. Our company should be part of the solution of the world's problems, not part of the problem. And I hate the rules of Wall Street and our attitudes to always make more money. This is not business; this is a casino.*

*It goes back to being in there for the long term. We're best placed to be the champion of sustainability, and I'm sure that others will follow. We're still under the radar. But eventually with the new balance of power, those who really add value to the world will be appreciated—well, that's the belief, the faith.*

*But it's also a necessity to keep our free market economy alive. If I listen to my grandchildren—they also are balancing between having a good life and having fun and it's not just sustainable—I think the next generation will be in that effort, that ambition.*

*There's a philanthropic tradition in the company, charity initiatives by employees. If they show that they are doing something, the company will contribute. If an employee of the company is active in charity work, the company will double his efforts.*

Emerging values of the rising generation about social responsibility can challenge business practices or even the business itself. For example, this family owned an oil company. As members of the fourth generation became involved in governance, they questioned that business:

*I think there's opportunity for our mix of businesses to change. The push might be in how the family invests or the businesses the family runs. For example, oil and gas, will that be something that my generation embraces? I think that's the big question mark, so redefining the family values and mission, that might be where the rubber hits the road. How do we get the fourth generation involved in some of these businesses, and what do we want to be involved in? It will be very interesting to see how some of the older family members either step back and let us step into some of those roles and make some changes. Or there won't be a lot of change but some addition to balance out the family's portfolio or focus. I'm not sure how that's going to play out yet, and it's being talked about quite a bit.*

As families worry about keeping the next generation engaged in the family enterprise and how to best train the next generation of leaders both formally and informally, some generative families use CSR to engage in cross-generational collaborations and build next-generation stewardship. An Asian G3 family member received strong encouragement from her grandfather in early discussions about the sustainability of their business as well as financial support to improve the sustainability of the family agrobusiness empire. Step by step over five years, she built her credibility as a business leader, challenging the family norms and stereotypes about the role of women as well as the age at which family members can have real impact and claim leadership in the community. The rise of impact investing gives the next generation in general, and women in particular, a unique opportunity to demonstrate that they can run profitable businesses with positive social and environmental impact.

The following European family had a long tradition of progressive social involvement, which had been neglected as the family diversified into multiple ventures.

Members of the twelfth generation remembered those values and began to realign them with their investments and business practices:

*It's always been done because, as a family member, the mayor had that socialist spirit in the sense that we were the first to fight against child labor, to create an educational center for youth, to give each worker a small house and plot of land. There has always been a familial, patriarchal spirit that included the workers and protected them and gave them the best. There was a workshop for handicapped children. It has always been done discreetly rather than flamboyantly. More "corporate." Like they do it today. That said, we would love to do even more.*

*There is this responsibility to make an entire region attractive and livable for our five thousand workers. The charitable spirit was always there at the foundation, even maybe a bit socialist. This consciousness that all of the hotels and restaurants in the neighborhood also depend on us. When there were hard moments with difficult decisions, when we had to sell one of the branches of the firm, it was managed and sold off to those who guaranteed sustenance for the community. That was always the first condition. They have this saying, "Not for us, for the others." They really had a great spirit. Unfortunately, it diminished at that point because that's how it was: it was the "crazy twenties"—you could get 25 percent from the stock market. It was a period during which, if you had power and money, you lived extremely well. But there were complications.*

*Today, there has been a readaptation. We have to keep this generosity, open-mindedness, and sense of responsibility while at the same time going through hard times where you may have to close a division. How do you do that? Bad moments for the family to go through. There never was a social plan . . . the tiniest decision taken without everyone being sick over it. That's not what we wanted to do. There's always been this human component and sense of responsibility. My father-in-law, who was very difficult, hated it. It was very difficult for him . . . .*

*The only way for the firm is to always show that our local roots matter. We make the business a link for people; we make the employees in China or India understand that they are also part of this local history. When they come and visit the homeland, they are very proud, too. To give an example, for four years it was very difficult, and the family didn't take any dividends. When we told our workers, "You know we put all our money in, we had to put more in . . . and we don't take dividends?" They went, "We have to power through."*

At its simplest, sustainability means shifting investments to tap into new opportunities and avoid being locked in an environmentally destructive or dying industry. One third-generation family firm is acutely aware of this, as its core business revolves around railway equipment where price drives purchase and foreign competition is significantly cheaper. As a result, this firm moved aggressively into two new opportunities: product as a service and wind towers.

CSR also involves a sensitivity to the impact of policies and economic hardship on people. Hermès is the independent luxury group best known for its leather goods and silk scarves. It is run by sixth-generation family member, Axel Dumas. Hermès starts its 2018 "Registration Document Including the Annual Financial Report" with a history of the firm, including its historical focus on craftsmanship and exceptional materials:

*This year's results once again reflect the strength of our growth model: a model of craftsmanship with humanist values, which has at its heart the creativity and inventiveness of each one of us. Creative freedom combined with exceptional know-how, the constant quest for exceptional materials, as well as the desire to offer outstanding services to our customers are our major assets.*[6]

The report continues:

*The points scored owe nothing to the luck of the draw. The opening of the Manufacture de l'Allan and the 250 jobs it will ultimately create, the success of the women's and men's ready-to-wear and home collections, the acclaimed launch of* Enchaînements libres, *the new high jewellery line, the confirmation of the* Twilly d'Hermès *success, and the dynamism of silk, leather and footwear are the milestones of a well-executed game, played out on embellished, enlarged and now digital playing fields. Once we have crossed the finish line, we can congratulate ourselves on these successes which enable us to share the fruits of this growth with those who contribute to it on a daily basis, to strengthen our territorial roots, and to develop employment opportunities. Thank you for the great game. Now, in 2019, it's time to dream.*[7]

Many of the largest and oldest generative families don't view social and environmental impact as an add-on, peripheral set of actions but as part of the core strategy. They use their core values and skills to solve the social and environmental issues they care about and create "sweet spots" where all three elements of the triple bottom line (profitability, social benefits, and protection of the environment) create cumulative effects rather than trade-offs. Also, today the urgency and danger of climate change and deep social divisions and inequality are hard to ignore.

One Latin American business leader puts it in these terms: *"We have a long history of very good labor relationships, so that's one part. And we also collaborate a lot with the locals where we participate. So it's basically taking good care of our suppliers, taking good care of our employees and the larger community where we live. And what isn't done by the company is done by the foundation."*

Another example of building on the family core competencies to pursue social purpose is from a European business leader, retired from the active family business and looking for a new purpose. He is building a new impact venture with his Indian partner to bring solutions for rural electrification to India, using the company's manufacturing facilities and core knowledge in electric systems. For him, this new venture is "just another way to carry on the family mission."

Another family business leader, after a distinguished career in a major consulting firm, returned to take leadership of the family business in his forties, and reflects on the difficult choices he must make. Although he is very focused on profitability in order to keep the family business alive and thriving, closing the business's first factory in a high-cost region is an absolute no-no for reasons of loyalty (*"I cannot close a factory where current employees have worked all their lives, as did their parents and grandparents"*) and social responsibility (*"We are the only source of employment in the region"*).

Instead, he adapted his business model to focus on innovation and fast-fashion and uses the legacy factory as a testing ground where top management can develop proofs of concept before sending the product to be mass-produced elsewhere.

This is reminiscent of Zara's business model. In this first-generation Spanish family business, the owners have developed a business model of runway to stores in three weeks. This timeline enables them higher margins than the industry norm while also creating and preserving jobs in the company's historical home, La Coruña. These social criteria for the preservation of livelihood are an integral part of the decision-making process for many family businesses.

For others, it is not enough to establish thriving communities and fight local poverty. One next-generation business leader notes that each generation of the family has a duty not just to expand incrementally but also to explore more radical ideas for business expansion. This view is shared by many of the rising generation leaders in this study who have family conglomerates in developing countries. Business opportunity plus social impact is a winning combination for their elders and the family office. One young leader just secured family investment for a social impact project based on this argument of new job creation for the community. To achieve this, he had to prove to the board that it was also a good business opportunity. Another young business leader interviewed for this study shared that he was given the explicit mission by his family and the leadership of his country to go to America and find *"the next generation of companies"* willing to invest in his home country in order to create jobs and lift his countrymen out of poverty. For our families, entrepreneurship and new business ventures are often framed as business opportunities and in social development terms.

---

### Career Path of a Rising Generation Family Leader Who Championed Social Responsibility

When a new family member enters family business leadership, he or she feels entitled to bring up CSR and environmental issues. This was not a concern for previous generations, but today this issue has deep urgency. Young leaders feel that developing sustainability and social responsibility is a life-or-death matter. This is the story of the career path of a new family leader in a Southeast Asian chemical company who dedicated himself to the values of environmental sustainability. In doing so, he faced many challenges:

> When I graduated college, I had an adventurous spirit, but I also needed a job. I picked the one furthest away in Papua New Guinea. I enjoyed it tremendously but realized that I'm not a biologist in the sense of sitting someplace and waiting for some bird to come by. The people I worked with were even more passionate about this than I was.
>
> When I finished my stint there, I spoke with my father. I said, "Since we've so many production-oriented businesses with inherent hazards like chemical distribution, we need an environmental policy and program, so how about if I do that for you?" He saw the potential, so he said, "Why not?" We had management conferences every two years, and he proposed to make the environment the key theme of the upcoming gathering. He invited prominent environmentalists and asked me to give a presentation.
>
> That was a great way for me to get exposed to the company and to meet the key executives. A number of them said, "Why don't you join? I mean, there's nobody else. Your father is getting older, and since you were a child you've always been interested in the business. Now you've this special environmental thing. Why don't you just join?"

*(continued)*

I went back to the US and did my master's in environmental management. The program focused on how business can reduce its environmental footprint. Then in 1995, exactly one hundred years after my grandfather started the company, my first job was environmental. We put it quickly together with health and safety because those things inherently go well together. I was the first manager of environment health and safety in the group; that's how my career started here.

We had a big warehouse storing sodium cyanide with other chemicals, flammable liquids, and oxidizing agents; a cocktail was just sitting there waiting for something bad to happen! That was the area in most need of finding proper storage methods with segregation, isolation, separation, emergency response plan, emergency prevention plans. We got all the companies certified to ISO 18,000, which was a new industry standard back in the nineties.

We started a number of new businesses that came out of an environmental impulse. We focused also on packaging because most companies were doing protective plastic packaging for the electronic industry. We decided to enter molded pulp packaging made of recycled paper as a new business. Some of them did not work out; we had a feather and bedding factory here in Singapore, and we went into organic cotton but found that actually the willingness to pay extra by the consumer was not there. So it was an experiment, but we stopped it, and the molded pulp packaging continues to this day.

[Doing this work] was very difficult for several reasons. First of all, this environmental movement was relatively new globally, certainly in Southeast Asia, and quite foreign to many. So that was one challenge. The second challenge was when you're a family member there is a certain inherent respect. They clearly knew that there could be a very good chance that I would become their leader one day, and I was the son of the then still very active chairman, so they clearly couldn't go against that.

For five years, I led our large crane business, and that was the best training for me because that was a real regional leadership role, and I was still quite young. When I came back to the head office, my father retired, so I became chairman.

One of the reasons we are able to manage such a diversified business is because we give a lot of decision-making autonomy to the individual managers. In some areas, there was a quiet resistance, which was difficult to deal with, and that, coupled with the fact that I was young, I had not been in a managerial position before [so] feedback was not easy to get.

Being the son of the chairman and crown prince, people are inherently reluctant to give negative feedback or suggest improvement, you know, ways that things can improve. That's even more so in Southeast Asia, so I had trouble getting feedback on the actions and the decisions and the judgment that I was having. There was a bit for my father, but I also stayed quite distant from my father [so as] not to have too close a reporting relationship.

We brought in a consultant, and once the case clearly highlighted how dangerously we were conducting our business, that message came home so clearly that everybody rallied around. Today, our chemical business is our largest. One reason for our success is our environmental program, the fate of [the] product once it leaves their factory gate, how you're storing, transporting, disposing, and how you ensure our end customers are not misusing it.

It's a completely different company today now that the environment is a key component of how we do business. We also are very pragmatic. There are things we do which are not against the environment but where one could also say we could actually be much more proactive but where for various reasons it just doesn't make sense right now. I think we've done well, and it's really part of the culture now. We've been carbon neutral since 2011, and nobody questions that anymore. We are known as a company that does this kind of thing, so I'm happy with what has been achieved. The family not in the business totally supports this. There was never any resistance.

Once in a while, I get an email or a note from somebody who has joined the company somewhere who says, "I'm so happy I joined the company. I found out all the environmental programs we have, and I really feel proud to be here." I got one the other day.

(continued)

*(Continued)*

> *We have a CSR program where we send people into the field twice a year. We always have many volunteers for each of these projects, which are about a week long. They plant trees and do things in nature. which is not necessarily within their comfort level, but they like doing that and think it's important, so that's where we are.*

## Impact Investing

Alongside projects within their philanthropic foundations and legacy business, generative families increasingly want to build investment portfolios that drive social impact. They invest huge amounts, especially following the sale of a business, and often under pressure from the rising generation, they seek social as well as financial returns. An earlier perception that social returns would lead to lower financial returns has now been challenged by new data, allowing older investors to come on board. Nearly half of the family offices surveyed worldwide by Bloomberg "believe that impact investing is a more efficient use of funds to achieve social impact than philanthropy."[8] The boundary between social responsibility, philanthropy, and for-profit ventures is less firm. Impact investing is an approach to profit that is linked also to social impact and values.

Current generations want to practice impact investing movement through portfolio structuring and impact measurement. They look both to filter out negative investments, ones that demonstrably cause long-term harm, and also to support businesses that are actively contributing to social objectives. One family leader explains that impact investing became his passion. The board and his siblings *"went crazy when I started to talk about leaving the family business; 'you can't leave the company,' they all said. I did it anyway. Dad was great all around with this process. The family agrees with this value emphasis. We agreed to take 5 percent of our cash for this purpose."* In addition to the desire for financial returns, the family also wants to consider the returns for society. This conversation may be received by older generations as an opportunity to expand their social impact or as a challenge to the family's behavior and even how the wealth was created. In other families, skeptical elders are won over by the combination of data and enthusiasm of the rising generation. But that evolution takes some time, and patient engagement of both generations is key to successful shifts of investment values.

Family offices are becoming proactive, rather than reactive, especially as the members of the next generation of young leaders are gaining influence. These young leaders ask, *"How can we contribute to building a stronger community, leveraging our social capital, financial resources, and skill set?"* rather than *"What do our clients want to see us doing?"*

Articulating a strong sense of mission is not unique to generative families, but they do it in a focused, authentic, and powerful manner. For example, one Asian family is managing a group of new sustainable businesses the family invested in, with a focus on job creation and infrastructure building. As one of the few large conglomerates in its home country, it is focusing on creating foreign partnerships to expand the job market at home and has refrained from expanding operations abroad, beyond sales, in order to prioritize job creation in its original territories. This focus is drilled into the next generation and is also communicated to employees, communities, and elected officials.

Members of the current generations, and particularly rising-generation leaders-in-training, want to go beyond walking the town with the *"I know it when I see it"* attitude of earlier generations, for whom impact was conveyed through individual stories and artifacts such as bridges and libraries and, of course, job creation and dividends.

But many generative families are struggling with how to measure social and environmental returns. Some approach this issue through collaborations with financial experts. They invest through impact funds or coinvest as equity partners with financial firms that focus on impact investing. Some family offices focus on areas they know best, at the industry and location level, and measure relevant inputs and outputs. For example, families are investing in renewable energy, both because they see the dwindling of their oil reserves and want to build the post-oil world for themselves and their countries and because they are aware of the environmental benefits and the potential for new job creation. Similarly, a fifth-generation family with expertise in the health-care sector is investing in promising start-ups through seed investments, both because they can leverage their domain knowledge to identify good business opportunities and because it continues to serve the family mission to further medical research. They know from past experience the key metrics for the industry.

Investing in education is also common. Some families set up the schools with donations of land, buildings, and equipment and expect the schools to pay for running expenses through tuition. An Asian family leader shares the strong traditions around impact investments in his local community but stresses that it is informal:

> We focus on especially the cities or the parts of the town where we came from, where my grandfather came from, where my grandmother came from, where our ancestors came from. We would want to contribute on the development of those cities or those regions, build maybe public facilities, sometimes schools, sometimes houses, and just contributing to the community there and to the closer community that we know and then, of course, we now also have setup. Even before, we didn't set up special foundation for our so-called CSR or so-called social activity.

Another popular area for impact investment is residential and commercial real estate. It is a natural progression from building workers' housing and community buildings, some for-profit, others not-for-profit, to mixed projects with low- or zero-interest loans, which are expected to be repaid and reinvested in other projects. This practice dates back to the company towns build by the Cadbury family in the nineteenth century.

Some families are exploring the benefits and drawbacks of green living and micro-living, whereas others are looking into sustainable tourist resorts to create more value from their land holdings. Some families are building or converting existing buildings into green buildings. And car-sharing pools, micro-living, and urban farming are seen as a natural extension of their mission to drive positive change in their community and to address new societal challenges, such as climate change and the increasing unaffordability of large cities from Dubai and Tokyo to London and San Francisco.

This is particularly strong in families where the real estate portfolio is driving future growth, as they realize the attraction of small residential units to millennials. This group, together with new retirees, drives the search for housing that is mindful of the environment and climate change. Several next-generation leaders in this study are driving conversations with their families and key nonfamily executives around sustainability as both a source of revenue and "the responsible thing to do." Green buildings and micro-living are seen both as possible drivers of revenues within the next fifteen years and a good fit with the existing family's values, such as value for money and building "friendly" communities by design.

Another important area is infrastructure building, particularly renewable energy and logistics, but also e-commerce platforms and banking platforms. Many families in Asia and Africa are aware that it is impossible for governments to build old-fashioned communications and logistics infrastructure, so they are instead using the potential of apps, cloud technology, and renewable energy to connect micro- and small entrepreneurs to the digital age. They are teaming up with impact experts or tech entrepreneurs to deliver mobile phone market information, banking and financial services, health care, or training for the masses.

For others, entrepreneurship seen as is the route out of poverty. Some support microenterprise with the help of leading organizations such as the Acumen or Grameen Foundation. But increasingly, next-gen leaders want real impact in the form of scalable firms. This reinforces investments in firms that create platforms and marketplace, as mentioned in the previous section.

For some families, tackling old yet intractable problems such as inequalities and poverty is not sufficient. They are turning their sights to new, "dirty" global problems that have proved impossible for governments and NGOs to get a grasp on, such as new diseases and medical treatments or climate change issues. This is particularly true around pollution, sustainable cities, and sustainable agriculture.

The latter is very popular among this study's families worldwide, with two main foci: how to introduce more sustainable farming practices and how to build higher added-value services, such as hospitality. One next-gen member who is operating coffee farms in Latin America spent part of her last year at university planning for the launch of a new family venture in a chain of foreign coffeeshops with the help of family members who emigrated at the previous generation. Sustainable agricultural practices, like renewable energy, often create both social impact (e.g., jobs, reduction of pollution) and environmental impact (e.g., better use of soil and water). Others are thinking more systematically and are looking at the impact of cattle raising or alternative sources of proteins.

## The Entrepreneurial Spirit in Impact Investing

André Mulliez is a third-generation owner of the French-based Mulliez family association. The family owns several major international retail chains, such as the sports
apparel brand Decathlon, supermarket chain Auchan, and home improvement/DIY
chain Leroy Merlin. In 1986, he launched Réseau Entreprendre, an entrepreneurial
network with the mission to create new jobs in northern France; it has since extended to
other regions. This has evolved into a foundation with three major areas of action: supporting new entrepreneurs through funding and mentoring, encouraging the growth
of French entrepreneurial spirit, and supporting the vision of entrepreneurs as creators
of social impact. According to their website:[9]

> *In the last years that I worked at Phildar, the situation gradually deteriorated. We had no other
> choice than to lay off 600 employees. It made me physically ill. I could not stand it. My family
> was used to creating jobs, not losing employees. I spoke to twelve members of my family who were as
> distressed as I was to see so many jobs go, and we agreed: "We have to lose these jobs. There is no other
> way, but we shall make amends by creating employers who, in turn, will generate employment." We
> invested our time and money and started Nord Entreprendre in 1986, the same way we would have
> started any other business. Here's how we operate: an entrepreneur comes to us with a new business
> project. We evaluate the candidacy, and if we believe there is a chance of success, we finance the
> project and support the entrepreneur.*
>
> *For each entrepreneur we find an experienced entrepreneur to be a mentor for three years.
> Mentors meet at least once a month with the entrepreneurs and are not compensated for their
> involvement. They do it because it is fun to be part of a new venture and also because they learn so
> much from the young entrepreneurs. We finance the projects by providing a loan between 15,000
> and 45,000 euros, free of interest and without guarantee, for a maximum of 5 years. Should the
> entrepreneurs succeed, they have a moral obligation not to pay back to the association, but to help
> new entrepreneurs.*
>
> *We do not support all types of business. What we want is to be behind businesses that will
> generate employment. We give preference to the 4% of all new businesses that will generate between
> 3 and 10 jobs. In we received a total of 2,850 requests, studied 855, presented 269 to our boards
> and accepted 205. The companies we support are from all kinds of business sectors, from production
> to distribution to services in all kinds of industries. Emulating the Nord Entreprendre model, we
> gradually opened new associations in different parts of France and grouped them under the name
> Réseau Entreprendre (Entrepreneuring Network). Today we have 21 associations, 1,400 members,
> 2,500 business-leader mentors and 870 winners. On average, we have a continuity rate of 86%
> after three years (national average: 62%) and 74% after five years (national average: 50%),
> which indicates that we have an efficient concept. A survey of our winners indicates that, after 7
> years, on average they employ 17 people. Extrapolating from this figure, today we have with all the
> companies we have supported a potential of approximately 11,000 new jobs—6,600 have already
> been created and the rest will be created in the coming years.[10]*

## Impact Investing as a Tool of Next-Generation Engagement

Impact investing comes into the family conversation as a natural consequence of
aligning values with business, financial activity, and investment of philanthropic
funds. A family has values about its stakeholders and responsibility to society; it
expresses those values both in family behavior and in the conduct of the business.
As the family does this, the members of the rising generation also look at how the

family invests its portfolio. The outcome of these conversations helps determine how deeply they want to involve themselves in the family enterprise. In order to get their commitment, the family builds upon its legacy values to move in new directions. This is an example of the generative alliance in action.

*"Why,"* they ask, *"do we not make sure that our investments reflect our values, just as we ask that our business practices do?"* Instead of seeing impact investment as just screening out negative behavior in companies they invest in, the emerging direction is to look at investments in terms of their positive impact. Liesel Pritzker Simmons prefers the more concrete "values-aligned" investing term to "socially responsible investing," explaining that they "have aligned 83% of their fixed-income assets and 50% of their equities" in 2013, with a full alignment expected in 2020.[11]

Impact investing is a strong focus of millennials looking for meaningful work, often because they don't share their parents' passion for an industry or region. One next-gen family member remarks, *"I have no interest in spending my life building light bulbs in the middle of nowhere. I want to live in a big city and chart my own path."* Parents who attempt to reengage them in the family business as it is, often fail, creating a major threat to family business survival.

If parents are willing to listen and adjust their expectations, however, they often realize that their children are opening new avenues for generating wealth through investment opportunities. Involving a family office—their own or a professional, multifamily one—they shift the conversation from *"Come home or we cut you out"* to *"What can you do to grow the family business in new directions?"* This often leads to the birth of successful global, diversified family conglomerates held together by a set of values and joint investors.

Generative families are good at recognizing the opportunity for dialogue and leadership building around the issue of social and environmental impact and have used it effectively to start discussion of what it means to be a business family. These cross-generational discussions achieve more than enabling rising-generation leaders to build credibility. They also transmit and renew values through discussion of past examples of the family social and environmental actions and the guiding values behind them. In particular, my research team and I observed several families in this study where grandparents and grandchildren became closer through discussions of what the family stands for and what it wants to be known for on issues such as climate change, alleviation of poverty, and fostering of strong local institutions such as sport clubs. Handing over the leadership of building an impact investment portfolio and deciding focus, instruments, and metrics, in particular, has helped several of our families build a better understanding of the mindset, skills, and values of the next generation. This process fosters discussion around innovation and entrepreneurship, as next-gen leaders explore whether they want to contribute as part of the family office—building investment portfolios, setting up equity/VC funds, or becoming social entrepreneurs themselves.

By learning how to select, structure, and sell their ideas for new social ventures to the family office based on a mix of profitability and family values and traditions, several of the next-gen individuals in this study have obtained family funding and support for these ventures in Europe and Latin America. In one case, the father himself is now engaging in client discussions by framing what the family stands for and what the next generation of venture with a social impact could be. In another case, two next gens from Latin America are now working as entrepreneurs and funders with a clear social and environmental mission as well as expectations of financial returns.

Some families struggle with cross-generational decision-making; when that happens, impact investing—seen as a useful add-on but not a key priority—suffers. One next-gen leader describes his frustration in trying to get a say with, or at least clarity from, his grandfather, the key decision-maker, on how social impact and environmental issues are assessed:

> In my family, that's really not important unless it makes a lot of money. All the focus on investments is on what makes the most money. It's hard to reconcile at times. It's like, "Well, you're not an advisor, so you're not part of the decision . . . ." Based on my experience, [impact investing] probably would be something that would be important for your family to formulate some thoughts around as G5 gets older. You'd probably see more questions and interests expressed among them, and you don't want to just shut it down by saying, "Well, you know, Grandpa is the advisor for our family, so you know, he'll take care of that." And they're kind of like "Stop asking that question—you're irritating us." Then it's, "So do you have a problem with the way we're doing things?" "No! I just want to know if there's a plan. And if we don't have a plan, we probably should have a plan." That's that pushback on the whole, that "we're controlling this, we're doing a good job, and it's none of your business even though your name is on it."

## Corporate Foundations

Another way family enterprises develop social capital is through dedicating a portion of their profits to corporate philanthropy. The family enterprise very often has a philanthropic foundation for the business, which often exists alongside a more personal family foundation. The family has many personal areas of interest to family members that lie far from the interests of their legacy company. Most corporate foundations give to causes that directly or indirectly support the business, for example, promoting health and wellness for employees and their families, endowing local schools with tools and technologies, or supporting the creation of specialized schools to teach rare skills that the company needs in order to thrive.

Generative families express their values about social impact through how they do business and also through foundations centered in their businesses. These foundations are connected both to the owning family and the leaders of the company, who may not be family members. The family shareholders create the company foundation and delegate responsibility but also retain the right to change that decision if conditions change. Here are two examples:

> 1: We agreed that giving is important, but we have different needs. The company also has a charitable strategy and a budget and our board and shareholders support, but we leave the giving decision up to management. It's management's responsibility, not the shareholders', to say what is going to be done with that money. But everybody has agreed that it's a good thing.

*2: My younger brother actually works with my mom in our foundation; we take 10 percent of the profit of our business and put it into a foundation. We have tried to streamline whole foundation activities. We also have an employee giving program, where they can give a percentage to the foundation, a yearly amount to give away. We'd slice and dice it up along with a certain kind of level and like longevity of employees' contracts and everything, so if you're a long time, you would have more money to designate to the charity of your choice. That is under review by our CEO; [it's] something that we as a family felt passionate about in the past, but we're looking at different ways to do that now. He might end up recommending that that still stays in place, so we're letting him take the lead for it being effective.*

In the following case, corporate giving is an outgrowth of the family's deep values and principles, passed on to the company:

*We have a philanthropic committee with four of the six older generation members, and we just appointed two of the younger generation. The chairman of the philanthropic committee works in a simple and straightforward way. The committee's goal is to use the dollars to further the gospels. They don't profess to be the Christian organization, but they're doing good works.*

*They also look at if it's in an area that we own or operate the business and if it is of special interest to the family. They'll put a different request and then manage it in that way. That's one avenue of giving that we do, and that would be done not to benefit the organization but because it's the right thing to do and that's what the Bible tells us to do. The company gives as well. Giving is more of a marketplace giving where they may partner with customers or related to the brand. We give 10 percent of our profits away—tithing.*

Company giving is not done only for the owners alone, but as a reflection of the values of the company, which includes employees. In addition to giving money back each year, a company usually has a mission statement about the purpose of its giving. The company often supports causes of its employees through matching gifts. Sometimes, it becomes involved in issues like education and homelessness that improve the community and make it more livable for everyone but also provide benefit for the company. A company foundation is often started by the company founder to support his or her personal values. While family members participate in this philanthropy alongside other company employees, the company foundation is not free to give to causes and ventures not connected to the company or its community. So family philanthropy may diverge from the company's philanthropy.

One company in a small community, where the family members are the leading citizens, adopted a dual foundation structure:

*The main foundation, connected to the company, funds works projects within the area. We're now expanding its governance. My grandfather set it up to include all his descendants in helping to decide what that foundation supports. It contains a gifts committee, which is everybody. They make donations to traditional and personal places, such as his kids' schools, Boy Scouts, buildings for nonprofits. We'll match people's gifts to schools and then have one major project. Typically, his focus was on local institutions, buildings, and was a popular thing. The other foundation contains just the family officers—my sister and me and our chief financial officer. We have not expanded governance of that foundation.*

Family and company are often partners-in-giving, which helps the family remain connected to the company and allows the latter to embody and align with the family's values. This approach is reflected in this two-paragraph account:

*Every family member is on their own to pursue their interest. What generally happens with our business is that we are so tied into this community. There have been in the past specific projects where a family member will be on that board and we as the board of directors agree to spend our budget for charity at that organization. We made big gifts to the Boys and Girls Club through the family or through the business but with the family's blessing.*

*Our CEO was on the board of the Boys and Girls Club. When it first formed, they were trying to start the organization; that was his pet project, a passion project. As a company, we agreed to give $60,000 a year for five or six years to support that. We do share when we make the pledge. I'm not sure we talk about it every year. It's been something we do consistently. Before that, my father was on the hospice board, and they were trying to build a new building, and we made a similar pledge.*

The following fourth-generation construction company has two foundations, with some overlap. They allow the family to pursue different directions in their personal family giving from the family office:

*A strong theme of philanthropy covers all three family branches. An endowed fund set up by my father in 1964 was always seen as separate from our company. It received $40 million each year from the company. We also had a company foundation that was governed just by current shareholders [and] set up in 2006. We see business as a force for good. In the communities we work, we support education, environment, and thought leadership. We have a CSR committee in the company that covers two-thirds of funding. The rest is funded by company profits and private shareholders for things they care about. We reach out to causes that our eight shareholders support. We have a peer group review of each shareholder's proposals. My nephew took over leadership of the endowed fund from me. It rotates among each of three families. The company foundation works from our family office across all families and is professionally managed.*

Causes are sometimes similar to those of family foundations, such as poverty alleviation and general education, but are nested in the business because they help build the brand as well as social capital for the enterprise. One Australian company supports the poor in its local community and has a huge impact through collaboration with the local business ecosystem, working hand in hand with other local businesses, as recounted in the next two paragraphs:

*We're passionate about education in the dairy industry. This is what the girls have come up with that they would like to do because they're at college at the moment. We would like to provide a scholarship for an individual to go through the four years of the course that they have here. Their second need was placement: within their second year, they will come back to our business, and they would work in the business for twelve months. They'd still have their scholarships that would give them extra income, plus they would be paid their commercial wage. That's the sort of business that we're trying to implement at the moment.*

*We lost our workers by emphasizing too much about education, and it's not that workers aren't educated; it's just that there's a different way of educating for those kinds of hands-on job[s]. We only graduate eight hundred students a year, Australia-wide, in agriculture, and there's four thousand jobs available each year; so we've got a shortfall before we even start. We thought if we have this scholarship program, it might encourage somebody that is trying to go somewhere else without university to think about the dairy industry.*

A second area of action for the corporate foundation is to provide better living conditions for the company's workers and their families in communities where the company has key operations. This is particularly the case for the legacy community, where the family built its wealth, but is also true for new countries where it expands its operations. Housing and health care are the most common areas of investment. Pollution, sanitation, and housing are other priority areas. Many generative families explore and invest in community building and environmentally friendlier communities.

For others, green sustainability is seen as the next generation of real estate diversification. Many generative families have large real estate portfolios and, led by their next generation, are considering testing the concept in their next wave of real estate development. For many, the focus is on technology and "green buildings" certification. These families are following in the footsteps of CBRE, the real estate pioneer, which has proven that the concept of green buildings, with water and energy-efficient systems, is both sustainable and profitable. Some are focusing on higher-end construction for environmentally conscious millennials. Another family, also under the impetus of the next generation, is focusing on building eco-friendly housing with rainwater harvesting and solar water heaters as part of the family portfolio of affordable housing in Asia. Historically, this family has been focused on creating affordable housing for the emerging lower middle class. They see sustainability primarily as a way to make buildings cheaper to maintain through more energy and water efficiencies. These projects are viewed as strategic investments and screened for a maximum fit with both family values and their core competencies.

A final endeavor of families, through corporate foundations, is the creation of more specific training programs and corporate universities focused on business skills, especially those perceived to be imperiled by societal shifts or lack of institutional support. They want to offer educational opportunities to their employees because they regard them as "members of the family" and also because this is an investment of human capital that benefits their long-term success. Many corporate foundations find that these programs are win/win: helping their employees develop marketable skills, which enable them to get promotions within or outside of their organization and also benefiting the business by providing a better caliber of employees, particularly in industries where skilled employees are hard to find and keep. These programs range from teaching craft and construction to engineering and hospitality.

## Enriching the Community

As the family moves away from direct involvement in company operations, there is a question of whether the family—now with many members who live in different places—can continue to hold a shared identity and work together. Many generative families launch new businesses, and corporate foundations grow with the business success. For others, community and philanthropic activities take the place of business operations, but the family brings its business expertise to focus on sustainable actions, for example, through a mix of gifts, loans, and seed investing in exchange for a seat on the board.

This may be encouraged by local incentives, too.

In the United States, a family can give stock to a foundation and use the profits for philanthropy. The company gives profits to the community but retains voting rights over the stock, keeping control in the family. As one such family member says, *"We have one shareholder that's not a family member, the Community Foundation. We've set up a donor-advised fund through them. The reason we did that is so that people could gift company stock to the foundation. Then over time, through an organized repurchase through the community, the company will buy back that stock."*

The following stories, from families on two sides of the world, exemplify the importance of recommitment to the community and the scale of the results that can come of these efforts.

## The Beacon: A Legacy Community Foundation

This legacy business has been transformed several times over generations, but it still exists after more than a century as a large public company. This is the story of how a fifth-generation family leader stewarded a community service project for the rising generations of the family as a vehicle to express family values and keep them connected to the community where the legacy company resided. This allows the family to build social capital after generations of success. This venture has now become the glue attracting far-flung family members to visit the company and continue to identify with their community of origin.

*There was tremendous symbiosis between a growing company and the small town. Its values informed the values of the company and helping the small town. Family members grew up with a very strong sense of responsibility and commitment to the community.*

*Philanthropy, started by my generation twenty years ago, is the mechanism to keep the family together and attract the younger generation. There was this tremendous symbiosis between our growing company and the small town where it was based. All the family branches grew up in the town with a strong sense of responsibility, commitment to the community and the company. The town felt the same way.*

*We saw philanthropy as one way to keep a family together. Out of one of our meetings came the genesis of what is now called the Beacon Fund. A few of us got together and raised $10,000 by passing the hat amongst our generation. We gave to the local area youth center, an organization my grandmother had been involved in, focused on kids at risk in the three counties where our wealth was generated.*

*Every year we'd raise more, from the assets of the sixth generation. Every year as it grew, we would write letters to the broader family, and we started to get more contributions from the fifth generation. In twenty years, the Beacon Fund has become quite large, and now we give away over $200,000 a year. We still raise money every year from family members, but ten years ago the fifth*

*(continued)*

*(Continued)*

*generation decided to merge one of their foundations that had some assets that were not actively managed, so we grew that way.*

*We give regularly to twenty or thirty organizations. We have ten board members from all branches of the family. At the beginning, it was blood, sweat, and tears where we were all very serious about it—each of us would read the grant proposals. The family office was incredibly helpful administering this, but we were just a board. Our board is separate from the family council, with lots of overlap; if you wanted to be on the board, you could be on it. The only requirement was that you have to give a little money and willingly contact organizations that applied for grants to learn more about them, write that up, make a case why you should support that particular organization, and then follow that organization. If we did make a grant, you were expected to continue to stay in touch with the organization.*

*It brought family members who didn't have a lot of connection with the area back there; people got quite excited about relationships with these organizations. Over time as we've grown, as we've had more assets and some capital campaigns, we hired a part-time executive director because none of us live there now. We've just made a successful transition to our second executive director, which made a tremendous difference, so we're giving grants directly to service organizations—capacity building grants. We're convening meetings of different funding organizations in the community, and we're about to go off to a big family gathering there. And while our "family council" has been difficult to maintain, the real glue has been the Beacon Fund because that's been an attraction for different branches. Those have gotten involved and excited, and the family recognizes that it's actually making a difference in the community where the wealth was generated.*

*We had a come-to-Jesus moment in 2010. I had just taken over as chairman of our trust company. We were all wondering, "What's the future, and what's the point?" If a new generation is going to step up, it can't be the same people doing all the work. The Fund is doing good, but that was chugging along on its own. It gathers every year, in person and lots of conference calls. New people became involved.*

*Our challenge is that we're spending lots of time planning social events but also celebrating our legacy, stories about the past, reeducating folks about the company and various family leaders. My cousin and I have been working on filming fifth-generation members still around and filling that in with memories from our generation of their parents and grandparents; getting lots of family photos. The focus from the involvement standpoint is going to be the Beacon Fund, where a core family value is giving back.*

*People get that intuitively and admire and appreciate what the Beacon is doing, but they also recognize this is the family effort. They're doing it with their families, and it makes people feel good as we enter our seventh generation. We started an internship program allowing college-age G7 folks to come back to work at some of the social service agencies.*

*We have a younger generation board that we give money to give away. They ask agencies to make specific requests for that group and when we gather—these are our children—and make decisions. We hope that this catches on. It's a mini version of the Beacon. Over the course of the year, they have one call with the director and talk about the areas they're interested in. They also are asked to give money directly to the Fund. We want them to give a little bit themselves, so then they've got to dig deep into their pockets and come up with some cash. And then that cash is supplemented. The executive director receives a few proposals from some of the agencies that we work with in the community, and they gather—when we have our annual Fund meeting, the kids come, too. They have a day where they talk about the proposals and visit the agencies and see it and then vote on where they want the money to go. Then they come back and present to the senior board, telling us why they gave the money. Some kids are more engaged than others. I am still on the board of the local company museum, which I enjoy, that brings me back to the community. The Fund also brings the various groups in the family and a growing group there every year. Our family trust company is still based there.*

## A Large-Scale Social Entrepreneurship Endeavor

The ethic of this Asian company means that the company is always aware that the dedication of many community members over generations has contributed to the family's wealth and success. They own the community because their continual support is a big reason for their success. Social responsibility is a recognition of respect for the "gift" it has received from the community. This is a characteristic of Asian businesses and families, who see themselves as deeply connected and obligated to their communities.

*My grandfather, the guy who started everything, began the social enterprise, the charity. He would support religious orders, people on the streets. My father formalized the foundation, so I am currently the president. It's forty-six years old; we have 160 team leaders on staff. We have major projects, which involve heritage, finance, education; it works with science and technology. The business needs skilled and educated workers.*

*We are firm believers in addressing and preparing youth to take advantage of opportunities in the future. We've been doing this for a long time, involve our employees in the programs, get the managers involved and part of the community. In [our country], where we don't have a social safety net, things aren't perfect, so we're pitching in and doing our share. It's done for other motives in addition to nation-building and leadership. A lot of family members have been involved in projects like that.*

*I got a phone call this morning from one of my cousins whose son has to go to Uganda for a mission; they are asking us to support his work. We encourage this; it provides us a wonderful reputation in the community. It's the way we work, it's tradition, formalized and institutionalized in our foundations, so we're very happy with every opportunity to engage in nation-building.*

*Our reputation is very important: how we are viewed, the way we operate, and the respect we've earned over the years. Our main success will be in terms of planning because we're a public company and we have responsibility toward our stockholders, the public. Being one of the larger corporations in [our country], we want to keep that trust investors have in us, and we do this by helping more people down the line in our community.*

*Those are the main issues in our foundation, which are national in scope. We meet regularly with the Secretary of Public Works because we are accountable for the success coming our way to the country. It's not just the business now; it's the country we're looking at. We have a growth rate of 6.5 percent last year; that's going to continue this year. We're the largest service [of our kind] in the world, more than India, and need a higher level of intellectual capital to staff the back-office center we're now engineering, so a lot of opportunities coming our way. As we create more and more wealth, we place more stress on the environment and on our infrastructure. We're addressing the next fifty years. We're also taking on the major issues and working with government, collaborating to get things done.*

*Our next generation are members of the foundation, on boards, and acting as operators that administer programs in their own areas. They're very much involved, and we do this with great respect and pleasure. It's not a person, it's part of our DNA, our work, and it's not just us, it's also our citizens, the community where we work.*

While not every generative family adopts all these practices, we see an interest in CRS, impact investing, and corporate philanthropy growing in almost all of our generative families. After generations of financial profit, they begin to focus on development of social capital. It is hard not to connect this focus, especially when it emerges more forcefully from the younger generations, as a key element in sustaining commitment and generating innovation in family enterprises. While this is increasing in nonfamily companies as well, the initiative and leadership for many of these practices is coming from business families.

## Taking Action in Your Own Family Enterprise

### Assessing Family CSR and Social Impact

To develop your enterprise social impact program, a family can assess where they are in relation to company and financial impact, CSR and sustainability, and in their community. Social impact begins with developing shared meaning and purpose on what social impact and sustainability means to the family. It includes the nature of the family's commitment to their values in relation to community service, investments, and culture of their businesses. To make these a reality, the entire family must together consider their values, how they are expressed in important areas, and how they act on them.

This assessment tool is for families to explore their current and planned future actions related to sustainability and social responsibility. It looks at **family** activities separate from their business, and how they, as owners, collaborate and guide their **business**. It begins with your preparation for a family impact meeting where the family meets to consider where they are and how they can expand their efforts to support and embody social impact.

As a successful business family, the family must look at how they use their human, social, and financial capital and the messages and direction that they give to the next generation. It is helpful to reflect where you are now as a family. This assessment can help you convene your family to define and review your family values, as you consider where you want to go, and which of the possibilities you want to embrace. We encourage family members from all generations to participate and be part of this conversation.

**Filling out your Assessment.** Each family member fills out the assessment as best they can, understanding that each family member experiences the family differently. Those who marry in and those of different generations may have different views. Members of the family can share their scores to begin a discussion together about their journey forward. For each practice, indicate in the **Current** column, on a scale of 1–3, how each statement reflects the practice of your family at this time. Circle the number for your response to each question, reflecting how you see your family:

3= Very true of our family

2= Somewhat true of our family

1= Not relevant or not true about our family

For the business and family assessment, total the numbers you have circled.

Rather than view a particular score as positive or negative, use the scores and differences to guide a family discussion of these areas, and how to expand family efforts.

| Support for Business CSR, Impact, and Sustainability | |
|---|---|
| As owners, the family sends a message to their business about what is important, both in terms of results and in terms of how it acts with employees, customers and the community. Without a clear message from the family owners, the company may not be clear to what degree and/or how to create a path to sustainability. | |
| 1 Our family has defined CSR and sustainability focus areas and goals for our family enterprises. | 3 2 1 |
| 2 Our family values are embedded in the culture, strategy, and policies of our family enterprises. | |
| 3 Family members have explored, and are aware of the impact our company has on the lives and livelihood of our community and the environment. | 3 2 1 |
| 4 Family members are aware of and actively support CSR and sustainability efforts in our business and investments. | 3 2 1 |
| 5 When required, the family seeks outside expertise on social responsibility and sustainability for our business. | 3 2 1 |
| 6 Family members who are board members or employees are active, visible leaders in company sustainability efforts. | 3 2 1 |
| 7 Board and company leaders brief the family on company issues related to CSR and sustainability. | 3 2 1 |
| 8 The family supports our business/financial enterprises in developing a clear and public values statement, which incorporates family values in its operations, products, and employment practices. | 3 2 1 |
| 9 The company reports to the family the outcome of its activities related to values, operations, products, and employment practices. | 3 2 1 |
| 10 Our family enterprises assess their impact and are accountable for results. | 3 2 1 |
| **TOTAL** | |

| Family Leadership for Community Transformation | |
|---|---|
| Because of their name, a business family is visible in their community. The activities and leadership of family members is important and reflects how others see them. Sustainability has to do with the way that the family takes on its role and leadership in community leadership and philanthropy and service. | |
| 1 Our family has cross-generational conversations about the purpose and use of our family wealth. | 3 2 1 |
| 2 The family considers social impact as well as profit in its financial and investment decisions. | 3 2 1 |
| 3 We take pride in our family's reputation in the community. | 3 2 1 |
| 4 Family members are active and visible in community events that support sustainability, community thriving and social responsibility. | 3 2 1 |
| 5 Family members regularly share with each other what they are doing in service and community affairs. | 3 2 1 |
| 6 Our family has policies to decide how much to give to investing in community needs and efforts. | 3 2 1 |
| 7 Family members receive support from the family to work in community service efforts. | 3 2 1 |
| 8 We have a shared family philanthropic policy that guides our giving. | 3 2 1 |
| 9 Young family members are engaged in and informed about family philanthropy. | 3 2 1 |
| 10 Family members are encouraged to be active on nonprofit boards. | 3 2 1 |
| **TOTAL** | |

## Defining Family Impact Vision and Values

The assessment will highlight many perspectives for your family about what impact means, and what you want to do. Your family should invite the family members to hold a family impact conversation to define their values and vision for their wealth. In addition to supporting and caring for each other, what do we want to see as the impact of our wealth? What is the purpose of our family wealth?

There are two parts to this conversation, which may involve different people. The family will consider how it wants to use its social capital to make a difference in the world. While different generations and family members have different roles in this decision, everyone in the family has an interest in this question. This may be more than a single family meeting. The purpose is to define a vision of what you want to see in the world, and how you see using the family resources to make a difference.

The other conversation is about the family legacy business, the family office or family assets and investment. This conversation may also include nonfamily business or financial leaders. Or the family might set some guidelines from their conversation and then turn the conversation over to the business and financial leaders to apply them.

Each of these conversations may begin with a larger group and then be passed to a task force that will define more clearly options and directions for family social impact.

## Notes

1.  In addition to accounts from the generative families in this study, this chapter also contains material that was gathered as part of a broader project. That material comes from interviews with social impact leaders and confidential interviews with families of Hult University students, (Hult) as well as historical and public information about social responsibility in family enterprises.
2.  Milton Friedman, "The Social Responsibility of Business Is to Increase Its Profits," *New York Times Magazine*, September 13, 1970, http://umich.edu/~thecore/doc/Friedman .pdf.
3.  Larry Fink, "2019 Letter to CEOs: Purpose and Profit," BlackRock, 2019, https://www .blackrock.com/corporate/investor-relations/larry-fink-ceo-letter.
4.  Sharna Goldseker and Michael Moody, *Generation Impact: How Next Gen Donors Are Revolutionizing Giving* (Hoboken, NJ: John Wiley & Sons, 2017).
5.  Carlo Caserio and Francesco Napoli, "Corporate Social Responsibility and Family Business: An Overview," *African Journal of Business Management* 10, no. 24 (2016): 594.
6.  Hermès International, "2018 Registration Document Including the Annual Financial Report," Hermès International, April 10, 2019, 5, https://finance.hermes.com/var/ finances/storage/original/application/c08f97609ecbee3439f50d89baaa5ff5.pdf.
7.  Ibid.
8.  Bloomberg, *The Future of Family Offices*, 2017, 11, https://data.bloomberglp.com/ professional/sites/10/The-Future-of-Family-Offices.pdf.
9.  https://www.fondation-entreprendre.org/la-fondation/.
10. Ibid.
11. Erin Carlyle, "Liesel Pritzker Simmons Sued Her Family and Got $500 Million, But She's No Trust Fund Baby," *Forbes*, November 17, 2013, https://www.forbes.com/sites/ erincarlyle/2013/11/17/liesel-pritzker-simmons-sued-her-family-and-got-500-million-but-shes-no-trust-fund-baby/#3ff4c1e3464c.

CHAPTER

8

# Owners' Mindset

## Stewardship and the Board of Directors

A family business is founded by a visionary who is also its chief executive. An owner/manager is lord of the mansion, answerable to nobody. Since both roles rest in one person, the challenge of aligning stakeholders is nonexistent. The founder therefore finds it hard to imagine the challenges facing future generations, where many people share or compete for these roles. When the family struggles to delegate roles and overcome differences, the founder offers little guidance.

Subsequent generations often continue to view ownership as connected with operations. However, as a third generation comes of age, and the legacy business is harvested, generative family members discover that ownership is quite different from operations. As owners, family members are now once removed from being hands-on. They must learn to delegate and trust others. Owners make decisions about the fate of the business, balance the use of resources, and recruit and oversee the work of non-family executives and advisors. They have to make major decisions together about who will lead the business, what direction it will take, and how it will use its resources. They also have to decide how to use their wealth: How much should be reinvested, used for the benefit of the family, or employed for other purposes like philanthropy? As owners, their focus shifts from operating a business to overseeing family and nonfamily leaders and making choices about resources. They must adapt and make strategic shifts that may supersede existing policies that have long been in practice.

So much to decide and so little guidance—this is the next-generation dilemma. A family enterprise can run on an ad hoc basis with little defined structure for at most two generations. But danger lies ahead. At some point, the business will become too complex to manage informally, and conflicts may emerge among family members. One third-generation family member notes, *"The key problem was lack of clarity in the organization about basic goals and mission and in understanding who decides these things. There were no job descriptions and no contracts for family members working in the business, so everything was up in the air."*

This chapter is about how the generative family transitions from operational owner/managers into roles as owners, exercising oversight over their family vision, values, and culture indirectly, through governance and board membership rather than as operating executives. A board of directors enables the family to exercise active leadership as they extend their ownership from one legacy business to several, or into a family office or portfolio of assets. Active oversight also enables members of rising generations to express their values and become leaders and enables a family with growing diversity to achieve alignment a cross generations.

To attend to the opinions, concerns, and needs of all the family shareholders, generative families convene multiple family or owners' groups who advise and raise issues to the family leaders (I will expand on this in a later section). Generative families must develop a unified *owners' group* with a long-term vision and perspective. The number of owners may become too large or may themselves lack the expertise to oversee the business. So they appoint a *board of directors*, which both represents the interests of the owners and provides the professional expertise to make the business successful. As an engaged board of directors is developed with significant input from independent, nonfamily directors, stewardship is expressed through governance and the oversight of family enterprises.

The third generation usually contains more family owners than can sit comfortably together around a table. Hence, they must organize some form of representative group to manage their interests. They can't all exercise direct oversight. Because young family members are continually coming of age, the elder owners also want to listen to the interests of those who will eventually become owners. To sustain a vibrant portfolio of business and financial activities, the multigenerational family develops business governance mechanisms composed of oversight entities. At its center, for example, the "board of directors" is a creation of the owners and usually includes both family members and independent, nonfamily members who are not owners. The board oversees, sustains, and develops the family enterprise for the growing number of owners.

Rising generations may not easily understand the difference between management and ownership. First- and second-generation leaders are often hands-on business owner/operators. They tend to see ownership as holding title to a property and doing what has to be done, not as a complex responsibility to indirectly oversee business operations. But as more family members who do not expect to be operators grow up, the ownership role becomes increasingly important. As members of the third and fourth generations come of age, they become more aware of the tasks and functions of their role as owners. Family members want to learn how exactly they can make appropriate decisions about their business while delegating operations to nonfamily leaders.

As we have seen in previous chapters, generative families' transition from family business to business family is more than a change in how the company is managed. Family members lose autonomy as they submit to the discipline of a professional business and adopt the role of responsible owners. They can no longer intervene directly, or use the business as a personal bank or employment resource. Even if there is one single family successor, the family has to move beyond being taken care of by this leader and exercise active responsibility for oversight. Leadership has limits as well as prerogatives.

To create, sustain, and adapt the family culture and values over generations, family members must be aligned, make fast and effective business decisions, and implement them. Shared cultural values, policies, and practices do not just emerge.

The family has to develop and sustain them by resolving differences and making painful choices. There is often family upheaval as owner/managers must change their behavior and become more accountable. The process by which the family owners collectively organize themselves to develop resilience by balancing internal family needs and external business challenges is *business governance*. Through each successive generation, generative families evolve more active and complex governance systems. They listen to many voices and resources and translate what they learn into effective operations, clear decisions, and adaptive responses to new challenges.

Family business leader Sir Adrian Cadbury defines corporate governance as being "concerned with holding the balance between economic and social goals and between individual and communal goals. The corporate governance framework is there to encourage the efficient use of resources and equally to require accountability for the stewardship of those resources. The aim is to align as nearly as possible the interests of individuals, corporations and society."[1] In the case of a family enterprise, governance has to link family, individual, company, and society, and hence adds an additional layer of complexity.

By G3, a generative family must manage a large growing family; many of their descendants are, or will become, owners. Governance emerges in both family and business systems, which interact and work together. I add to Cadbury's formulation by defining family enterprise governance as creating clarity and alignment about purposes, boundaries, agreements, participation, policies, and roles to help the whole family work together effectively across generations, to transfer its business and wealth while maintaining family harmony, good returns on investments, and the desired social impact.

Business governance is the structure by which disparate elements of the generative alliance become aligned and integrated to set a clear, expansive, and unified path for business and financial entities. The family needs to balance the voices and perspectives of each group of stakeholders: mature family owners, young family owners-to-be, married-in spouses, key family executives, and advisors. They often don't agree. Different views are raised and balanced within the family ownership group and the board. Out of this, decisions are made that serve the multiple purposes and constituencies of the family.

In a public company, the major responsibility of being an owner is to make sure one's self-interest benefits by the choices made by the business. However, ownership in a long-lived generative family enterprise is more than just a business role. As we have seen, the family has other goals for its wealth and resources. Family owners must balance the needs of the business with the other needs and desires of the family. In addition to making profit, family enterprises want to create value in their human, relationship, and social capital. To do this, the owner's role is defined more broadly as that of a *steward* for the family. While the owners look after their personal self-interest, they also factor in the long-term interest of the family as a whole. A steward is not just benefiting personally but also taking care that the business is sustained and ready for the next generation.

Because owners have ultimate control over family ventures, they must exercise it actively and responsibly. They have to stay informed, make tough choices, and ensure they are implemented. Even when they appoint a board, there remain areas where family owners must decide and act. The board asks the owners to tell them the general direction they want for the business, how much risk and reinvestment there will be, and what values the enterprise will be based upon. As each generation adds new owners, they return to these questions at regular intervals. Agreements that limit voting control to those with special classes of stock or to trustees must be taken into account. But because this is a family, the formal owners usually want to listen to views and concerns beyond a narrow leadership circle. Unlike a nonfamily company, they listen seriously to the views and ideas of their rising generation who look forward to future ownership.

## Beyond Self-Interest: Becoming Stewards

What does it mean to be an owner of a family enterprise? Family members go through a learning process to take up this complex role. Responsible family owners develop the capability to oversee businesses and investments that may have grown to huge proportions. In many family businesses, serving on the board is a passive activity: attending an annual meeting, hearing a report from the CEO, and then having a good dinner. Taking this stance, however, defers authority to the CEO, who may or may not be a family member, with the board just making sure that profits are delivered to the owners. This does not allow the board to oversee the broader goals and values of the family, or to push the enterprise in new directions.

Every family enterprise must consider what kind of owners that family members want to be. A generative family embodies active, engaged ownership, actively engaged in the values and culture of its family enterprise. They are informed and create a vision for their various ventures. The family owners see themselves as stewards, producing wealth that has lasting and appreciating value with an eye toward providing for generations to come. Together, family owners share values and are aligned about what they want and where they are going. As owner/stewards, they are active, thoughtful, vigilant, and resilient in how they exercise their care for the family enterprises. Stewardship is difficult to mandate; it is a complex conception of responsibility that is part of the culture of the family enterprise. It is learned, absorbed, accepted, and internalized by the whole extended family, and it needs both time and talent from family owners.

Even though ownership is dispersed among many family members, the family wants to ensure that control over major decisions is in the hands of those who protect and look after *all* family members, not just the most prominent current owners. Many family enterprises are weakened because individual needs are not subjugated to those of the family as a whole. Stewardship arises when owners shift from maintaining a personal agenda to considering the best interests of all the family stakeholders. Such owners may even go beyond the family, adding concern for nonfamily leaders, employees, and others in the community. Stewardship is a form of self-interested altruism.

Active owner/stewards see themselves as answering to several nonowner stakeholder constituencies:

- Nonowning family members, especially the rising generations of young family members and married-in family members

- Employees, suppliers, and customers who can be deeply connected to the family
- Community members who are affected by them and who influence their actions

A steward is more than a fiduciary who looks out for the best interests of the individual business. A steward also feels a responsibility to future owners and others who are affected by the enterprise. This is a broader perspective than that of a passive, less involved owner. It leads the steward to be concerned about conflicts between short- and long-term goals and disagreements among different stakeholder groups. Taking this broad a view of one's actions is not a natural or easy practice; one must be emotionally intelligent enough to move beyond narrow self-interest and search out future consequences of actions.

### Stewards Oversee Family and Business

By G3, the extended family has formed a family "tribe" with shared values, personal relationships, and shared family assets. Therefore, when the board members (and/or the owners and trustees) make business and financial decisions, they feel a responsibility to be attuned to the views of constituents who may not be owners. This sense of responsibility differs significantly from the approach of a board in a nonfamily business, where responsibility is defined more narrowly.

Business governance is only one facet of the governance practices of a generative family. They must also develop a parallel structure of governance and regulation of its activities as a family. This is *family governance* and will be the subject of chapters that follow. A generative family contains both of these "two pillars" of governance:

- Family organization through a family council and assembly of all family members
- Business organization of the business by a board of directors and perhaps an owners' council

These two pillars—family council and board—are highly interconnected when it comes to overseeing the family enterprise. With these two governance entities, the family now requires not just a single business leader but multiple leaders for different governance entities.

Here is an example of one family's governance process and the documents that define their interconnection and boundary:

> We have a shareholder agreement that lasts ten years, and then we update or renew it. Company bylaws guide the business. The first document the family council developed was a family charter. It talks about what we're committed to—our core values and purpose as a family.
>
> The family charter sets the direction for the family within the family council. One of the big distinctions it makes is between the "business of the family" as opposed to the "business of the business." If we ever have to ask at a meeting if a topic is something we should be talking about or just the business of the business, somebody will say, "Wait a minute. I think we're almost crossing the line here." We can always get clarification if we need it.

*We've also developed an owners' plan, a document the family council generates and presents to the board each year. This plan gives direction about the interests of the family with regard to the business. We've found this to be quite useful, and the board has acknowledged that they find it useful to get the family's input on the direction of the company. The plan includes things like the level of risk we're comfortable with. And if, for example, the family says it's comfortable with moderate risk, the plan even defines what we mean by moderate risk. This owners' plan hasn't changed much year to year, but we tweak it a little to get clarification based on the feedback and questions from the board. We've found this to be a valuable document for both sides.*

A family enterprise may also become a public company, which includes non-family owners. Even when the family has majority control over the business, the owners must balance family and broader interests. When a family business goes public or when ownership is placed in a trust, the new status often means that previous family perks and practices can no longer continue. The family has to understand why this is necessary and learn other ways to balance personal and business needs. The owners' role radically shifts with the form of the business, as this account illustrates:

*From 2004 onward, the family council started evolving toward the trust structure. In the past, my grandfather simply decided how to use the money through an informal system of family benefits he provided to his children. Back then, it was just his children; the grandchildren, like me, were very young. When we went public in 2004, we had to clarify the share structure. When your company is not listed, management can mingle personal and company money, but the listing process required us to clean up the share ownership process and the trust.*

*Two days from now, we're going to sign the family agreement that governs the relationship between my father and his trust and the rest of the family. My parents still control 35 percent of these shares, but the remaining 65 percent are in a trust to benefit future generations and provide liquidity for every branch of the family. The 35 percent funds the family office and will be used for family benefits and philanthropy. It also provides a single voting block for business decisions. The trustee, my father, has 35 percent voting rights. He named me successor trustee, so I will have to manage family involvement in the future. I will have control not only of my own shares but also the voting rights of the trust.*

*Another distribution goes to family owners whether or not they work in the business. Family members that work in the business get a market rate salary and bonus. The trustee balances family and business needs. Our challenge will come thirty years in the future when more family members may demand a high dividend.*

*Our investment committee meets quarterly, more often when there is an investment decision. I told my dad after the signing, "Dad, you cannot be in control of all these decisions. You must allow for a democratic process and let me manage the business with my brothers." We presented the case for major investment decisions and a secret ballot to approve them. We stated that the minority must respect the majority and that vetoing should be done very, very seldom. We told him, "You must allow this process to happen because you won't be around forever. It's best that we start to work on this now while you're still here."*

## Transparency and the Voice of the Family

Another quality of the initial wealth-creating generation is a tendency for the founder/leader to hold back information. Since he is the sole decision-maker, he isn't sure why information should be shared or why family members need to know. If they want information, he feels they don't trust him and are "checking up" on him.

In this paternalistic view of many founders, informing family members is low priority. Even the second generation may not discuss business issues with the nonowning family members. Instead, family owners may be kept in the dark by elders, as this family member reports, *"I went once a year to an event there, but I was sometimes ashamed because I knew so little about it. Dad didn't really tell much, and we didn't really ask. We didn't discuss how the family and the business intermingled until recently."*

But as more family members become owners, they must have access to layers of business information. The family shifts from a closed, secretive system to an open one, and this shift represents a cultural transformation. Since the older generation are majority owners with control, it is sometimes difficult for them to understand why they should share information with other family members. Generative families report a cultural shift in the second or third generation from a closed to an open, transparent approach to business information. The family becomes more comfortable sharing information and initiating some give-and-take about business and financial operations. This is particularly important as the older generation prepares the rising generation for leadership.

By the third generation, the family has learned the importance of sharing business information beyond the circle of major owners:

*Transparency obviously has been a huge push for us even in our business meetings. We start with just us—none of our executives—and we talk about our vision for the company, where we're going in the next year, what things we think are important about last year's performance, and plans for the future. We field a few questions from the audience, then go through the financials with our CFO. Next, the auditor comes in, and they get to ask him questions. Finally, the executives come in and present plans for each division.*

Generative families create policies and activities that actively include family shareholders in governance, even if they have no formal authority or just a small ownership stake, as this family illustrates:

*Every six months, we have a shareholders' meeting in which all family members from age sixteen and above learn about the financial performance of the business. We present the key strategic issues in each area of the business. We start with the vision and values, and we keep reinforcing them. Each time a new young member enters, we stress them vigorously to inculcate in them where we're coming from and where we've been.*

*We have a family council, ownership council, and advisory board. The ownership council comprises those members of the family who have been working within the business; most of them evolved from the former business eighteen years ago. The ownership council ensures that the advisory board oversees the appointment of the CEO and gauges his or her performance. The ownership council also oversees the bigger picture; deciding on the direction of the business is part of their role. The ownership council created the family constitution and periodically reviews and modifies it. For a while, it met quarterly; now it's every six months.*

While the family owners and their designated board control the business, generative families are unique because they also take pains to communicate with all family members. They are prepared to listen to concerns and ideas from all parts of the family, including younger and other nonowning family members and those whose ownership is in trust. Feedback from the family helps the owners to become aware of significant disagreements.

For example, there might be disagreements about important matters like the sale of the business, major new investments, or new directions for the company. Listening to feedback can also make them aware of new ideas and opportunities. This transparency is important because new-generation family members—the children of these nonowners—will eventually become owners. The family realizes that informing them about the business and including them in discussions is critical for responsible future ownership. But this transparency and listening must also include the understanding that their input is strictly advisory and that the business leaders must make their own decisions.

For example, in one family led by two third-generation leaders, several talented G4 members were coming of age. While the board and ownership were in the third generation, they had a policy inviting young G4 family members to attend board meetings from the age of 18. Two young sons attended every meeting, and with their professional education and outside experience, they began to propose new opportunities for the family, which had recently sold its large consumer business and was seeking new directions to restart growth. The sons wanted to be part of the future and were not particularly concerned about when they would become owners or join the board formally.

Here are two accounts of how transparency invites family members to become involved and promotes family engagement and an attitude of stewardship within growing generative families with many family ventures to oversee:

## Transparency as a Path to Greater Family Engagement

Other generative families go through stages to develop transparency. Small family shareholders may not be fully informed about the business. Since all family members can't serve on the board, the family must develop opportunities to communicate with the board, learn about the board's decisions, and have a voice within those decisions. Here's how one family accomplished this:

*During our annual family meeting, we have one day in which the managers spend eight hours with the family talking about what's going on with the business. Then we do a half-day roundtable with the CEO and whoever he brings with him. Five or six people from management give talks to the family. That's a much smaller group, so you get a better sense of what the family is thinking about*

*(continued)*

*and what the business is doing. As the family chair of the board, I personally do presentations. This year, we are also going to all the sites around the world to talk about what the family is doing in terms of the transition. They know that the nonfamily CEO is reaching retirement, so we want to make sure that we close the circle in terms of communication.*

*We have a family information meeting and lunch every second Tuesday. We get all family members working within the business to join us for an update on what's going on. The things we discuss may not all be business-related; the purpose is just to keep the family working together, involved together, and knowing each other.*

*It's critical to our success that communication channels with family members remain transparent in both directions; that's the only way to ensure that there's trust and harmony and support from the family. The day that trust breaks down is the day we'll lose the support of family members. Things will start falling apart if this becomes a widespread failing.*

*The next generation voiced their concern for a more explicit system. It's been a learning process for everyone. I got involved very young because my parents told me that you're in a better position to participate than us, so go ahead.*

*The family has a high level of integrity about our planning and structure governance. Those who choose not to be actively involved in the family can get information about why the family money is being handled in a certain way or why we're involved in certain businesses. We always try our very best to have individuals at the top of the industry involved alongside us; these include outside board members and directors.*

*G5 members said that they wanted to be more involved but acknowledged that they never opened the board packets. So a number of years ago, we went electronic with our board packages so everyone in generations four and five gets a copy of a packet before every meeting. These packets include budgets, financials, investment portfolios, the minutes from every committee meeting, and all the ranch management board issues they are drafting. Many family members that aren't on the board don't open the board packets, but each person has to acknowledge that the information is there and decide how they are going to use it.*

*When we started, there was zero visibility on the value of the business—no transparency or actual figures to review in terms of margin or five-year plans. We would just have a very short presentation of general figures and dividends, and that was it. Then some family shareholders started to ask questions about the management and the structure of the company. My family Group A has been much more directly involved than family Group B. So, shareholders in Group B started asking, "Why aren't you more transparent to shareholders?"*

## Who Is Responsible for Transparency in a Huge Family Enterprise?

A sixth-generation family with several hundred family shareholders operated with high transparency and inclusiveness. But the whole family together was too large an entity to decide business policy directly, so it created a full-time role of family president. As the family president explains, his role was to organize the business so that the family could give responsible and thoughtful input:

*In terms of the board of the company, there is always a preference given to family members. They make up the majority of the board, but over the years we've also welcomed nonfamily board members. We hired our first nonfamily CEO twelve years ago, and he's worked out extremely well. At that time—around 2001—my position as family president was created. People didn't know the new CEO very well and weren't confident that he could handle both the business and the family side of*

*(continued)*

*(Continued)*

things. Every CEO before that had been a family member and wore both hats. At this time, however, we decided to split the position into a two-leader system of governance: CEO and family president.

Having a family president then gave rise to the idea of a family council. The family president is essentially the chairman of the family council. Before that, we had a human resource committee of family members who would advise the family member president on family matters. Now, with the family council, we have a more formal arrangement for discussing family issues. One responsibility of the family president and the family council is to maintain the interest of the family in the business.

I sit on the board of directors. My job, along with the other family directors, is to make sure that business decisions track with family values. I'm asked, "How would the family feel about this?" Then I go back to the family council and use it as a sounding board to test ideas in the family. I also run family programs, including the big annual meeting. I have some staff allocated, and a family council committee helps plan it. This is a big part of our job because it's a huge meeting, and it's always pretty complicated.

There are now more places for family members to be involved. Someday we might have a new family member step up and be our CEO. Our nominating committee is unique. It's not a nominating committee for the board, but a hybrid of board members, family members, and family council members. Board members from the family are elected by this hybrid council, as are associate directors. The nominating committee nominates the family president, the board endorses the nomination, and the family votes on that position.

We have the same problems that everybody does: people apply, and if you don't give them the position, they're not happy. When it comes to the family council, we're usually looking for a certain talent. We try to home in on that in the job description so that when people apply, they get that we're looking, for example, for a younger person with social media skills. I think all nominating committees struggle with how people feel when they're rejected; we certainly don't have that one figured out.

We're trying to be conscious of the future through a strategic long-range planning exercise we do every ten years. We try to look at what lies ahead so that the new leaders of the business and the family will be ready and committed to both.

## Designing a Professional Board of Directors

A board of directors is the core instrument for a family enterprise to sustain its distinctive culture and exercise values-based oversight. It upholds the family's legacy and values and defines the relationships among owners and across generations. It also is the vehicle for anticipating and initiating change to take advantage of new possibilities or respond to crises. In its formative stage, the board usually contains just the owners. But as time passes, the board takes on an expanded role. While the board represents the owners, it eventually adds independent members who have the requisite experience to implement the intentions of the owners (and in a family, sometimes also the owners-to-be) in the most professional way. Bringing independent members to the board is important because the business needs skills for oversight that may not reside in the family. They are a resource representing the owners, not the owners themselves. As a generative family develops, the board evolves through several stages; as the business and family become more complex, the board moves to a higher level of development.

### Duties of Board Members

Because this is a family enterprise, the board has the added responsibility of considering the concerns of family members. The board needs to keep family members informed about decisions and the reasons behind them while remaining mindful of the concerns, ideas, and values of all members of the family. Family members who serve on the board need to adopt a different mindset. Instead of looking out for their own family or branch, they now are asked to consider the needs of the entire family. A family member must be tutored in this ownership mindset before going onto the board.

Board members are expected to be capable, competent, and committed to the entire business entity. They have the following duties:

- **Duty of Care:** remaining diligent, staying informed, asking questions, attending meetings, and reading board materials
- **Duty of Candor:** sharing concerns and observations truthfully even if they are difficult or unwelcome
- **Duty of Loyalty:** showing undivided allegiance to the organization's welfare, avoiding conflicts of interest, and making decisions in the best interest of the business while putting aside self-interest
- **Duty of Obedience:** staying faithful to the organization's mission and avoiding taking any actions inconsistent with this mission

### Evolution of Boards

Boards develop over generations, from an informal group of owner/managers to eventually include other family members, then nonfamily advisors, and finally independent directors. By the third generation, most generative families have a board with both family and independent, nonfamily directors. The development of the board parallels the development of family governance that takes on the work of managing the family activities and input. The board answers to the owners' group and also listens to the advice and concerns of the rest of the family, young family members and married-ins, who are not owners but deeply engaged with the family.

During the era of the founder/owner, the board is passive if it exists at all. It is a congratulatory group that meets periodically to give thanks to the founder. After the passing of the founder, the group of owners finds the board is important in appointing and overseeing the work of the family CEO, whether he or she is a family member or not. The nonworking owners have to discover their role. More time passes, and the board wants to get advice from nonfamily professionals and appoints board advisors. At some time, most families appoint one or more of their nonowner advisors to be part of the board, and in some generative families they become a majority. Since the independent directors serve at the pleasure of the owners, they can always dismiss the directors if they are not satisfied with their guidance.

Generative families increasingly bring on independent nonfamily board members to add to their expertise. On average, there are more family directors than independent ones, but some older families have a majority of independent directors. Over generations, generative families tend to increase the number of independent

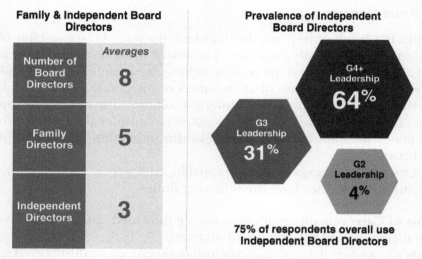

**Figure 8.1    Prevalence of independent board directors.**

directors. As we see in Figure 8.1, only a third of our families that have the third generation in leadership have independent directors, but that doubles when the family moves to G4. North American generative families are more likely to have independent directors, even though the average size and age of the North American families are smaller.

The board of a family enterprise evolves across generations through several steps. (See Figure 8.2.)

Each family board has its own trajectory of development as it responds to business and family challenges. The following account illustrates this development in one family:

> *As the second generation became older and started professions of their own, the board started to grow as well. But as the board grew, it had to deal with concerns about maintaining family values and practices. The second and third generations continued to add to these rules and structures. Philanthropies were often initiated by the third generation; they had a say because they were represented early on the board. They're looking now at the fourth generation to enforce and strengthen what they have been doing. There is even an idea that we could put together a junior board for high school and college kids, so they can prepare for these responsibilities.*
>
> *The board oversees everything: the company as well as internal family decisions. Most members of our family office board are also board members of public companies, so it's run like any other boardroom. In addition to making decisions about companies, investments, and structuring new divisions, they're also developing education for the next generation. So it's very inclusive.*
>
> *The original criteria for being a board member was simply someone who achieved an executive level in the outside world. Those who came on the board at an early age were already accomplished in their fields. The most recent changes state that if you are responsible for a significant portion of the family's holdings, you should be on the board. Now, new family members are included as well.*

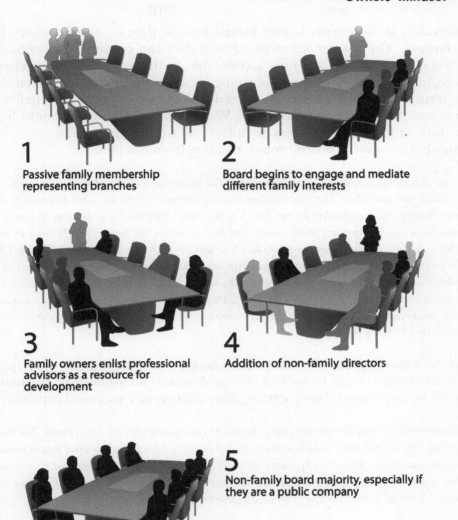

**1** Passive family membership representing branches

**2** Board begins to engage and mediate different family interests

**3** Family owners enlist professional advisors as a resource for development

**4** Addition of non-family directors

**5** Non-family board majority, especially if they are a public company

**Figure 8.2    The stages of board development.**

Even though family shareholders may not have management roles, they can be involved in defining and sustaining the family culture as shown in this account:

*We are very involved in the business, though nobody in the family has an executive position. All family owners are on the board, and we have a board meeting every month. That's how we relate to the business. We are also involved with many other activities in the company. At the end of the year, we do strategic planning for the next three years. Each company does its own strategic planning, but we are all very involved with what we call the values and vision process.*

Founders initially resist having formal boards; they see them as intruding on their control. They prefer informal advisors they can consult with confidentially. This works because they are only accountable to themselves. As new generations emerge, however, family owners and young future owners expect and even demand more transparency and clarity. They need to feel that ways exist to challenge the leaders and initiate necessary changes. Without this challenge, it would be much more difficult to achieve business discipline and strategic innovation.

Another account of board evolution comes from this family:

*Until this April we only had family members. The third generation had six family lines—one son and five daughters. Three sons-in-law and a grandson ran the business. Eventually those four turned into two leaders in the fourth generation. My father was the son of one of the sons-in-law in the business. Each family line had a seat on the board for fifty years or more. This policy of one board member per family line was an understanding from 1970. In 1999, we put in a fairly elaborate voting procedure and changed the bylaws; now it's part of the bylaws that each family line gets a seat on the board. When we did that, we also allowed for up to three additional, nonfamily directors. Since the sixties, the secretary/treasurer has always been nonfamily. The guy who was secretary/treasurer became the first nonfamily member on the board in 134 years.*

In the following family, a business challenge—new technology—precipitated a shift from family control to control by a professional board because the family saw the need for experienced oversight by those with greater technical capability:

*We transitioned from 100 percent family hands-on control and operation to a blend. The family maintained control over fundamental issues, but we created a board made up of family members and independent outsiders. This board provides critical business leadership and management that is a blend of family and nonfamily. We don't have an exact formula for this blend; over time, it's shifted from more family to more independent outsiders.*

### Complex Business Governance Structures

There can be a board for each business entity, and sometimes boards report to other boards. This fifth-generation company has a unique two-board structure:

*For the last twenty years, we have operated in a dual board structure. Some may call it a family council, but there is actually a corporate board of directors with some family members and some nonfamily members that handles the week-to-week business. The philosophy and direction of the company is handled by what we call the family board of directors. Some might call this a family council, but we operate differently than a family council. We make motions and pass them; we act in a somewhat more official capacity than a family council. We all grew up in a very business-like atmosphere, so that works best for us. The openness of both of those boards allows family members a certain "internship," for lack of a better term. Any family member over the age of twenty-one can commit to being on either of these two boards for a couple of years.*

*My mother is eighty-four and has pretty much already turned business operations over to our family board. It still operates under her philosophy, but we're running the show. There are two things that our family is trying to reinforce now that we're through our generational change: expectations and the quantity of time spent together. Sometimes that time is filled with conflict and argument and even some pain, but the only way we get through that is by working through it together.*

*The family board provides guidelines and criteria for the corporate board. This includes things like where we look for properties, final decisions on forming trusts, donations to the foundation, how many money managers we'd like to see—everything down to monthly decisions. That's why I say our family board of directors is not really a family council. It makes actual decisions; for instance, we tell the president of the company, "This is the direction we're moving in. We need you to help us get there."*

By the fourth generation, the number of owners can be quite large. For example, one non-US family conglomerate began to ask how to stay connected with over two hundred family owners. They created four governance boards to manage the complex relationships:

- An operating business
- A family office (a subsidiary of the operating business)
- A foundation (a charitable arm of the family)
- A family council (formed in 2004)

A family with a public and private company had boards for each one, working with their family council:

*The responsibility of the family council is high-level oversight. They suggest potential new board directors in a prescribed process. We want the most qualified people serving in those positions. First, because it's a very large enterprise and, second, because it's a public company, and we want to make sure we are operating in the best way and have the best people making the key decisions.*

*The second part of that oversight is the parallel planning. Parallel planning considers the concerns and desires of the families as majority shareholders and presents these to their board. The board is made up of primarily independent board members with family members as chair and vice chair. We present to the board where we see growth, risk, liquidity, profitability, and what we are comfortable with. They review that and tell us, "The strategic plan we are working with addresses every one of those things." Alternatively, they might say, "Our plan does not address liquidity. What should we be doing to look at that?" Or they might ask, "Do the goals you are looking at make business sense?" As we discuss these things, the six family members out of the eighteen on the board (plus the chair and vice chair who are family members) represent the family's parallel planning process. At the same time, we have a majority of independent directors and a nonfamily CEO, all of whom are trying to come up with what is best for the company and for the rest of the shareholders as well.*

### Forming the Board

Because they are the central governing entities for the family enterprises, generative families spend a great deal of time considering how their boards are constituted. A good board must balance several factors, starting with the interests of the owners (both major and minor) and future owners. Then there is allocating the fruit of the enterprise; this includes the need for investment in innovation, development of business discipline, and returns to family owners. A good board represents the owners, but it must also obtain professional expertise relevant to the current and future needs of the business.

Boards often have different categories of members. Commonly, in the beginning of their evolution, boards select or elect a member from each family branch. By the third or fourth generation, the importance of branch identity declines. In addition, by this time most family boards develop a mechanism for selecting family members. Sometimes selection is done by the board or major family owners and sometimes by some form of family election. If there is a private trust company, the board must contain a certain percentage of independent directors.

Generative families often have two classes of stock: voting and nonvoting shares. This is done to preserve and focus authority over the business when there are many owners. A family often controls a public company without having majority ownership by having the voting shares held only by members of the family.

A family with two branches with a sixty/forty share of ownership felt that having independent directors was the best way to protect the rights of the minority family branch. Another European family had six branches, each with a board seat and control of one of the family businesses. As members of the fourth generation came on board, they overhauled the process, with an appointed board deciding whether business leaders should be family or nonfamily members.

Because of their personal relationships and family nature, some families, like this one, move away from one share, one vote to other ways of voting that introduce more equality for family members:

> *The person with two shares has the same voice, the same questions, and gets the same attention as the person with 20,000 shares. I think I've been able to accomplish this because I come to it without much personal baggage. I'm very inclusionary. If you call me up with a list of ten questions and you own two shares, I'll answer your questions with the same vigor that I would if you had 20,000 shares. We don't see shares; we are a family.*

One model seen in large families with multiple businesses consists of a family holding company with family "managing directors" of individual business entities. This arrangement keeps family members from directly competing with one another. It also allows for diversity in managing individual businesses while creating alignment and integration at the whole family level. Here's how one family made this work. They had six family board members (this number can vary) who are also trustees of the trust. This includes three members from the fifth generation, ages eighty-six, sixty-four, and sixty-three years old, and three from the G6, in their forties. Each of the six runs a division of the business. They are active owners.

They meet formally once a year in July for two and a half days and informally when decisions need to be made. The six make decisions together. One member of G5 would like to bring on an external nonfamily holding company leader at some point.

Sometimes, the businesses are relatively independent of one another:

> *The business has become increasingly diversified over the generations. It's become almost a conglomerate at this point, and several families have exited. We had a liquidity event in 2006 to 2007 when we sold a manufacturing plant. We now have four contracting-related businesses: agriculture and real estate partnerships and a couple of investment vehicles. We also have an ESOP [employee stock ownership plan] through the construction businesses. Each business has a separate board.*

Some families, especially older families outside of the United States, limit ownership to the family members who work in the business. Other family members are compensated for their shares, as in this example:

> *My brother, my cousin, and I share a certain personality and interest in adventure. We have this rule: you can only be a shareholder if you are active in the business. With that rule, we avoid a situation where you have many shareholders who are there just to collect dividends. These shareholders might have a more conservative approach and say, "Let's conserve what we have. We don't need any new experiments or risk, please. Dividends come before reinvestment." We've never had to deal with that kind of attitude because nobody can join who is not working in the business.*

As the business grows over generations, requirements for board members become more stringent. Members of each generation find they must set the bar higher for board members. One family has a board with four family representatives, one from each branch. The board actively seeks and recruits good candidates, and these are not elected, but selected. The board is always looking for good future prospects.

Over time, families may get more explicit as they develop fair, transparent, and effective selection processes:

> *We have a formal process for electing family directors by the whole family. The family nominates the family director for the seat coming from the family side and then the whole family votes. This is not a one-vote-per-share system but rather one-vote-per-family-member, so every family member has a vote.*

To anticipate conflict, this family defines the criteria for selecting family board members:

> *We discussed guidelines for good board members with our next-generation board members. What should a good board member study? What does he or she need to know? What kind of experience is expected? It's amazing how much energy was put into refusing to deal with this discussion.*

*Many people didn't understand what it meant. They said, "How can anybody oblige the parents to put or not to put their kids on the board?" We answered, "Nobody is obliging you. We just want some guidelines for fourth gens to know what is expected."*

A board oversees the company, family office, and/or foundation. But in many cases, the family council chooses family board members for the owners. One family uses "back channels" to dialogue about who would be good nominees; this is sometimes contentious. The family council then interviews prospects and makes recommendations to the board.

In other situations, the family and board split the responsibility of appointing family board members:

*The terms for the board of directors are basically one-year terms, but there's no term limit. There's an age limit of seventy. Right now, we've got three family members on the board, and they're all going to turn seventy at the same time.*

*When there's an opening, a letter goes out to the family, people apply, and the council interviews the candidates. It's a pretty structured process; a set of questions are sent to those who are interested. In addition, there's an interview process with the family council. After that, the council makes a recommendation to the board. The council does not choose the family director, but the board pays a lot of attention to the recommendation. So far, they have gone with our recommendation every time.*

*The council is also very involved in selecting the CEO. They interview prospective CEO candidates and then make their recommendation to the board. Recently, a family member and two nonfamily members were up for a position. The family council did not recommend the family member. That gave the board permission to decide for one of the nonfamily members. It was a five–four vote, but it ended up being absolutely the right decision. But if the council had said, "We really want this family member," I think that would've swayed the board in that direction.*

Another family had a unique dilemma. A highly qualified in-law was proposed for the board, but the family felt this person was not connected enough to the family; he didn't come to family reunions and didn't know what the family wanted. Both of these were expectations for board membership; it was not just a business decision. He was not selected. Instead, he was told that before he could serve, he would have to interact more with the family.

There is a danger that family board members, who are usually major shareholders, will see their terms as lasting for life. Many families face this tendency, and they either anticipate it or respond to it by creating term limits. Even if board members are routinely reelected, there is a time when the family can decide that a director's time is over. This family has one-year board terms, so the directors have to be reelected every year:

*Right now, we have a system for choosing board members, with deadlines and a formal evaluation committee. Everything is transparent and based on best practices. We're trying to head off conflicts and encourage as much family involvement as possible.*

Another family with many shareholders has an elaborate process of checks and balances:

> We have 135 family members and eighty-seven shareholders, but we only have two people employed in the business. Five of our eleven directors are family members along with nine on the family council. Our policy is that anybody in the family can nominate a family member for the board of directors. The family council gathers those names and résumés and decides which individuals are qualified to be board members. We then send two or three names to the nominating committee.
>
> Since the 1950s, our policy has been that there will always be more outside directors on the board than family members. Outside directors interview family nominees and decide who will be on the board. This selection process avoids hard feelings among family members; for example, they can't accuse another member of vetoing their favorite candidate. It also allows the family to be free of an entitled mentality, as in, "I want to be a director, and therefore I get to be a director." A director is a professional position and should be decided on merit. Having the outside directors make the final decision ensures that the most qualified people will be chosen.

To prepare for board service as a steward, young family members need to learn about the business, the role of the board, and skills required for board membership. Membership is not a prize but a responsibility; it's a professional role. As young family members learn how to be professional board members, there are other avenues for that learning than just being voted onto the board. For example, several families formed a *junior board* made up of family members who wanted to develop their skills and knowledge. Junior boards help the business to achieve transparency while teaching and preparing younger members for roles on the board. They met regularly with family leaders and board members, but their purpose was to learn and to slowly begin to offer advice. A junior board enables the family to recognize capability and develop it.

Another family formed an *advisory board* comprised of family members who met with the board as learners and, occasionally, provided informal strategic advice. These informal board observers or advisors then became potential candidates for formal membership. Here's how this worked in one family:

> A year ago, we decided it would be to our benefit to have more family members on the board. We thought this would encourage the education of more family members about the business and ensure that board decisions were aligned with the shareholders' values. At the time, there was only one family member on the board, along with six nonfamily members. We decided we didn't want to replace any current members, so we added two more family members. Assuming that my cousin and I become full board members, we'd then have three family members out of nine directors. We've learned that being a board member has a big learning curve, especially in this kind of technical business. It takes a long time to get up to speed to be useful, so we really don't want people rotating off that quickly.

When a strong leader died in a company, the successor wanted to develop the next generation. He selected not the oldest but the most qualified to sit on the board, and that caused some tension. Another family developed seven competencies required for a board member. The board solicits prospects via letter, and the candidate then states how well he or she fulfills the criteria. The board then selects the best candidate.

Another family had a discussion of board responsibility and structure and then passed the baton as the old board resigned and a new one was installed. The board went from two brothers to a board of eight, all of whom were well qualified for the position.

The earlier generations of leaders teach their heirs that board service is a responsibility, not a perk for family members:

> *I'm trying to inculcate the perspective of what it means to be a good owner. When I reflect on the problems of the past, we've always had sort of mixed management and ownership, and that's created a lot of fights. The idea that their responsibility is to be a good owner is fundamental to what we're trying to achieve. We're in the midst of developing a new approach in which the main task of the board of directors is to oversee the entire enterprise. We're looking at our businesses as a true portfolio and empowering separate boards for each underlying business. We have flexibility in shaping the portfolio for the future. This can also present opportunities for subsequent generations to be involved in the businesses in many different ways.*

As generations pass, each new generation must learn its roles and responsibilities:

> *We're trying to consider how to bring in the fifth and sixth generations. Board membership provides a forum for engagement and a way for stockholders to move to the idea of stewardship. Our challenge has been to define clear roles and boundaries between the family council, the board, and management. That's been tricky. When I first came on the board, our board and management were pretty antagonistic toward family stockholders. When I walked into my first board meeting, I was suddenly on the hot seat about something that involved my uncle; this was an awful experience. I realized that we needed new board members, but the current structure for electing them was not going to work. Most stockholders didn't even know who the outside directors were.*
>
> *We named an ad hoc Board Selection and Election Task Force to develop a new structure for electing board members. They established term limits and considered a retirement age. Up to then, it was like being appointed to the Supreme Court: you had to die to have your seat open up. This process took two years. All the old directors got the message and resigned, so we didn't have to throw them out. We created a robust search committee, and now we have a great new board and CEO, and we are mostly on the same page. There are five family members on the board, if you include the CEO, who has a seat.*

One family member developed insight into the role by serving as an independent director of other family businesses:

> *I am an independent director on the board of two family businesses; I do this because I want to support the family in protecting their wealth. I also want to listen to the things they want.*

*I feel that I can do this better than family members who are owners of these businesses because I'm not involved emotionally; I can make impartial decisions.*

### Independent Board Members

The inclusion of independent board directors is part of an overall transformation of the family enterprise, as illustrated here:

> *We created a board last year that includes outsiders. We are integrating all of our companies under a single board and CEO. We approved our new structure in 2013 and named two co-chairs—two of my cousins—to guide us through the transition. For the first time in our history, we hired a nonfamily CEO. We wanted our cousins to work side by side with the new CEO for the first six months to make sure he learns everything and can take full advantage of their support. Then they will relinquish all operative functions, and the CEO will be fully in control.*

When independent board members are appointed, the family faces a challenge: Should the family be committed to implementing good ideas suggested by the new, independent board members? Suppose they suggest an idea that makes good business sense but doesn't have the support of the family. One family that had a majority of independent members solved this problem by requiring every decision to have at least one family member in agreement.

In this family, the widows of the second-generation siblings transitioned to a professional third generation that included several independent board members:

> *Our purpose in having a private trust company is to manage the diversification of the family's wealth rather than leaving it up to the institutional trustees who may not know us. We recruited our first group of independent board members, and this allowed us to retire my aunts from the board of directors (they were well meaning but not well versed in business strategy). After the independent board was in place, two things happened. First, the independent board asked me to become president and chief operating officer. Second, they suggested we put forward an offer to family members who were unhappy with the changes to liquidate some of their ownership. We ended up purchasing 57 percent of the equity of the company.*

We can see that governance is the unifying and integrating process that sustains the generative alliance—and that this in turn sustains the long-term family enterprise. Having an active board that acts as a group of stewards and contains independent directors and competent representatives of family owners allows the family to focus on the business goals of craftsmanship and innovation. Business governance is the ringmaster of family organization and continuity.

## Taking Action in Your Own Family Enterprise

This chapter outlined the developmental arc of business governance for a family enterprise. You can conduct an audit of the state of your own family governance to see how far along you are. The key is to develop the appropriate governance process to fit your current state and anticipate and prepare for the next generation. At each point in time, you should consider the approaching challenges in your family and in the business and then begin to develop a structure that fits where you are going, not just where you are now.

You can look at where you are right now along the developmental arc of board/governance development and see what will be needed to serve you in the near future.

| GOVERNANCE/ BOARD QUALITY | HAVE NOW? | HOW THIS MIGHT BE USEFUL | WHAT WE MIGHT NEED SOON! |
|---|---|---|---|
| Insiders Board— Owner/Operators | | | |
| Board with All Major Family Owners | | | |
| Board with Representative Family Owners | | | |
| Cross-Generational Representation on Board | | | |
| Non-Family Advisors to Board | | | |
| Independent Board Members | | | |
| Independent Board Member Majority | | | |

Next, you can consider how the family is engaged in business governance by answering these questions:

- How transparent to family members are the operations of the business and the changes that are being considered?
- How are the growing members of the rising generation informed about the business?
- How are young and inexperienced family members educated about what is happening?
- How are family ideas and input about business policy accessed and listened to?
- How can new family members become involved in governance?
- How visible are the qualifications and selection of board members?

## Note

1. https://www.ft.com/content/2f99b24a-5328-11e5-8642-453585f2cfcd.

# THREE

# Inside the Family: Family Governance to Create a Great Family

This section shifts focus to the family. It highlights a realm of activity that is private and unique to a family enterprise: the organization, governance, and activity of the family separate from the business. It begins with Chapter 9, which talks about the nature of the unique family "tribes" that compose generative families, and how they gather in the form of a family assembly, which is the beginning of family governance.

Each chapter that follows describes a key element of family governance, including the family council, owners' groups, and the board, and finally, in Chapter 12, how they are all tied together in a family constitution, a master agreement that defines who the family is, what it does, and how it works.

# Inside the Family: Family Governance to Create a Great Family

**CHAPTER**

**9**

# The Family Tribe

## Creating Purposeful Extended Family Community Beyond the Enterprise

**B**uilding a successful business is the first creative act of a business family. But that is not enough to ensure a future for the extended family. Building a strongly connected extended family, organized around shared values concerning the use of the vast family resources, is the second creative act of the family as it crosses generations. The family has an active and creative role in the enterprise that is largely unknown to families who do not own large businesses or family assets.

A generative family desires much more than financial wealth. Its long-term achievement also lies in how it builds the extended family and the collective impact of what the family members do together, and what they do in the world. The opportunities are endless. But how do family members get together, uncover opportunities, set priorities, and make their ambitious plans actually happen?

After several generations, even the wealthiest families inevitably grow apart. Relatives live far away. Despite their shared holdings, they may not feel compelled to get to know each other. They often become uninvolved shareholders, strangers to each other, not wanting any additional contact as a family. Unless someone does something to pull people together, no force will counteract disengagement and fracturing.

Generative families, by their nature, avoid this fate. They find a reason to endure and develop active personal relationships and shared projects. They prepare for the future as a family as well as a business. Despite increasing numbers and distance, they share a common identity and a commitment to sustaining it. To do this, they actively and consciously work to establish a community. Building on their shared legacy of values and practices, they renew these ties each generation with the many new extended family members. As social theorist Thorstein Veblen noted nearly a century ago, "The wealthy are the most tribal group in modern society."[1]

Tribes grow naturally when related families share a village. They have a common day-to-day experience, livelihood, and need to regulate their affairs. But when a tribe has a shared heritage but not a common location, relationships and trust do not grow spontaneously. They have to be created, by finding times and places for shared experience and for building a shared meaning and purpose for their bonds. As family members grow more distant from their common heritage, this becomes more of a challenge. Generative families are up to the challenge.

This chapter looks at how generative families develop a thriving community of caring, meaning, and purpose as they cross generations, countering the tendency to disconnect and disperse that is usual across generations. Building a tribe allows the family to generate deep personal bonds between households and generations, among a far-flung group of relatives. By building community, the family can affirm and sustain its shared values and culture and adapt its family enterprise to a changing world. This tough challenge gives birth to a lot of shared activity across families.

## Building a Great Family Tribe

A tribal extended family is very different from an individual household. For most people, the image of a family is a small loving related group that lives and grows up together. Because they care about each other, they know and trust each other (though there are tensions), spend time together, do fun things and learn together, support each individual to find his or her own path in life, respect differences, use their resources wisely, and look toward children in the next generation. A nuclear family is direct and personal.

A tribal extended family contains linked households with varying degrees of personal connection and shared experience as well as a long-term obligation to work together as partners. Relationships must be built and developed actively; they do not take root naturally. Tensions, rivalries, jealousies, and differences emerge. If these obstacles are to be overcome, family members need stronger measures than just being together from time to time.

Members of an extended business family build a new kind of tribe—one not sharing a physical community but united by personal bonds, shared investments, meetings, social media, and shared work projects. While physically dispersed, they consciously work to stay connected and develop personal and working interrelationships. They often share a family vacation home, in the mountains or on the water, with a set time each year when they all are in residence.

As earlier chapters have shown, to reach this goal family members need to transform the structure from the sole leadership of a family patriarch into a partnership with leadership distributed among several family members. Rather than a single leader, they have a leadership group. While there may not be direct democracy, there is a transparent and participatory environment where every voice is heard and respected.

This community is not just collaborative; it must also be responsible and active. Many business families are concerned that rising generations will become entitled, looking at what they will get rather than what they can give. The core purpose of creating a family tribe is to redefine the role of rising generations from being heirs and consumers to being responsible, accountable citizens. Stewardship is akin to citizenship in a tribal community. By becoming citizens, members affirm their responsibilities as well as their benefits. As this section of the book will show, one of the primary purposes of family governance is to be clear about family members' responsibilities and hold people accountable. Only with responsible behavior can the new generations continue, sustain, and add to the family wealth. Citizenship entails responsibilities in order to sustain the benefits.

As new family members join the "tribe" by birth or marriage, there are three challenging tasks:

- Renewing, updating, and sustaining the family's legacy values
- Building personal relationships so that the newer rising generation family members can remain comfortably aligned and trust, value, and respect each other
- Using the family wealth in a meaningful way that builds positive identity in the family as a whole and within each family member

Generative family members build their community by initiating programs, practices, policies, and actions to serve their goals, and react to emerging adversity and challenges. To develop this level of trust, cousins and new spouses must get to know each other, not just socially but also as business and financial partners, making decisions and acting together.

Coming together as a tribe becomes a designed event as the third generation reaches adulthood and asks what the family enterprise means to them as family members. If they want to become a generative family, they need to do more than just have a family reunion; they need to define themselves as an operating entity that begins with personal relationships but becomes organized to take on many shared tasks.

## Reclaiming the Family Legacy

Here is an account of how G3 built their tribal identity:

*My grandfather passed away in 1993, and all the third-generation members, nineteen of us, got together for probably the very first time we ever saw each other. We did not grow up together. We decided we wanted to do more, and we took the opportunity several months later to get together and try to learn a little bit more about each other. It was kind of a touchy-feely type of thing, but we got to know more about each other. We've heard stories about each other—some are good, some are bad—but we had to go through and listen and understand each other better. And we decided that we were okay. My belief is that that participation by the next generation is what brought the family back together again. Questions started being asked about if we truly are a family—because this generation feels that we are—what do we need to do about the businesses to include those as a family? So we brought in a consultant, and we started talking about a family council and cooperation and coordination and listened to each other. We have only been doing it about fifteen years, but we have come a long way.*

*Over the third generation, ten of the nineteen were involved at some extent. It boiled down to a handful doing most [of] the work, but everybody else participated. So they are all part of it for the most part. A few of them are kind of outliers. We hold a family assembly once a year and what we call a cousins' camp at the ranch. We bring people to the ranch for three days with no meetings to show conservation and environmental concerns and what the ranch does. Nobody works for the*

*(continued)*

(*Continued*)

*ranch now, but it is a long-term legacy asset. We want to make sure everybody has a chance to see and appreciate what the ranch means to the family.*

*But we said at that time if we are talking about a family council, it included not only the ones here today but those not even born yet. The family has grown quite a bit since; we are about seventy-eight people right now. We have thirty-five years between oldest and youngest of G4. About four G4 members are older than the youngest of G3. We talk about twenty-year generation ages now. We use the word "generage" versus generation because we have a group of fourth generage that are fifteen to thirty-five. We are trying to get that fourth generage group to be involved. We formed a committee manned by themselves. We give them some things to do on the philanthropy side of it and opportunities to get to know each other better. They have a meeting once a year where they spend the weekend learning about themselves, about one of the enterprises, and what we do. As we make decisions for this next ten years—I'm using ten years as the older of the third generation start winding down, the younger start picking up as well as the older of the fourth generage, that next twenty-year group coming up.*

A tribal community is not for every family. Indeed, many family enterprises split, sell, or discontinue their shared identity and ownership by the third generation. For many families, the path of individual freedom is the best way to share and build wealth. Generative families make the opposite choice.

## Sustaining Legacy Identity

Since the family does not share a physical community, it builds its identity and personal bonds from its history, especially the origins of its good fortune and wealth. Family members tell stories to one another and pass them down across generations; their story gives them a shared purpose beyond making and spending money. This is the family's mission and values, which lead family members to a vision of what they want to be and do in the future. Family members must come together frequently enough to bond and develop a sense of why they are together. With all the other things they can do in their lives, what is the reason for staying together?

One important tie is the history of what the family has done. The family has a reputation and status in the community, and because of the family's wealth, more is expected of the family members. New family members find that there are projects they can do together that they cannot do alone. And indeed, they find that their parents and community expect them to do things together.

The family is connected to the past and building for the future. It has amassed great wealth, but each new generation faces the question of what the wealth is to be used for. Is there a shared project that matters to family members enough for them to work together? The motivation for becoming a family tribe comes from fulfilling the promise of what the family has done in the past. If the family has created great wealth, family members want to do something with a positive impact in the future. Just running the business isn't enough; today's family members can do more than that as a great family.

New family members may not be fully aware of the family story and history. Families share family history and stories while they are together. While the family may have moved further from their ancestral home, family members often have special spaces where they gather. They may have a wonderful vacation home or a tradition of gathering for holidays or in the summer. They may have ties to the community where the business lies, and they may have created a community presence or foundation to serve that community.

But in order to remain in touch, the family has to do the work of getting folks together, not just for a vacation or social gathering but to undertake the generative work of the family. The challenge is that each household has its own commitments. As family members become more numerous and distant, the family has to be more active in convincing family members to take the time and make the effort to connect. This connection has three aspects. First, the people must know, like, and respect each other personally. Second, they have to discover a shared purpose that is more compelling than what each of them can do individually. Third, they have to develop trust in each other's competence, motivation, and good will. Luckily, the potential generative family has the means to do this. The family can allocate money and time for family gatherings and for shared projects designed by the family.

## The Family Assembly

An assembly is a gathering of the whole extended family; its existence creates the tribe. It allows old and new tribal members to get together. A *family assembly* usually takes place yearly, but if the extended family is larger and more dispersed, it becomes more expensive and difficult and is held less frequently. It is a form of community building where the extended family forms a temporary "village." Relationships grow, information is shared, family history is celebrated, fun activities and vacations are planned, and a shared vision for the family and its various family ventures emerges. If there were no assemblies, the foundation for the shared identity of the extended family as a family might be lost. While the ownership of the legacy business, family office, and other ventures would continue, the shared meaning that is part of being a family enterprise could not be reproduced.

While nonbusiness families have their own family reunions and assemblies, when a multigenerational family shares ownership of valuable family enterprises, the assembly allows the family to sustain a common family culture and identity. For example, one family leader recounted how she had attended family summer camps for fifty years since she was a child. She got to know the scores of cousins to the point where she knew who was competent, who was talented, and who was ambitious. Young people would pressure their families to attend because summer camp was such an important part of their lives. This family can move into its seventh generation because of the deep commitment to this community-building event. With more than one hundred family members attending, the event is a major cost to the family. Taking on this cost is a sign of the family's commitment.

A family assembly is provides a regular place and time for cousins to get close and find common purpose. They develop a common culture, language, and liking for each other. They can then look for new opportunities to help co-create the family's future path. By doing this together, when the time comes, they are already bought in and open to becoming partners; they form a generational identity with fresh ideas about the family enterprises and dedication to building upon their shared legacy.

An assembly goes by different names in different families, but the purposes are similar: business review, education, fun, and relationship building. Here are examples from three different families:

1. **Social gathering:** *We have an annual family reunion where all family members, including spouses, are invited. They are usually done during the summer, and it's more of a social gathering. We rotate that around. Some years we skip it for different reasons, but in general we try to get together once a year, socially.*

2. **Business review:** *We initiated what we call family camp, a three-day weekend over the summer where we educate the family about the company. We have a budget for these events that pays airfare for people coming from out of town to facilitate 100 percent attendance. At this camp, you can go through family documents like buy–sell agreements. It also facilitates bonding and social time so that shareholders know each other and can work on their relationships.*

3. **Community building:** *We had yearly family social reunions and board and business, but the family gathering that we recently had was nothing like we had ever done before and it was all about transitioning and communication, involvement, fun. We had a talent show where G4 could meet, and G5 met as a group with another facilitator, where ideas were shared. We came together Sunday morning in a wrap-up session to compare what each group felt was important. G5 has already begun setting up their own network for communication and forming an education committee. They've already begun working on their goals, and then we primarily focused on the ranch because most of us in G4 grew up there and spent a lot of time there. It's changing now that the family is growing so much. But we focused on access to the land and trying to create more opportunities, as we get large, for the family to be there, and so we're adding additional houses to the main headquarters so more family members can be down there at the same time.*

As the family moves from an informal gathering to a formal assembly, one of the first tasks is to define clearly what the family is all about and the values it stands for. Here are two accounts of how this started:

1. *To start the values piece, we sent out an email and said, "Put down what your values are. What do you think should be included in our mission, vision, and values?" And everybody could give input and we incorporated ... you could only imagine with twenty-something people giving input, how many values we had. But we incorporated it because we felt like it was important that everyone had a voice.*

2. *We went through a process of developing a family vision a few years ago led by somebody in my generation who sent a list of a hundred values to the assembly with an invitation for them to mark the ones they thought most important related to the family and the family business. Based on that, we developed family values that ultimately were memorialized in a constitution completed five years ago. It was the first document with force and significant buy-in.*

One of the most important issues for a family assembly is to consider the relative primacy of business and family interests in making decisions. A family leader remembers, *"I did a survey with my family and one of the questions was, 'What do you value the most or what do you consider is the most valuable to our family enterprise—the business or the family?' I had 130 respondents, where 51 percent said family and 49 percent said business. If you've got the family equally committed to both, it's a beautiful thing. That's how I would define success, where the family is equally supportive of the business and the family."*

By assembling, the family realizes that much that they want to do is separate and independent from the business. The range of areas that the assembly can consider include getting to know each other deeply, building a common culture and family identity, learning from each other about common interests, and learning the skills of working together as a family team. The family then faces the need to develop family governance in addition to and alongside business and financial governance.

At the assembly, a family can define ongoing tasks and select representatives for committees and task groups. By doing this, the assembly is more than just a fun family vacation. It is a working community, demanding more from its citizens than just showing up. This emerging infrastructure is what is referred to as family governance.

The process begins informally but over time becomes more formal and organized:

*We spent a few days asking, "Do we want to work together in a family business?" And there was a unanimous yes. If so, why and what do we hope to achieve out of it? And we set some vision out of that of what we wanted to achieve together. We looked at a document that identified the values going back generations. We went through that document, and I identified with it and still feel very connected to it. Some elements were more important, and we incorporated those values of what we are today. So we've got that very strong cultural and historical link with where we've come from.*

*So we sat around in the larger family and chatted about what we liked about working together, why we thought there was benefit, what the negatives were, and there was very strong unanimity that we wanted to work together, we liked working together, and we felt there was benefit in doing so, and we wanted to continue to do so.*

*Given that, we then said, "Okay, what are we going to achieve together?" And we went through several different areas in terms of wealth preservation and generation or growing it into the future. We looked at roles for family and opportunities for family, and we looked at the family's sense of identity. And we picked on each of those areas and identified some goals or longer-term vision of what we wanted to achieve in each of those areas. And we spent quite a bit of time chatting about that.*

Most of all, families noted that the assembly was active and fun. They mentioned activities that included the building and racing of boats, family Olympics, a ropes course, team building, building model planes or boats, a quiz about family events, and other family competitions where older and younger generations could compete. There were prizes and celebrations, talent shows, family awards, and formal dinners. Younger generations made presentations of their entrepreneurial ideas as well as ideas for the family. In many ways, the family assembly is like the holiday celebration of a close community, where people enjoy each other's company and get to know each other on a deeper level. They create fond memories, which become part of family tradition.

Some smaller families who live close to each other are able to have more regular family meetings. Any family can have weekly or monthly family dinners, and many generative families continue that practice. But there is another dimension of meetings where the family is also a business or financial partnership. They need to talk through family conflict, and explicitly address needs, desires, and intentions about how the family wants to remain together as a community, and what they want from their various ventures.

In initiating family gatherings, the greatest challenge is to sustain inclusion. Large families are often satisfied if they get more than half of the family members to attend, but they always strive to get greater involvement. It is especially important to get younger family members, just coming of age or starting families, to bond with the family. If not, they can be lost forever to this shared effort. There is also a challenge when one branch or household lives far away. Setting up the habit of participation is essential if those family members are going to be available to commit to and participate in family activities. Families set up social networks, they hold family branch meetings and dinners, and they call and persuade close family members to set the time aside for gatherings. They are always reaching out.

## Cross-Generational Engagement: Role of Older and Younger Generations

The tribe provides a setting where family values, practices, and traditions can be passed from the older to the younger generation. To do this, the differences in style and values in each generation must be addressed. Together, older and younger generations must develop trust and find common ground.

Building tribal extended family community is not the work of a lone family leader or generation. It arises from ongoing exchange across generations. While it may occasionally begin with the intent of the wealth creator, it can also arise from the inspiration of a member of a younger generation. Extended families train and initiate their next generation in cooperation in order to sustain their partnership. This can only happen with a great deal of engagement and communication across generations. In order to build cross-generational communication, each generation must come to understand and respond to the concerns of the other generation. Family gatherings and assemblies often focus on how each generation sees the world differently and ways they can better understand each other. (See Figure 9.1.)

### Elders

The patriarch of the family often has a vision of the future. As one family member says, "*It goes back to Grandpa; it's a requirement to be a responsible steward. He instilled in everyone that this is something you need to nurture and make sure it works for the good*

## DIALOGUE ACROSS GENERATIONS

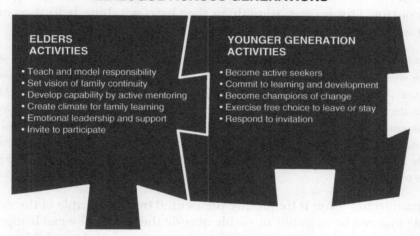

**ELDERS ACTIVITIES**

- Teach and model responsibility
- Set vision of family continuity
- Develop capability by active mentoring
- Create climate for family learning
- Emotional leadership and support
- Invite to participate

**YOUNGER GENERATION ACTIVITIES**

- Become active seekers
- Commit to learning and development
- Become champions of change
- Exercise free choice to leave or stay
- Respond to invitation

**Figure 9.1   Activities of elders and the younger generation.**

*of everyone."* While elders help, a family thinks ahead by creating policies for the next generation. The vision of the elders may be incomplete. Generations need to engage in dialogue and blend their visions. Another family member says, *"My grandfather would sit down with people and talk them through things, preempt issues, and encourage us. He was the strongest proponent of being international so that the increasing number of family members in the fourth generation had enough room to take leadership without stepping on each other's toes. He created simple rules like not having more than three family members in a city. Sometimes we made mistakes despite having those clear policies because as every generation moves on, people forget some of the common-sense concepts that were put in place at the time."*

Keenly aware of this challenge, family elders actively engage their children and grandchildren. In this way, the generative family is a learning system, with a focused intention for one generation not just to pass on money and a successful business but also to sustain and develop what the family has. This takes the form of encouraging focus on all forms of family capital. Young family members learn and grow by taking part in activities that add value in family relationships, in their own careers, and in the community.

The most important feature of cross-generational activity is that it allows the family to develop an informal link to a key aspect of the generative alliance. While the older generation works closely with nonfamily advisors and leaders, in order to develop the full alliance there must be a strong connection between the older and younger generations, even if younger generations do not have formal ownership or participation in the family enterprise. The alliance grows as members of the younger generation are asked for their ideas and taught about the family enterprise. By sharing their ideas and testing them with their elders, they develop trust and become comfortable with each other. Both generations of the family learn from each other.

The elders must also realize that capability development means giving up a modicum of control. This is often something they have not done before, as one patriarch notes:

> *Reflecting on what you can control and can't control, many people have that dynastic dream, but it is more of a dream. In the end, one can't control what is going to happen ten generations from now. Attempts to do so can backfire, whereas I can control the choices I make right now, such as the way I communicate with my family members, the advice that I give them, and the environment I help create to foster various strengths and bring out the best in them. But when they come into their own and into positions of authority, I see them as entitled and authoritative to make the choices they deem right at that time, and I can't control that, nor would it be a good idea to try.*

The patriarchal vision is frequently augmented by the example of the matriarch, whose role may not be as public or visible outside the family. She can bridge the gap between the father's dream and the different experience of their children:

> *She has always been the one that wanted her kids to be independent and stand on our own. She's always fostered us to grow wings. Having the trust company and giving up sole fiduciary responsibility of trustee did a couple of things. It's been a challenge with her as trustee sleeping with the grantor every night if they don't see eye-to-eye on something. So I think the trust company alleviates some of that controversy. She's very social. She has a great group of friends. She loves to travel, so I think they will end up planning everything.*

Here is a description of another matriarch who helped the next generation build community:

> *For all the initial things that we would do as a family, my mom's generation was in control. She focused on bringing together the fourth generation to build relationships, and so they would refer to a family value because there's been kind of a list of family values that have been created at that point. She would say, "If philanthropy or connecting to nature is one of our family values, let's bring the kids together on a backpacking trip and then help them, encourage them to pick a charity and we will fund it."*

### Youngers

The emerging generation can be active or passive in response to these messages. They can listen silently or engage and challenge with their own questions and views. To become generative, active engagement by more than just a favored few is needed. Many families in this study contained rising generation leaders who actively initiated change in their families ("family champions"[2]) as well as family members who felt they had no voice, needing to be almost pulled into engagement. One goal of governance was to increase the number of active, informed family members.

The initiative to formalize family governance can come from anyone in the family, not only the leaders. A rising generation family member can initiate governance if he or she can make the case to the family:

> *I'm going to credit one of my cousins as being a trailblazer from early on. About fifteen years ago, she was already speaking to my uncle, who was the CEO, about family involvement and what*

*the future might be in that regard, "planting the seeds" for how we, as the third generation, need to step up as the owners of the company and start to learn about it and be responsible owners. She contacted a consultant who came to our annual meeting. She said, "Let's get a group of people to look at how we might put something together" and then spent a year doing that. We knew we needed to have it all set in place so that we can present it to the family in a way that we know what we're talking about. We've got a clear direction for it, and that's how the council got started.*

Another account by the eldest member of a fourth-generation family shows how young family members may need active invitations to become engaged:

*As a family entering the fourth generation, we stepped back and reviewed the company legacy and collective family values. Its operations were going beyond the scope of what we do well, and from a business perspective that was huge. From a family perspective, it created curiosity around family governance, which then led to the family council and to our generation being an impetus for change and a need for education and emotional engagement at an earlier age, better preparing for transitions, and grounding our generation in its relation to the company.*

*I certainly did not enjoy it at the time, but looking back on it, I am very appreciative and grateful to have been dragged to those shareholder meetings, business events, and family events even if I thought it was the equivalent to waterboarding at the time. I am now very glad that it was done.*

In every family, some rising generation "cousins" may want to leave the family partnership and go off on their own. As some family members elect to leave, family governance must make clear what it means to exercise the option to stay, what benefits and responsibilities accompany remaining with the partnership, and if family members do chose to leave, how these departures should be done and what these family members will and won't be a part of in the future. If guidelines are not clear or explicit, family members cannot make informed decisions about staying or leaving.

## Taking Action in Your Own Family Enterprise

### Celebrating the Family Legacy

There are many ways that your family can tell its story to younger generations and build its legacy. Here are some activities that can be done at family gatherings.

- **Stories:** Each family member, from oldest to youngest, can share a story of something that represents the core of what the family means to him or her. Individuals can also bring a family picture, or an object, that represents the family. Storytelling is a wonderful way to begin a family assembly.
- **Time line:** On a large wall, family members can begin at the beginning and share what they know and what was important, for the family and its business, at each period. The stories make up a history of the family. Other family members can share stories of what they remember that was important.
- **Interviews:** The younger family members can interview, maybe with video, elder family members about what they remember and want to share with the younger generation.

- **Picture books and histories:** The family may commission someone to create a written, audio, or video history of the family. Many generative families have books that tell their story; these books are shared within the family—or even with employees and the community.

### Conducting Cross-Generational Dialogue

These questions can be posed to family members in order to begin a conversation related to the key ideas of working together as a connected family and family enterprise.

| Elder Generation | Rising Generation |
|---|---|
| • What do you want from the rising generation?<br>• What have you been doing to help members of the rising generation achieve what you expect from them?<br>• How can you help them move in that direction?<br>• What process are you going to use to select the next generation of family leadership? | • What do you want from your parents and elders?<br>• What do they expect from you?<br>• What are you doing to prepare for your career and life goals? |
| • What messages about money and wealth do you want to pass to your children?<br>• How do you talk to your children about the family wealth and how special it is to have it?<br>• What values do you want your children to develop, and how have you consciously helped make this happen?<br>• What are the messages that you have to help your children set off on their own life journey when they finish their education (or before)? | • What values did you learn from your family about money and wealth?<br>• How does the presence of family wealth affect your life choices and future?<br>• What help and support do you need from your family?<br>• How are you considering becoming involved in family activities having to do with the family ventures? |
| • How do you help members of the rising generation feel part of the larger extended family descended from the G1 wealth creator(s)?<br>• Have you informed them about what the family offers and what it needs from them?<br>• What are the opportunities available for the next generation to become engaged in the family? | • How have you become informed about the activities of the various family ventures?<br>• What makes you want to participate? What holds you back?<br>• What is most exciting about being part of this unique family?<br>• What is your plan for contributing to the family? |
| • How do you keep open the possibility of family engagement for all members of the rising generation?<br>• How are members of the rising generation informed and invited to participate in family activities?<br>• How have you created a fair and open process for selection and accountability for roles in the family enterprise?<br>• How do you offer your guidance, help, and support to members of the next generation without them feeling the pressure to please you and do what you want? | • What are the benefits to you of being part of this family?<br>• What attracts you about becoming engaged in family activities?<br>• What do you offer the family that might contribute to its success in the emerging generation?<br>• What would you most want to see the whole family accomplish in the coming years? |

## Notes

1. Thorstein, Veblen, *The Theory of the Leisure Class: An Economic Study of Institutions* (Macmillan, 1899).
2. A member of the research team, Joshua Nacht, has written his PhD dissertation and some articles elaborating on this role. He discusses this concept in his book, *Family Champions and Champion Families: Developing Family Leaders to Sustain the Family Enterprise,* coauthored with Gregory Greenleaf (Chicago: Family Business Consulting Group, 2018).

# 10

# Governance

## Organizing the Interconnection of Family and Business

**B**y G3, a generative family has become a very wealthy, loosely connected tribe of families with a common interest. They manage huge resources; hence they are more than a social group. Because of their shared legacy, they need to organize a tribal government, to manage assets, resolve disagreements, manage family and business affairs, and create a common vision and purpose. Each family member must become a citizen of the tribe and take responsibility to participate. This government consists of a tribal council that oversees and organizes personal relations, and other councils that oversee their business and financial resources.

As a tribe of dispersed families, the family needs to sustain harmony, community and continuity. They need a well-developed family organization that runs parallel to its business interests. *Family governance* is one of the major achievements of a generative family. It enables the family to steward and use its wealth to fulfill its values and purpose, and maintain appropriate communication and influence over its business governance.

Governance takes the generative family beyond business and legal requirements for financial oversight. The family initiates special activities outside the business but taps into the resources and opportunities offered by its business and wealth. Many incredible activities become possible to this type of family. A family can remember and preserve the family history and legacy, educate and enrich the lives of the children, have great family vacations, serve the community, establish philanthropic ventures, and advance the values and principles the family wants embodied in its businesses. In this chapter, the central questions are: Who makes all of this happen? How do these things happen? The family, not the business, develops a "tribal council" to manage these activities. Family governance signals a separation of activities of the family from those of the business.

Developing governance is a challenge and family drama that takes place over the course of generations. If individual family members have different interests but want to work in concert, they need clear agreements, councils, and working committees to implement them, and they have to be accountable to each other.

This chapter, and the two that follow, present how and why generative families develop family governance.

## The Purpose of Family Governance

Family members are stewards of wealth in trust not just for their own use but for future generations as well. The future is safeguarded by people who benefit in the present. The family is growing in number and usually contains several ventures with different degrees of complexity. They must develop a system of organization, policies, and decision-making entities that together form the governance system. To manage and safeguard the family's growing wealth, governance allows family members to add purpose, organization, and focused activity to their lives.

Governance is an element of all family business: a board is needed to manage business entities for the owners. But for a generative family, governance takes on added importance and complexity: the owners share values and intentions and want to influence their assets and ventures and develop their connection as an extended family. Governance must be implemented in the family as well as the business. With the passing of the lone autocratic family leader who is able to impose his will, conflict is inevitable. Generative families must resolve differences in an acceptable way by developing processes for working together and making decisions. However, it takes commitment, creativity, hard work, and practice to make governance work.

Families new to wealth may find governance a confusing concept. It was not on the radar of the wealth creators or even their children. Family governance is a unique and highly demanding endeavor not needed by most nonfinancially linked families. If it does not own valuable assets together, a family has little cause to develop formal policies, activities, agreements, and working groups. However, a family with newly acquired wealth discovers much that must be done as a family to become effective stewards at managing all types of family "capital" beyond the third generation. Family members cannot just be a family; they have to organize and commit time to take care of their assets, build a shared identity and community, and hold each other accountable.

Generative families develop structures and processes to manage the natural tension between each person's self-interest and collective interests. When the family reaches a certain size and wants to continue to act in unison, the process must be managed consciously and clearly. The personal values, expectations, interests, concerns, and feelings of each family member are the foundation upon which governance is based. As a family tribe, the family takes on projects and tasks separate from the business.

Why does a third-generation family need to govern the family at all? Generative families often refer to the adage, "With great wealth comes great responsibilities." Even if they aren't active family leaders, family members should learn to be good citizens, engaged, responsible participants in family activities. They can't ignore their wealth, nor can they just sit back and enjoy the harvest. While family members have different degrees of ownership and levels of influence over decisions, every family member should have a voice in what happens. Because they care about one another, family members want to listen to other members. Each family member has a responsibility to be informed and thoughtful in offering his or her ideas. Unlike public companies, in a family enterprise the next generation of owners is already in the room. The process of family governance allows the family to anticipate and debate everyone's ideas.

Many family inheritors are not very well informed about their business or financial situation. The legacy family business may have been sold, and the family may now share a variety of investments. Perhaps the family opens a family office to look after its assets (as was true about half of the families in this study). If the whole family shares ownership of business, investments, land, or a foundation, whose values or vision guides the family? While each business and or asset may each have its own governing board, the family members as owners or owners-to-be want a voice in what direction the family goes and what it does with the wealth that flows to the owners and beneficiaries.

Family governance is a blend of need, opportunity, and possibility. The work of the family is not about increasing wealth but about what the family does with its resources and how working together leads the family to achieve more than any family member can achieve on his or her own. This added value is often in nonfinancial areas: human, relationship, and social "capital." As the previous chapter showed, the generative family creates an extended family community that expands upon the family legacy, builds trusting and enduring relationships, educates young people, and offers them roles in philanthropy, management, and family ventures. Family governance is how that is achieved.

Governance is the process by which the family makes these choices and develops the structure to put its decisions into action. It is not democracy; regulations and policies define the precise rights and responsibilities of different types of stakeholders. They may limit the available choices radically. A few people may have all the votes, but because they are part of a family, they want to inform and listen to one another. The essence of governance is balancing the perspectives of each group. The generative alliance contains elders who are majority owners and leaders, advisors that bring skills and loyalty, and excited rising generations who offer new ideas and energy. All these voices need to be heard, aligned, and integrated. This presents a huge challenge for a growing, extended family with a portfolio of ventures and assets. Governance is not an option; it is a necessity.

Business ownership is not evenly distributed. Some family branches inherit larger shares of ownership, and family members may sell all or some of their shares. Other family members—including young people, trust beneficiaries, and married-ins—are not owners. One major reason for creating family governance is that family members must learn that while being part of a family of wealth has its perks, every family member has a different claim on the family wealth and role in influencing it.

This first-generation matriarch looks toward her grandchildren and observes that family is more important than the family's huge business. Her legacy work has shifted to the family:

*I thought, "I will make a strong family organization while the business organization will be quite loose." Grandchildren can decide on their own what they want to do. The family is to me the most important element. In business, everything starts with the family. You must take the time to develop each member to their potential. That takes time and education. People don't understand how important that is, and they underestimate the time, care, and devotion it takes to build a strong family. But for me that's where everything happens, so that's where we spent most of our time. I guess if you look at our family business, it would be a combination of individuation combined with collectivism.*

## Values That Underlie Family Governance

While there are diverse paths to governance, there are common elements to the cultures and values of actively governing families. To succeed, family cultures must become transparent, inclusive, future-focused, and accountable. They echo qualities of family enterprise culture reported in Chapter 6. The following quotes from families illustrate qualities and values that emerge with family governance.

### Inclusiveness: A Unified Voice of the Family

*It's an important value and one that has made us strong during difficult times. Where a lot of companies might have just blown up, we've been able to create processes where we . . . give people the opportunity to voice their opinions at these meetings and try to work through stuff. They have an investment in the family as well as the business. There's a lot at stake if this doesn't work. We faced that a couple of times where some of the business decisions were very difficult. We weren't aligned. It's more about being proud of who we are that carries us through during those times.*

### Communication and Transparency

*With regards to leadership, it's critical to our success that communication channels with family members remain open and two-way transparent because that's the only way to ensure that there's trust, harmony, and support from the family. The day that that breaks down into mistrust and lack of transparency between the business and the family is the day we lose the support of family members to want to continue being shareholders. Things start falling apart if it becomes a widespread failing in the family.*

### Developing and Recruiting Family Talent

*We identify and support upcoming talent, identify people that have an interest to learn about the business even if it is just on a family-ownership level or if it's somebody, they think to themselves, "I might want to work at the company." How do we go about fostering that? One of the ways is getting them involved with the family council, then trying to have them learn about the business and see if it's something they might want to do later in life. The family council meets four times a year directly after the board meeting.*

### Competency and Accountability: Saying "No" to Family Members

*The board nominating committee is composed of family council and board members. I was the nominating committee chairman, so I know this stuff pretty well. People apply, and if you don't give them the position, then I've got to tell them why, and some people aren't happy about that. So we constantly work on how to be clear about requirements for a*

*(continued)*

> *position. You try to home in on that in the job description so that when people apply,
> they get that we're looking for younger people with social media skills, etc. So people that
> apply when they're told no hear, "Well, you didn't really fit the slot." All nominating
> committees struggle with how people feel when they're rejected and the consequences. We
> certainly don't have that one figured out.*

## What Ignites Shared Family Governance?

Rudimentary governance is always present in the family; as it gets more complex,
it must become more explicit, collaborative, and inclusive. G1 already has its own
form of governance, but it is autocratic; one or two wealth creators make all the
decisions, with no oversight or review. When the family contains a single household,
governance can remain informal with few explicit policies and roles. The second
generation expands to include more people and greater complexity, as this family
member notes: *"We often say the founding generation's philosophy is 'follow me up the hill,
my way or the highway.' To survive, G2 needs to learn more about working in an interrelated
sort of way."* The G2 siblings have grown up together, but they need to learn to collaborate in making good decisions because they no longer have a venerable "father"
to direct them.

To survive together, the third generation must go further. G3 may face a maturing business with increasing global competition and need for professional management, as well as pressure to raise capital or sell. This changing landscape often means
finding ways to challenge family members who have become too comfortable doing
things in a certain way. The family must establish a professional business but also an
aware, competent, and engaged family of owner-stewards. The family does this by
making the rules more explicit and detailed so that family members know what they
can and can't do.

To finance its commitment to philanthropy, a G4 family realized it needed a
profitable business. The family evolved from seeing the business as the place for
the family to act on its values to seeing that the business was also the vehicle
for greater projects:

> *Our Christian heritage was the reason the company existed, so that the family can contribute
> to charity. While sales were growing, profits remained flat. We asked: "How come we don't
> have as much money to give away? What's going on?" We told the older generation to look at
> whether we keep the business, sell, or restructure it. We had all family branches involved in
> that discussion. One thing that's important about the vote is that it had to be unanimous;
> everybody had to agree on the next step. We looked at everything from selling the business to
> going public to the status quo. We want to do the right thing, and that is sustain this business
> for future generations.*

The need to adopt explicit rules and clear policies for decision-making seems
reasonable, yet in a growing family, some family members may not initially grasp its
importance. That is why there must be education. If they are not informed, newer

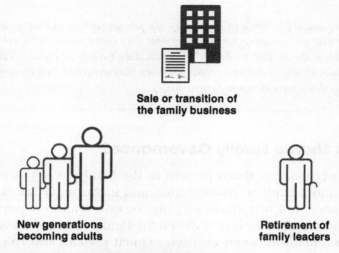

**Sale or transition of
the family business**

**New generations
becoming adults**

**Retirement of
family leaders**

**Figure 10.1   Three "triggers" for family governance.**

family members do not understand why things are being done in a certain way. They may become disengaged or even hostile to change:

> It's been a challenge trying to get everybody to understand the need for a more formal governance process. My younger brother and my mum are not as connected to the business. My mum has been on the board for a long time and wanted to retire and separate herself out of the whole process and just be a grandmother and do her thing. So it's been a challenge trying to get us together and say, "How are we going to engage the in-laws before we get to that fourth generation?" and making sure we have a plan for the next ten years.

Many families hire advisors or consultants. While outside advice is important, family members must still be informed and engaged. They can get good advice, but they can't outsource responsibility for making it happen. The family should not become dependent on advisors, who can become an interest group of their own. As one family member observed, *"It's a real challenge to choose what we do as a family and when do we look to outside helpers. The more somebody from the outside does it, the less the family must do it. It sets up a cycle. I'd like to see our family take more initiative to do these things that we're paying someone else to do. It makes me uncomfortable."* Other families are clear that they value working together to design and implement governance. By doing that, the family members buy in and feel emotionally connected to the work that needs to be done.

A major business transition can lead them to initiate family governance. While business leaders negotiate the business aspects of the deal, the sale of a family business changes the personal relationships of family members. The loss of the legacy family business can be traumatic to family members and the family as a whole. The sale can lead to family members losing their jobs as well as to a shift in leadership as the family decides what to do with its assets. This is a major governance project for the emerging younger generation:

> *In the eighties, we sold our original operating company. The fourth generation were all in our twenties or thirties, and our parents were getting older. We owned all these assets, but some issues and debates were going on in the management of the merger. We got involved, but there wasn't a clear family strategy. To deal with the transition, the older generation called for a series of "All Hands on Deck" meetings. They were held every two years. Very few third-generation members attended, so it was mostly the younger fourth generation from all over. We got to know each other. We debated the issues, looked at as basic an issue as who is considered a family member and who isn't all the way through to redefining our family values.*

A transition to formal governance may also be triggered by the passing or retirement of an elder-generation leader who took care of everyone without training a successor or letting people know what he (most usually) was doing. If not before, then after this departure, the family is forced to rethink how things are done. As this fifth-generation heir says, *"We're revisiting how our family office is managed and supervised. That was done for years by the patriarch, who had a certain way and didn't want to change. But we had conversations about the need to change into something more responsive to everyone."*

## Embedding Governance in the Family

Sometimes there is a lot to overcome before a family can accept or welcome governance. A family like this one may be passively involved and let things happen until they become aware that governance would be helpful to them:

> *I was on our corporate foundation board when we first started bringing in representatives from all branches of the family. It was our first opportunity to talk about anything. About fifteen years ago, we got a new nonfamily CEO from another family company, who said, "You guys need a family governance system." He announced this to the foundation board because it was the only place where the family members convened.*
>
> *Nobody knew what family governance was or what it meant. I was the only member of my family that wasn't involved in some way, and I felt a bit guilty about not giving back. One of my brothers was working in the business at the time, my other brother was on the board, and the husband of my sister was also working in the business. I was serving on the foundation board but not in the business. I initially met quite a bit of resistance at the board level because nobody understood what it meant and didn't see the need for it. Later, when they heard that family governance involved creating a family council, they got nervous because they were concerned that the council would become a "shadow" board and interfere with the operating company board. The first thing I did was go to an educational program to find out what exactly it is. That began the process of gathering all our family members, creating a family directory, and getting people to come to our first family meeting.*
>
> *The challenges along the way were huge because the board didn't understand what we were doing, seeing me as an agitator, akin to a union organizer, organizing the masses. They thought*

*(continued)*

*(Continued)*

*that was a bad idea. Their view was run the business well, keep the shareholders at an arm's length, and everything will be fine. The less we hear from the shareholders, the better. So it has been a long, long process for the council. First, convincing the board that we weren't going to interfere with the running of the business and were just trying to provide a service to them.*

*We created a family purpose statement for our governance:*

- *Foster a community that is connected and engaged, respects individual perspectives, and works together on shared goals.*
- *Facilitate communication within the family and between family and company.*
- *Represent the family in working with the board and management on projects of common interest.*
- *Nurture strong and effective leadership.*
- *Promote and provide continuing education among family, board, and management.*
- *Uphold our family's values.*

*We were in the position of continually having to prove ourselves to the board and to our family, who didn't understand what we were doing either. The family liked the idea of having a voice. But they were skeptical and didn't understand why they had to do anything. They had never had any sense of responsibility for being owners. They just were receiving dividends.*

*It's been a challenge of gaining legitimacy and credibility with the board and with the family. The family began to gain a sense of, "Oh, my god, we are owners of this company. That's a big responsibility, and there are certain things that I need to do to be prepared to be a good owner." The sixth generation have been coming to the meetings, and that's been the theme. Now that's kind of part of their DNA. They understand that's what's necessary in a family business. The fifth generation, those of us who were involved in the beginning, keep feeling a need to beat people over the head to justify our existence and keep explaining why we're doing what we're doing. And the next generation, especially the ones on the board, are saying, "Why are you doing this? It's not necessary. We get it. We get what you're doing," and it's just a matter of how we then move forward.*

## Building Blocks of Family Governance

A generative family begins with developing a boundary to separate interconnected family and business activities. Family governance is different from business governance, but they overlap. They can be seen as two "pillars" that work together. Each pillar has a purpose and must be organized around that purpose. Previous chapters have presented the business pillar as well as the organization of business governance. This chapter is about the family pillar. As the family becomes more extensive and has more people and more resources, it can do much more than just oversee business and financial assets. Emerging family members can be a creative force, supporting family members and the wider community. These activities are clearly separate from the business. (See Figure 10.2.)

The leaders in family activities are different than the family business leaders. Wise families discover that their business leaders have a great deal on their plate—they don't also need to be family leaders. Other people can step up to family

| "TRIBAL" FAMILY<br>Family Assembly and Council | PROFESSIONAL BUSINESS<br>Board and Owners Council |
|---|---|
| • Develops personal relationship. | • Long-term commitment. |
| • Regulates relationships to family<br>office and wealth. | • Patient capital. |
| • Builds family trust. | • Professional managers. |
| • Engages across generations. | • Nonfamily CEO option. |
| • Supports legacy values. | • Independent directors. |
| • Administers family property. | • Family employment policy |
| • Celebrates rich history. | |
| • Develops human capital. | |
| • Shares philanthropic efforts. | |

**Figure 10.2    "Tribal" family versus professional business governance.**

leadership. Family and business leaders each organize different areas that together support and create the family.

The second generation grows up together in the household of the wealth creators and finds it natural to take roles in the business. But the third generation may not directly know what the family business needs or offers—or may not even feel welcome. In their upbringing, many young people from business families are told, explicitly or implicitly, to be passive and not ask questions; they are told that they will be taken care of. G3 family members have always lived with the reality of the family's wealth and community visibility and respect. While they may know "Grandpa" as a kindly person, they do not experience the scope of his achievement in building the family enterprise. They know their family has significant wealth, but they may have different ideas of what the family should do or invest in. Do their ideas have any standing? They need clear direction about how they can legitimately participate.

Members of the younger "rising generation" inherit benefits of the family wealth, but they face many competing possibilities for their time and energy. They ask, "*Why should we work together at all if there are so many great things we can do with our wealth and inheritance outside the family?*"

To remain partners into the fourth and later generations, the generative family must attract each emerging generation family member to give of his or her talent, time, and energy. Generative families do not just expect new members of each generation to contribute and be part of the family; they use governance to invite these new members in with an attractive offer. Such families begin family assemblies and education programs to make membership more attractive and meaningful. Their goal is to recruit young family members to actively engage in family pursuits.

They also prescribe how a family member who does not want to be part of the family enterprise can leave and sell shares back to the family (see the section on pruning in Chapter 5). In every generation, some family members do not want to be pressured into family governance. Almost every one of the families in this study offers an exit mechanism whereby family members can leave the family enterprise and claim their share of the assets (with clear limits and guidelines for doing that). As James Hughes describes them, generative families are not any more a family of all blood relations but a *family of affinity*, actively choosing to be together. While they inherit wealth, family members in a family of affinity must actively "sign up" to be "citizens" of an active governance body of engaged family members, adding new ideas and new energy to develop and utilize what they have been given.

When all family members work in the business, they are in daily contact and can collaborate on policies and decisions. After family members disperse and increase in numbers, with many not directly engaged, governance allows them to create a bridge to the family enterprise and learn about their opportunity to contribute and become leaders. When trusts, trustees, and family advisors come between the family and the rising generation, family members must create their own personal entity to define their place. Family governance offers engagement opportunities to family members who are not employees or board members.

Governance is not completing a checklist of tasks; instead, all of its elements are interrelated. For example, a family council needs to be defined with goals, values, and policies; these form the foundation of a shared family agreement called a *family constitution*. The council is selected and represents the wider family, which must meet as a whole group. The process of holding a wider family meeting as a whole group has been called family assembly. So creating governance includes three almost universal building blocks—a family assembly, a council, and agreements in the form of a family protocol, charter, or constitution. The agreement and the council are like yin and yang: the council can't work without a protocol, and the protocol does not make sense if there is not a council and other active family gatherings (such as a family assembly) to make it a reality. The two chapters that follow look at each of these entities.

Many families feel that governance lies in the agreements and legal documents that outline how they hold and manage their assets. While this is a central aspect of governance, generative families view it in a larger context, consisting of an integrated, interconnected system of agreements, activities, policies, practices, and values. An agreement means very little if there is no meaningful path to put it into action. It is a social system, containing the elements seen in Figure 10.3.

All of these elements are interconnected. To start, a governance system must offer transparency and a free flow of information because people cannot exercise oversight or control when they can't see what's happening. Transparency is not always part of the original generation. The beginning of governance comes with the regular sharing of financial and business information that was formerly

Transparency

Councils

Agreements

Boundaries

Accountability

**Figure 10.3    Elements of family governance.**

confidential. With transparency, there must be policies, practices, and rules specified in documents adhered to by all family members. The agreements are administered in family councils and boards that work in concert. These entities and agreements define boundaries and roles, which clarify and differentiate responsibilities and accountability and which define how representative leaders are responsible to the whole family. Unless all five of these elements are present, the generative family cannot operate effectively.

A G2 or G3 family with a strong and thriving business (or several) realizes that potential family activities will not happen unless the family takes initiative. Such initiative can arise from anywhere in the extended family, not just the formal leadership. The family learns that assembly of the whole extended family is necessary for staying in touch, building relationships, and airing concerns, but it is not a good setting for making decisions or creating policies. For that, they need a smaller, more focused working group. This family council is convened by the family leadership as a sort of executive committee, listening to all of the family voices to help the family define what it wants to do together and setting up a family foundation, shared property, investments, or family office. Since the family has grown in numbers, the council is a small, dedicated group *representing,* and responsible to, the others.

The family council allows the family to conduct the "business of the family" having to do with business oversight, goals, and resources for developing family, human, and social capital. Family members may erroneously expect the business leaders to carry out these responsibilities, but they are usually busy with other commitments and do not have the time or the motivation to manage these responsibilities, so they fall through the cracks. The result may be family tension, conflict, or just lack of attention to things that are important, like assessing the capability and commitment of the rising generation to enter family leadership. The family creates a family council to have a nonbusiness mechanism to accomplish this. This will be explored in the following chapter.

Family governance separates family issues from those of the business, which are addressed in a parallel governance structure. There are many areas of overlap. As we will see, the family council, while not having formal authority over the business, may contain some owners and other influential family members. Their values, concerns, and voice are important messages for the board of directors. There are many ways that the family connects to the business, some formal and some informal, and governance organizes this input.

To operate effectively, the family council needs a working agreement defining its purpose, values, policies, and practices over what can be a huge, multigenerational set of family enterprises. The family has several preexisting agreements: trust documents, shareholder agreements, corporate by-laws, and policies, all of which guide the family enterprise. But family members don't often read these documents or fully understand what they can and cannot do or how various financial events will happen. These documents often raise more questions than answers.

Also, while these documents specify rules and practices, they often don't include the purpose and values that guide the family. And they have many holes. For example, documents may talk about rules regarding transfer of ownership, voting, or distributions, but different interpretations of these rules can lead to conflict within families. Drafting a detailed family constitution, charter, or protocol allows the family to formulate clear instructions for how these agreements work in practice. These questions include who makes decisions, about what, how they work, who is included, who implements decisions, how these individuals are paid, and how family leaders are selected.

## Increasing Prevalence of Governance Practices

In pursuing the family's financial, individual, and social goals, each generational transition develops common practices. These practices are advocated at academic and business conferences and by family business consultants. One of the primary questions in this research was whether successful families actually use these practices and attribute their success to them. An earlier study[1] looked at the use and importance of eighteen practices in two hundred successful multigenerational families.[2] The current research study found several of these practices were reported as factors in intergenerational success. The focus of this study is on families beyond the third generation. These findings shine a light on practices and conditions rarely if ever described this way before.

**Table 10.1 Family practices by generation.**

| | G2 | G3 | G3-4 | G4 | G5+ |
|---|---|---|---|---|---|
| **Family Governance** | | | | | |
| Family Council | 63% | 71% | 100% | 85% | 100% |
| Family Constitution | 25 | 43 | 71 | 96 | 100 |
| Next Gen. Education | 13 | 43 | 71 | 75 | 100 |
| Exit Policy | 0 | 43 | 43 | 85 | 100 |
| **Enterprise Practices** | | | | | |
| Independent Board | 25 | 71 | 85 | 96 | 100 |
| Nonfamily CEO | 25 | 28 | 43 | 25 | 100 |

*(continued)*

 The current study found that these practices were increasingly important with each succeeding generation. The practices are divided into those that have to do with family policies, roles, and decisions and those that have to do with the family enterprise. The number of families that use each of these practices greatly increases over generations, until by the fourth generation, nearly every family uses every practice. (See Table 10.1 and Figure 10.4.)

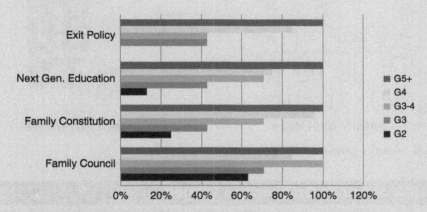

**Figure 10.4  Evolving family governance practices over generations.**

## Linking Family and Business/Ownership Governance

The link between family and business should be open and fluid. Family members own the business and feel deeply and emotionally committed to what it does. They can move into the business by visiting, working there, or taking roles that relate to the various family ventures. Key purposes of the family council and owners' groups are to link family and business governance and educate and prepare family members to perform their proper roles. Figure 10.5 depicts the relationship of the two pillars of governance—the family and the business.

 The family council is a parallel organization to the business's board of directors, which represents the owners. But family members are often owners, so the family faces the reality that while their governance structures are separate, the membership of these two groups overlaps. One of the key functions of the family council and family governance is to manage the relationship with the owners, who in turn create their board of directors and other oversight mechanisms. The family council and assembly are connected to the business and boards of directors via the owners' council and also via direct connection (and often cross-representation) between the family council and board.

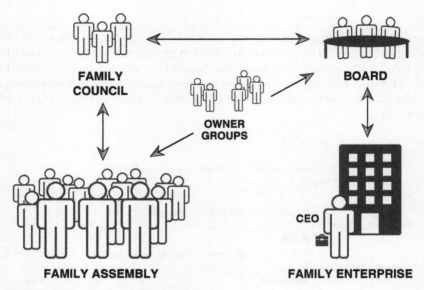

**Figure 10.5  Family governance structure.**

## Overview of Family Governance Entities

Previous chapters introduced the family assembly, board, and owners' council as important elements of family governance. The chapters that follow will explore the family council and describe the family constitution.

Table 10.2 defines the differences between the family assembly, family council, and owner's council, three elements of family governance. The table begins with the family assembly, described in Chapter 9. It also includes the owners' council, presented in Chapter 6 on business governance; the owners' council is a subgroup of family members who have direct ownership of the family enterprises.

**Table 10.2  Comparing family assembly, owners' council, and family council.**

|  | Assembly | Owners' Council | Family Council |
|---|---|---|---|
| Definition | Gathering of all family members | Oversight group to specify and safeguard the owner's interests | Representative entity to organize and conduct shared family activities |
| Purpose | Building community, adopting legislation | Defining intentions, values and overseeing assets | Organizing and overseeing family activities |
| Meeting Times | Annual | Quarterly or less | Several times a year |
| Constituents | All family members, inclusive | Owners of family assets | Voted on or selected to represent family members |

*(continued)*

**Table 10.2** *(continued)*

|  | Assembly | Owners' Council | Family Council |
|---|---|---|---|
| **Activities** | Having fun together, initiating activities, defining values and policies, building relationships, providing education | Appointing and overseeing board of directors for family assets, defining business and financial goals, creating strategic vision | Setting up committees to organize and carry out family activities, proposing policies to assembly, coordinating family activities |
| **Definition** | Gathering of all family members | Oversight group to specify and safeguard the owner's interests | Representative entity to organize and conduct shared family activities |
| **Purpose** | Building community, adopting legislation | Defining intentions, values and overseeing assets | Organizing and overseeing family activities |
| **Meeting Times** | Annual | Quarterly or less | Several times a year |
| **Constituents** | All family members, inclusive | Owners of family assets | Voted on or selected to represent family members |
| **Activities** | Having fun together, initiating activities, defining values and policies, building relationships, providing education | Appointing and overseeing board of directors for family assets, defining business and financial goals, creating strategic vision | Setting up committees to organize and carry out family activities, proposing policies to assembly, coordinating family activities |

## Weaving Family and Business Governance

The board and family council each play a role in overseeing the family enterprise. The dividing line between the two is a moving target, set and maintained not by fiat but by negotiation. The family initiates a cycle of high-level advising and deciding but then defers to the board. The board listens to the family and makes the difficult choices and explains those choices to everyone. Here is an account of how a manufacturing business entering its fourth generation deals with this interplay:

> We're trying to come up with criteria for family board members. I've been on a number of other boards, so I know something about how boards work. We're also developing criteria for replacing the four family board members. None of us are planning to go anywhere soon, but we need to decide the criteria so that the fifth generation will know where to look if they want to be involved. They can learn what it means to be a board member. When I entered the board, I had no idea what I was getting into.
>
> At every board meeting we have a summary report from the chair of the family council. At the family council, we have reports about the board meeting. They're usually back-to-back: the board meeting happens one day, and then the family council meets the next day. In addition, we have a family relations subcommittee. This developed because our board chair wanted us to review our values. I began with a review and an updating of current family values.

*The family council does several key things. They develop the values that the whole company lives by, elect board members, and build family relationships that encourage stewardship. So that's the family council. The family assembly is held every other year, and anybody can volunteer to help out with that. We encourage stewardship and involvement, so a lot of people want to participate.*

*When I got on the board, the selection and election task force was in major crisis. There was a lot of screaming by family members about this. We needed to develop our credibility with management as a family. We had gone through two CEOs in four years. I could see that the current CEO was not good for the company. This led to a big split in the family, though eventually everybody agreed with my assessment and he transitioned out. The next CEO did some good things but was also not in line with the values of the company or the family. That was a very difficult transition, as once again the family was split.*

*The most recent hiring of a new CEO finally led to a good one! But it also produced problems. These days, only a few family members work for the company. We have seven hundred employees and only three full-time family employees. Because one of them is my brother, I hear from him what's going on from the perspective of the employees. But he isn't in top management; he and my cousin are just below the top. Their presence can be a little tricky because my cousin and I on the board hear from family members who work in the company, but the other two family board members do not have that link. That's one of the complexities of being in a family business.*

The nature of the link between family and business is often discussed in the start of a family council:

*One thing our new council is considering is what roles should the council play in representing the family in the board of the company. Some of us believe that the family council should have members knowledgeable about our businesses so that when the family council expresses the family's desire or when there are issues regarding the functioning of the board, there will be council members who are knowledgeable so that their opinion carries weight.*

Most family councils have clearly defined functions, but it is easy for the family to push the boundaries too far into business operations, as this account shows:

*The family assembly meets every other year to develop the values that the whole company lives by, to elect board members, to build up family relationships and encourage stewardship. Anybody can volunteer to help, and a lot of people do. Because we encourage stewardship and involvement, a lot of people want to participate. But that has its limits as well. For example, we had a big to-do recently about salaries of family board members. The family council got involved trying to analyze the salaries of the board members. And that was not appropriate because they didn't have the experience. They just didn't have a clue, and so the board chair had to take that back and say, "These decisions actually get made at the board level," and that was fine. We must maintain those clear role definitions.*

This family realized that family members, especially young people growing up, often do not fully understand the responsibility of ownership. What is their role and responsibility if they become an owner or an employee? What if they expect to become an owner but are not yet one? One of the major tasks of a family governance system is to educate each family member in his or her role. The media is full of stories of how wealthy families interfere in their businesses, causing the business to lose value and even forcing a sale. Learning the appropriate role of a family member and having a clear plan for governance seems to have helped the generative families in this study avoid this fate.

This leads to one critical difference between family enterprises and public corporations. In addition to family owners, there are family members who expect to inherit ownership—*owners-in-waiting*. They know this will happen, and it is in the family's interest to have them understand the business and learn their future role as owners. There are also beneficiaries of trusts, whose business decisions are made by trustees; the trustees have a voice in the business future and the use of its assets. These potential owners and beneficiaries are important to the family and participate in governance. Family governance usually includes education and communication about the business, and these family nonowners also can share ideas and suggestions even though they are not formal decision-makers.

The council formalizes the connection between family owners, owners-to-be, and the business board often by having shared meetings. The family has things that it wants to know and suggest for the business, and the company wants to know where the family stands on key strategic issues:

> *Every board meeting has a report from the family council chair. She comes to the board meeting and does a summary report of what's going on. Then, at the family council, we have reports about the board meeting.*
>
> *They're usually back to back. The board meeting happens, and then the next day the family council meeting happens. We've done it the other way, the family council meeting first and then the board meeting, and there are pros and cons to both ways. Not many companies have a family relations standing subcommittee. That developed because our board chair wanted us to review the values in the family. This led us to begin a review and updating of the family's values and how they want them expressed in the company.*

Frequently there is another intervening governance entity composed of the family owners called, appropriately, an *owners' council*. This group has several functions that differentiate it from the board. It contains the owners, who may be too numerous to all be on the board. This group is especially important if the family has several ventures. The family might, for example, own a ranch and a publicly held community bank. Each has its own board. The family might also have a family office or a holding company containing a portfolio of businesses. The owners' council acts as an umbrella organization to define and integrate the goals and policies of each entity. It typically consists of family members who are actual owners (and maybe trustees of family trusts) and does not contain outside directors.

Boards, as we have seen, frequently have nonfamily independent directors who are not owners but whose expertise and wisdom helps guide the business. These directors want to know the goals and values that are held by the family owners, and they want to hear it in one unified voice. The owners' council is where the family aligns its goals, values, and priorities, airs conflicts, and then speaks to the board with a unified voice. It is needed in addition to the board when the family owners become more numerous and have concerns to share with the board.

An important function of a family council is communicating what the family wants from the business. Boards of family enterprises often hear different things from different family branches and individuals; they want a clear statement of the family expectations and intentions for the business. Here is how one family makes that clear to the board:

> *We have a shareholder agreement that lasts ten years. Then we look at updating or renewing it. Company bylaws guide the business of the company. One of the first documents the council developed was a family charter; we sought outside consulting guidance on this. It fundamentally talks about what we're committed to as a family, our core values, and the purpose for us gathering as a family within the family council as well as sets the direction for the family within the family council. One of the big distinctions is, as a council, we're really dealing with the "business of the family" not the "business of the business," and so if we ever get on the line of "Is this really something we should be talking about or just the business of the business," somebody will notice that and say, "Wait a minute. I think we're almost crossing the line here. We can always seek to get clarification if we need it."*
>
> *Within the last three to four years, we've developed an owners' plan, a document the family council generates through a committee. We present it to the board each year to give the direction for the board of the family's interests regarding the business. We've found that quite useful, and the board has acknowledged they also find it quite useful to know for the direction of the company. It talks about everything from what level of risk are we comfortable with and even when we talk about moderate risk, what does that mean to us exactly? The owners' plan hasn't changed much year to year, but we tweak it to try to get clearer about what that is for the board based on their feedback and questions that they have for us. I think we found that to be a valuable document on both sides.*

The level of formality and organization of governance increases each generation to accommodate a larger family and more complex set of family enterprises:

> *The council is separate from the board. The council is about the governance of the family. They have nothing to do with the business governance. The board is the oversight piece for the business. They're like a business board even though they have family members on, but there's more independent members than family. It's completely different. The family directors on the board report to the family council at their meetings about the business, and the president of the family council reports to the business board about the family council, but the family council has nothing to do with running the business at all. Each of them has about ten family members that they call constituents, and each family council member reports to their constituents about what is going on in the business. They're elected by the family, not by branch.*

The family above has four coordinators for education, governance, communications, and the annual meeting. The family council chair reflects, *"I can categorically say, we would not have our business today if it had not been for the family council and the reunification of the family."*

As the family enterprise becomes highly professional, family members becoming stewards must in turn become more professional in their oversight. To serve in governance groups, they need a certain level of skill and need to do a certain amount of work. The family council creates that education for their younger members and defines qualifications for different roles, though sometimes the business also offers education activities, such as internships and seminars.

The family, through the council, has a voice (but not always a vote) in the direction of the company, but their ideas do not go directly to the business. The family's voice is transmitted through the owners' council or board. Some families allow individual family members to make input informally, but family governance usually specifies a formal process for the family to communicate its values and intentions to the board:

> *The owners through a lot of education have developed a written document that's given to the board every year. It's reviewed every year by the family council. If they have some things they want to change or if the board has a little pushback on something, they reconsider. This process tries to divide as clearly as possible the risk and return parameters that the shareholders wish to have in the company.*

The following chapters will look in more detail at the family council and the family constitutions, family governance elements that work in parallel with the boards of family enterprises.

## Taking Action in Your Own Family Enterprise

If your family has not considered governance, has tried to set up a board or council and not been successful, or initiated governance activity but feels it is not doing as much as it can, this book has offered a range of possible paths and practices you can draw upon. Governance is a platform to prepare your family to act as a creative force to develop the potential for wise, thoughtful, and productive use of its accumulated wealth.

Generative families outline a direction that you may not have considered for your family. While many of the families interviewed for this study developed governance in their third generation, it is never too early to do this. If you are in your second generation or living with success beyond anyone's expectations, family governance may not yet be part of your future plans. You may be working with advisors to invest or create an estate plan or trust. This book suggests that you can use this opportunity for a larger purpose: to consider the future of your family and your family enterprise, not as a task to complete but as a wonderful shared opportunity to see what your family can do as a shared cross-generational project. It is about possibility.

The first step toward engaging a family is to hold a family meeting for all family members, with a purpose other than just socializing. It can have a theme such as philanthropy or talking about the family's vision for the future. Families differ as to whom they want to include. Some start with just the blood family; others start with a value of inclusion and invite spouses. The goals of the meeting are to have a good discussion, not necessarily to make any decisions, and to create a safe and welcoming environment for each individual to have a voice and feel good about being part of the family. If the first meeting is successful, the family will decide to meet again and will begin to create a purposeful family community.

To begin to initiate governance, you need to get your family together, with older and younger generations considering what they want in the future. With all your family resources, they can imagine far more than the status quo. You can look at the future with two mindsets. First, you can think about what you need to do to anticipate future challenges as you have more people and cross generations. Second, you can consider what you might do, what you could do, that is creative, expansive, and worthy of what you have together.

What can you do as a family to move forward? We believe that you can invite the old and new generations of your family together to ask yourselves, "What is possible for us as a family together?" This is not a question with a single answer but rather an invitation for all family members to embark on a journey to consider what they can and want to do together and then to make it happen. Building a family council, holding regular family assemblies, and developing a family constitution are all interconnected and important in that they formalize and organize the good intentions of many family members.

### Assessing Your Family Enterprise Best Practices

This offers your family a "snapshot" to discover how much you engage in practices identified as important to sustaining your family across generations and using your family wealth to make a difference in people's lives. It focuses on best practices in three areas—the family, the family enterprise, and the human capital of the next generation. These practices were developed in several research projects over the past decade.[3]

You can complete it yourself, with your own view of your family; or several family members can complete it and compare responses. Different family members—having different places in the family—view the family differently.

You may not agree on the presence of a practice in your family or on its need for the future. That can lead to a productive discussion, not argument. Your responses represent your **perceptions** of the degree to which your family has adopted, or needs to adopt, each practice. This sets the stage for a **Family Conversation** about how your family can grow, develop, and prepare for the succession and stewardship of the next generation.

If you are a family advisor, you can use this tool to assess areas of strength and those that need development in the future. If several members of your family complete this inventory independently, they can compare responses in a **Family Conversation** to explore areas of agreement, and where scores or perceptions do not agree. Then, as a family, you can proceed to develop a **Strategic Family Roadmap**, to design and implement the practices that enable your family to succeed across generations.

## Best Practices for Multigenerational Family Enterprise

For each practice, indicate in the **Current** column, on a scale of 0–3 (0 = our family does not do that; 1 = we have talked about this; 2 = we are beginning to do this;

3 = we utilize this practice in our family), the degree you see your family using that practice at this time. In the **Future** column indicate how important you believe this practice will be for your family to develop that practice in the next three to five years (from 0 = very low to 3 = very high).

| Practice | Current | Future |
|---|---|---|
| **Pathway I: Nurture the Family** | | |
| 1.1 Clear, compelling family purpose and direction | | |
| 1.2 Opportunities for extended family to get to know each other | | |
| 1.3 Climate of family openness, trust, and communication | | |
| 1.4 Regular family meetings as a family council | | |
| 1.5 Sharing and respect for family history and legacy | | |
| 1.6 Shared family philanthropic and social engagement | | |
| **Pathway II: Steward the Family Enterprises** | | |
| 2.1 Strategic plan for family wealth and enterprise development | | |
| 2.2 Active, diverse, empowered board guiding each enterprise | | |
| 2.3 Transparency about financial information and business decisions | | |
| 2.4 Explicit and shared shareholder agreements about family assets | | |
| 2.5 Policies that support diversification and entrepreneurial ventures | | |
| 2.6 Exit and distribution policies for individual shareholder liquidity | | |
| **Pathway III: Cultivate Human Capital for the Next Generation** | | |
| 3.1 Employment policies about working in family enterprises | | |
| 3.2 Agreement on values about family money and wealth | | |
| 3.3 Support and encouragement to develop next-generation leadership | | |
| 3.4 Empower individuals to seek personal fulfillment and life purpose | | |
| 3.5 Opportunities to become involved in family governance activities | | |
| 3.6 Teach age-appropriate financial skills to young family members | | |

## Notes

1. Dennis Jaffe and Jane Flanagan, *Three Pathways to Evolutionary Survival: Best Practices of Successful, Global, Multi-generational Family Enterprises* (Chicago: Family Office Exchange and Family Business Network, 2012).
2. These practices are contained in the final part of the chapter, so that a family can use them for a self-assessment.
3. A summary can be viewed in the paper "Three Pathways to Evolutionary Survival: Best Practices for Multi-Generational Enterprise," published by Wise Counsel, 2012.

# The Family Council: Conducting the Work of the Family

The family council is the "executive" branch, representing all family members and carrying out the work of family governance. When there are family activities beyond the business, who will make them happen? Where will the funding come from? Who decides, and who is in charge? The assembly has too many people and not enough time. If the assembly has a vision of what they want to be, they empower a group of family leaders to make that happen. The council contains the "worker bees" of the family who want to build the family's future.

During the first two generations, the whole family is small enough to assemble around a dining room table, and family meetings are often informal and unstructured. But as the number of family members increases, the family needs more coordination. Organizing family meetings and events and preparing the rising generation lead to the designation of a small group of family members as coordinators.

A family council is one of the most unusual and unique features of generative families. If we think of a family as simply a collection of loosely linked households, it is hard to see why a family council would be needed. Does a family really need a social committee to organize family activities? But a generative family is larger—many households and many functions. Family governance can best be understood as the government, or executive council, of a growing tribe with many goals, ventures, and shared projects.

A family council starts informally and evolves as the need for explicit policies and activities becomes clear. For example, one family member says, *"We had many family members and eight family members on the board. The whole family would have dinner the night before a board meeting and discuss all the family issues and talk about that stuff and that eventually became the family assembly. We muddled on to address social needs, family unity, and harmony, and there is a component, which I think is turning out to be brilliant, of personal development."* After a satisfying family conversation, family members wonder, what's next? Who will be responsible for carrying out their ideas? In response, an active family council emerges.

The creation of a family council marks a stage of development after the generative family has expanded and owns several shared assets. As more people enter the family, with less shared history and values, family governance enables them to define their collective rules, policies, and expectations and to organize activities. It also expresses and supports a shared family identity that energizes and sustains the family through tough times and conflict.

The emergence of a council expresses a clear separation from operating the business. Family members can be part of the council and can share opinions and concerns separately from the business. The council includes family members who are not owners or active in the business and enables them to be part of the family identity and activities and to be knowledgeable about the business.

The great majority of generative families, 77 percent, developed as a family council.

**Do You Have a Family Council?**

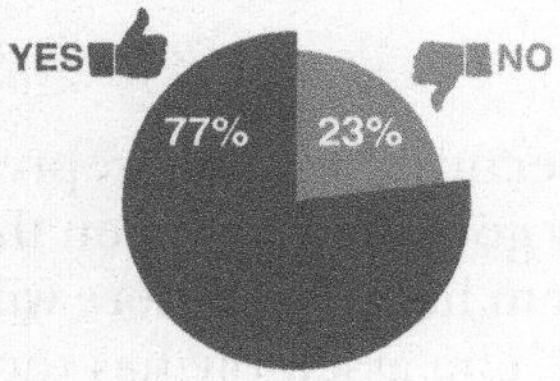

|  | G2 | G3 | G4+ |
|---|---|---|---|
| Have a Family Council | 8% | 32% | 60% |

**Figure 11.1 Prevalence of family councils and when they develop.**

The council forms the bridge between family values, relationships, and intentions and the business. The council distills the voice of the family and passes it to the board, the regulating mechanism of the business. While family governance is differentiated from business governance, there are areas of overlap. For example, the family members as owners have values and goals they want to impart to the business.

The family enterprise must abide by many legal documents: corporate charters, shareholder agreements, trust documents. These documents often are not fully understood by all family members. The family council helps family members learn and understand these documents as living agreements between old and new members of a business family. A council is a place where the family can consider the meaning of obscure or hard-to-understand materials. While the family council cannot suspend or contradict existing agreements, it is intended to help the family elaborate on them or suggest a need to amend them.

The council initiates many activities for the family not directly related to running the family businesses:

- It organizes family gatherings, sets the agenda, and records what is decided.
- It arranges educational activities for the family so that family members can become responsible, capable, and committed stewards of the family wealth.

- It brings family members together to talk about what they want to do with their wealth, in line with their values, and how they will do this. Through the council, the family can take on shared projects and initiatives. The council can also hold family members accountable for their behavior. It can deal with conflicts and set standards for family behavior.

The council can debate and explore family perspectives about business options such as selling the business, buying new ones, and making major investments. While these may seem to be business issues, they also impact the family.

The council offers a place for the family to initiate and amend shared activities, above and beyond those that already exist. While a vast difference exists between a legal document and an informal but shared family policy or wish, because of the respect and personal concern for each other, the council's view is taken seriously and often acted upon by trustees, owners, and board members. The family council helps and serves the business by making the business's operations more transparent and available to family members. The council makes the generative family a family, despite its size. It makes sure that the family relationships develop, that each person feels fairly treated and respected and has opportunity to participate. It is the heart and soul of the generative family.

## Emergence of the Family Council

The family council arises when the family becomes too large to be guided directly by a full family assembly and when the complexity and number of people dictate greater coordination of family activities. This account from a third-generation family leader illustrates how a family council evolves in response to the challenges faced by a successful business:

> We formed a family council about fifteen years ago. Originally, it was just my two sisters and myself. In the last five years, our objective has been to engage our fourth generation, who are in their forties. None of them work in the business. We are trying to bring them into the governance of the business and leadership within the family. We're about to complete our first family strategic plan, which our fourth generation has provided most of the input for. We are a work in progress as far as nurturing the family and trying to make sure our fourth generation gets involved with our strategic plan. We started having extended family gatherings and interactions. We talk about family openness, trust, and communication because we realized that is the only way we're going to stick together and maintain this business. We've created a legacy committee in our family council to try to formalize and provide more information about the family and business history. We don't share philanthropic interests. Some years ago, we talked about whether we wanted to share them, and we agreed that we all had different directions, so to some degree, we do share. We share our differences.
>
> Today we're finishing up our family strategic plan. I'm the chairman of the board, but the family council head will be one of the G4s, and we will have a G4 family office chair that will be the main liaison between the family council and the business. So both of those responsibilities have been removed from me and given to the next generation. This is their steppingstone into the governance leadership of the business. That is a great

*accomplishment for moving the family forward and passing of the baton from one generation to the next. It's easy to give you a three-minute summary, but it's been a difficult exercise for all of us.*

When most family members no longer have the opportunity to work in the business, there can be a loss of commitment and connection, unless a council is established to sustain that connection:

*The family council provides a forum for engagement of family members not employed or otherwise working with the company on the board. I think it has helped to have family members at least know each other because we organize things like a family assembly every other year and occasionally other activities. So there's a connection between second and third cousins twice removed they just wouldn't have otherwise because many of our family members are scattered around. It provided a forum for engagement and a way for the stockholders to move to the idea of stewardship.*

*The challenge for us has been defining the roles and the boundaries clearly between the role of the family, the family council, the board, and management. That's been tricky, as a family member can be in any of these roles. When I first came on the board, we had a board and management. Both were antagonistic toward the family and the stockholders, kind of looked down their nose at them.*

*We now have our first fifth-generation chair of family council, and there's awareness that the family council is a place to develop leadership skills and learn more about stewardship. We're hoping we start to put out a newsletter with family news and articles about things like stewardship. Right now, it's a little haphazard, but it must have some benefits and terms of that kind of stewardship mentality.*

Here is an account of how G3 in another family discovered the need for a family council:

*Love isn't enough. In the case of the family business—even if everybody loves one another and has trust, certain processes must be in place in the business itself to ensure that problems are worked out and things are discussed on a business-like basis. An example is the family council. We talk about what business issues are important. We ask, "What are our major decisions?" and from there we make the decisions. That's one process. The other topic for the council [concerns] our social lives and other problems that we're facing. We developed a protocol—the agreements of what is required from each one of us. We tried to find models to draw on, but we couldn't, so we just sat down and wrote them. Every few years, we modify them.*

*Mechanisms in place have allowed a smooth transition process. They include the family mission—what the family believes in, what they want their employees to believe in, and what they want to do for the company, the people, and the society in general. They also have a family protocol, a set of rules, which govern expectations of each other. They have a monthly executive council meeting where they discuss family matters, how they are doing in terms of communication, how is each person's leadership, what feelings are involved. No business, just interpersonal relations. This is the grease that keeps them flowing. If there are any conflicts, they come out.*

It's not easy to get the family to buy in to set up a family council. The need must be made obvious to the family members in order for them to set aside the resources and take the time to organize one. A family champion who steps up and sees the potential of a council must overcome family resistance:

> The biggest hurdle in setting up a family council was the divide in the family between having a council and fear that it would interfere with the business as opposed to add value to the business. Since then, everyone's in agreement. It adds value! Occasionally, something will come up where they'll debate whether that's a topic for the business or the family. But that was by far the biggest hurdle in getting a family council approved by the family. There was just a great divide in what it was meant to be and what it was going to do. So our charter is quite specific about the role of the family council, the role of the board, the interaction between the board and the family council, etcetera.

While every family develops a boundary between business and family activities, there is overlap. The family council differentiates itself from the business board and business activities in different ways. A one-hundred-year-old East Asian family with a family office and many ventures established its council in 2004:

> Our family charter defines the role of the council to uphold the vision and mission statements, to ensure stewardship, and act as a communication link between the family and its business interests, whilst encouraging engagement via family-led initiatives. In 2009, we had 125th-year celebrations. We have an annual general meeting, family assembly, and family dinner; and family members are encouraged to attend and participate. The council meets quarterly, with rotating membership, providing an opportunity for cousins to get to know each other and build closer relationships.
>
> We differ from perhaps some other family councils in the US, in that it is not an umbrella body sitting over the top of all the operating businesses. It sits alongside the businesses, and it's a more of a forum to voice views and hear difference of opinion. In a wider sense, it keeps relationships going.
>
> Going back to the inception of council, while it was not responsible for governance, it had visibility over a lot of what the family office did. Over time, that involvement has evolved with the establishment of a dedicated family office board. With it, perhaps the level of detail provided to the council has changed in that there is more confidence from the family that an appropriate level of focus is being applied to the family office business. With the establishment of the family office board in 2010, a large part of what council did was allowing a shift from focusing on the family business to more focus on the business of the family.
>
> So what would an agenda look like? The council receives presentations from executives of the family office, the operating business divisions, and the foundation. The council has a role regarding the family heritage assets, engagement, and education, and so there are several work streams being progressed by family members at any given time. A big part of its role is as a representative body of the wider family. Members are expected and encouraged to keep those communication channels open. If anything, it increases and encourages interpersonal family relationships.

Family councils evolve in unique configurations. For example, here is an account of dual family councils in a large fourth-generation family with a large legacy business and many investments:

*We have two large branches of the family descending from two brothers. Both of those have specific family councils, and each one of those councils probably has close to thirty members from two generations. Each council provides a voice for each family member, whether that person is a shareholder or not. The goals of the councils are to address any family concerns, priorities, and projects that might or might not be connected to the business. That's to keep the family cohesive, communicating and enjoying each other. It's also to impart information about the family business and how to be an effective shareholder. Each of the family councils have their own committees that focus on governance, new ventures, asset management, family activities, and education. The purpose is to foster personal and shareholder development so that everybody's voice, whether they are shareholders or not, is heard in the council.*

*Our ownership council comprises the entire shareholder group from both family councils. On top of that, we have a whole family assembly, which comprises all family members from age sixteen and spouses. That integrated council is designed to provide meaning and purpose to the family and a vehicle for education and development of family members. So the ownership council is governing and leading the family's interest, and the integrated council is about meaning and purpose and education and development. There is also a history committee that preserves photos, video, and newspaper articles on the family. Hopefully, they'll all be maintained well into the future.*

A family council often originates following the sale of the legacy business, as the family decides it wants to sustain regular connection even when the business is gone:

*The better I can get the family council to own the areas of legacy and education, the more it allows the family office to focus on the investment side, whether it's estate planning, accounting, or taxes. We could be a lot more efficient if we didn't get caught up in areas that belong to a council.*

*The family connection is purely financial right now. That has been the glue. And the way I've done it is getting everybody together for these family meetings. We've changed the name to family reunions or retreats, so there's no such onerous feeling around it. We have three days of everybody enjoying being together, and it's a matter of how you maintain that momentum when they leave. That's the challenge because everybody buys into it, everybody loves it, everybody loves being together, but I go back to when my dad gave up when he couldn't schedule that next meeting. Part of my life now is to not give up when getting faced with that.*

*The family council is about what the family wants to do when they are together. Why are we together? I called a meeting last year partly out of a sense of frustration. I said, "Let's all sit here and decide we want to be more than pooling our assets."*

*If we want to do any of this extra stuff and be a family rather than just a bunch of people who happen to have the same last name and invest together, what are we going to do? We had a one-day meeting where everybody came together and said, "Okay, we want to do this, we see the purpose," but they walk out the door, and I don't see much from anybody until the next time we're all together. I see that attitude in the council, the place where the family gets to be together and decides what they want to be or if they want to be or what type of family is it going to be. Is it going to be Thanksgiving-plus or is it just going to be Thanksgiving and then we'll do the family office on the side? The challenge for me is support because I've already drunk the Kool-Aid. But I need to be on their side of the table when it comes to deciding these things. I can't be the family office guy.*

Family councils contain many moving parts and roles for family members, as we see in this highly dispersed European family enterprise:

*Everybody can be a council member, but they participate for different reasons in different areas. In one branch, for example, they agreed, "Okay, you go on the foundation, you go on the corporation, and you go into the family office," which is another big company. You're looking at roles for sixty people, four in the corporation, four in the foundation, sixteen on the council. We also have several families with a department running their nonbusiness affairs, and they get larger and larger and larger, and finally, you've got to incorporate it, put in directors, independent directors, different management teams, and we've got different directors of that.*

*Family office and corporate executives are paid. Everything else is volunteer. That gives us opportunity to have family business meetings and assemblies, and we invite the younger generation who are not yet shareholders to see that. We have regional meetings where we combine briefings on the corporation's affairs with family office affairs. We have an enormous ski weekend where everyone gets invited. The family council has been setting up groups to do various things. For example, one is called Family Engagement and Development Group, which includes some in-laws, to develop education programs for sixth-generation family. Some of G6 have already been on council, so that's the very first sniff of a generational change. It's a complex structure that you have in terms of engagement, and it gets to about half of the current fifth generation.*

*Council members circulate. In my branch, other than my two siblings who live overseas, every single member of the fifth generation has been on council. And some of the sixth. Because the council spots rotate every two years, we will eventually rotate the entire family through the council. And some people go, "Yup, well, I know it's going—I don't know what's going on, but I decided that I'm not interested at all," and that's for them. Not everyone's business orientated. We invest in your potential, but your potential could be anything. It could be violinist. You could be a painter. You don't have to be a businessman. And of course, they might go on to the foundation, which has a longer term of service.*

*It's going to get harder with the seventh generation. I suspect the branch structure might start to break down at that point. I was chair of the council four years ago. There was a bit of crossover. Council had a role in our business portfolio. Management will come and present new products and portfolio weightings and ideas to the council. And we wouldn't vote on it. Simply, the corporation would recommend, and the council will endorse, and we found that made people's heads explode because the portfolio management was getting a bit complex for some of the newbies. But I think the most important aspect of the council is people talking about problems and socializing who wouldn't normally, so that's an avenue of family to meet and work together. And getting business presentations, that's very good.*

In early generations, the family leader is also the chairman and perhaps CEO of the business. A watershed moment occurs when the family brings in a nonfamily CEO. In this case, the family business leader usually becomes board chair. Having a nonfamily business leader means the family council takes on greater importance. One large many-generational family created what it calls a two-president system of governance. The family chair describes her role and how it evolved:

*The family president is essentially the family council chairman. That's a more common struc-ture. Before that, we had a human resource committee of family members who advised the family president. We could bring up family issues within a council-like structure, but we formalized it in 2001, so it became the family president with a family council. The responsibility and roles of the family president and the council are to maintain the interest; I sit on the board.*

*    My job in addition to the other family directors is to make sure business decisions track with family values. I'm asked to test how the family feels with this. Then I go back to the council, and we would be a sounding board for family members and test ideas to the family. I'm a conduit from the family council and the family to the board as are the family directors. I also run family programs, which include the big annual meeting. That's under my supervision. I have staff allocated, and I also have in the family council a committee who helps plan that, and it takes about a year. This is a big part of our job because it's a huge meeting and it's always complicated.*

## Governing a Family Conglomerate

By the fourth generation, the family enterprises can be huge and include several wealth-creating entities. As the business and family grow, governance must evolve to match them, not just as a business but also in relation to the oversight role of the family council. This detailed account outlines the steps taken by a family adapting its governance process in response to new challenges:

*The family council was created thirteen years ago. Our consultant had us instituting policies, procedures, and entities in place without understanding the reasons for it. We did a good job of putting them in place, but it was not until later we started to understand the reasons for governance as we experienced growing pains.*

*    We were fortunate to start before the third generation was old enough to voice their opinions. They were fifteen years younger than they are today. At that time, they just went along with their parents, so we could get a head start. I have talked to other families where that generation is a lot older, and it is more difficult to understand the one-family concept and get that trust. Certain members are doubtful about doing it. In our case, the second generation was willing to trust each other and that passed down to the next generation, but the effort broke down when we tried to implement it.*

*    The older members of the third generation worked closely with this whole process. We have a thirty-five-year difference between the oldest and the youngest of the nineteen G3 players. The older G3s were involved because their parents wanted them to be involved, because this was for them. If the family and the enterprises are important, we need to make sure that this next generation*

*(continued)*

understands that—not only about the businesses but also about the family. The direction we set is that the family is the most important. If certain individuals are no longer a shareholder for whatever reason, they are still part of the family.

The family is the overarching umbrella over the enterprises, philanthropy, and family connection. To do that, we created a family council. Our first attempt was only to work on family harmony to implement education and development for the next generation. After a couple of years, we decided that if these enterprises are so important to keep in the family, then the family council needs to have some responsibility for this. So we rechartered our council to include high-level oversight of our enterprises and to start development plans, the process of having next generation members involved with direction, board positions, management in some cases, employment. That all took place at that second reiteration of our family council.

In the past, the council had nine members, two second-generation and the other seven were all G3s. We have an age term of sixty-five on our family council and seventy-two for all our enterprises. We are down to one second-generation member under the age of sixty-five, who has been the chair since we started. He and I originated our work toward family unity and education fifteen years ago. But he was of the belief that we should be efficient. The family council should be efficient at the expense of not being inclusive. And as we go into a third-generation family council, one of our decisions is that we should be less efficient and more inclusive. This family council wants to be involved with every decision, every process that takes place at the family level instead of the chair being responsible and doing everything and the family council saying, "Yes, that is a good idea," in a rubber stamp. The chair's new responsibility is to lead the family council into getting everything done where they do the work. We want to set up accountabilities, which means changing our processes, charters, and work committees. Two G4 are now on our council. It is a big learning curve for them.

I asked six council members to conduct a governance review. I said, "Nothing is sacred. Review every committee, every charter, every policy, every procedure, and see if this is the right thing we should be doing as we move forward for the next generation because you as the council members will be the ones responsible for this, not the chair." In the past, the chair came up with the policies and procedures, and everybody agreed. I want this younger group to take ownership, reviewing and changing everything.

We are making substantial changes to our constitution. We want to leave it fairly the same but change our competencies to include accountability. We need to make sure that the best people are on the council. They are educated and knowledgeable. We are working on development plans for them to make them better family leaders. We have term limits so they can only serve six years. As we bring in somebody new, we want to have a good orientation program. Changes are coming up because this next generation wants to take ownership of what we are doing.

We support a culture of change and the attitude of, "Hey, you guys are going to take this over. This is going to be yours. You need to make it your own, and it is okay to evolve and develop things. We don't have to keep it the same as it was from this previous generation. You guys need to take responsibility for that."

Feedback told us that older third-generation members felt disenfranchised even as they served because it is more of a reactionary process to the chair's decisions and leadership. There was nothing wrong with what he was doing. But his leadership style was different from what this next generation wants it to be. We spent two years trying to make this transition just in the chair position. The past chair was not paid. Second generation did not need the funding. But now we are talking about a position that may end up being three-quarters-time to run the family council and head our family office. How much time is that going to take, and can you have somebody working full time somewhere else and still be the best family leader? We decided to make this a payable position. We set up accountabilities. The big change in our constitution is to add the competency of accountability. We pay our family council members $5,000 per year. If they are being paid to make decisions

(continued)

*(Continued)*

*and communicate with the family, they need to be accountable to respond to questions within a forty-eight-hour period. We are trying to put in measurements, to measure these competencies so that I as a chair can work with them and say, "You are not very strong here. Let's help strengthen you in this competency."*

## Building a Family Council

Families are practical and want to know the nuts and bolts of organizing councils. Who is included, how do they operate, how often do they meet, and how does new membership enter? While councils evolve differently as each generation has more people and resources to manage, my research team and I found a great deal of similarity in the general principles of how they operated.

Family councils usually meet several times a year, most often in person. (See Figure 11.2.) Several choices face a family when it develops a council. These include selecting members, organizing the council, and conducting council activities. We will look at each of these areas in the following sections.

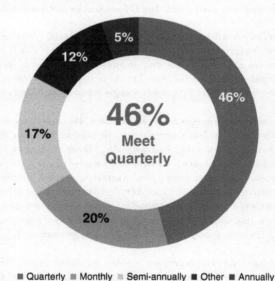

■ Quarterly ■ Monthly ■ Semi-annually ■ Other ■ Annually

**Figure 11.2  Frequency of family council meetings.**

### Selecting Council Members

If there are more than a dozen family members, every person cannot be on the council. By the third generation, the council begins to select members to "represent" the others. Whoever proposes its membership, whether the younger or older generation or both, a council is intended to be inclusive. Since the council is for the family and relies on the energy of family volunteers, it must generate engagement and commitment from the whole family. While the business can have a smaller core group of major owners who run the business, the council must reach out to all generations, branches, and ages of the family. Even if the business is run by one person in a top-down fashion, the family council can be collaborative and inclusive. Families that try to impose family governance from the top are generally not successful.

While organizing, the council may need to meet every month or two. After creating its mission, charter, and meeting format and after appointing committees, it may shift to meeting quarterly or twice a year. The council often meets jointly with the board of directors a day before or after the board meeting, for cross-communication and to discuss shared concerns. Each entity tells the other what they have been up to, and raises issues that involve the other. In a fourth- or fifth-generation generative family, the council may take on parallel and equal status to the board of directors and finds itself working in concert with the business in several areas, as explained below.

A G4 family leader describes the makeup of the family council: "*We have thirty-six people in our family assembly, twelve people in our family council, and four standing committee chairs—which are part of that twelve, and then we have my role as family council chair.*" In this family, people are eligible for membership when they reach age twenty-one, though another family inducts new family members at age fifteen, provided they prepare and demonstrate that they are ready.

A council is often organized by the larger "legislative" group that is the family assembly, which selects council members as its representatives and proposes family activities and priorities. Family shareholders or the older generation may initially appoint the council, and it usually begins with all or mostly older generation membership. But as younger members mature, they want to participate. Some councils start with volunteers, and this seems to work out well as a dedicated group of natural leaders steps up. The most long-standing councils have an effective term-limit policy, which leads to many family members circulating into council membership.

The size of family councils ranges from a handful of members to a dozen. They can be selected by the family or by their constituency (branch, generation, or role in the family) through either consensus or election. This study revealed a progression from branch representation to generational or at-large selection of council members. In the second or third generation, representatives usually are selected from each family branch. In or after the fourth generation, the council shifts to different types of representation, for example, from generations or at-large membership. Some councils define one representative, for example, to be a married-in family member, and another perhaps represents the rising generation. The salience of membership in a second-generation branch becomes less important than membership, for example, in a generational cohort.

By the fourth generation, some branches come to be larger, and the branch system frequently gives way to at-large election or election by generational groups:

*Nine of us are in the council. It was originally set up so that there would be representatives from all five branches. There would also be at least one in-law and one emerging generation representative. Each branch selected their representative. That's gone by the wayside because some branches weren't reaching out to their family. So the council itself had to reach out, saying, "Oh, we don't have a representative from this branch. Let's see if we can get somebody." If nobody steps up—and that is the case with one of the branches—then it's like, "Well, sorry. We tried. Nobody wanted to step up. That's fine." We still try to get representation from all branches. We try to keep the number at nine. That seems like a good number for us. There are enough people to do stuff. We started at the very beginning paying council members a nominal stipend, and I know we're one of the few that do.*

Smaller families tend to have governance activities undertaken by volunteers. As the work gets more complex or demanding, the family realizes that those who step up to leadership should be compensated for their time and energy. The council may begin to compensate the council chair or its members, perhaps not at market rates but as a symbolic way of saying "this is important work." Also, the question arises of paying expenses for family councils and even family assemblies, to which some families must travel a long way and for which younger family members must take time off from their jobs. Encouraging family members to be part of governance means making sure they do not feel exploited.

Since the council represents the family, it must set up a regular process for communicating with the rest of the family. Since the whole family assembly meets infrequently, the council usually sends out minutes of its meetings. In families where each member "represents" a constituency, that member reports to the constituency. In some families, this takes the form of a family branch or generation meeting or phone call. The key is that the council initiates a chain of two-way communication so that the council is an active focuser of, initiator of, and responder to family issues. The council also connects actively to the business.

As time passes, a family faces the challenge of the same few people volunteering all the time. This is acceptable at first, but it can also lead to patterns where new people don't feel invited or encouraged to step up. And the initial leaders can burn out. For that reason, families limit terms of service and encourage different family members to step into leadership roles:

*We don't want to have any one person taking on too many roles. Family members on the boards are supposedly capable for certain things, but you may also need that at the family council. There is a likelihood that some of the people might be the same in an ideal world. But on the other hand, you want to separate the power, and you want to have independent supervision. So we have some people who are active or who have been active in the business, but they're a minority. There are other people who bring their competence despite not being in the business. I would say that the family council is driven by a competent minority and followed by a wider democracy.*

One source of talent in the family that can be overlooked or ignored is the married-ins. To avoid conflict many families prohibit married-in family members from certain roles. They may not work in the business, have any ownership, be on the board or family council, or even attend business meetings. This certainly is a way of limiting the possibility of conflict, but it also limits opportunity. In some of the most successful families, in-laws stand beside family members as leaders in boards, family councils, and management. Some families begin with a policy limiting participation by in-laws but find over the years that they have come to feel trust and respect for these family members by choice. Other families begin with a value of inclusion.

Here is an example of a new family member who added value to the family talent pool:

> In 1992, we formed a family council and had successive annual meetings over time at the company as well. That set us on the pathway of understanding the importance of those regular gatherings and regular interaction and, later, transparency about what was going on with the business and a collective decision-making body. They were soliciting nominations, and I wanted to be as involved and as informed as possible. It was rare and out of character for them to elect a nonlineal descendant to the family council, and I was only able to do that because the relationships and trust were built already.
>
> We were meeting once a year. We moved to twice a year as we had more topics to cover and people became more interested. At this point, we're meeting four times a year because we're experiencing leadership succession and transition issues along with a consultant to help guide us. We've been focused on that for the last two years. There are five people in the family council, and they're nominated and voted on by the family assembly, which is usually held when we have our annual meeting.

## Organizing the Council

Council operation is like other representative organizations. The council's first order of business is to select a chair, set an agenda, and draw up its mission and priorities. In initial meetings, council members define what the council is, what it will do, and how the council members will accomplish its tasks. These decisions are written down and form the core of what will become the family constitution.

### Mission and Values

Before the council can decide on its operations and policies, it must formulate its *mission*—who it is and what it is about. Since family governance concerns the use of the family resources that come from the original wealth of the business founder, families often begin with a statement of the legacy mission and values of the founder. These are often more about the business than the family, but most families identify core values and intentions of the founding generation that they want to build upon. Family governance often begins with the legacy mission and values, which the third or later generation must consider and apply to their new realties. Chapter 12 focuses on family constitutions and presents examples of these family mission and values statements.

A family council commonly has a purpose statement setting forth its overall goals and intention to:

- Create a connection across generations in the family
- Provide an organized family voice to business and financial ventures
- Develop the human capital of family members
- Have impact as a family in the wider community

The process of explicitly defining mission and values is intensely personal and meaningful to a family. It often includes several large and small family meetings where family members argue about how to define each value and what they want the family to do—its mission—for the coming generation. While the outcome statement may seem bland outside the family, internally these are deeply meaningful to family members.

When family members become aware of the legal or trust documents, shareholder agreements, and business policies, they may feel that some are unclear or even unfair. The council becomes a place where family members consider how the policies work in the life of the family and debate or even adapt the policies to fit their family reality. The council must explore the policies and communicate with the rest of the family to get input from other family members; this process is neither quick nor easy.

### Operating Principles

When its purpose becomes clear, the council then sets up its operating principles and policies. This includes how membership in the family is defined, how council members are selected, how often they meet, what they do, what their roles and responsibilities are, what compensation will be for family governance work, how decisions are made, how their role as liaisons with the business and the business board will work, how family employment policies will function, and which subcommittees will be formed.

The council defines what it will do; this is included in what becomes the family constitution. Councils meet fairly frequently, especially when they are starting up, usually three or four times a year. They draw up an agenda, usually soliciting items from the whole family. Some councils are very connected to business issues, especially if the family runs a business with family members involved in management, while others, where the family has sold its legacy business and has a family office or several ventures, have a more formal relationship. As one fourth-generation family notes, *"Because we are such a large family, the family council is a group of nine people elected by the family for a three-year term—so they are on a three-year rotating cycle—and they can serve for two consecutive terms, and then you have to get off for a year."*

Generally, the council names committees to do its work, which opens further opportunities for participation. A family council member is often the chair of each committee, with other family members either being appointed or volunteering. One family has four standing committees to do its work: education, medical, recreation, and charity, each chaired by a G3 uncle. Another family has similar committees for education, philanthropy, family relations, and governance. These committees report in turn to the council. Members of the fourth generation (and sometimes in-laws) are invited to volunteer to join any of them.

If a family is widely dispersed, it can be difficult to get all members of the council together. With emerging technology, families are using electronic communication to do their work:

*Initially, we met much more often face to face, but people are just too busy. They can't do it. So we tried to do a lot of work online. We've got somebody on the council now that is good at leading virtual teams. She set up a whole family council website so a lot of family members and advisors can provide feedback to documents. A lot of work gets done virtually, online. We're still refining that. We're trying to find the best way to convene, whether online or by phone. We're getting better. The family council website has been fantastic. Now all our key documents are there, so whoever takes over as a council chair, everything is in place.*

### Conducting Council Activities

The family council can initiate activities that members feel are useful or wonderful, using family resources to fund them. The council helps the family develop human, financial, relationship, social, and legacy capital. It helps the family define and set in motion activities to develop each form of capital.

Several families use the council to record the history of their family and family enterprise—and even celebrate their founders. For example, one notes, *"We created a family directory with pictures, a family handbook, and a history book of the first one hundred years. They've contributed to the creation of our community center with its museum."*

The council can coordinate vacation property and plan events like holiday gatherings. For a family enterprise, doing this in a council is important as it differentiates family from business activities. This is especially important when the family company becomes public or only includes some family members as owners:

> *Our family council has been in place for quite some time and primarily contains generation five, who are preparing for leadership succession. Two members from each of the three branches are on that, so there's six members that elect the chair. It was primarily set up to help plan family events and oversee any family issues. Every weekend, a family member is going down to the ranch. A managed ranch calendar is set up at the beginning of the year, and the time is fairly divided up. Things happen at the ranch, and over time, the council has taken on more of a policy-making function, addressing things that have happened down at the ranch or hunting guidelines, policies, and less about nurturing the family. Another area that needs attention is that it's not too much fun for those family members on that council. Some of them are young, maybe even in their twenties. It can be very stressful managing such an incredible resource.*

A major focus of the family council is education, development, and learning appropriate roles for the emerging generation of family members. For generative families, this function takes on more and more significance. Here are accounts from three families of how this was done:

1. *We came up with some new ideas for how to make this happen for us. One of them being, we make a G5 committee that has a seat at the table at board meetings, that reports to the board. Its job is to represent our generation, what we're thinking, what we want to know, bring questions to the board that we have. And then also report back to that generation. That was an idea we had about gaining voice and learning about the business.*

2. *Five years ago, our fourth-generation group was in our middle twenties, and Mom's generation were in their sixties. Both generations began to recognize that they wanted to pull the fourth generation in and start involving us in governance and family business even*

> *though we're still young. So they've expanded the family council to include three at-large family members, elected by the family as a whole.*

3.  *The important matters are entry of a generation, what we expect heirs to do, values we wish for the parents to inculcate to their kids, the role of the family in foundation programs. If they want to get involved, we have summer jobs that put them in so they get a bird's-eye view, whether they're in high school or grade school, community projects that come from our foundation—we send some of our kids to do some hospital or Habitat for Humanity work.*

By creating a place where information can be shared and decisions made openly, with representatives of each household or branch present, the council allows family members to be more secure about whether family resources are allocated fairly. While trust and other documents detail how resources are distributed, family members can misunderstand or question them. Perceptions of unfairness are a leading cause of tension in extended family enterprises. The trustees and board members often meet with the council to explain and clarify what they do. Creating a council allows the family to experience greater trust in each other and the work of the leadership. The council performs an important function by clarifying and explaining what is in place and by openly designing further polices and criteria for dividing family resources. These range from the establishment of salaries for governance activities to suggestions for how to allocate profits for reinvestment and philanthropy to deciding how to fairly allocate time at a family vacation home or football season tickets.

When family members have conflict around such issues or even about personal relationships, the council can help mediate them or find resources to assist them. One family has a conflict resolution committee that deals with conflicts referred to it by family members and helps them find appropriate resources that may be offered to an individual or to two conflicting family members—or even engage the whole council around the meaning of a policy.

Conflict in families is often based on fears and concerns caused by lack of transparency. The council allows the family to share what is being done with concerned family members:

> *We got challenged on dividend policy and came up with data that showed that our policy was excellent. We demonstrated that dividend per shareholder has remained constant or increased over time. So we came back to the family and said, "If you want to increase the dividend policy, you're going to be taking food out of your babies' mouth. Is that what you want to do—starve your children?" I mean I thought that was a pretty good way to address that. We didn't, but that was kind of fun. That was a good presentation. It worked very well.*

## Family Council Activities

The council develops policies and practices in many areas. Every family selects its own focus, with the following being the most common.

1.  **A voice for family members.** Family members need a place where they can ask questions and get answers and find out how they can be involved in family activities.

*(continued)*

2. **A plan for the future.** The council can look ahead and create a strategic plan for the development of the family and the various elements of its governance.

3. **Links to the family business.** The family council contains family owners but also nonowners, and the council must develop a clear process for communicating with the business board and for hearing what is happening in the business. The family has a personal connection to the business and also depends on resources from the business. Through the family council, the family has input into the way the family enterprise is run and its goals.

4. **Family legacy and history.** By assembling family mementos, pictures, and documents and interviewing family elders, the council can create a family history that is available to new family members who do not know directly about how the family developed.

5. **Development of competence and capability in the rising generation.** The family council can create training programs for family members as they learn how to conduct their roles as family stewards and prepare for service as directors or members in family and business governance.

6. **Allocation of family resources.** The council must decide how financial and other resources are shared and how the family reinvests in the future.

7. **Conflict resolution.** As families diverge, different perceptions of opportunity and fairness can lead to deeply emotional conflicts. The family council can offer a mediating mechanism for a family to air and resolve these grievances before they become public.

8. **The family social network.** The connection of the family and the resources held by the family create the possibility of a family network that offers family members a common identity through their connection, information, support, and leverage not available to others.

9. **Community good.** The council looks at the family role in the community, in shared service, and in giving back through service and philanthropic projects.

10. **Management of shared family assets.** The family often owns vacation houses, access to special community, arts, and sports events, and other resources that must be allocated equitably.

By having a family council, a generative family remains a family. The activities of the council take them beyond being business partners, to forming a vital, creative community. While many of these activities are not business-related, they make it possible for the family to exercise its unique, values-based role in its family ventures.

## Taking Action in Your Own Family Enterprise

### Holding a Family Meeting

A family council begins with a family meeting. If the group decides to hold regular meetings and discuss issues of shared concern, they have begun to form a family council. Holding a first family meeting is a challenge. It must go well if you are going to move toward setting up a family council. Following are some steps for setting up a meeting.

**1. Get everyone's agreement to hold the meeting.** It is important to approach the family elders/leaders, who may be anxious or concerned, and help them become comfortable with the idea of a family meeting. Usually, one family member has a concern and hears about the idea of family meetings from another family, at a conference, or in an article or book. If you are a family member (or an advisor) who wants a meeting, you might start with your allies—the family members most likely to agree on the need for a meeting. Get their help to approach other family members. To set up a meeting, the initiator will have to involve everyone in the family, with the possible exception of one or two highly skeptical or suspicious members.

After getting agreement from the family leader to hold a meeting, the next task is to get the rest of the family to participate. Invite selected members of the next generation to become part of the planning process and ask them to communicate with their siblings and other family members. The goal is to calm any fears and concerns by creating a positive environment and clear expectations.

**2. Have a clear purpose and goal.** Defining one big task based on current family needs and challenges helps keep the meeting manageable and overcomes the tendency of families to jump from one issue to another. It also motivates people to participate. Any topic in a family triggers emotional connections and associations. It is incredible how quickly a meeting can lose focus when someone says something that upsets another family member, dredging up past hurts. Keeping a family meeting on track is difficult for most families, especially when the topic is a difficult one with emotional overtones.

The purpose of most family meetings (especially the first one) is to communicate, not to make decisions. Many family members are anxious about having a meeting because they feel there will be pressure to make decisions that are outside their "comfort zone." By stating clearly and directly that the purpose of the meeting is to get to know each other, hear what everybody thinks, and not make decisions, the participants will be more relaxed. A result of a successful meeting is that the family feels good enough about what it has achieved to schedule another meeting.

**3. Design the meeting collaboratively and create clear expectations.** The advisor should hesitate to define the agenda alone or with help solely from the family elder. The convener or advisor should, if possible, work with a small group of two or three people who act as the steering committee, representing different roles and generations. The steering committee should in turn reach out and talk with all family members about what they would like to accomplish in a family meeting. The committee can then define a theme, or big task, and craft an agenda so the family members know the purpose and what will be discussed. There may also be discussions about whom to invite—whether to include in-laws and if children should attend (and what is the appropriate age for those children).

The steering committee can meet with the advisor or on its own. The steering committee plans the meeting, periodically reaches out to the rest of the family for information, shares ideas, and sets the date, format, and agenda of the meeting. If the family is widely dispersed across different regions, the steering committee can work by telephone conferences and share notes with the rest of the family. The more the committee members share, the more they will engage the family and build commitment to the meeting. In fact, by working together, the process of communicating is set in motion for the family even before the meeting is held.

The agenda should be written and given to everyone well in advance of the meeting. Sometimes, materials are shared in advance—perhaps a family trust agreement or a letter from the grandparents about their legacy. Also, there may be tasks that people are asked to do to prepare, such as complete a questionnaire or read an article.

**4. Clarify format and expectations.** Decisions must be made about the setting, format, and participation expectations. While there are some best practices for meetings, each family is different. A family should try to accommodate everyone's concerns from the beginning.

The invitees will depend on the topic. The family should try to be as inclusive as possible because everyone in the family has concerns and questions about the family enterprise. Families need to consider whether they want some family members to hear about things firsthand or secondhand. They may limit whom they invite to the meeting, for example, by excluding married-in spouses, or they may exclude those topics from the meeting.

Families should select a time and place where people can be comfortable and talk freely with no distractions. Often, the meeting is an electronics-free zone. Note that the first meeting should not be a marathon. It is a chance for people to learn something and to share some of their own feelings and perspectives. The meeting should only last a half day or a day, as anything shorter will not offer enough time for people to learn or share. If the family is large or there are a lot of difficult issues that could arise, working with an outside facilitator is recommended.

**5. Invite participants and gather information.** It is important that everyone is clear about the purpose of the meeting, as well as the date and time. As with any important gathering, everyone should have time to prepare and respond. An invitation letter can be very useful in providing the purpose of the meeting, describing its importance, setting the tone, and indicating what to prepare and think about.

**6. Create a "safe" environment.** Psychological safety is needed for people to build trust and to participate in an open manner. Holding a family meeting in a place where individuals feel comfortable will let them be authentic, open, and unafraid to bring up conflicting or controversial perspectives.

There are physical and psychological elements of creating a safe space. This type of meeting is usually held in a place outside the home and office. The space should have windows and be light, airy, and open. It may be an advisor's conference room or a conference center. To be physically comfortable, the meeting room should be arranged so that people can have eye contact with each other. A conference table or a semicircle of chairs will suffice. If there are more than a dozen people, the room can be arranged with a group of round tables, where smaller groups can have discussions.

### Holding Family Conversations

A family council begins with a family meeting to discuss an important topic. It is usually defined as an exploratory conversation where no decisions will be made.

The meeting should have a clear focus and often an outside person to act as facilitator. Everyone invited should know the purpose and agree to a set of ground rules for how the conversation will be conducted.

**Wealth and values conversation:** A conversation where a family that has created wealth shares and explores its values and concerns with the members of the next generation.

This type of meeting is an opportunity for family members to talk about the meaning of money, their personal and family goals, and what they want to achieve in the future. It is not a decision-making meeting, where estate plans are created or action steps are taken. This is often the first time the family has come together to talk about money and wealth in a focused way.

This meeting is about achieving understanding between the elder generation of wealth creators and the younger generation, who will be the inheritors and who are creating their own life paths with the family resources. The discussions will include much more than just financial wealth. They usually feature an exchange of questions, concerns, goals, and desires by members of each generation. These topics may be difficult to talk about, especially if the family has had a custom of not talking about money.

The goal of the meeting is to discover shared family values on which to collaborate. It's not just about the legacy values of the parents and wealth creators. It's also about the values that are important to the younger generation. These values then form a framework for personal and family decision-making about areas of shared concern; this framework then leads to expectations about family behavior.

**Ownership and inheritance conversation:** A meeting in which family elders share basic information about their wealth and family enterprises, estate plan, and/or principles and expectations for the future and in which they also learn about prospective heirs' expectations for the future.

Without necessarily sharing the full details of their plan, the family elders can share their view of what is fair for the next generation and how they are approaching gifting their wealth. This information is usually followed by questions, concerns, and reactions from the next generation.

These meetings may discuss the family business, inheritance, grandchildren, how to use income, philanthropy, giving, and responsibilities that come with inheritance. The purpose of this discussion is to increase transparency among family members, anticipate issues, understand the meaning of fairness and differences in siblings and their families, and plan for the future.

**The future of our family enterprise:** An often difficult conversation that deals with the management, control, and future of a legacy family business and how the wealth creators view the next generation being involved.

This type of meeting looks at the options for the family business's future, life goals of new family members, and issues such as whether the next generation has the will and the skill to manage and own the family business. This is often an area where family members have very different views and perspectives.

After understanding each other's perspectives, the family members must decide:

- How are family members involved in the business?
- Who has a say in major decisions?
- Who is on the board and management team of the business?
- How will family members inside and outside the business be treated?

Ultimately, the meeting will lead to an understanding about the future of the family business and how the next generation will assume control. If there are several family businesses or a family office or foundation, similar issues need to be discussed in relation to those entities as well. This is rarely a single conversation. A series of meetings will need to take place over a period of one to three years in order to make decisions and come to agreement.

**A difficult issue or conflict:** *A problem-solving session when a serious issue or difference has come up in the family.* This meeting may concern an individual problem, a financial setback, or an issue of fairness or family hurt. As feelings and emotions are at the forefront, there is need for a skilled facilitator and a commitment to several meetings to air the issues, listen to different perspectives, and then slowly come to a decision about what to do. Each person feels that he or she is right and that the others are wrong. These differences can easily lead to litigation, negative publicity, and further hurt. The challenge for an advisor is to help the family decide to try to resolve the issue within the family and outside of public scrutiny—in such a way that the family members can maintain their relationship after the issue is resolved. The family should go slow, get help, and expect to do its work in steps.

# CHAPTER 12

# The Family Constitution: Governing Document of the Generative Family

A generative family is a huge endeavor. It brings together many people and a portfolio of businesses and financial ventures. It can contain a foundation, family office, vacation houses, and hold an important role in the community. Its reach is often global. The family can have multiple ownership agreements and several trusts, each with an operating document. It can contain multiple boards, a family council, and an owners' group. It convenes periodically as a whole family, has task force and committee meetings, and offers education programs for the next generation. And at its center, legacy values and mission statements from older generations that define the family's purpose, identity, and commitments. Even those in the center find it hard to track and absorb all of these agreements.

Where does someone go to discover or consult the rules of the game, the operating principles and practices for how this huge entity works? Nearly all generative families create some sort of guiding document that clearly sets forth these values, policies, and practices. It expresses, definitively and clearly to everyone, what the family does, what it stands for, and how it organizes its family and business governance activities. This chapter looks at the nature and development of this *family constitution*.

Constitutions outline the shared policies and understandings that family members are expected to adhere to. Each adult family member, as a signer, becomes a participant in what James Hughes calls a *compact across generations*.[1] Adopting the constitution is akin to claiming citizenship of a vital and working community. With benefits and privileges also come responsibilities that all family members need to observe.

A *family constitution* is an intergenerational document created and agreed to by the whole family. It clearly and explicitly states the values, expectations, principles, procedures, activities, and decision-making procedures that regulate family activities and use of its resources. Legal, shareholder, and trust agreements are integrated, summarized, and explained within it. The constitution defines the role expectations—rights and responsibilities—of a family member citizen. It organizes and binds the family into a working community as it grows, changes, adapts to new circumstances, and overcomes conflict.

But it is more than an organizational framework; it begins with a call to action, an inspirational statement of who the family is, why they are in business, and what they stand for. It is a private and personal document that is intended only for the family. Therefore, while newer families and advisors hear about them, they have not often seen one and therefore find them hard to visualize.

The families in this study report that a constitution most often emerges in the third generation. More than 80 percent of the families in this study have formal constitutions while the others have similar guiding agreements. Family constitutions and guiding agreements are a global phenomenon, appearing in equal measure in every country. While some look and sound like legal documents, the majority are more inspirational and personal. Constitutions range from a few pages to a booklet with fifty or more pages. They often contain family pictures and mementos such as letters from the founders. My research team and I collected about twenty examples, and this chapter draws from them.

The working groups composing the elements of family governance—business boards, family councils, and assemblies—are recognized with purpose, policies, and practices collected in this master document, which can be simple and aspirational or very detailed and elaborate. The constitution and the family council are two sides of a coin. Each is necessary for the other; together they constitute governance. This chapter explains how constitutions (or charters or protocols, as some families call them) are created and what they contain.

Generative families work together across generations to develop a statement of core purpose and values. While each family statement is different, there are some common themes and values. It is contributed to and agreed upon by all current family members. New family members who reach adulthood and those who marry in can learn from studying it, and are asked to sign on. It forms a charter for the extended family that makes them more than a clan or dynasty but a shared family enterprise.

The constitution is an evolving document. It is usually not a legal document, but a personal, moral document, with some aspects of it duplicated in legal shareholder documents. Each generation, drawing on the version of the previous generation, amends or develops its constitution. The members of each generation usually do this together, over a period of a year or so.

## The Constitution Defines Business and Family Culture and Organization

The constitution often signals or affirms a deep change in the family culture. In political bodies, the constitution marks the end of a monarchy and instills a new regime of defined rights and responsibilities and collaboration within the community. For a family, signing a constitution signals a similar shift. It affirms that the family has moved from a single, often closed, culture where rules are random, hidden or implicit, to one based upon transparency, dialogue, and public deliberation. It also signals a shift from a single autocratic family leader to one where the leadership is constrained by rules and obligations that include participation of all family members. Otherwise, if one person decides everything, why would the family need a constitution at all? The creation of a constitution reflects cultural changes already under way as it formally recognizes that change is beginning.

The adoption of a family constitution, echoing a transformational social event like the signing of the Magna Carta, represents a shift from a patriarchal to a collaborative cultural style for the family. Such a culture shift, as we have seen, is difficult and often fraught with conflict. The process of writing a constitution offers a platform for different family perspectives to be integrated and to define rules, practices, and a structure that allow it to grow and adapt. (See Figure 12.1.)

**HOW CONSTITUTIONS TRANSFORM FAMILY CULTURE**

| from ▶ | to |
|---|---|
| Patriarchal Agreements ▶ | Collaborative Agreements |
| Legal Presentation ▶ | Meaningful Presentation |
| Ambiguous and Implicit ▶ | Explicit |
| Strict Rules ▶ | Values and Principles to Interpret |
| Fragmented and Disconnected ▶ | Integrated |
| Fixed Policies ▶ | Flexible Policies |

**Figure 12.1   Movement toward a family constitution.**

## Moral Agreements: Elaborating on Legal Documents

Every generative family has many legal documents, such as shareholder and trust agreements, wills, estate plans, and corporate charters. These are often inaccessible, hard to understand, ambiguous, and even obsolete or designed for an earlier time. As family members come of age and select marriage partners, they need to understand what their new family is all about.

Family members discover that they need to build upon the original family "compact" and legacy that led to where they are now and how things work. To create a constitution, family members do the following:

- Review existing documents and update them to current realities.
- Define the context in which the family has arisen by making explicit the values, intentions, and principles espoused by the founders for their successors.
- Define operating entities that make the agreements workable and operational, make decisions, and deal with differences that arise.

The result of this is governance, expressed through the master family governing agreement—its constitution.

For the most part, constitutions are not legal documents, though like such agreements, they are written, agreed to, and signed. They are often referred to as *moral agreements,* in that family members voluntarily agree to them because they care about each other. They do not substitute for or contradict legal agreements in place. Rather, they explain the existing legal agreements so that they are clearly understood and elaborate upon them in areas that are less clear or not mentioned.

For example, there may be an ownership agreement for a vacation property, but the family must allocate funds for its upkeep, select and buy furniture, pay for property ownership and upkeep, and allocate its use. Every company hires its employees, but family owners may specify special qualifications for family employees or executives. So the family may end up using the constitution to help family members understand, apply, and work with legal agreements, though they can, of course, consult the original documents as well.

Constitutions don't even look like legal documents. They are usually written in personal language by and for the family members. They begin by presenting the values, vision, and mission—what the family is all about—and then specifying how the family will work. What follows are sections about family policies, the organization of the family council and assembly, the foundation, input to the business, employment, education, and family meetings. Legal agreements often don't feel clear or fair to some family members, and they need to be explained or modified when the family considers how these agreements work in practice.

Legal documents are linked to specific entities, and do not usually explain the guiding purposes or values that lie behind them. Also, a family can contain many legal entities, each with their own guiding documents, that are not connected and may even contradict each other. By addressing the family as a whole, the constitution joins and links documents and allows the family to consider themselves as a single entity with many subentities. It can clarify or clean up ambiguities and contradictions. The constitution begins with a definition of the nature and purpose of the whole generative family, and then proceeds to detail the different parts and entities and how they fit together and link to each other.

Constitutions celebrate the legacy of the family, inspiring family members to be active in family governance and making implicit agreements transparent and shared by all. The examples my research team and I obtained contain pictures of the family founders, businesses, and homesteads. They frequently include early statements of values and vision. A few contain letters or documents from founders or elders about their experiences and hopes for the future. These are often a revelation to younger family members, who learn new respect and understanding of the family origins.

The constitution sets forth how family membership is defined, the roles of a family member, the purpose and activities of the family assembly and council, and activities that relate to the family and the business. It starts with a *preamble,* defining the family's core purpose, mission, values, and vision. Crafting this beginning is the most challenging task and takes the longest time. Family members need to reflect upon their legacy and history—the values and intentions of the wealth creators—and add new elements now needed to address the greater numbers of new family members, who have emerging values and changing circumstances that have emerged from the family's success and the growth of its business and financial resources.

Every family experiences some conflict when some members feel slighted and not treated fairly. Defining fairness is a challenge for every family. A constitution expresses the principles and values followed by the family, and how they are observed. Constitutions help family members understand what the family defines as fairness and how differences may be surfaced and resolved. They often are the result of contentious and difficult family discussions and the resulting resolution is hard won.

The constitution is a working, living document that guides the family in its regular interactions around its assets or work. It can be amended and updated by a process outlined within the document. Creating the constitution can also be the product of a process by which the family transitions to a new level of collaborative organization. For example, it may reorganize the family after the sale of its legacy business or the creation of a family office. It may be compiled to explain and clarify legal trust and corporate agreements as third- and later-generation family members grow up and marry. Every family has such agreements that need to be tied together as circumstances get more complex.

## What Does a Constitution Do for a Family?

Like all governance activities, the constitution solves a problem for the family. It is based not only on legal or abstract needs but also on practical realities. A European third-generation family explains how the constitution evolved from the work of the family council and assembly:

> The assembly elected a family council, organized by branches, empowered to do several things: preserving family values, understanding and keeping contact with the family business, education, philanthropy. There are four members from each of the four branches, a total of sixteen. And it was packed with the fifth generation.
>
> Our charter had family values and powers of the council and assembly. On your twentieth birthday, you're presented with a charter and sign it. It's got a list of values and a code of behavior. We used it to restate the corporation's values to align with family values. One of the lessons we picked up overseas was that as a family grows, they lose interest unless there's something holding them. Quite often, it's legacy, history, or values that link people to their business. As soon as you lose those, the business goes. They'll go, "Ah, yeah. We'll just sell the business. I'm not interested in that. We've lost interest."

Governance cannot be created *for* the family by a consultant. An active, committed, and responsible group can't be organized in absentia. Several families in this study note that they initially hired someone to write a constitution for them or work with a single family leader. They frequently discovered that this was the right thing done in the wrong way. In each instance, the family rejected or ignored the document. This third-generation Asian family elder learned the following:

> We had a weekend discussion, and I thought it was going to take us somewhere. But when I proposed a draft of the constitution that our consultant had written and I had commented on, they didn't accept it at all. They said, "We don't need all this." They were dismissive and negative, and basically, they felt it was Anglo-Saxon hocus pocus. "This is too formal, too serious. Who do you think we are?" They took it very badly, and I was very disappointed.

If a small group begins to draft a constitution, the group needs to periodically step back, slow down, or start over again, being sure to include other family members in the process. That means that in drafting the constitution, the family leader, who as business owner can pull many strings in the family, must hang back and work with other family members inside and outside of the core business. A constitution is often organized as the family looks ahead to generational succession; the family creates documents organizing the pathway ahead. Some say they are writing the constitution for future generations, not the ones that currently exist.

The families in this study report that effective constitutions positively accepted within the family are most often created by a representative task force of family members from at least two generations:

*I joined the working group called a family council task force. We would sit together and go over the examples of other family constitutions. We met every month for a year and a half to discuss the different policies and outline. It was a lot of discussion and debate. Now we have a document that has been accepted and approved. At the first family assembly, the family voted in the first family council. They've been quite active so far.*

Another European family had just sold its legacy family business to a global conglomerate. Developing the constitution was an inclusive and evolutionary process, offering an opportunity for the family to redefine itself and come together in a new form. The family elder reports:

*The ownership council created the family constitution and from time to time reviews that and potentially modifies that as required. Initially, vision and value evolved out of the history of where the family had come from. We endorsed and identified activities we felt most strongly about. We worked on the vision together.*

*I wrote a lot of the framework for the constitution, and we then fine-tuned it together in the ownership council. We chatted about it on a regular basis, and it took several years. It wasn't a five-minute job. The process of creating it was more important than the end document. It gave people an opportunity to discuss and raise issues, and we make decisions by consensus, not votes. It took a bit longer, but we got better buy-in as a result.*

Since the constitution is an "operating manual" for family and business governance, some guidance and education must be provided to the family to learn how to use it, as this family leader notes:

*First, they must take an interest in the process of ownership. We record our policies in what we call our family council notebook. For example, we have a board training policy, a training program for those who want to be on the board. We also have a code of conduct, conflict of interest policy, decision-making policy, a family employment policy, and a family loan policy. Our G4s developed the policies. They patiently sat through meetings as we "wordsmithed" the drafts to death. The good news is they haven't been turned away from it. Over that time, our objective was to bring them into governance and leadership. Something rubbed off—maybe this was something that they should be interested in. We commenced distributions/dividends a few years ago, and we have included them in the financial discussion of not only their trusts but also the business.*

*We do a business strategic plan every four years that contains a distribution policy. Fourth-generation members have taken great interest in the distributions. Thus, they became very interested in the success of the business, and they have taken responsibility toward business governance. Through the financial exposure and preparing the family council policies, we ended up with five fourth-generation members that are very enthusiastic about their future, the legacy, and protecting it. As annoying as some of the steps and processes might have been, the two generations stuck with it, and in the end it has been a success.*

A challenge for a family is how to keep the constitution accessible and available. One way is to post it and other family information on a shared web portal. In a large and dispersed family, this new technology enables a far-flung family to remain actively engaged and connected:

*The portal is maintained by the corporation. Initially, it was a printed agreement that we called the family guidebook or handbook. It had everything you wanted to know about us. The portal now has several different tabs. A family tab that has that statement. It also has a family employee statement of values, a section on our business history, and the history timeline. We have videos and information from shareholder meetings and teleconferences. We keep our family tree and directory up to date. We have the family photos gallery that also has photos from our family meetings.*

*Then we have a whole section for the family council with a statement of purpose, council contact information, information from the family meetings, family surveys, finances, next-gen programs, newsletters. We do a newsletter twice a year. Then we've got a section on family in business; within that section, we have family surveys and roles and responsibilities. We have key policies and procedures and describe the summer internship program. Then there's a whole section on communications from the corporation—announcements, newsletters, quarterly reports, directors, biographies, governance, board committees, key contacts, general overview of the corporation, and the leadership team. Then there is the family foundation tab with policies, annual reports, directors, grants, and recipients.*

## Elements of the Constitution

Almost every constitution begins with some sort of preamble, statement of the purpose, what the family is and stands for. These often come from the first or second generation, perhaps amended by members of G3, and are meant to remind the family of who they are and call people to be part of all the things the family does together.

The constitution then clearly defines the often vague border between the board and management and the inactive shareholders. For example, one family's corporate bylaws provide for an advisory board of directors and a formal board of directors. The charter goes into detail on the role of the advisory board and how family members can participate. This is viewed as the official pathway for family shareholders to learn about and influence the business and deal with their concerns and differences. There are requirements for participation that the family member needs to adhere to.

The constitution separates the family's governance from business governance by defining the purpose and place of each family entity and clarifying the nature of the overlap between them. The experience of a generative family is that a constitution must be created collaboratively by the family and actively pursued by all the members.

The family's distribution policies for profits from its business and investments are usually explained in the family constitution. These policies are often embedded deep in trust documents and may not be shared with or clear to everyone. Family members need to know what these policies are, how they are administered, and how they may change over time. These policies make clear what a family member can expect from the collective family wealth. While trusts and boards make these decisions, if family members are not clear on the criteria and free to express their preferences and desires, conflict can easily arise. Some family members may feel that the agreements are not fair or that family members who work in the business are benefiting from reinvestment of profits in ways that family members whose lives are taking other directions are not.

One Asian family describes how its constitution clearly spells out family policies:

*In 2004, our company became public. So the ownership structure must be even more clear because we are required to be very, very transparent. We needed a governance structure to run the family and the business and policies for how to manage the wealth within the family. I said, "Yes, we believe that the family should pay for education, but what is the standard?" Okay? Should the kids fly business class, or should they fly coach? When they travel, do they stay in a dormitory, or [do] they get to stay in a hotel? If we buy them a car, what is the standard? We were seeing our standards abused by family members. Some of them fly their children on business class and buy them a BMW for school. And I sense that this thing about the education, the family pays for education, if the family pays for medical, somebody gets sick, what is the right thing to pay? Somebody gets sick, and some Chinese friend said, "Oh, you need to eat this kind of crazy turtle that costs $10,000 apiece." As the family grows, if you do not have a proper structure, then you start to have abuse. Some people will say, "Oh, I do not know this is a benefit. How come I never claim it?" and "Oh, do this and why I cannot do this?" You start to have more in-laws; you start to get more children.*

*We designed whole family governance policies and procedures and divided the benefits. For example, we have policies about supporting kids in school. We say that, okay, every university will tell us the cost of the tuition and living, and we provide more than the cost. We created a standard. If you go to United States, this is what we are going to pay. If you go to UK, this is what we're going to pay. If you stay in Hong Kong, this is what we're going to pay. And then we start to identify what kind of car we're going to give you. And then we say, okay, if you do not have a 3.5 GPA, you don't get a car and you fly coach.*

The constitution can go into detail about special family activities. For example, there may be a section on philanthropy and social investment that outlines the family's values about the community and the environment to guide the investments and business practices of the family and its policies for contributing to the community. These social values express how the family allocates its *social capital* and are increasingly important to the rising generation as they decide how involved they want to be in family activities.

Another important area covered in constitutions is how the family deals with conflict and disagreement. It can clearly define the principles of fairness that apply to each individual. As the family grows, conflict about what is fair or how rules are to be applied is the largest risk factor in sustaining the family connection and governance. How does the family deal with a major conflict without making the argument public and having a negative effect on the family's business? The constitution makes clear what happens if there is disagreement. Some families have begun to experiment with creating a judicial element to go along with the legislative function of the family council and assembly, and the executive function of the business management team. They set up something like a *council of elders* whose job is to listen to parties who are in conflict and guide them to finding common ground or to exercising the right to exit if the conflict cannot be resolved.

The family is at its core a community. The role of the constitution is to organize the activities of the community so that it can keep order, inspire and recognize contribution, and creatively initiate new activities to extend the family capital.

---

## Outline of a Family Constitution

Given the common challenges that arise from the biological inevitability of a family and the desire to sustain the legacy values of a business founder, it is not unexpected that my research team and I found many common elements in family constitutions around the globe. Following is a generic outline of the common elements found in dozens of constitutions.

Part I: Core Purpose: Vision/Mission/Values of Family for Business and Itself

The initial statement is the purpose of the family and the family enterprise and the reason for setting up a governance structure. It is usually drafted by the whole family together, working across generations. It contains:

- Legacy letter or statement from elders
- Family origins and history
- Family values and mission
- Business values and mission
- A statement of what the family wants from the business and the family ventures
- A statement of why the family is embarking on the journey to explicit governance
- Family code of conduct

Part II: Overview of Family Enterprise Organization and Policies

This section defines the family's reason for having its businesses and indicates how the family connects to these ventures. It may outline the operation and policies of a shareholders' council as well as the values, intentions, and expectations of return for

*(continued)*

*(Continued)*

the family from the business(es). It also makes clear how family members can become involved in the various family ventures as employees and in setting up new ventures:

- Family's expectations and relation to business
- Owners' council and its role
- Makeup of board of directors
- Defining areas of interest and values for the business
- Policies for family member employment in the business
- Family funding and support for setting up new ventures

### Part III: Governance and Legal Structures

This section clearly outlines the legal and financial structures that bind and organize the family and how these structures work in practice. This section is usually drawn from the shareholder's agreements and corporate bylaws, but the section is written to clarify how the family is organized, how the shareholders are involved, and how trusts work. This section helps each family member know the rules for how resources are allocated, how decisions are made, and what they can expect:

- Roles of shareholders and appointment of boards and trustees
- Role of trusts and shareholder agreements
- Distribution of funds to shareholders
- Transfer of ownership
- Guidelines to review and change parts of the constitution

### Part IV: Family Council and Assembly—Mission, Organization, Responsibilities

This section outlines the family governance structure of family meetings, the family assembly, and the family council. It explains what the council does and how the family meets, decides, and creates practices that evolve out of its mission and values. It includes elements such as the following:

- Purposes and activities of the council
- Assembly of whole family—when it happens and what it does
- Council purpose and membership
- Voting and decisions
- Officers and committees
- Education and support of next-generation family members

### Part V: Philanthropy and Social Mission

This section describes how the family defines and acts on its values in its role in the community and gives back. It covers such items as:

- Family foundation or other philanthropic activities
- Decisions about family giving
- Social values and social ventures

## Writing the Constitution

Writing the constitution begins with the existing legal documents. They are read and explained so that they are clear to the family. This is more difficult than it seems, and often there are several drafts before the meaning and mechanics of each agreement is understood, consistent, and clear. Then, the drafters look at the informal policies and activities that have been created by the family council and other operating entities, like the foundation or family office. There are several parts to a constitution that refer, for example, to the family values, the activities of the council, business governance, trust agreements, and philanthropic activities and entities such as foundations.

The constitution is an amalgam and expansion of several individual agreements—created by the council, the owners' council, the trust, and the board of directors. The constitution is a unifying document used by the whole family. Family leaders may start to draft a constitution but soon discover many reasons to include other family members. They need to know what is on their minds, what their expectations and concerns are. Families that develop the most useful and accepted constitutions report that the process of creating them was *inclusive,* proceeding through several drafts over a period of a year or more. The constitution draws from many documents—legal and shareholder agreements, for example—and expands upon how they work in practice. By searching out and carefully reading these documents, the drafters are able to explain them to the family, which often leads to the need for clarification and even change.

*Which comes first: the constitution or the institutions it defines—the council and the assembly?* The families in this study report that these elements evolve together in parallel. Sometimes the family members begin to meet and write a statement about who they are and what they are doing. So the constitution is drafted by this self-created group. Other times, family leaders begin to write a constitution and soon discover that they need to include others to consider what they want for the future.

This cannot be done by a lawyer or consultant. When family members read and reflect upon existing agreements, questions occur, gaps are located, new conditions are recognized, and contradictions surface. Different family members see the agreements differently and raise different questions, especially members of the rising generation. To make a constitution that all can live with, everyone must have input and questions must be responded to.

Constitutions do not last forever. Enterprising families face major changes each generation as a new group of family leaders emerges. The constitution often starts as a short document, a few pages of values and polices, and then over each generation further sections are added. After a new generation, a constitution adds policies as well as family history and traditions; it can grow to become a small family monograph.

A constitution evolves as the family faces new challenges and as old rules and policies are reevaluated. Here is one evolutionary story:

> *The first version was for the second generation only. It was a three-page paper where they wrote things that they could or could not do as brothers and shareholders. It was very simple, but they put that into practice. That's what amazes me: they have very strong personalities, so they got*

*together for almost three years to build this family constitution. In the beginning, it was a lot about separating family, business, and ownership, so they had simple things. For example, a shareholder's wife cannot bring her car to get fixed in the company; she cannot use the gardener to work in her house. They each could have a company car.*

*Last year, we signed the second family constitution, created by the second and third generation together. It covered all five of our major family holding companies. A working group from each holding would nominate one person to represent that holding in the constitution task force. The new constitution grew from three to more than forty pages.*

*I think the rules also grow. It's amazing because our constitution has a lot of policies that we may not use, that we hope to never use. For example, if someone wants to leave the family business, to sell their shares, how are we going to do that, how are we going to pay for that? Now we have all the little rules that the third and the fourth generation understand and can live with. For example, right now the business can no longer give a car to all shareholders, so we understood that benefit was only for the second generation.*

## Mission and Values: A Call to Action

Unlike legal documents, constitutions begin with a statement of the family's purpose, principles, and values. This takes the form of an inspirational call to family members about their nature as a family and as a family enterprise. It is especially important for family members to be involved in defining this core statement of the mission and values they share as part of a generative family, as this family reports:

*A group within the family took that task. It took about a year to develop the mission statement and values. This committee put something together and then sent it out to the family at large saying, "Give us your input. What do you think?" We started the values process by sending an email that asked each person to "put down your values, what you think should be included in our mission, vision and values." You can only imagine with more than twenty people giving input how many values we had. But we incorporated it because we felt like it was important that everyone had a voice.*

*The constitution came from the same group. I gathered examples of other constitutions to form a template. The committee filled in the blanks. Once we got to where we felt like it was in a final format, we shared it with the whole family during the annual business meetings of the family assembly, and they came back with revisions. We revised and shared it again, and it was enthusiastically approved.*

As a family becomes a multi-household tribe that includes its rising generation, it can draw from everyone's personal values and mission to create a shared mission statement:

*We came up with a family mission statement that evolved out of all our individual mission statements. That's one of the activities the family council worked on. Everyone came up with their own personal missions. Based on that we developed a collective value table, our values, and then a group mission. We have a family employment framework we worked on at the family council and then took to the operating companies for feedback and tweaked it a little bit to make sure it was connected to their human resource policies.*

A South American family emphasized the role of values as a guide to their life together:

> *In the community and with each other, every family member is clearly aware of a set of values that guide their personal and business dealings. Each of them feels that these values form the foundation for their continuing success. The values are clearly and explicitly honored in action, not just rhetoric. The close attention to defining core values came from a family tradition of studying philosophy as well as commerce.*

Another family drafted a constitution[2] in a half dozen family meetings over the course of a year. The family's charter and mission statement was created by two generations: the second-generation family CEO and his two sisters, one of whom also works in the business, and the nine adults among their eleven third-generation offspring, ranging in age from the twenties to forty. Their constitution begins with the charter and mission statement:

> *We are a family committed to our members and descendants being responsible, productive, well-educated citizens who practice the work ethic and make constructive contributions in the local community and the world at large.*
>
> *Each member is encouraged to develop and use self-supporting, marketable skills that contribute to the enhancement of their own self-esteem and independence.*
>
> *We urge family members to adopt lifestyles that are healthy, personally satisfying, and at such a profile as to preserve the maximum level of family privacy, given the public nature of our business.*
>
> *We urge the continuation of the orientation of prudent, careful investing with a long-term view of outcomes so all descendants of our founders may enjoy the benefits of the foundation they built.*
>
> *We believe clear, constructive communications are at the core of our long-term success as a family. We encourage all efforts to further harmony, develop humor and perspective on life, balance long-term concerns while enjoying the present, and to enhance communications, caring, and amicable relationships among family members.*

This mission statement is followed by concrete guidelines for family employment and creation of a family business advisory board. The family all signed off on it even though the family CEO was clearly in charge as controlling owner. Now he has handed the chairman and CEO roles to the next generation while remaining on the board as a member.

## Family Values Statements

Every constitution contains core values the family stands for and teaches to each new generation. They often appear to be addressing family members, sharing the intentions

*(continued)*

(*Continued*)

of founders for the continuation of their family enterprise. Here are excerpts from values statements from six different generative families:

1. The reason we unlock our doors every day is what my mother and father taught us and what their grandparents taught them is your family business: it exists to make the community a better place and to make the family closer and happier. If it's not providing those things, you're just kind of spinning your gears. Our family business is a tool that brings the family together in a pursuit that gives us all some opportunity and some happiness.
2. Our great-grandfather passed those values down to his sons, who carried on that dream: church, schooling, and community.
3. Honoring God and helping people develop in pursuing excellence. They were the foundation of how our business went along and grew.
4. Creating a community that has value to the society.
5. Integrity or ethics integrity and stewardship. That's who we are; we identify with that. And if you would go and ask all 258 shareholders what our core values are, 99 percent of them could tell you.
6. The values our family has stood for over four generations are integrity, professional education, nonmaterialistic family cooperation, respect for different skills of each family member, free choice to enter the family enterprises, and community service.

Why is defining mission and values so essential for a business family? The family has a legacy of values and mission from the founder and second generation. While the members of G3 want to respect this legacy, they face new challenges to sustain themselves as both a business and a family. They may feel some values need to take on a different meaning or find that the mission and values are primarily about the business and that they need to adapt and extend them to the new arena of family governance. And the new generation may have new emerging values and principles they want to add to the family. We need to integrate these "roots and wings," legacy and innovation, as described in previous chapters. For example, some rising generations want to incorporate sustainability or social responsibility into their business or investing. So the process of defining mission and values is deeply collaborative and involves negotiation across generations.

A creative tension sometimes exists between the old and newer versions. Some families ask the members of G3 to come together and adopt their principles for their generation as they enter leadership. One family had the elders of G2 write "legacy letters" to the members of G3 before they met to begin work on the family constitution. Then, the members of G3 were free to express their own reinterpretations and even take the family in new directions.

One global fourth-generation family found that creating a family constitution led the whole family to see the enterprise differently:

*Separating the business from the family allowed the family narrative to shift. Gradually we developed a new narrative of who we were and what we were doing beyond just the business.*

*It's difficult. How do we do it? I started working with my siblings first. But G4 has thirty people when we included their children. I proposed to them, "Well, since we didn't grow up together, would you like to grow old together?" That was the invitation.*

*Because we live in different parts of the world, we are very individualist. We got together every quarter to talk a few days, and after three years, I said, "We need closure with the family." We talked about another initiative to draft the family charter, which includes the whole family so that there's already a consistency and understanding from the generation above to a generation below us.*

*Doing the family constitution enabled my three siblings who'd grown up together in the early years, but who now lived far apart from each other, to get closer together. From a generational standpoint, to get the patriarchal generation to change their ways is not going to happen. It's up to this generation, in their forties and fifties, and their children, in their twenties, who've been studying abroad, to say, "Yeah, we know about this concept of corporate governance or a family-type constitution." So I think there is increasing awareness and acceptance of these concepts.*

## Code of Conduct: Encouraging Respectful Communication and Behavior

Closely related to the values statement is a code of conduct, which links the values to resulting behavior and communication style expected from family members. As new family members become adults and others enter by marriage, the code of conduct explains that being a family member entails some clear standards for behavior that accompany the benefits.

It must be remembered that generative families are families first. Old patterns of communication and memories of past hurts are often raw and emergent in interaction. When there is stress an individual often regresses to old and childish behavior, especially when they are family. While a set of rules cannot enforce respectful communication, they offer a clear statement of what is expected, and sometimes are linked to provisions for how family members can challenge inappropriate behavior. Generative families find that codes of conduct provide a common foundation for asking family members to overcome bad habits and let go of old slights and grudges.

Here are the principles from one family's code:

*We want to maintain the traditional values in our family system but modified to meet changing business conditions. Staying together was a key point of the code and to maintain a high moral standard, honesty, and values, then to cultivate and strengthen the bonds of trust in each other and in the family. Then to recognize the continuing family security and growth was from hard work, initiative, and frugality and accept, honor, and follow decisions arrived at by consensus; to give each individual maximum opportunity, morally, educationally, and professionally, to develop both for the family and for himself; and to enable senior members to reside or retire in their countries of choice. There are eighteen "principles," but that's just the flavor.*

In a fractious or divided family, the code provides principles that define how to deal with emotional or difficult issues and specify how the family can act together. It defines a safe space, a way for the family to interact even when there is stress and conflict. The family has to affirm that the code is an aspiration and that some may find it difficult to adhere to, but having it written down allows family members to hold one another to behaviors and call each other to account.

A European family leader recalls, *"The family created a set of rules to address conflict and build unity within the ownership group. This code of conduct set a standard of positive behavior for all family members to follow. It also translated into a set of values and guidelines for nonfamily managers to set the tone for the culture of their businesses."*

In another family, a third generation of several siblings had a family legacy of lots of conflict and rivalry across genders and those working in and out of the business. They were finding that this tendency was passing to their children as they developed their family governance. They convened a task force to define standards that family members would aspire toward in their interaction. This code did not end conflict, but it set some useful and practical standards of behavior that they could challenge each other to follow:

> *The Code of Behavior is designed to promote harmony and unity among all family members. It is intended to help the family reach its highest goals.*
>
> 1. *We strive to maintain a sense of gratitude for the gifts from our ancestors, those currently generating wealth for the Trust, and for all family members.*
> 2. *We strive to offer support and appreciation to one another.*
> 3. *We desire to listen when others speak and wait our turn before speaking.*
> 4. *We aim to keep a light heart and do our best to keep the mood pleasant, respectful and productive.*
> 5. *We want to respect that diverse opinions exist and acknowledge that very few things are completely black or white, right or wrong, good or bad. We know that coming to an understanding may take time.*
> 6. *We strive to address family, and family business conflicts privately and not argue in front of a client, employee, customer, or advisor.*
> 7. *We value the importance of respectful communication when trying to find understanding. If needed, we try to arrange a meeting, set a date and time limit for the meeting, arrive prepared to listen to the other person and do our best to reach a peaceful resolution. It is helpful to use equal timed speaking turns with listener remaining silent, and reflect back and acknowledge what you heard the other person say before beginning your turn to speak.*
> 8. *When conflicts arise, we try to recognize and acknowledge our feelings and take a break until we can remain calm and work towards resolution once more.*
> 9. *We never want to speak negatively about anyone behind their back, but rather speak directly to the person we are at issue with.*
> 10. *We understand that blame and accusations are not productive places to start conversations. We want to approach each other with dignity and respect. We ask to be heard and try to remain inquisitive.*
> 11. *We recognize that the Family Council has developed tools and resources to assist with intra-family conflict. We try to take advantage of what the Family Council has to offer.*
> 12. *We want to take responsibility for our actions and mistakes. We try to use mistakes as learning tools and reflecting back to acknowledge.*
> 13. *When offering help or advice, we strive to inquire first to confirm that it is welcome.*

14. *We make every effort to abide by the agreements we have made; we will aim to not make changes to agreements unilaterally. Instead, we make changes with the people involved.*

15. *We make every effort to honor our time commitments, to complete tasks on time, arrive at scheduled meetings and events on time and be ready to participate.*

16. *We try to acknowledge when we have over-committed our time or energy. We seek to be willing to speak up and ask for help if we need to lighten the load of our responsibilities. If we remove ourselves from a responsibility, we want to allow others to proceed as they see fit.*

17. *We do our best to hold ourselves accountable for our actions and decisions.*

As with mission and values, the code of conduct is negotiated across generations. As families include new generations in governance, this enables them to agree on and share expectations for responsible behavior. For example, several families mentioned the need to be clear and explicit about the meaning of confidentiality of family information. The behavior of family members in public situations was also included in these codes. One family stated clearly that family members were expected not to be written about in the local news and social media. Others specify when and how a family member can comment on family-related business issues.

## One Family ... United Under Shared Values and Purpose

From the many examples my research team and I gathered of family constitutions, one particularly stands out. Here is a very detailed and evocative values and purpose statement that encompasses many of the core values and elements of family enterprise expressed by the generative families in this study. It is a family whose business has grown and developed over one hundred years to become a global conglomerate of businesses owned by an interlocking series of family trusts. To define their shared values and practices, the family members came up with this document:

**To the family members of the fourth and fifth generations:**

**Purpose:** As members of the fourth generation, our mission is to grow the business and carry forward the family legacy as a diverse yet united family of owners.

We are fortunate to have been born into a multigenerational family business, started by our great-grandfather almost one hundred years ago. Every generation has contributed years of sweat equity and reinvestment to the business, shaping it into a successful company that will become our generation's responsibility.

Just as those before us, our duty is to act as responsible stewards of the company, prioritizing what best serves the business and all its stakeholders over what best serves a particular individual. To that end, we have agreed to the following principles, shared goals and values that embody how we commit to conduct ourselves moving forward.

We recognize that we are unique individuals with different ways of thinking, so this document will serve as our north star, reminding us of our common values and commitments, so that together we can navigate challenging decisions, resolve differences, and propel the business to greater success.

We agree to live and act by these principles, holding ourselves and each other accountable, all with the shared goal of doing what is best for the company, owners, and all stakeholders.

*(continued)*

*(Continued)*

**Legacy:** Our goal is to respect the family's legacy and to preserve it by perpetuating its historic employee-focused culture and the values that previous generations embodied.

Close family ties have contributed to our success as a family-owned business. As the family grows larger and more dispersed, we will need to focus on cultivating our family bonds.

**Values:** Our great-grandparents, grandparents, and parents built a solid and reputable business founded on the principles of service, fairness, and integrity. These principles earned the company and its ownership respect and loyalty from employees, customers, business partners, and the community. This yields direct benefits to the business. We commit to live by these values, which include:

- Stewardship: We don't think of ourselves as the absolute owners of the family business. Rather, we view it as an intergenerational resource that we are entrusted with. The value of the family business was not created in one generation, and we think that it should benefit more than one generation of all stakeholders.
- The Golden Rule: Treat others as you would like to be treated. Empathy will guide our dealings with fellow owners, employees, and other stakeholders.
- Humility: Remain humble and be thankful for what we have, but never forget the responsibilities that go with it.
- Integrity: Be honest and trustworthy. Always do the right thing, even when no one's looking.
- Candor: Be forthright. Communicate respectfully, but don't let that deter you from discussing difficult or uncomfortable issues directly.
- Hard Work: Never underestimate the value of ingenuity and hard work. Be willing to "roll up your sleeves" and get the job done.
- Think Long Term: Make decisions that will benefit the company in the long run, even if they're more difficult. Be patient and do not be distracted by the short-term view.
- Lead by Example: Be the ultimate example of values. Inspire the behavior and action that we want to see in the employees and the company.

**Goals**: Our goals are to profitably grow the business and to carry forward the family legacy. We recognize that these two things are not mutually exclusive, although in certain situations, one may take precedence over the other.

**Importance of Profit and Stakeholders:** We recognize that being profitable is essential to our success. Profitability results from the combination of employee effort, effective management, sound strategy, and the patient capital of shareholders.

The company may have started with one person's goal to make a better living for his family, but we recognize that its success and scope means that we should seek more than the singular aim of shareholder profit. The company is a source of livelihood for thousands of employees (and their families) who are vital to its success. Without profitability, our goals for stakeholders and family legacy will come to nothing.

So while we aim for profit, and achieve our aims through profit, profit isn't our only aim. The company exists not only to make profit or to enhance our employees' lives but to achieve both.

*(continued)*

In seeking to do so, we'll remember that it's often necessary to sacrifice short-term gains for long-term profitability. We'll also be mindful that sometimes leaders will need to make decisions that negatively affect stakeholders now but that contribute to the long-term profitability and longevity of the business, which is ultimately in the best interest of stakeholders.

**Owners and the Business:** We aspire to be a family and ownership group that embodies the values of the business. Owners should be a source of impetus, not an impediment, to the business. We've seen how the third generation is trusted and respected and how that motivates employees. Family owners can add a personal touch that inspires employees to do their best. We aim to be owners who bring out the best in our employees.

To do this, we will embody the traits which have contributed to the company's character and success, like humility, sacrifice, hard work, leading by example, and a long-term mindset. These are character traits that should be a way of life for us. They cannot merely be adopted or discarded when convenient.

**Roles:** For our family business to succeed, we must maintain the distinction between ownership and management. We believe this is especially important as ownership transfers from the third to fourth generation.

Ownership is responsible to select the Board of Directors, who will oversee the governance and management of the Company.

Management is responsible to develop and execute the strategy of the business and to operate the business consistent with the policies and objectives established by the Board of Directors. A management role should be gained through experience and qualification. The business must always seek to retain the best management available to it, whether it is family or nonfamily.

Ownership should be supportive of and trust managers, and managers should be committed to values consistent with those of the owners and capable of achieving the desired objectives.

Owners contribute to the business by supplying patient capital and by supporting the reinvestment of profits to grow, evolve, and diversify the business. Owners are responsible to select the best representatives for the Board of Directors, regardless of whether they are immediate family, extended family, or nonfamily.

Status as a shareholder does not confer an owner with the right to determine the day-to-day management of the business. Status as a director or employee does not make someone more of an owner than another.

Owners entrust the Board of Directors and management to guide the strategy, management, and operations of the business and should be cautious not to disrupt the Board or management.

An owner who serves as a director or employee and who has additional decision-making powers and access to information has a heightened responsibility to be trustworthy and to act for the benefit of all owners, not just himself or herself.

We will be careful about entitlement in all of its forms, whether it is the owner who thinks that the company only exists for his or her enrichment or the owner who feels that a management role gives him or her a proprietary right to the business over other owners.

*(continued)*

*(Continued)*

In all things, we will live by the Golden Rule, and treat those in different roles the way that we would want to be treated if we were in their place.

**Owner's Lives and the Business:** Ownership brings both benefits and responsibilities. Sometimes there aren't easy divisions between private life and business life. Our responsibilities to the business make demands on our personal lives—requiring the devotion of weekends, evenings, holidays, and other personal time to the business and subjecting us to a higher level of public visibility and scrutiny. However, the business has also enhanced our lives, providing livelihoods to parents and employed owners, contributing funds for education, and distributing business earnings from time to time.

We will strive to achieve a balance between living lives consistent with our collective family values (like humility, hard work, and gratefulness), while recognizing that individual personalities, values, aspirations, political beliefs, and other views will be diverse. Our lives may be influenced by the business, but they should not be dominated by it.

We recognize that decisions about where to live, where to work, and how to vote are deeply personal and should not be subject to family pressure. However, we have an obligation to be cognizant of how our actions affect the company.

However, we also recognize that our publication of opinions, our possessions, and our experiences can reflect on the family and the business, often without our knowing it. Therefore, we will be mindful about ostentation and cautious to avoid conspicuous display of wealth, especially with social media.

We will recognize that well-meaning, reasonable people can differ over these issues, and we will be understanding and accepting when we don't see eye to eye.

If we feel we are experiencing unreasonable sacrifices, we will speak up so that resentment doesn't build up over time.

**Managing Conflict:** We believe that maintaining healthy family relations is paramount, and we commit to not letting what happens with the business harm our relationships with each other. Many family businesses have been ruined by owner conflict. Living according to our values will help us avoid disagreement, but we should still expect disagreement and conflict.

We believe that a group with diverse views will be more effective than a monoculture vulnerable to groupthink. We will be candid with one another, rationally and honestly articulate our divergent views, truly listen respectfully, disagree agreeably, build consensus, compromise, and respect the outcomes of decisions that we disagree with.

We will try to understand others' viewpoints before trying to debate or dissuade them, and we will consider the possibility that we're wrong. We will try to keep owner egos from influencing decisions.

We will accept disagreement but be intolerant of conflict. We will embrace differences but not divisiveness. We will remember that unity and harmony are fragile but vital to our success.

We will address conflicts early on to avoid them festering and compounding over time.

We will avoid escalating isolated disagreements into clannish conflict and intervene when we see signs of that happening.

When we do have differences, we'll talk directly with the person involved. We will try not to involve other family members in the disagreement before talking to the other person. We will avoid the natural inclination to be a sounding board for others and

*(continued)*

redirect to the "conflictee." We will hold each other accountable to do this, which is important, because it doesn't come naturally to us as a family.

Direct and forthright communication is important, but so is continuous communication.

While we value our privacy and the value of appearing as a united group, we will involve a third-party mediator when appropriate, recognizing that harmony and conflict resolution are more important than privacy and pride. During conflicts, we will work as a group to resolve them, rather than allowing one person to manage the conflict alone.

**Commitment:** We have been fortunate to be a part of this, but the company's survival is never guaranteed.

We believe these goals and values have contributed to our success thus far, and they are vital to the perpetuation of a successful family business. It is our responsibility to carry them forward.

Each of us agrees to remember, act, and live by these principles and to hold each other accountable to them. This is our solemn pact as owners, about which we will never be complacent.

This is an expression of the shared goals, values, and principles that we pledge to uphold and remember.

A family constitution is an impressive achievement. But whatever form it takes, to become a generative family, a family must have a meaningful mission and purpose for being, prescribe behavior, and create policies and practices to guide itself. A generative family is more than an intention; it is a complex vehicle to achieve many aims and goals for the family. Each generation it grows more complex. The existence of an evolving family constitution is one way that the generative family is able to thrive across generations.

The constitution is not a product or something that can be drafted and then implemented by a family. As we learn from the examples of generative families, it evolves and is developed by the family as it designs its governance process. It does not take place before or after this, but at the same time, alongside it. In addition to codifying and explaining family legal and business documents, the constitution is a shared activity that, by their participation, inspires and invites rising generations to become involved. It vividly shows how to do that, and the benefits and responsibilities of taking on a stewardship role. The constitution also helps the family navigate and overcome differences and conflict and integrate all the different activities and ventures that are emerging in the family. Without a constitution, the family risks working at cross-purposes and not being able to align and continue its long-term success.

## Taking Action in Your Own Family Enterprise

The constitution is the outcome of many family activities that can be done separately, but ultimately, they come together to produce the intergenerational guide that is the constitution. Here are some of important activities that help build a constitution.

## Legacy Letters (or Videos)

There is much wisdom that the older generations can share. It is often implicit, or tacit, in that their actions reflect it but it is not really known or useful to the rising generation. Family elders can share their learning and expectations with new generations in the form of a letter or a video. This is very moving, especially when young people who knew them slightly or not at all view it after they have passed. It also adds vitality and emotional expression to what might be dry expectations or directions in trust documents. Often these letters are included in the preamble or beginning of the constitution.

## Finding the Meaning and Practical Relevance of Legal Documents

Legal agreements, corporate by-laws, trust documents, and shareholder agreements too often live only in family or lawyers' offices. They are thought to be arcane and irrelevant, when in reality they are the foundation for family organization. Each new generation should be introduced to them and have an opportunity to meet with advisors and family members to become familiar with them. This briefing often precedes the drafting of a constitution. The briefing usually raises questions and areas of ambiguity that have to be addressed. Many family disagreements and feelings of unfairness arise because young family members do not understand these agreements. After reviewing and understanding agreements, a family gathering can define questions to ask advisors or family leaders, and also areas where further development is needed.

## Convening a Family "Constitutional Convention"

Creating a constitution is not a one-step process, or something that an advisor can draft. Advisors can help, but they can only emerge from a body that represents the leading voices of the family. It is not separate from or different than the starting of a family council or other family governance processes. It should rather be considered one of the first activities in a new family council or assembly, or the beginning of these groups.

The process can begin by bringing the family together at a family assembly and presenting the nature and reason for developing a constitution. It is meant to clarify the values, rules, and practices that guide the family enterprise. It is done by a group of family members that represents each branch, key constituency, and generation, but includes the older leaders. This group of from 4 to 8 family members gathers the existing documents, and begins the process defined above for generating the constitution. They will want to communicate in person with the family, to share drafts and ideas. After their work together, they will convene a large family session to read and consider the constitution part by part. This may take several meetings.

You begin with the big picture, the mission, purpose, and values of the family. Then you might meet to talk about the nature of each key family entity—council, board, and other ventures, and how they are organized. This process is not a one-time event and often takes place with large and small meetings until a workable draft emerges. It can then be used and tested over a year and then revisited to make mid-course corrections.

After a constitution is drafted, it is important that there are regular opportunities to review it and a process for making changes. No family constitution can stand without regular updates.

## Notes

1. Jay Hughes, *Family: The Compact Across Generations* (Hoboken: John Wiley & Sons, 2007).
2. With the help of consultant David Bork.

# PART FOUR

## The Rising Generation: Sustaining the Future

Family enterprise is about the future, and the future rests in the hands of the next, rising generation. Perhaps the greatest desire of a generative family is to raise an educated, creative, socially responsible, and committed generation to form the next generation of family leaders. This final section discusses how the family takes up the special task of preparing family leaders to sustain and move the business into new generations. It looks at how the family invests in and prepares members of the new, rising generation to become new family leaders and owners.

Chapter 13 explores how each individual family develops their children as responsible, creative contributors to the family enterprise. Chapter 14 talks about how the family learns and grows together, by engagement by teaching and sharing the work of the family enterprise. Chapter 15 shows how generative families build social capital through philanthropy and community engagement. Finally, the book concludes with some reflections on the implications of what we learned from generative families, and some predictions about this group in the future.

# Releasing the Potential of the Rising Generation

## How to Develop Capable Successors

One quality that showed up in almost every generative family is a deep, ongoing, active engagement in developing the skills and commitment of their rising generations. They realize that these young people are their most important resource, and they will not spontaneously grow up to become good stewards. They have an important, impactful, and unique opportunity in the family enterprise, but to make good use of it requires engagement, investment, and active measures. Family elders realize that wealth can have negative impact on their offspring, and so they thoughtfully invest in many programs and practices. This chapter begins with the challenges facing wealthy young people in general, and then looks at how parents, and collective generative families, develop capable, committed stewards for their enterprise.

Every family, wealthy or not, faces the daunting challenge of raising children to become productive members of society. But following the adage "to whom much is given, much is expected," an extraordinarily wealthy family with many shared assets faces additional challenges. Since young members of such a family expect to become responsible for a large and complex set of financial and business entities, they have to learn skills that the less fortunate never encounter. They also need to learn and accept the family's values about work, responsible behavior, lifestyle, money, inheritance, and social responsibility.

Generative families educate and prepare the next generation to take care of their assets as well as use the freedom and opportunities they have been given to make a vital contribution. No family wants to feel that it created great wealth so that its children could be lazy, wasteful, and unproductive, spending the money as fast as possible. Generative families want to develop character in young family members, and they want to see it develop without coercion. We look here at how actively and explicitly this is done.

They view a responsible inheritor as having the following qualities:

- Working at a productive career or life task valued by others that they care about and have become skilled at

- An informed owner (or owner-to-be) of the family assets
- A good family citizen who is committed to family values and participates in family governance

Meeting this challenge involves more than having good intentions or designing a trust with restrictive spending rules. Generative families adopt family development practices that can be even more time- and energy-intensive and demanding than creating a successful business. That may be why there are so few of these families.

Financial and business success enables new paths to open for the rising generations. Elder generations take a long-term view of the future, an essential element of which is preparing their children and heirs for a good life. This has always been a concern of wealthy families, as US founding father John Adams affirmed in this letter to his wife:

> *I must study Politicks and War that my sons may have liberty to study Mathematicks and Philosophy. My sons ought to study Mathematicks and Philosophy, Geography, natural History, Naval Architecture, navigation, Commerce and Agriculture, in order to give their children a right to study Painting, Poetry, Musick, Architecture, Statuary, Tapestry and Porcelaine.[1]*

This letter highlights the fact that members of the elder generation may envision a very different future for their children than simply continuing the legacy business. They see their family success as offering wider opportunities for their children, ones that are not open to everyone.

But with infinite possibilities ahead of them, their children may find it difficult to decide what to choose. In addition to skills, they need to discover life purpose and develop their own values for living that build on the family's legacy values. Every generation of parents would like to be able to control the positive effect of their wealth on their children. In reality, control is limited, and parents can only hope to influence, set an example, and talk together with their children about the future. This final section looks at how generative families develop activities to set this positive climate for their rising generation. Each time a new generation takes leadership, they demonstrate how well they have succeeded at this goal.

One of the core findings of this study is that a generative family is focused on creating opportunities for and encouraging the development of its children through active investment of family resources to develop skill and commitment. One third-generation family leader reflects:

> *You have to take the time to develop each member to their potential. People don't understand how important education is, and underestimate the time, the care, and the devotion that it takes to build a strong family. But for me that's where everything happens. So that's where we spent most of our time. If you look at our family business, it would be a combination of individuation and collectivism.*

An Asian family leader explains the many facets of this "project":

> *The important matters are entry of a generation, what we expect heirs to do, values we wish for the parents to instill in their kids, the role of the family in matters, and the access to the foundation programs. If they want to get involved, we have summer jobs where the kids get a*

*bird's-eye view, whether they're in high school or grade school. We have community projects; we send some of our kids to do hospital work or Habitat for Humanity. We give them a flavor of the business stuff that we think is important.*

Generative families mention several reasons for developing the next generation:

- To have their successors sustain and oversee family assets to use them wisely while being stewards for the next generation.
- To use family resources to develop the potential and capability of each individual.
- To develop and install a cadre of successors to carry on the family legacy of profitable and productive ventures, following the family's espoused values.

Families without a legacy business or substantial shared assets handle the tasks of raising productive offspring privately, within the nuclear family, preparing them to go their own way in life. The same is true for generative families—with an additional wrinkle: given their shared resources, generative families need responsible and competent family members to steward these resources in future generations. Therefore, they must teach additional skills and instill sensitivity in their successors as stewards of the family wealth or risk losing that wealth through inattention or incompetence. The financial skills they need to learn are far more complex than budgeting or balancing a checkbook. For this reason, they often provide this education as a collective family activity.

Many generative families also feel that the primary responsibility for this development belongs in each individual household. As one leader observes, "*Our different families have different perspectives on how much information people should be provided with and in terms of the attitudes toward money and spending and what kids should have or not have. And so those kinds of things are left much more to the individual families or branches.*" The extended family then builds on the foundation of values and character with shared family activities agreed to by everyone, designed to add specific skills and commitment to the family ventures.

My colleague Jim Grubman and I[2] previously described the journey of a family new to wealth. Wealth creators usually come from modest circumstances and are new *immigrants* to the experience and use of wealth. As we saw in Chapter 4, they are self-made and remember what it took to achieve their wealth—hard work, individual initiative, personal drive, and high control.

Their children and grandchildren are born into an environment of family affluence. They are *natives* to family wealth; wealth is always part of their lives, and they grow up in a world of wealth that conditions their everyday reality. But they are also aware that they did not create this wealth. Lacking awareness of where it came from, they often have anxiety about what they would do if it were not there. They hear from their parents that they should be prepared to go their own way, but because they have grown up in an affluent household, what this actually means may be more theoretical than realistic. What they experience is anxiety, rather than direction.

When parents look ahead to what they want their children to learn, they tend to emphasize skills of independent action that served them well. Their children must learn self-reliance and be able to create their lives on their own. Parental intention is admirable, but parents' knowledge of next generation needs is incomplete.

In addition to learning how to find their way in their career and personal relationships, young family members of generative families need to learn about additional areas related to their family assets and wealth.

Because their family is linked by trusts and shared financial entities, they must learn skills to oversee and manage these assets and learn how to work together in harmony with siblings, cousins, and spouses. Inheriting wealth does not mean a person has the ability to use it wisely. Careful use of wealth must be learned. Younger members of the family need collaborative and team-oriented skills to oversee, steward, and add to the family capital. They must learn what it means to become a responsible family steward, and work together to achieve it.

## The Developmental Path of the Young Family Member

### Inheriting Wealth: What Is Its Intended Purpose?

*"It's all about the money,"* one family leader observes. While this view is held by many family elders, generative families for the most part view this notion as limited and short-sighted. Although money looms large in the life choices of a next-generation family member, continuity depends as well on developing all forms of family capital. Money alone is not a strong enough glue to compel family members to dedicate themselves to each other. They need a compelling purpose to pull themselves from their individual lives to commit to the family enterprise.

Financial rewards are not just for immediate enjoyment but are also to be sustained for future generations and used for values-based endeavors. Family members must develop a balance between current and future needs and between consumption and service.

By remaining united across generations and reinvesting profits, the family enterprise can remain large and profitable. Wealth is not a goal in itself. Its value lies in what it allows individuals and the family to do and in how it is used. This is something that the family determines together. At some point, often at the initiative of the emerging generation, the family begins to ask each other what all this family wealth is to be used for.

This young successor in a hundred-year-old South Asian family with 450 family members observes:

> *The first eighty years were basically surviving and building up wealth; we reached the point where we're doing very well—more cash flow, higher dividends. With more wealth, there could be a change in behavior with the way the younger generation deals with it, so we have to be very conscious about how this wealth is deployed and how we manage to keep our values in the midst of all of this seeming success.*

With the growing family infrastructure of shared activities and practices, a young person growing up in a wealthy household can't help but wonder about the family wealth. Young people in such families wonder about:

- What they can expect in their lives
- The rules for using and benefiting from the family resources

- What the family enterprise contains and how it works
- Roles they might look forward to in the business and family
- What they have to do to attain them

The family can constructively engage this curiosity and offer answers so that its young heirs can move forward with their lives and make thoughtful and relevant decisions.

Family wealth, as noted in Chapter 2, also includes human, relationship, social, and spiritual "capital." These forms of capital can endure longer than the original financial wealth. In addition, developing non-financial capital adds meaning and shared purpose to the family.

One of the most important practices for a generative family to develop and affirm values and purposes for its various family ventures and its wealth. The family struggles with the question "What is our financial wealth for?' in a way that engages the members of the rising generation. The presence of shared values and mission is necessary so that the family, with new members entering regularly by birth and marriage, agrees with or modifies what it is doing together.

With so many family members, the expectation of living a life of ease may no longer be realistic. But the children should not be the last to learn this. Aside from a very few (but highly visible) members of the global leisure class, fourth- or fifth-generation family heirs can look forward to a nice "lifestyle supplement" to their income, enabling them, for example, to work for a lower salary in a rewarding career but not enough not to work at all:

> *Family wealth enabled me to live comfortably and put my kids through college. My kids definitely see it in the same way. My son owns his own business. I have given him a lot of support, but he knows it comes from our family business. The family definitely sees that. And that is our success. Not only that, but the family stories are continuing.*

Young children growing up in a wealthy environment cannot be expected to understand these limits; the family has to help them overcome unrealistic underestimates or overestimates of family financial wealth. These children may not respond well to an ultimatum. They need warning and active guidance from their parents to prepare them for their future role as stewards.

Families have different ways of distributing wealth. Each approach deeply influences the mindset, motivation, and development of the rising generation. Traditional cultures, spanning regions such as southern Europe, the Middle East, and South America, offer an allowance or regular distribution to each family member, usually allocated by age. Only a handful of the legacy families in this study operated this way, and they all reported finding this approach counterproductive. When income is not connected to ownership or family engagement, its presence gives the message that there is nothing the rising generation needs to do to qualify for it. It makes family organization more difficult. The majority of generative families pass inheritance to individual households, even if it is owned by a trust; each household or family branch allocates inheritance in its own way. One legacy family can therefore have several approaches to inheritance.

G1 wealth creators usually create a complex set of financial structures—trusts, holding companies, and a foundation—which form the reality for each successive generation. As one sociological researcher observes:

> In generational aging and transition, a family must create a transcendent, controlling version of itself in the organization of its property to achieve a coherence of organization that can preserve the mystique of its name and ensure its continuing exercise of patrician functions in its social environment. This coherence does not come as much from commitments made by its members to their common lineage, as from the application of law and the work of fiduciaries whose primary responsibility is to protect the founder's legacy from divisive family quarrels.[3]

These arrangements can be seen on a continuum of tighter to looser control. On one end are purpose trusts that use resources only in clearly defined ways. In the middle are pools that can be accessed, with rules and limits and often a nonfamily trustee. Then there are inheritances that are more loosely controlled but with voting control of the asset assigned to a single family leader. And finally, there is no control, where the family owners are free to decide together how to use their wealth. Each family must teach and come to terms with the degrees of freedom handed over to the new generation.

Between the heir and the family wealth, then, lie trusts and financial entities, as well as family advisors, all of which inheritors must understand, accept, navigate, and eventually oversee. Learning about this legal structure, young people can feel devalued or distrusted if, for example, they are offered a beneficiary role with limited power or influence. The successful family must provide the training to make this relationship harmonious and satisfying and may also look for ways to allow more flexibility. Each young family member must understand these options and learn how to relate to them in a mutually beneficial manner that may not be immediately clear. By understanding, negotiating, and engaging, these young family members may discover areas of flexibility not initially apparent. To avoid acrimony and conflict, the family must develop caring relationships and commitment to work together so that the family wealth serves the family goals.[4]

### Parenting and Developing Character in the Wealthy Household

The primary responsibility of parents is to raise productive adults. If the family is also an economic unit, the family usually prepares its children to fulfill their responsibilities in the family ventures. Generative families report that this task is made more difficult when the family has substantial wealth. Wealth can be seductive; it deeply affects the reality of how children grow up and how they learn that the wealth is not just something to make them special and comfortable. The family has to teach values about children's responsibility to be stewards of the wealth, ensuring it will be wisely used.

An added challenge is that wealthy children grow up with a sense of specialness that sometimes translates into feeling that wealth makes them better than other people. This is called *entitlement*; its opposite, a sense of service and responsibility to sustain the wealth and add to it, is called *stewardship*. The goal of the privileged household is to help its children move from entitlement to stewardship. This chapter explores two facets of this endeavor: first, the active role of parents before their children begin university, and second, the journey of the young adult to develop a personal identity. The first stage is the prime time for active family engagement, teaching, and learning; this time is followed by a period of gradually letting go as young adults find their way through higher education and into their first work experiences.

Parents set examples about values and teach responsibility even when they are not conscious they are doing so. "Messages" are passed in family conversations about what is and is not important about wealth and in life. For example, one young woman proudly showed her father her first paycheck, earned from working in a service project. Her father's response was, *"Why are you working? You don't have to work."* The effect of this message was that she always felt vaguely guilty about working because she was taking money away from people who needed it.

Most generative families report that they are successful in sending the message to many, if not most, of their rising generations that they must develop a work ethic, and an ability to take care of themselves if the "golden goose" stops producing:

> *We are focusing on what the family members want to do. We're encouraging the family members, by saying clearly, "Look, you're getting a check from the business and if you don't want to be in the business, it's fine. But go do something. Learn what you want to do and pursue it." That way they learn the skills of how to survive because we don't know what happens if the wealth supply runs out.*

Young people develop values from their parents' indirect messages and examples. They may learn that a person's worth is measured by how much money they have or that people who have money do or do not do certain things. These messages can be conscious or unconscious.

Money has many meanings for a young person. Children are especially curious about where money comes from, as it is very abstract and almost magical. They have to learn that some people do not have nice houses and schools. Their experience may be that when you want money, you just stop at an ATM and get some. Parents may use money as a reward or give children gifts when they leave for work or a vacation on their own, leaving their children to learn that money can be a barely adequate substitute for love and engagement.

Values about wealth, the families in this study report, arise from engagement and example within the family, rather than policies and rules. Here is an account by a South American family of how one parent influenced his children:

> *I raised my children to be leaders and live by the family values. We started working with the children when they were very young. We went with them to sports activities, and every single day of my life, I talked to every single child. Every night, we'd have a little chat. Two very important things came out. One was the ability to communicate. We have excellent communication skills among ourselves. Communication didn't start when they started in the business. It started when they were four or five at the breakfast table or basketball court. We try to have dinner together every night. Every Sunday, we would go to church. I think that strengthened family values. My wife is great. She's the chief emotional officer. When you give people security and enough love to*

*go around and respect them, they are secure. When people are anxious or nervous or worried, they are that way because they're not given enough love.*

*Those values were transmitted to the children. My wife and I insisted on excellence in education. I guess if we had had a child that didn't want to study, we would have had to force them. But we really tried to mold them to do well in school. They went to the best schools here, but every summer we sent them to the US for summer programs. Since my grandfather never had an opportunity to have a good education, he used to tell me, "I told your father that I'm not going to give him that inheritance from me. The only thing I'm going to leave him and your uncles and aunts is an education. That's the only inheritance that no one can take away from you." That was a very nice message.*

He helped his children see that despite living in a highly affluent community, they would not have everything other kids had. While they were richer than most of their peer families, his children were taught to be thoughtful about their spending.

Young children learn about work by doing chores and helping around the house. If there is a family business or family office, they may experience work by helping there. This may also be the first time they get paid. By visiting the family business and seeing how work is done, they directly view the source of the family legacy and imagine their own possible future. Similarly, if a family engages together in community service work, children learn about other cultures and the challenges of a world where some have and others do not. This is a difficult moral lesson.

*"We know what a drug money can be as it stopped children from becoming the best they could be. I didn't want that for our children,"* says a matriarch of one branch of a large multigeneration family. *"I was very conscious that I wanted my children to make it on their own."* This desire in turn led her and her husband to work actively with their own family branch, developing a strong family organization to introduce a contrasting culture of excellence for their children.

Sharing family values and discussion about money and wealth is a critical task for a wealthy family. One South American family heir reports how the family established a "counterculture" that challenged the prevailing materialism seen in their peers, a difficult lesson for them to learn:

*I noticed a lot of children are given polo lessons, yachts, sports cars very early. We have stayed away from that. The first car they got was a Volvo. No yachts, no polo. It's about work and helping your neighbor, loving your family. When our friends at school would get something like a fancy new bike, my mother would say, "Well, that's not necessary. You can have a simple bicycle. It will do the same thing." They never tried to match up to the advantages of other people. So if somebody had a car, we had a bicycle. Or if somebody had Nike, we had Converse. In that sense, money was not important. It was never discussed until we were older. We learned to be moderate with money, have control over it. Don't overextend yourself.*

*I remember I had a savings box made out of paper-mâché. Every day, they gave us seventy-five cents or a dollar to buy a coke or candy. I never bought the coke or candy. I saved the money and put it in my savings box every day for I don't know how many years. I saved almost $2,000 like that. Then I bought stocks. I was about fourteen or fifteen, and I said to my dad, "Why don't you buy some stocks for me?" So he bought me some stock that*

*I still have. I also collected auto stickers and sold them at school. With that money, I bought a croquet game with my neighbors, and we formed a croquet league.*

One challenge of long-standing family wealth is a by-product of its success. Over generations, the family establishes a public image of values and service to the community as well as a vibrant and successful business. The outside view is of prosperity and service. The next-generation family members benefit from this perception by experiencing respect and community status but also sometimes envy and jealousy.

Young family members may need help to respond to this public perception:

*In terms of values, I keep stressing why we want to stay together. Very few people in my family have anybody to relate to with this wealth other than ourselves. We're not the Rockefellers. We all live with the fact that people assume that we have private jets and live this grand life, which we don't. But we're much better off than most of our friends, so we're very fortunate. Nobody wants to complain about having money or the issues that come with it, so there is a big void of how you discuss this or who you discuss it with. By getting together, we earn a comfort zone that we can talk about it. We need to rely on each other that way. Share experiences, thoughts. How do we deal with that as it goes to our kids? We all are guinea pigs.*

While the "family" is wealthy, individual members may have no control over or access to that wealth. The outside community may regard them as rich, but as individuals they feel constrained and of limited means. This may make them anxious and uncomfortable. How do they react when someone asks for a loan or expects them to always pick up the check at dinner? Several heirs mentioned the importance of not having their family wealth known to their peers; one family member changed his name when he entered college so that he would not be associated with his parents' generous endowments.

Families all over the world share one quality in relation to wealth: they don't talk about it or do so with great difficulty. Many generative families experienced the distrust and incapacity that came from keeping it secret from their children. They came to learn (often after a struggle) how to talk with their children about money, wealth, and inheritance. Rarely does a family do this from the start. A second- or third-generation leader, nonfamily leader, or advisor can guide the family to this conversation. One family in this study had difficulty with its first attempt at a family discussion. But the family tried again and was more successful.

If the family does not allow the children to talk about money and wealth, the children's feelings and struggle will have no outlet, and they may make self-defeating life choices. Several family members talked about feeling a vague sense of guilt about having money. "*I didn't earn it,*" said one family member, "*so I didn't feel it was really mine.*" While family wealth provides many benefits, members of wealthy families are always aware of the double-edged nature of inherited wealth. Young people need guidance to deal with these mixed feelings, and this guidance is best delivered in personal discussions.

Generative families learn to meet regularly to talk about money and wealth; this stands in strong contrast to most families, even affluent ones, that do not talk about this. Parents recall conversations about the future. They try to take a light touch, making it possible for the next generation to become involved, but also establishing clear values and expectations for members of the next generation.

Explaining the meaning and use of family wealth is difficult. It demands a high level of engagement and give and take. Here is a creative example from a European family patriarch. He holds regular meetings with his two sons, who work with him in the business:

> *It's still small enough to do that on an informal basis, but we realize that in the future that's going to have to be more formal. Me and my sons (the third to fourth generation) have over the last ten years formalized meetings about transition. Twice a year, we sit together for twenty-four hours. We call this the "how are you meeting." We exchange views of what kind of things we are going to work on for the next generation in a formal way. It's like a business family meeting. We do it here in my house.*
>
> *The basic question is: How are things going in general, what are the top preoccupations in your head? What can make the other parties happier? We look at what do you like and what you don't like, what went wrong, or what can I do to make you happier? I make mistakes, and you make mistakes, and you are going to do that every week, and you have to accept the way you are. You cannot change that, but it's good that you know that so you will try to avoid these negative things.*

What causes parents and children to start talking? It could be a crisis, a sudden or untimely death, or a financial windfall or loss. Or it can be a question voiced by a young family member. The parent can either open up or shut down the conversation.

It is difficult for parents and their offspring to talk freely and candidly. One reason is that young people feel that their parents are looking for specific responses and have a hidden purpose in what they are asking. So in order to have family conversation and to convey that they are open to hearing what their children think, parents have to ask more questions than state their opinions. Parents have to make it clear they want to hear the answer and not interrupt. If they get a one-word answer, they gently probe by asking further questions. This is called "having an attitude of inquiry rather than advocacy." While parents do in fact have an agenda and opinions, waiting to learn from the young people what they think and feel first is a path to a successful family conversation.

Instilling values is rarely a formal process. Rather, through their own actions, parents set an example. However, several legacy families also initiate conversations with their children specifically about the meaning of family wealth. There seems to be no set age for doing this. Most families adopt a graduated method of conversation—sharing information and teaching skills at different ages as appropriate. "*We've talked about where happiness comes from, having a good solid family, good solid friends, good food, a happy life at school. Things that are very tangible that you can call on all the time,*" says an inheritor who is now chair of her family's council.

Most families who have been successful over multiple generations develop an ethic of thoughtful spending, setting limits on how much the family spends in an external environment that enshrines consumption. It takes the concerted effort of a parent to instill this sensitivity. This sixth-generation family, with a long history in several countries, embodies the following values:

*Our values are focused on trying to live in a frugal way, trying not to abuse family wealth, and respect other people. We're distributing relatively modest amounts at a relatively young age. I've heard of other families where at age eighteen, they come into a trust fund where they're rolling in millions of dollars. It's important for us not to do that because that way, you're causing major issues for future generations.*

## Desired Values for Successors

Surprisingly, my research team and I found that the values legacy families desire for their children are remarkably similar in every part of the world:

- **Generosity:** Young people should give back to the community.
- **Respect:** Young people should value people of all wealth backgrounds.
- **Work Ethic and Skills:** Young people should have the capability to earn their own money and to find work they care about and at which they can succeed.
- **Self-esteem:** Young people must learn to find value in themselves independent of their wealth.
- **Financial Literacy:** Young people should learn how to handle money.
- **Responsibility for Wealth:** Young people should not be spoiled by affluence and should understand that wealth is a tool, not an end in itself.
- **Frugality:** Young people should exercise prudence in their spending.
- **Pride:** Young people should appreciate the opportunity wealth offers.

The efforts described here are largely aimed at creating a family climate for these values to emerge. The founding generation's values are influential, as a third-generation family leader of a European family states:

*The dividends are not something we've actually earned. Prior generations put together this company and did a lot of hard work, so we need to be responsible and wise with the money that we are given, not live extravagantly. We give a lot philanthropically and live modestly, like my grandfather and grandmother, who created the company. They chose to live in the same one-story brick house they've lived in for fifty years rather than deciding to upgrade to some kind of extravagant mansion. They were happy and content and satisfied with what they had and spent their money in other ways, whether it would be taking family and friends on trips to places or cultural things. There is an overriding mentality to not take for granted what you have and use it for education and long-term value.*

Grandparents (elders) can be powerful teachers and models. Their venerated history and their special relationship with their grandchildren allow them to share their special family legacy:

*We get together each summer for two weeks without the parents; it's our opportunity as grandparents to give back to the next generation some of our values, pass along some of our traditions, and nurture that history and those traditions. Every five years, our family has an important ceremony. We dress up. It starts at age five when the child is five years old; we plant a tree for them at our country house. At age ten, they get the treasure chest, filled with all of the history of the family and the DVDs and all the artifacts.*

## The Three-Box Tool for Teaching Money Values

Values education begins early at home. One tool mentioned by several families is the "three boxes." When a child is first given an allowance, he or she is asked to allocate the money into three boxes: one for spending, one for saving, and one for giving to others. This distinction is difficult for a young child to understand at first, but once learned, the principle will have lasting impact on his or her life.

Here is one parent's account of adopting this activity and its impact:

*Our kids have been raised in a household that embodied "to whom much is given much is expected" [and] has been modeled. We began when they were probably four years old. They got an allowance and had a spend jar, a saving jar, and a giving jar. They had to cut it in thirds and put it in each of those jars. Then through school activities, church, and other things, they began giving their giving jar money at a very early age. Over the years, whenever we have made a significant contribution, we ask the family to come together. They have attended numerous philanthropic events and functions. We have a governance agreement that you can't come to the company until you work two years outside of the company. When he finished college, my son went to work for Teach For America and supported inner-city kids in very difficult circumstances.*

Here is another account:

*A lot of people wonder, "Well, my kid's only ten now. There's no need to teach him anything until he's eighteen, right?" But I think the real answer goes right back to when they're age four or five. We latched onto the three piggy bank idea. We give the kids an allowance each week, but they have to remember to ask for it, which is a little twist that not many people do. They actually have some responsibility to ask for it and remember so that it's not like a dividend check that just shows up every year. We give them three coins, and they've got three piggy banks. One's got "spending" written on it, one's got "saving" written on it, [and] one's got "charity" written on it. Each week, they put a coin in each one. That leads to great learning opportunities and teaching moments. So if there's a bushfire on TV or something and the kids think that that's bad that somebody's house got burned down, then we say, "Let's use some of the money in your charity piggy bank and put it toward people that they're going to help." They go to their piggy bank and see they've got $10 in there. Then there's a decision on how much to give. "If you give it all to this one, you don't have any more for others." They can start to think about all these different issues when they're really young, and it comes naturally to them.*

*They learn the value of money. Some of my kids' friends don't know whether a car costs $1,000 or $1 million. But in their spending piggy bank, if they've got a certain amount of money in there, then when you're in a shop, and the kids are always saying, "I want this Lego" or "I want that toy," the discussion can come back to, "Well, how much do you have in your spending piggy bank?" "Oh, I've got $10." Well, then, that $50 Lego box doesn't look so good, does it, if you have to buy it?*

*My kids spontaneously decided to set up a store on the curb, selling anything they can get their hands on, whether it's rocks from the garden or flowers or palm fronds or paper planes or whatever they can do. They set up a sign and say it's for charity and stop people in the street.*

*(continued)*

> *They've made a surprising amount of money. They enjoy doing it, putting the time in. And then we have a great discussion about, "Okay, how will we spend it?" With some charities, you can say, "Well, you can buy a sheep for one family or you could buy 20 chickens or you can buy fruit trees." Then you have a discussion about what will last longer, what's most beneficial, all these things. It all leads to great discussion, and I'm hoping it becomes embedded in the kids from a really early age.*

## Developing Identity as a Child of Wealth

Even with parental support and engagement, a young person growing up in a wealthy household must develop a positive identity independent of the family.[5] While there are many examples of materialistic, entitled, "spoiled," even self-destructive and lost young people, the accounts by families in this study indicate that an engaged, values-based investment in the next generation by the family elders is a strong antidote to this tendency. Such an investment begins in the household and then expands to the extended family "community" of cousins growing up in the shadow of the family enterprise. The extended family reinforces the message by offering membership in a wonderful community that shares a business and commitment to positive social values. Membership has rewards but contains responsibility. To prepare to join the extended family enterprise as a steward, the young person first embarks on a journey to develop a personal sense of purpose and capability that in turn enables a positive role in the family enterprise.

The trappings of wealth are omnipresent for young people. This reinforces a sense that they are "special" in undefined ways, affecting expectations, questions, choices, and concerns about their future. This upbringing potentially provides inheritors an unusual amount of freedom to define themselves. But this same freedom and privilege also complicates making good choices and feeling good about their fortune in a world where people with inherited wealth may feel devalued by others with less who resent them. The way a young inheritor integrates the presence of money and wealth into his or her work, personal relationships, and life choices creates "wealth identity."[6]

Knowing their life is subsidized, how do these young people motivate themselves among so many possibilities and choose what to do with their lives? Living in the outsize shadows of their parents, they wonder what they can do that will be significant and important. The opportunities of wealth can be lost if spent on meaningless, self-defeating, or destructive pursuits. Wealth can be a source of confusion if inheritors are not sure what it means to them, what they want to do with it, or how it fits into their lives. They find themselves doing a little of this, a little of that, and not having enough motivation to stick with anything.

Money alone is not the issue. It is also the status and recognition that comes with wealth, potentially leading to feelings of power and entitlement but also feelings of entrapment and isolation. Having and inheriting money has a marked impact on young people's core identity—on the beliefs and values that map how they view themselves as well as how others see them. Inheritors can experience guilt or feel that they do not deserve these gifts, complicating their ability to move forward with a positive relationship to their wealth. After learning from their parents, they have to work on their own to develop their own personal identity. Identity development does not emerge fully from parents' teaching. However, the experience of being part of an extended family community can aid their journey immeasurably.

Wealthy heirs nowadays grow up in a bubble, a "gilded ghetto"[7] where they mostly meet others like themselves. Being protected, they do not experience diversity or have much opportunity to manage their own affairs. They do not go out or even play on their own. "Helicopter" parents watch and program their every activity, leaving little space for self-discovery.

With all of their wealth, their life experience is thus limited. Entering college may be one of the first times they are on their own, sharing space and getting to places on time without reminders. They may meet and learn from people different than them and may expand their horizons or remain secluded within a tight circle of other heirs. They need to be prepared and encouraged to take the first path—that of expanding their horizons.

This developmental journey can be described as a triangle, with contributions from both the parents and the young person. (See Figure 13.1.)

A young person begins by learning from parental example and teaching. There can also be contribution via extended family activities. But the young person must then go on a personal journey—college, travel, relationships, work—to develop a sense of personal identity, capabilities, self-confidence, and a personal mission. As this journey unfolds, the young person then returns to the family, entering the family assembly and other family activities, in a variety of ways. This inside/outside/return model needs support from the elder generation.

Several family practices help young people in generative families navigate this path. First, the elders let go and allow young adults to find their way. Young people are encouraged to set out on their own, with appropriate support for things like education or travel, but not so much that they don't have to do some things for

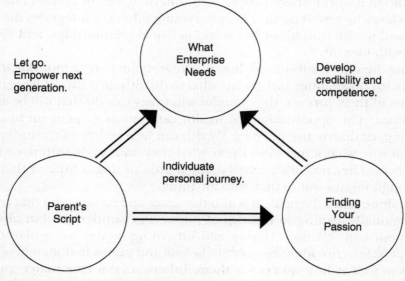

**Figure 13.1   Developmental journey of heirs.**

themselves. Particularly important is getting their first job outside the family, which is not given to them, and at which they have to perform on their own. Parental expectations should be made explicit, and parents should try as much as they can not to give mixed messages that show disapproval of the young people's choices. This can be tough for parents who feel strongly about certain directions.

Young people want their families to be interested and supportive of what they do; they want their parents to limit criticism and control over their choices. As their kids move toward maturity, parents can be appreciative but should exercise less direct control. They should resist their desire to use money to control choices and behavior. Young people develop best when they feel that while there are resources behind them, they are also expected to be on their own, even self-supporting. The family should have a clear agreement about what can be expected from the family and what the young people are expected to do in return. The presence of trusts and money is a problem if the rules for what is theirs and what is not are unclear.

Many young people report difficult experiences that propel them to learn and grow. If they don't struggle, they cannot learn. So parents who are rescuers, or who support their children in avoiding the consequences of difficulties, prevent learning. When a crisis or difficulty leads the young person to struggle, a common developmental sequence of identity development emerges that follows the lines of the "hero's journey"[8]—a person sets out to find something, encounters setbacks and difficulties, and overcomes them with some help from outside, all to end up with the prize that includes a sense of achievement, personal identity, and life purpose. Identity development can be viewed as a personal journey of difficult lessons and obstacles overcome, leading to public achievement and recognition as the young person returns home.

Young people who grow up with wealth inhabit a cocoon of safety, protection, plenty, and attention that has been called a state of "innocence"[9]—where they feel special and omnipotent, as if nothing can happen to them. Then, maybe on their initial journey outside the family something happens—a personal failure, a difficult relationship, or a challenge—that signals they can't rely on their parents or their money but have to fix it on their own. They are hurt and troubled, and this sets them to learn, reflect on, and come to terms with what they want to do with their lives. They may have to overcome bad judgment or habits. Doing so, they develop on their own some confidence, self-acceptance, and sense of purpose.

For parents, anxiety and desire for the best for their children can lead to rescuing them from any nascent difficulty, setting up a cycle of codependency where the child knows parents will always be there to take care of them. Parents who find their young adult children in trouble or hurting have to be able to apply positive tough love—emotional support along with the message that they have to solve their problems without unlimited parental resources. This lesson must first be learned by the parent.

Parental engagement is tricky at this stage. A parent should find a way to be in regular contact, as a sounding board for some (not all) experiences but taking care to be supportive and ask questions rather than preach or tell the young person what to do. Support does not have to mean solving a problem or intervening. Using one's means to smooth a path to college or a job is almost always counterproductive. For a parent used to having direct impact and taking action, this stage of support can be difficult to learn. Such a parent is not used to such an indirect role.

Young people who emerge from their own journey develop a sense of self strong enough to be ready to become involved in family ventures. They return home with their own success at doing something well and a set of skills they are ready to offer to the family.

## Learning About Business and Work

Families usually expect and require family members to work. But the definition of work was flexible. As one family leader says, *"We have a requirement for work, but we don't have a requirement for a salary, so if someone chooses their life work to be a volunteer coordinator for some charity, we consider that work."*

Another family developed what they call "the passion project," in which each young family member was invited to develop a business or project, funded by the family, doing something he or she was passionate about. The goal was for the young person to demonstrate persistence, capability and commitment and to have his or her work recognized in some way by the relevant community. These projects were not necessarily remunerative; the family supported arts or social service projects if the receiver demonstrated its worth to the community.

Education about the family business happens informally and is important in developing expectations and focusing on career goals. This member of a Middle Eastern family with widely dispersed relatives recalls:

*I was dragged to meetings since I was five or six. If there was a meeting on the weekend or I was on holiday, I would just get dragged along. So that was one way. Second, there were always business guests at home. There were always family members staying at home, nephews or uncles or people visiting for business. We lived with my grandfather, so there was always conversation between my father and my grandfather or my father and his brothers that were visiting. You couldn't help but hear although you didn't always understand it until later on. You heard and were involved passively.*

Wealth opens up special opportunities for the rising generation to pursue rewarding career directions not open to less fortunate families. Noticing the musical talent shown by a young family member, a family elder—without the young woman's knowledge—asked the trust to invest in a rare instrument that was being auctioned. It was a good investment in a valuable antique and also a way to support a special talent. The young family member has gone on to teach and play all over the world. Other families report that they invest in the human capital of family members when they show special motivation or ability.

## Skills for the Rising Generation

Substantial family wealth, generative families report, is a great challenge as well as opportunity for members of the next generation. While they pursue their own path in life, the many possible forms of shared family "capital" present family members

with some inviting opportunities. In addition to the legacy businesses and investments, there is the possibility of founding new ones. Inheritors can look beyond
personal benefit in their gift from prior generations. There are also service opportunities arising from family philanthropy. But to be useful, each successor has to
develop professional skills and a personal commitment to become a steward (even
when also pursuing their own life path).

What skills and capabilities are needed in the rising generation of a legacy family?
Since the family enterprise looms large in the family psyche, young people's active
focus on preparing for leadership takes three major forms:

- **Business:** In the second and third generation, family successors emerge who
  can work in the business (whether as executives or on the board of directors).
  By the third generation, the family has often either sold the legacy business or
  transitioned to a role where it oversees the business as owners with nonfamily
  leaders to guide the company. With a family office or extensive investments,
  the role of board member, trustee, or steward of assets demands different
  kinds of family leadership.
- **Family:** By the third generation, with many households comprising the
  extended family, successive generations must take active roles sustaining
  family connection and promoting cooperative relations and shared family
  activities to align, inspire, and educate the extended family. The family must
  develop collaborative, relationship skills to do this.
- **Community:** Family resources lead to many opportunities to serve the
  wider community, by partly supporting service careers and by initiating
  philanthropic and social entrepreneurship ventures.

Each of these endeavors is complex and demanding, and the generative family
has a limited talent pool. The family must take steps to reap the most from each
person by educating, guiding, inspiring, and inviting the most talented of the next
generation into leadership.

Members of G3 or G4 growing up in separate households widely dispersed geographically may not know each other personally or feel connected to the family
legacy or business unless they are actively engaged. In order to function as a unit,
the generative family must renew its shared identity as a family enterprise in each
new generation, aligning their many households.

As we have seen, generative families do not include *all* blood family descendants.
Households and family branches may drop out of the shared entity while at the same
time young people and new spouses enter. Each individual member, and the family
as a whole, must develop a positive identity and reason for working as partners in
the future. Family efforts are directed at using family resources to motivate and focus
growing numbers of family members. "Generativity" means that the next generation
does not rest on past success but commits to do more. For example, the next generation may take the business in new directions, perhaps starting new ventures that
express the family's values in areas like social investment and entrepreneurship.

At some time, every member of the new generation must make a choice—to commit to the future of the whole family or to exit and go his or her own way. Generative

families provide the opportunity to say "no" to the extended family. In every generation, some may take this opportunity to go their own way. By the third generation, the family may contain many smaller shareholders; some will be happy to sell their shares and use their capital in their own way. To ensure a robust future, the family must *recruit* them to join, and the family must do this by giving these young people a good reason to commit to be together as a partnership.

Great families see their rising generation as future leaders as they train and furnish them with personal and professional skills. It is no easy task to develop these leadership capabilities in several next-generation family leaders. A person with all these qualities might sound like a superhero! This looks like the wish list for a corporate leadership development program—and that's precisely what it is. All the efforts discovered in this study, from individual family learning to shared educational and development programs, are aimed at this level of development of leaders whose role is that of family "steward." These outsize expectations for the next generation can be inspiring but also overwhelming. The key is to create programs that offer the right amount of challenge.

## Developing a Positive Work Ethic

One aspect of raising new generations that almost every generative family agrees on is that they want them to develop a positive work ethic. Even if they work in social service roles, they want them to be passionate about something that makes a difference and become good at it. They find ways to encourage this.

Here is an account by a third-generation father about developing work values:

*My older sister was born in a small apartment. I was born in a nice house. Then my younger sister spent her formative years in a much nicer house. All of us saw an incredible work ethic from my dad and uncle. A big challenge for me is how does my kid know how hard I'm working?*

*I knew clearly that my dad busted his ass. He was gone from six in the morning until ten at night six days a week. Sunday he'd sleep in until seven or eight. He made it to my games. One of the benefits of working in the family office is that I can take my kid to school every day. I don't miss a game. How does my kid see that work ethic? That's one of the struggles my dad never had. He just did it. My generation hopefully will struggle with that and hopefully have good answers, so the next generation is more comfortable with their wealth. Not that we're uncomfortable, but I think we're just learning how to do it. My dad couldn't teach me how to be born into wealth.*

*Family members have to rely on each other, to teach them the values that need to go with it. The reason my generation struggles with it is because we saw it, we lived it, [and] now it's ours. I've got to figure out how to make sure that my kids have a strong work ethic or understand the value of money. I went from a six-figure marketing job to teaching high school for 28,000 bucks yet still living the lifestyle of a six-figure marketing guy in Manhattan. That's not a reality for most people. How do you bridge that gap and let a kid understand? It's important that we educate our kids and rely on each other. That's where the family comes in. I see my responsibility for my niece who might not be getting that idea. I have to step in somehow because I think their mother is doing a poor job of it.*

Several parents noted that they were especially active when their children transitioned from university to their first work experience. With the cushion of family wealth, young people looking forward to inheriting or working in the family business may have lower motivation to struggle and learn from adversity in their early work efforts. Indeed, adversity may be a new experience:

> *Their parents help them through those critical stages—the end of school and through university in their first years post-university. I think their critical stage is that first post-university job. They'd better start somewhere although it's not easy or pleasant. Both our daughters had first jobs at interesting companies but with terrible bosses. They learned really good lessons about life in the real world. They didn't stay very long with those jobs, but when you're starting out, you've got to get your hands dirty and start at the bottom. But some family members think, "I don't need to do it. I can sort of skip" that first phase out of university. But I just don't think you can. I didn't. I started working in a public works project as a young graduate engineer. The transition from university where it's still partying and fun to the real world where you often start with a pretty crummy job. They're going to start with a pretty basic job that's not going to pay them very well.*

One second-generation elder sums up his generation's work with the following vision for the next generation:

> *I wish the next generation can see what we are and where we've come from merely as a background to who they will become. There is no sense of entitlement to either position or income. I hope they see it as part of their roots, something they're pleased about. And we'll give a little bit of time and intellectual bandwidth so they can be effective shareholders and owners. I don't want to look beyond that generation. Who knows what might happen; I'm not particularly dynastic. It was up to my generation to do the rational things when we crystallized the wealth. And in due course, it will be the opportunity for the next generation.*
>
> *I want them to be able to function as a unit that enables them to avoid defaulting to "let's stop doing this because we don't know each other and can't work together, but let's make an informed decision about where we're going now as a family group." I do think that there's value in that just because it's nice to know where you come from as an individual and as a family. There's a sense of identity and connection that gives people a good foundation to live their lives with knowledge about where it's come from. I always say we're not special. We just got lucky. If you're lucky, then what measures your success is how you capitalize on luck. In other words, be the best you can, then don't sit around. The disease of the inheritor, we all know, is the propensity to undershoot their potential because the inherited capital allows them to do that. Most humans are pretty lazy. I hope that would only be the minority of cases in this family, that they'll just get on and enjoy life and live life to the full. We don't need to go ten generations. We just need to do a good job each generation and see what happens.*

## Educational Programs

How do members of the rising generation actually learn and develop skills they will need to serve the family? Because of the size of the family and its special needs as a business family, the larger and longer-lived families in this study frequently develop custom-built educational skill development programs. These programs go beyond information sharing to developing the *capability* to take on leadership in the many facets of the family enterprise. They teach the specific skills to become a productive steward of the family enterprise: leadership, relationship, financial, and business skills. These are not skills they are likely to gain in higher education, or if they do, the special nature of the family enterprise makes it useful to supplement their education.

Family education programs focus on interpersonal skills like communication and can be similar to experiential corporate training but with the trainees being family members. Like executives, young people learn to work more effectively as a team, overcome (sibling) rivalry, and avoid bringing in conflict from the family:

> *Over the decade, we have done age-appropriate work across myriad subjects, including self-development, leadership, understanding self, and basic entrepreneurial practices. We reviewed every acquisition we've conducted over that decade. We review our financials twice a year formally with them. They've gone through our tax return in detail, and they have been to events that launch a new product, new rotation, grand opening, expansion of a site. When they were fourteen years old, we started talking about if they wanted to have a car, they had to make $5,000 on their own by say lifeguarding or cutting grass.*
>
> *We also designed a summer experience for teenagers where you spend time in all the finance, IT, HR strategic planning, human resources, and small business initiatives. Some of them returned to their company and worked in areas that were particularly exciting to them. They entered college with an unusually deep appreciation for the complexities and opportunities it would take to be in the business world. I would call those very rich windows. You had a young person in an adult environment, listening and seeing the inner workings of a four-business-unit enterprise.*

The family above appointed a family member full time as family relationship manager to oversee the development of the human capital of now hundreds of family members:

> *Parents need to make sure they're talking about the vision and values around the dinner table. That's key. Once they get older and they become inquisitive, we have a whole set of things we do with the family. We start at age twelve and categorize them from age twelve to twenty. We want some of the twenty-year-olds to be the mentors to some of the twelve-year-olds. We do functions with that age group two to three times a year. We call it "cousin-palooza." Education doesn't revolve around what we do; it revolves around who we are. You get these kids together and introduce them to each other and like, "Hey, I know you; you sit next to me in science class. I didn't know we were related."*

Education programs are frequently geared for age cohorts. Younger children and teenagers attend gamified activities, like going on a scavenger hunt or creating a family tree. One family used the word "generage" to refer to family members who were of similar ages regardless of their generation. They designed programs for each generage.

Another family created a financial skills seminar, initially offered to family members over twenty-one. The first topic was about how to pay taxes. The second year the topic was budgeting. Younger family members expressed interest, so they lowered the eligible age to eighteen. Even more family members attended. Finally, for the third year on the topic of investing, they lowered the age to fifteen and had their largest attendance. This family has a tradition of family engagement, but they have been struck by the interest of their younger members. They have begun to add to their pool of "future family leaders."

---

## Desired Capabilities in the Rising Generation

Generative families have already created a thriving business and extensive wealth. Their expectations for their children are similarly broad. They want their children to be prepared to pursue their own calling or contribute to the family enterprise and to society. From the accounts of family in this study, my research team and I generated a set of desired capabilities ("Cs") that these families' education and development programs aim for:

- **Character:** ethical sensitivity
- **Competence/capability**: financial and governance/ownership skills
- **Commitment/caring**: stewardship; productivity as part of the family; a good partner
- **Connections/community**: trust in and personal commitment to each other
- **Collaboration/compromise**: ability to work together with give and take
- **Communication/transparency**: shared information and understanding of family enterprise
- **Changeability/resilience**: ability to adapt and change
- **Curiosity/creativity**: ability to seek out and discover novel possibilities

---

To ensure its future, generative families need to develop their successors in each new generation as capable stewards who are committed to the family's purpose and values, and are ready, willing, and able to take this on. Since the family enterprise is complex and demanding, every rising generation member must develop a positive personal identity and life purpose, and also find ways to serve the whole family enterprise. While in every family, some will not reach this goal, the family wants to create a climate where many if not most do. Parents in each household share this commitment and the collective family creates supplemental programs and activities to further these aims.

Parents in generative families must learn how to practice high involvement in these activities while exerting progressively less control. The next chapter will look further into how the generative family invites their rising generations to learn about the family enterprise and participate in what it does.

## Taking Action in Your Own Family Enterprise

### Developing a Personal Development Plan

As young family members complete college and graduate school and prepare for their careers, it is helpful to develop a plan for personal and career development. Many books and resources can help with this. One way to focus your growth is to

create and manage a **Personal Development Plan**. To take personal responsibility
for your future, it should have the following elements:

- Assess Your Skills and Capabilities
  - What do you want/need to learn?
  - How will you learn it?
  - What preparation and experiences do you need to develop your capability?
  - How will you assess yourself in these areas?
- Move Out of the "Bubble" of Family Privilege
  - Leave home and discover the wider world through work, travel, and education
  - Support yourself
  - Take risks and try to learn about overcoming adversity
- Find a Mentor, Guide, or Coach
  - Elder who has been there and can support and guide you
  - Who are the best mentors? Where do you find them?
- Develop Credibility
  - What is most important in your message to the family?
  - What is the difference between interest, capability, and credibility?
  - How do others know what you can do, how you can add value?
  - How do you develop your credibility in the family and the family business?
  - *What is your plan for learning and developing your role?*
  - *What do I have to learn in order to be ready for this role?*

### Wealth Messages

We earlier offered tools for having a family conversation about money and wealth.
This conversation can take place one-to-one between each set of parents and each
child, not as a single event but as an ongoing process. When a young person is choosing college or looking at a first job, family conversations can be helpful. When they
are away at college, regular family phone calls or visits can offer a young person
support while still allowing privacy for them to manage their own lives. Family agreements about support and help can be part of these talks.

### What Is the Family "Deal"?

A key question for every young family member, and one that often is left unstated,
is "What can I expect from the family in terms of resources, support, and aid just
because I was born into this family?" This support may also be conditional on taking
up certain responsibilities, having certain values, or behaving in a certain way. As a
whole family, or in individual conversations, each young family member should be
able to learn what he or she can expect and what the conditions are.

In this conversation there must be some exchange. Often young people grow up
with certain expectations about fairness and what they were told. The family has to
make the reality clear but also be willing to listen to the situation from the young
person's perspective.

Often this can be done with a cross-generational family meeting, rather than individual ones, so that it can be clear how the expectations are similar or different for each person.

### Assessing Basic Money and Wealth Management Skills[10]

Family education programs often teach young people core money management skills. These skills are important to all young people, but because these young people are expected to become stewards of family wealth, the family teaches these skills to the family together. These skills include how to:

- Feel comfortable with wealth.
- Talk about wealth in personal relationships.
- Manage personal wealth.
- Work with advisors.
- Save.
- Keep track of money.
- Get paid what you are worth.
- Spend wisely.
- Live on a budget.
- Invest.
- Handle credit.
- Use money to change the world.

Each young family member can respond to this list by checking the skills they have learned and those they want further help to learn. This can be done together as a family and the results used to develop family education programs and offer coaching to individuals.

## Notes

1. John Adams to Abigail Adams, May 12, 1780, in *Adams Family Correspondence,* eds. L. H. Butterfield and Marc Friedlaender, vol. 3 (Cambridge, MA: Belknap Press of Harvard University Press, 1973), 342.
2. Dennis T. Jaffe and James A. Grubman, "Acquirers' and Inheritors' Dilemma: Finding Life Purpose and Building Personal Identity in the Presence of Wealth,"*Journal of Wealth Management* 10, no. 2 (2007), 20–44. This model was amplified and described in greater detail in Grubman's book *Strangers in Paradise: How Families Adapt to Wealth Across Generations* (Northfield, MA: FamilyWealth Consulting, 2013).
3. George E. Marcus with Peter Dobkin Hall, *Lives in Trust: The Fortunes of Dynastic Families in Late Twentieth-Century America* (Boulder, CO: Westview Press, 1992), 55.
4. Hartley Goldstone, James E. Hughes, Jr., and Keith Whitaker's book, *Family Trusts: A Guide for Beneficiaries, Trustees, Trust Protectors, and Trust Creators* (Hoboken, NJ: John Wiley & Sons, 2015), explains the opportunity to expand this relationship.
5. The observation that it is difficult to grow up in a wealthy household and to develop a positive identity is an insight that comes from a group of researchers including John L. Levy, Joanie Bronfman, Joline Godfrey, Lee Hausner, James A. Grubman, David Bork, and Madeline Levine, who have each written extensively on this topic.

6. Stephen Goldbart, Dennis T. Jaffe, and Joan DiFuria, "Money, Meaning, and Identity: Coming to Terms with Being Wealthy," in *Psychology and Consumer Culture: The Struggle for a Good Life in a Materialistic World,* eds. Ted Kasser and Allen D. Kanner (Washington, DC: American Psychological Association, 2004), 189–210.

7. Jessie H. O'Neill, *The Golden Ghetto: The Psychology of Affluence* (Milwaukee, WI: Affluenza Project, 1997).

8. This concept, developed by mythologist Joseph Campbell, suggests that over the course of a life, a young person often follows a common developmental journey told in different ways across cultures. The hero's journey is a quest. The young person sets out into the world, faces a deep challenge and danger, finds allies, overcomes the challenge, and returns home as a hero. See Joseph Campbell, *The Hero with a Thousand Faces* (Princeton, NJ: Bollingen Foundation, 1949).

9. This term was coined by George Kinder in *The Seven Stages of Money Maturity: Understanding the Spirit and Value of Money in Your Life* (New York: Dell, 1999) to denote those who enjoy wealth but have no idea where it comes from or how to manage it.

10. Adapted from Joline Godfrey's book *Raising Financially Fit Kids,* rev. ed. (New York: Random House) and from conversations with James A. Grubman.

CHAPTER

14

# Family as a Cross-Generational Learning Community

Consider a young third-generation family member from a wealthy and successful family. She grew up barely knowing her cousins who lived in different cities. She is proud of the business that bears her mother's maiden name, but neither her cousins nor the family business are a day-to-day reality for her. Her parents and siblings are her anchors, but she has never seriously considered any specific role in the family enterprise. Not that she isn't capable—it's just not on her radar.

When she is about to start high school, the extended family holds the first of what becomes an annual family retreat. She spends fun time with her cousins and discovers how much she has in common with them. Upon learning the history of the family's legacy business and the role of the new family office, she has the notion that perhaps she might study business and eventually have a role in sales and marketing. She then takes a mini-course with her cousins about budgeting, household expenses, and credit cards, topics she had never thought about, as her parents paid for everything. She loves the summer meetings and volunteers to join the committee to plan next year's meeting. This is how a third-generation family initiates the opportunity for the next generation to become a legacy family.

By learning with her extended family, she became aware of new opportunities and found a possible path for participation in her generative family. The previous chapter presented the personal development of identity and values in family members as they grow to adulthood. This chapter continues by looking at the special ways that generative families use their collective resources to bring family members together to learn and grow. While family assemblies and gatherings are fun, and enable people to get to know each other, such gatherings are also the source for a variety of educational and learning activities.

The extended family tribe prides itself in creating events like this for family members to learn together as they invest in developing the capabilities and commitment of their rising generation. We will look here at what they do and how they do it.

Development and education for the rising generation is a dual responsibility of the individual household and the extended family. First comes informal learning within the individual household, as reported in the previous chapter. Due to the scale and complexity of the needs and responsibilities of the large family enterprise, more guidance is needed. Hence, by the third generation, the extended family takes up the task of creating shared efforts, coordinated by a self-initiating group of family members who form an education committee or task force, usually growing out of (or sometimes into) the family council.

While members can be appointed to a committee like this, no one can impose commitment. Most families encourage a few family members to volunteer and step up. The education committee usually contains members of more than one generation. Its primary tasks are creating curriculum, employing resources, finding venues, and getting family members to attend. Families make use of outside advisors and frequently call upon family office executives to help. Some families pay a family member to act as the coordinator of their educational programs. They often take place as part of the family assembly, presented in Chapter 9.

## Next Generation Activities

Extended family activities include the following elements, which will be described here:

- Cross-generational community meetings
- Business/financial briefings
- Mentoring and career development
- Junior boards

### Cross-Generational Community Meetings

Relationship building and education begins when the extended family meets to define itself as a shared community of interest. By the third generation, the generative family contains branches, households, and dispersed family members who do not know each other well. From a group of related kin, the family must generate an active desire to be together and develop a common identity concerning who the family is collectively and what it is doing together. Otherwise, forces of separation will overcome the family's shared legacy.

Building extended family relationships often begins with summer gatherings for young people and teenagers:

> *Because they live all over the place, we have a gathering every summer for the teenagers. This last summer was our third year, so we had a whole family reunion. The summer before that, my daughter and her husband, who are in the fourth generation, hosted the teen reunion at our family cabin. We had fifteen teenagers show up. I was the cook, stayed all the way. Even living all over the place, they're instantly friends.*

How can these simple gatherings foster individual development? Members of the rising generation meet and discover how their shared legacy draws them together. They then consider whether they want to work together and perhaps get excited about future possibilities. Out of their growing sense of connection and community, they initiate leadership and engage the older generation in their ideas for the future.

At the turn of the twentieth century, wealthy US families often developed family summer encampments, wilderness spaces for the whole family to gather. Many legacy families today maintain this tradition. As a family moves away from having the legacy business as its center, it often invests in a setting that physically houses the extended family. While it can be a resort, the tradition of a shared family "place" with artifacts and spaces holding special memories for young people helps develop an identity beyond their particular nuclear family. It is passed down by the founders, a grand old family home dripping with tradition.

Next-generation programs don't originate spontaneously. They originate when a family member emerges to become the initiator or driver. This person can emerge from any generation. This person can be:

- A family elder, perhaps a grandparent, who champions an active program for the next generation
- A parent who sees common challenges in other branches of the family
- One or more young family members who want to know each other better and look to the family to develop meetings that include their generation

The fourth generation of a European family (with approval of the third-generation elders), led by the head of their family foundation, began to hold such meetings for several days every two years. This family had about forty people in the fourth generation—ranging in age from forty down to ten and residing in a half dozen countries. The family shares a heritage, a family office with a nonfamily CEO, extensive investments, and a very public and extensive philanthropy program. The goal of the fourth generation, says one family member, was to "*establish their own identity and debate their own issues.*" Some of them don't know each other well. They formed several committees—family governance, philanthropy, and education—to develop themselves as the next generation of leaders in the family. A common vision emerged to anchor their commitment to sustain family unity for another generation.

Extended family gatherings often include more than two generations. Today, with life expectancy rising, the family may contain three or even four adult generations. The passing of leadership, responsibility, and governance is not from one generation to another but across two or more generations. It may involve different generations sharing leadership in a complex power and responsibility arrangement. It is not a single event but an evolving process.

One major feature of these intergenerational activities is sharing and telling family stories. Older family members are invited to talk about their experiences, and family members use drawing, writing, video, and social media to record these stories. By sharing the legacy, young people develop as a community, and they are able to build upon the legacy as they reenvision the future.

An extended family gathering enables the members of the rising generation to decide whether they want to be partners and, if they do, what form their involvement will take. It is a fundamental building block of the one-hundred-year family, as this family describes:

> *Every two years, our generation [G3] would all come together. Fourth-generation children would get to know each other. We looked at who is considered a family member, all the way to family values. There was a good turnout, so it must have tapped into a real need.*
>
> *We always use nice places, the mountains or beach. Four or five of the thirteen members of the third generation were driving it. We had a very high attendance. We talked about transition to third-generation membership of the board, what we should do as a family office business, and how we should look after investments.*
>
> *Control of the family had not yet passed from one generation to the next. The second generation controlled the estate, still the major shareholder in the holding company. The initiative came from our generation agitating upward rather than the second generation saying we're ready to pass it on.*
>
> *Our generation was more entrepreneurial, more direct in what we wanted. I advocated we should have internal investment management skills around this pool of assets. It took fifteen years to complete that transition. We debated the structure of the holding company board, should there be a representative from each of the four family branches and should there be a family and a nonfamily deputy chairman. Gradually, all these governance arrangements evolved. We thought carefully about who should replace whom, when. That 2G to 3G transition took a decade.*

Several families mentioned how nicely grandparents fit into this role. One family has what it calls the "grandparents project," where grandparents teach and mentor their grandchildren. The grandparents retired from the business but now want to share their experience and spend time with their grandchildren, sharing what they know as mentors and learning from their grandchildren about things like technology:

> *The grandparents' camp came out of a meeting with an Indian family who had businesses. They were private businesses, and they had businesses in different parts of the world. How do you get them to work together? We make sure that they have to share the same kitchen. We send the cousin generation away together. Because they're the ones that are going to be working together. And unless they get to know each other when they're young, they're never going to be able to work together.*

The family meetings and the availability of family resources, like the family office, lead to specific action plans. For example, one fifth-generation family offers young people three pathways for engagement:

- Plant tours and business events
- Participation in the family council or a committee
- Application to become shareholder observers of the family's independent board

By the third generation, the members of the elder generation have limited authority to dictate to the next generation. They have to adopt a more invitational, collaborative attitude in getting their children engaged:

*But it's the fifth generation trying to drag the sixth generation in, and there isn't the same authority that comes from those older generation folks saying "thou shalt gather." When you have all these cousins spread out, they're like, "Yeah, I like you, but I get on a plane and go home; I got kids in school" and all that. But when the grandfather was right there, when you have the senior guys and they were the big business leaders, this was very powerful. We don't have that anymore. And that was a lost opportunity from my father's generation.*

Traditional societies hold rituals to mark major milestones, where an individual faces the community and is welcomed into a new role or status. The formal entry into family governance is one such transition that has great importance for the generative family and the individual. Several families developed formal rituals to mark this passage, as seen in the remarks of this family:

*We offer an invitation to younger family members when they turn eighteen to be a part of these annual meetings. We've done some really good work around tradition and initiation and including younger family members, inviting them in a ceremony. It happens at the annual meeting for any new fourth generations. If you're born into the family, when you turn eighteen, you're invited to be a part of the business side. We hold a ceremony to introduce you, pairing the younger family member with a mentor from the older generation in a different family branch. We've had mixed success with that mentor program, but I think the idea is really good and helping build relationships between generations and branches. That mentor introduces the incoming fourth-generation family member to the family (enterprise), and that fourth-generation member receives a ring that all of us have gotten at age eighteen. It's like a puzzle ring, and it represents the six branches of the family all living together. That's a wonderful symbol.*

*My great uncle would always tell the story about the pioneers moving West and how they would throw their hats across the creek if they were traveling in their covered wagons. By throwing their hats across the creek, it's showing your dedication and commitment to cross that creek because a hat back in the old West was a big deal and you didn't want to lose your hat. You get a ring and you get a cowboy hat, and we find a little stream and make sure you have to cross. There was a lot of symbolism and connection, and this initiation ceremony has been really valuable to younger ones. It's kind of a big deal to be invited in and to have all the family there to welcome you. The family office does an orientation to give you information on investments and business before you show up. It's a lot of support around what am I getting into, and this welcomes the family as well.*

Shared service activities offer another avenue for young people who have grown up with wealth, and may feel uneasy or conflicted about it, to focus on giving back to the community, helping build a further rationale for working together in a new generation:

*Going through this process creates family glue, which helps everything hang together in the future. Everybody has a hand in the creation, which means they bought into it more. This is another reason why it's got more likelihood to survive, as opposed to something created by one or two people. If others aren't involved in it, it doesn't have the same level of traction with the broader family. Also, the broader family doesn't have any perspective to comment on or even identify the hidden issues throughout the whole plan. That was a function of our distance apart and [lack of] communication, which was difficult. Even though it sounds like we've done everything right, there's a lot of challenges to get it really right. The key is to have everyone involved.*

Learning about the business can be active and experiential, especially for younger family members. One farm and food retailer has a unique way to promote its young members of the fourth generation as "family ambassadors":

*We set up a store visit policy where we provide them with business cards as the fourth-generation family member. We have a process where they visit a store as an ambassador for the family. We actually give them a little compensation for doing that. They can choose to do it if they want, as one way they can be involved. The company has stockholders. They have a travel fund, so they're encouraged to attend a food show or a family business conference. At the food shows from the time they were little, they could be in the booth meeting people, walking the show with Grandpa or with Dad or Mom and seeing what the business is like.*

Family learning might include educational travel. For example, one family conducted what they called the Asia Project, a cross-generational family group traveling for several months learning about social investment. Their learning has since had an impact on the expansion of the business and also the development of their philanthropic mission, less centered on their own home community. During these expeditions, family members react to the deep emotional experiences of human need and social projects and think together about what projects to adopt for their own family.

The members of the rising generation become more than dutiful preservers of tradition. Generative families recognize that they have to focus on adaptation and change, rather than the status quo. Here is an account of a G3 family leader about teaching G4 the need to focus on the future:

*When working for the family, one of the things I've always tried to convey to them is you have to think of the office and process almost like an architect. You want to figure out what your end result should look like and work backwards to figure out how to build it. An architect is drawing a beautiful building, but you never start with "Hey, let's look at our wiring and plumbing and cement."*

After the fourth generation, there are more dispersed families having less connection even to their family branch. An important developmental activity in these families is getting together as a generational group. By doing this separately from their elders, they can comfortably develop their connection to each other. They often discover that due to their legacy, they have many shared values and things in common. They also find they like each other.

Getting together as a generational community offers an opportunity to make requests to the elder generation. As millennials, they have a particular way of seeing the world. Upon learning the family legacy and values, they have questions, concerns, or requests. Several families report that after a meeting of the younger generation, the members of the younger generation become comfortable sharing their concerns with their elders. By sharing them as a group, rather than individually, they do not risk one person being singled out as having a "problem"; instead, as a unified generational group, they gain credibility that they should be seriously listened to.

As family social and educational activities diverge from those of business oversight and governance, the family can comfortably become more inclusive. Families discuss how, for example, to more fully include married-in spouses. One family evolved toward more inclusiveness as it developed an explicit, formal governance process:

> *For our cousins' camp, a decision was made that there would be no business meetings. We all grew up with our parents, the five branches. We would get together with our grandparents on Thanksgiving and Easter. After the meal, my grandfather would grab all of his kids and take them in another room and close the door, leaving their spouses outside and the kids outside. There was never a participative type of thing for the rest of the family. The third generation said, "We don't like that approach of separating spouses. Spouses need to be included." We have made that change, but we also want to make sure that everything that we do as a family is not strictly business. We want to make sure we still have social time. Since we have a two-day family assembly that is mostly meetings, we have another time that is strictly social, on the ranch. We want to share what the ranch does environmentally and taking care, stewardship and all the stuff we are doing. We don't want to have formal meetings at that time. We get everybody together, just for the fun of being around each other and enjoy it.*

### Business/Financial Briefings

Traditionally, family enterprise leaders and trustees are reluctant to share information with family beneficiaries and the rising generation. The elders have a tradition of "taking care" of the younger generation and do not feel they need to be informed. This paternalistic model is common in many places around the world. But the family members interviewed for this study found this tradition did not properly allow for the development and engagement of the next generation. If young people were not informed, how could they learn the legacy and prepare themselves not just for possible employment in the business or other family activities but also for acting as owners/stewards in overseeing the assets or contributing, often without compensation, to shared family activities? The generative families in this study *all* hold some variant of an annual business meeting, where family members of all ages are invited to attend and learn from the business and financial leaders.

These annual events can be traditional one- or two-hour presentations of business figures and charts, but many families have found ways to make them far more elaborate and interactive. One family with a large business "*produced a very detailed annual report, not unlike that of a public company, which we circulate to all family shareholders. The CEO and CFO present to all shareholders semiannually. We have quite a detailed regional meeting. On the structured capital side, we distribute most of the profits as dividends, but if people want to reinvest, there's a dividend reinvestment plan.*"

Meetings include visits to businesses, the family office, or a foundation as well as conversations with key employees. These visits are increasingly interactive and feature more than information. As one family member says, these activities include "touring the company farms, plant tours, business center tours, and the museum so that there's a good bit of hands-on activity to create interaction with what's actually going on in the company."

Family business education is not simply "delivered" by the elders to the younger generation. It combines leadership from the elders and active engagement from the younger generation:

> *Having a family that's committed to family education is essential. There needs to be a driver within the family pushing it. In the early days we held workshops on understanding personality types, communication skills, and financial things. Utilizing an outside source to provide some programming makes a huge difference because if you're trying to develop these things on a one-off basis, it's incredibly time-consuming. Years ago, we developed a longer-term curriculum of what we cared about having our kids learn. Then we looked at the components and identified the things we thought made sense for the kids to learn together in a common space or place. We then identified the things that we felt were better taught and learnt within the branches of the family.*

Part of the education is learning about activities and roles that do not exist for a nonbusiness family. The briefings clarify the differences between working in the business and being an owner. An *owner* has certain rights, with others delegated to members of the board of directors. An *employee* works in the business and receives a salary but does not necessarily have a say in oversight or business policy. A family member can be an employee, an owner, or both. This can be very confusing, especially for young people initially exposed to the concept. Briefings define the roles of an owner, manager, board member, trustee, and family council member. For example, one family had a training program for prospective trustees for the family trusts. They had dozens of such trusts, and each one needed successor trustees. The family wanted to appoint family members, but to do so, these younger family members needed to learn how to act as trustees.

Another G4 family created an extensive business leadership class to orient new adults and married-in family members to the complex family enterprises:

> *It's a seven-week summer class held once a week where folks from our company come in and talk about their area of responsibility, what they do, and what they have in their history. They come to learn about the business. We hope that prepares them for college, so they'll know what they want to do. Once you graduate from that class, you can spend a week in the business shadowing people, doing a little deeper dive at what you heard and a better understanding. We call this Production Group Experience, and they work with people in the business and get exposure. Some employees work with them in the company. We say to them: "Tell them about who you are and your education. Tell them the challenges and only what you're doing in the department. Get them prepared for life a little bit." That's another way we expose the kids before they get here.*

Many families offer sessions where family owners, and some owners-to-be, ask questions and share ideas. Families also have longer sessions, where young family members (and sometimes people who have recently married in) learn about the family and its various ventures. In larger enterprises, these seminars may last several days. The level of transparency is generally high, as families realize that new generations will not feel connected unless they are informed. They usually ask that those attending understand that what is shared is confidential, not disclosed outside the family. They view the next generation as their future owners and leaders, and educate them accordingly.

The interactive nature of the family meetings, where information is shared and family members air concerns or differences, also helps the family develop mechanisms to resolve conflict. As they get to know each other more deeply and share values and experiences, they develop a level of caring and trust that allows them to broach and even resolve differences that arise:

> Ten years ago, our annual family meeting was fraught with conflict and stress, which was a real burden. We began to implement a process for dealing with conflicted relationships or disgruntled family members; we call it our task force process. That is where we would get a question which in the past would have caused an argument or a challenge. Instead of allowing that to be our pattern, we spent time answering that question. If it wasn't a ten-minute response, we would actually get into a lot of the history and understanding the person's concern or complaint and the policies or procedures that exist today that support whatever we were looking at. For example, one of the questions we got was why the dividend policy is the way that it is, which everybody knows is really the "how come I don't get more money" question. Instead of shutting them down, we spent a year answering that question of why we give dividends, how do we determine what that number is, can the company sustain its growth with this current policy, can the family sustain its growth with the current policy. It took us six years to get through all of the major questions and to demonstrate that we were willing to take people's concerns seriously and address them rather than allow those concerns to blow up into family conflict. We use that process today for implementing any kind of change. It's one of those really big moves that we made in our family. Through that task force process, we built working relationships. From those working relationships, friendships developed.

Family education may not only be about business. Other families have seminars on topics like natural resources or sustainability. When several members were moved by a new novel, one family invited the novelist to spend a day with them. These special learning activities are possible because of the commitment of the family to use its resources for shared learning.

These programs represent a significant investment of time, energy, and money. Families report that they receive continual feedback about their value from young participants and their parents. Their goal is education not just to work in the business but also to take responsible leadership roles in governance, for example, as board, family council, or family committee members:

> Now that our family is bigger, more people are engaged in educating and developing skills that make them a viable board member. Our board changed because our business has changed. The board oversees investments that are more complicated, and there is more to know and a lot more business experience needed than back in the old days when it was just a board with family members who just were there because they were family members.

*The next-generation program has its highest value because it is building a cohort of people who are getting educated about what we do, how the family council is structured, and family history. They're getting educated about why we're awesome and why we need to continue to be who we are, embracing the values and emotion around being connected to a family like ours. The next-gen program is inspiring the next generation of family members to pick up the flag and keep marching forward.*

As households diverge, the family ponders how to promote attendance and participation in shared family events, with so many competing elements in family members' lives. This fifth-generation family leader observes:

*Several things encourage people to come. Their children are now making relationships with their cousins, and this program is built around the zero to thirteen-year-olds, and they beg their parents to go. Sometimes we hear back that the parents don't really want to go, but the kids are very anxious to engage with their cousins. Not only are they getting their parents to come who might be on the edge; they're also creating this relationship with each other so that by the time they get into the boardroom or the family council or wherever they're going to plug in, they have relationships and know each other.*

Over the years, more and more family members elect to come. Many families pay expenses and travel, and some even reimburse for missing work or babysitters. The concept is that if this is an event that serves the family, people who are supporting themselves should be compensated for their time and expenses. If there are one hundred family members, this can be costly, and the family has to decide what the benefit is for the family. Many decide that it is what they want to do.

## The Family Academy

One US family entering its second century has developed family activities that exemplify the complexity of building a connected, capable, and committed emerging generation:

*We have a very extensive internship for high school and college kids. We have a mentoring program. At age sixteen, they attend the meetings, and they're given a family mentor (other than their parents) to sit at the annual meetings with them and meet with a couple of times throughout the year to answer any questions they may have. We started the annual Family Academy to educate kids four to fifteen years old. The family council works with the company to set up the agenda for the annual meetings; we get reports from our manufacturing and real estate divisions. Through the education committee and the coordinator of the family council, we have a cycle of topics for years to come.*

*We're a global company. We own land overseas and a shipping branch. We hear reports about what's going on and have activities that involve fun things with the company employees and the board who attend the annual meeting. Somebody in our family does videos to introduce the family to family members and things that they do. There's a lot of high interaction as we've gotten to know each other better; it's been really interesting to see the branch divisions dissolve. At first, we didn't even know who each other was, so one of the activities to get to know family was a placemat of the family tree. We would go around and try to figure out where everybody was. The young kids made*

*(continued)*

*a 120-foot-long family tree, and everybody stood on their square. We take our annual picture on it, and every five years, they update it. Everybody could see where everyone was. When we first started big annual meetings, we had 110 people attending. When we started, people would come in and sit in their own little nuclear family group. Now, it's completely broken up.*

*We were hearing from people, saying they didn't know how to read a financial report. The CFO and I put together a session on "How to Read a Financial Report." We have a cycle of topics, and it came up to be a finance year. We asked, how do you teach business finance to a five-year-old? Every year, the kids produce something. First year, it was refrigerator magnets. They've done birdhouses, book bags, using their imagination. The oldest members take on the role of CEO, CFO, COO because everybody has to be an officer. They take on these roles and do production teams cross-age because we have from five to fourteen years old. At the big dinner, they sell what they produce, and the next day, they count their money. We've opened a bank account for them. They borrow from the company for their supplies, and they have to repay. They figure out their retained earnings and then take a percentage and donate it to charity. They make a financial report to the adults. They learn about all sorts of things. It's always great fun to see how the kids account for the foreign money. The first year, they just wanted to disregard it, and I said, "No, you can't just count that as a dollar. It's not a dollar. You've got to look up the foreign exchange. What's that? Let us show you." So they now know about foreign currency exchange.*

## Mentoring and Career Development

Mentoring is the pairing of a young family member with a more senior person who guides them to develop skills, a trusted nonjudgmental person they can confidentially open up to about their misunderstandings and anxieties. The mentor can be another family member, an independent board member, a nonfamily executive, or a community member who is a friend of the family. Mentoring can be offered with the goal of working in the family business, but some families also offer mentors to those early in their careers who are considering several options, as this young leader of her family council reports:

*Our G4 are now reaching the age where they're ready for summer jobs and summer internships, as juniors or seniors in high school starting college. We created mentorship programs and summer job opportunities. We've made it a point to create opportunities for G4 to work in the business or to be exposed to the business at age fifteen. We've also been focusing on ways that we can educate our G4s about the business, what they're a part of, and what they've been born into, along with talking with them about wealth and stewardship and being good human beings. We're trying to improve ways to pass on our values.*

Mentoring and career development serve a dual purpose: they help prepare for one's career of choice, and they also develop qualified family members for part-time governance roles. These programs offer an added benefit: being part of these efforts develops bonds of connection to each other and what the family is doing. They also offer visible opportunities for the members of the rising generation to add to the family, social, and business mission and demonstrate their leadership abilities to the rest of the family. Some elders report spotting family talent to recruit from the quality of their engagement and dedication to family education and meetings.

Mentoring can be informal or formal. It may begin informally within a single household:

*Once a month, we get together with my three children just to touch base and see whether the different activities of businesses are growing. Then twice a year, we have a full gathering, typically about one day, one day and a half in some place. We are quite spread around, and we get together, including all members of the family and the spouses and children.*

Mentoring is a special opportunity that a family can provide for even high-school-age family members to prepare them for the challenge of career selection:

*We try to meet and connect with each one of those kids in their twenties. We have a team called the Family Sustainability Team. Our goal is just to get to know them, find out what they're doing in high school, what their goals are in life, what they want to do when they grow up, and where they want to go to school. And at the same time teaching what options might be there in the business. We try to connect with them before they start to get too far along in their college career or in the business world because we were having people apply for our business. I had guys and gals coming to me, and one of them has a degree in landscaping and the other one's got a degree in music and history, and I'm saying, "They're not the skills we can use." We were the employer of last resort, if they couldn't find anything else anywhere else. We want to stop that from happening. If they're interested in the business, let's make sure that they get the right education before they get here.*

Young family members may feel the opposite of entitled. They may be concerned about whether they measure up and may need support from others to make effective career and life choices. This support can come from inside or outside the family. This family member sought support from a network of peers about developing confidence when starting work in the family enterprise: "*I think it is more; can I really do it? Of course, working here it is quite a big thing. It gives me a lot of sleepless nights. It is about getting at peace with the whole thing. Yes, it works, it is possible, and I know it is a big thing. Even with this, even if you want to do it, it is quite a challenge.*"

When asked whether his (or her) father had confidence in them, this family member replied:

*Yes, but still I have a lot of friends, and I think it's helpful to be part of a family business network because you always think you are the only person in the world who has such a crazy family, and there are quite a few more who are even crazier. We say a lot of times that if someone would retire or my dad retires and he would look for a successor in the free market, you would not be chosen. Because of that gap, you get the feeling "I can do it because I have the skills and I am prepared.*

Career development does not come with an employment guarantee. Just being kin in a family enterprise is not sufficient qualification to work in a professional capacity. But with some training, a young family member may find a role in family governance or service. Their ventures demand a high level of capability, even as a volunteer. Since the needed skills are somewhat unique to a family enterprise, they are not easily learned in formal education.

By knowing each other across families and spending time together, family members learn about the skills and interests of older family members in other households and become comfortable informally seeking them out. So, in addition to parents and siblings, a wider network of cousins, uncles, aunts, and elders can be called upon. This is "relationship capital." One family in this study mentioned that there was hardly a college where a family member could not be found who knew someone who attended; this network might be of some help in learning about schools.

Some families utilize nonfamily board members as mentors to family members in the business. Another family member, running the family office in a large sixth-generation family, mentioned how young family members often came to talk with him informally. One family leader reported that he spends 60 percent of his time mentoring, meeting each week for an hour with each of a dozen family members working at various roles in the business.

Mentoring and career development take place both inside individual households and within the extended family. Some parents take the initiative to speak with their children about careers and help them develop a career plan. This is important in legacy families as each young person needs to consider the important question of how he or she will participate in the family enterprise, whether as an employee or in governance. Elders help their children look at the issues of entering or not entering the family business as compared to other opportunities, like working in the family foundation or serving on governance committees. Other families accomplish this by creating a whole family program.

Career development can become the focus of family meetings, with the opportunity for the younger generation to learn from the older one:

*One time, we gave the next generation the planning of an agenda, and they ended up creating a process where different people from G4 told stories about our careers. G5 was on one side of the room, G4 was on the other side of the room, and there was an interesting dialogue back and forth about the things that are helpful at certain stages of careers. There has been an informal approach. It is hard, particularly with people at that stage of their careers, to be involved in all of this family governance work. Almost all of G5 now have active careers.*

The generative family actively prepares the next generation for roles on the board, in family governance (such as on the family council), or with the family foundation. In first- and second-generation families, the board may include all or most family members. However, as the business and family grow and the board begins to include independent nonfamily professionals, family board members themselves require a higher level of professional skills in financial oversight, strategic planning, and business development. The family has to develop such skills for future board members rather than just have the larger shareholders wait their turn to serve. Board membership becomes a responsibility, not a right, of family owners.

As more people participate in governance, members of the next generation have to learn to make decisions together. Many families do not want to have a formal vote for policies but instead want to build consensus. This is difficult to achieve; working consensus requires a real commitment to compromise and listen to others. One fourth-generation family leader notes how difficult this is for the emerging fifth generation:

> *Leaders are emerging, but everyone's afraid to give anyone power because we saw what happened with our parents, and we don't want that to happen to us. It might be with the best intentions, but if one person takes it the wrong way or it's misinterpreted, you might lose that person's trust forever. And you've lost credibility because things don't really work in the family. Things have to be unanimous to work, which is very time-consuming. If you're not looking for consensus, you're going to fail; fifty-one percent isn't going to cut it. We had an opportunity a while back to install our water on the ranch. Not the water rights, but pump water, and sell it for various drilling activities, which could have been a huge income source. But because it was viewed as something different, there's risk associated with it, and it's not going to happen. How do you overcome that? There's absolutely no easy answer. If there was, there wouldn't be books and books and books on this stuff.*

Another family is more specific about how to prepare next-generation leaders. By documenting the competencies needed for various family governance roles, the family targets its education programs to develop those skills. As an investment, the education program is accountable for results just as its business is:

> *We've outlined the expectations of each role in our family. We have expectations for our family assembly that give us a baseline for how we need to move that fifth generation up in order for them to be good functioning family members. We've also articulated expectations for our family council role. We have twelve people in our family council who meet quarterly, and we see them as leaders of our business and the most active family members we have. In our governance model, we have standing committees, four people in charge of each standing committee. We've created expectations for all of these, and we're working with a curriculum developer to build an education program.*
>
> *There's a lot of different ways a person gets developed. We provide a curriculum. We have coaching and mentoring available. We have assessments that one can take advantage of to see their baseline capabilities. We have a development education committee that helps individuals put together development plans based on where they want to go. We have also an evaluation process to be able to measure whether or not an individual was successful in achieving those expectations and what additional support they need to meet those expectations. It's been very deliberate in developing our family, and it's something the family agrees is vitally important for us to continue to be good stewards and to grow to be the stewards we need to be over time. This is now an ongoing process because as the business achieves its goal, it's going to have another goal, and that's going to be the moving target for us to keep moving ourselves.*

## A Roadmap for Family Development

Figure 14.1 is adopted from a family with over one hundred family owners, including many who work in one of the various family businesses. It outlines a developmental sequence of activities that are offered to family members as they grow up and begin to exhibit interest and capability. The goal is to invite them to consider whether they might have the desire and capability to take a role in the family ventures and, if they do, to plan their development accordingly.

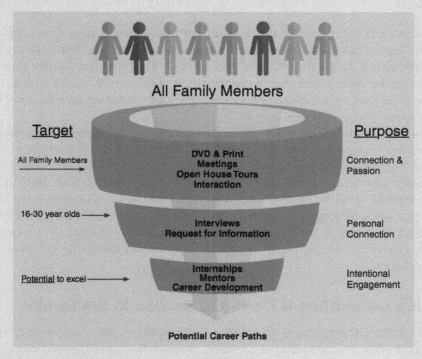

**Figure 14.1   A roadmap for family development.**

### Junior Boards

It is critical to prepare young family members to serve on various family boards that oversee and develop their various ventures. Board membership, while open to owners, is reserved for the most capable people, including nonfamily independent directors. In order to serve on a board, family members must learn the role and prepare for it. One way they can do that is by observing the board in action.

Several families have created a program to give young family members an initial experience with governance, where they learn what is needed and decide if they see this in their future. This "junior board" takes several forms. Some families select young people who seem interested and capable and then offer themk a role as an observer at board meetings. Other families open this group to volunteers, feeling that this is a way to discover a talent pool that has interest in serving the family. This is not just for those who want to work in the business. Some family members are needed to be part of governance by being on a board or family council. These roles attract some family members in graduate school, working at other jobs, or at home raising young children. The junior board may observe the board meeting or have its own meeting that includes briefings and discussions with key members of the family business. One family had a quarterly seminar on "the business future" open to those who were willing to prepare by reading reports and reference material.

Junior boards represent an entry point for becoming engaged in family leadership. Some legacy families have several businesses and entities with separate boards. One family with a large foundation and family office invited family members to observe from the time when they were fourteen. The family leader notes, "*We don't have a family farm or factory that people can visit. So this is what we do, and before they enter college, we want them to know what we do.*"

A generative family may offer membership on one of these boards to younger members who express interest and capability. The effect of such engagement is to move from information sharing and education to putting what is learned to visible use. By participating in these efforts, a young family member can both learn and also demonstrate what he or she has learned. By taking on a project—for example, overseeing a philanthropic investment or helping a small company owned by the family—they develop a track record within the family. From these candidates, the family can select next-generation members for membership on various boards and committees.

## The Rising Generation Is Called to Service to the Family

The goal of family education programs is to develop an empowered, inspired, capable, and ethical generation of stewards prepared and dedicated to continuing the family enterprise. The members of the new generation are expected to add to the legacy, grow the many forms of family capital, and make their own mark in the world.

Every young person in any family has the opportunity to go forth and make his or her own way in life. "Find your passion," parents instruct their children. "Prepare and develop skills to do something that will support and engage you." This is no less true for members of generative families. While the shared activities and business and service activities of the generative family have much to offer, successors can always go off on their own, and many do. Yet legacy families have an added potentiality. The rising generation also has opportunities to serve the family. This final section describes the "call" of these special opportunities within the family, which figure strongly in the life choices and developmental paths of young people growing up in generative families.

Generative families frame a family or community service invitation to attract those who are ready, willing, and able to get involved. Keeping family ventures strong and vital demands an increasing level of skill in each generation. Each generation wants successors who innovate as the business environment and family both change. The role of educational programs is not just to prepare the members of the next generation but also to frame the message that calls them to take creative roles within the family and its multiple ventures.

Elders can only create a *climate* consisting of inviting opportunities for the rising generation. In response, each member of the rising generation makes a *choice* to become part of it. Young millennials today have been educated and raised in a cyber-world where they are globally connected. Growing up with wealth, they develop values about doing something significant. If they join the family enterprise, they usually don't do it just to honor the past and fulfill an obligation (though this may weigh heavily on them). They join to do something they cannot do elsewhere. They want to set their own stamp on the family enterprise, even as they honor and respect legacy values and practices. They can always choose to go their own way and separate from the family. Joining is a commitment to give up some of their freedom in return for becoming part of a shared legacy and future success.

Family education and development efforts do not compel the new generation to serve the family. But by creating an offer, a "call" for them to serve, the family can make it attractive for these young people to engage. A generative family can offer two unique "calls" to the rising generation:

- The call to serve the family and family enterprise
- The call to serve the community and the world

The ultimate success for a generative family occurs when a critical mass of its rising generation answers each call to step up and become family leaders.

The "offer" is that by virtue of their membership in the legacy family, members of the rising generation can do something extraordinary. The development and education process shows what has been done, how these young people can contribute, what might be done in the future, and the demands of the role. Each individual must make an active choice to respond to the call, and each does that in different ways. But the individual cannot make that choice if the family has not created the resources, structure, and opportunities for him or her to be part of something great. We now look at how the rising generation can answer the call of the opportunity. Only if the new generation steps up can the family succeed for yet another generation.

### Choosing to Join the Family Enterprise

Members of the rising generation must prepare for roles in service to the family. The larger challenge for the family is to develop young people's capability and desire—the "will" and "skill"—to take on various family and family enterprise leadership roles. All of these challenges fall to the emerging young family members.

A single family successor within the rising generation is expected in many parts of the world. But this expectation is disappearing as more families take a broader view of their family leadership needs. Generative families look at the capability of the shared generation as a collective resource; several family members emerge in different leadership roles, for example, in the business, in the family, and in the family's philanthropic efforts. The many members of the next generation want to understand how to develop leadership capability and how they will be recognized.

Globally, the traditional expectation of ascension by the eldest son is being replaced with an expectation that each member of the new generation will make his or her own choice about candidacy. Leaders are selected from this self-defining group. One elder remarks:

> *I don't want my kids to feel an obligation to work here. They certainly need to feel the responsibility that ownership brings, and that responsibility is there whether they cash out or own everything. There's a responsibility that comes with life that they need to learn. The degree to which they are involved I do not want to try to dictate nor even premeditate. All I want is the flexibility for them to pursue what turns them on and to live the best life they can.*

The resounding view is that no young family member should feel coerced into partnership. As one family puts it, there should be a "free choice" to choose one's role in relation to family assets or even to leave the partnership. This is made more complicated by the formation of trusts that can tie them together for a generation or two. But by the third or fourth generation—in all of the generative families in this study—there is a mechanism to "free" dissident family members. This *exit policy* is a resolution for potential conflict that can otherwise tie up a family and make it difficult for the family to function as a coherent business. Knowing they can always leave, sometimes family members can then agree to remain and see what they can achieve together.

Most families expect their adult children to go off and "seek their fortune." In a legacy family, the fortune is already there, posing both a challenge and an opportunity. The research my team and I conducted made us aware that the members of the rising generation of a legacy family must decide how actively and directly they want to be engaged with the family and its enterprises. Family education offers a grounding for making informed choices.

This is not a single choice but a reality that always lies before them as they become responsible and productive adults. We see them making life choices in relation to the family, as they answer the following questions for themselves:

- How do I responsibly draw on the family wealth?
- How will I be involved and engaged with the family and its enterprises?
- Will I initiate or get involved in family-supported philanthropic and community ventures?
- Will I take on a leadership role in some aspect of the family enterprise?

To consider whether to "join" the family enterprise or how much to be involved in governance, each young family member has to first spend some time outside the family. Young people going off on their own and working outside the family is one of the most common early developmental steps the families in this study mention. Absent a crisis, most families discourage family members from entering the business too soon:

> *I think the ones that are successful have done it by moving outside as they transition into adulthood, through college and all that, in particular when it comes to business. To be outside the family, live on your own, do your own thing, find your own friends, move out of town. One of the most important things that all of my nieces and nephews have done, and I hope what my daughter does, is that she gets a paycheck for a few years from somebody else to prepare her for what the real world is like.*

Only a few family members can be employed by various family ventures, and the family wants to select the most capable, those with the best "fit," and those who are prepared to serve. Most third- and later-generation successors draw upon the advantages of education and social contacts to develop independent careers. These careers are often aided by supplementary income from the family, income that allows them to work below market rates on something they care about:

> *One family member formed his own music label and now runs that. Another started his own nonprofit, and another was in the early stages of forming a larger nonprofit. So many people have been able to take that philanthropic ball and run with it because they have the flexibility for the plans and perspective to do what they wanted to do and pursue that passion.*

Lessons learned at home and on their personal journey help develop personal capability and life direction. With so many possibilities, the members of the rising generation need guidance to discover and channel them:

> *Our biggest "idea bin" is trying to find an opportunity for future generations. It's more of an intellectual than a physical opportunity. We have a dozen fifth-generation family members between sixteen and twenty-six, and their parents (of which I'm one as I have an eleven-year-old) feel this tremendous need to look at developing opportunities for them. We're not trying to pick their job or buy a business they like. We're trying to let them know that "you have an important tool in life that allows you to make a better life for yourself." The family business provides some resources the fourth generation put in a package that younger kids in G5 see as a meaningful opportunity.*

In return for being offered special opportunities, each young person is asked implicitly to develop credibility and demonstrate capability within the family. Family membership adds pressure to making life and career choices; it never makes these choices easier. Here is one account from a G5 entering business leadership along with his generational peers:

> *When I started working, I was thrown in the deep end. To enter our family business, you have to have some store of experience, build a business, etc. Your responsibility grows as you show*

*your capability. I worked outside for a few years at a private equity fund. Then I came back into the family business. When I came back, I could see that few of our larger, global businesses had someone involved from the younger generation. So I told my uncle who's driving those businesses, "I'd like to get involved." I came on board as the next-generation guy.*

*I've been in those businesses now for fifteen years, and my uncle is still there; he's seventy-something now. I've proven myself, built my credibility. At the last executive committee meeting, I told them, "Listen, the last few meetings he'd been absent, and I'd effectively chaired them." So for one specific business, "I've already done this, and maybe it's time that you let me do this and you can add or comment afterwards if I've missed anything." He actually said, "Okay," and the next meeting he stepped back and said, "You drive it." It's not easy; these guys don't like to let go. You have to push them a little. If they're comfortable, they'll step back. It's not easy; they still meddle around once in a while. But the CEO of that business passed away. The new CEO got the message that I'm the guy who's driving it, so he calls me now. The transition happened over fifteen years. It didn't happen overnight.*

### Service to the Family and Enterprise

Being born into a business family offers the opportunity to work in one of the legacy businesses or with other family ventures, such as a family office or foundation. Career choices in any family are heavily influenced by the positive example of parents and relatives. If a parent is an actor, politician, craftsman, teacher, lawyer, or farmer, one absorbs values and learns informally about these professions. Also, the benefits of having a network of people in that industry or profession enable an heir to enlist personal contacts for a possible job or career. Admission to the best schools, consideration for the best internships, and the ability to meet the "right people" are all advantages to being part of a generative family.

Each generative family is continually remaking itself, forming new business and social ventures and renewing or selling its legacy business. The members of the rising generation have to become change leaders and be creative about the future.

Some generative families have nonfamily CEOs and instead offer opportunities to members of the rising generation to:

- Serve on the company or family office board of directors
- Serve on governance committees and task forces
- Start new ventures
- Serve as volunteers, employees, or board members of family social ventures

The invitation to the members of the rising generations is conditional on the specific young person being professionally qualified and having the skills to be competitive in an often large, complex, and specialized business. Almost every family in this study has formal, or at least clear but informal, rules for employment. The families dictate standards about qualification, background, and preparation for entering the family enterprise. As the number of family members in each generation grows, competition for positions becomes greater and the demands higher.

The families in this study reveal four pathways by which the members of the next generation become employed in the family enterprise:

- **They were asked to join by the business leaders.** The young prospects had visible success outside the business, and the family actively recruited them.
- **They could ask to join.** They had to apply and be accepted by family and non-family leaders. They often joined at a low level with the expectation that they would be promoted as they demonstrated capability.
- **They "fell in,"** joining the business for convenience and then finding it comfortable and just remaining there.
- **They were "pulled in."** It was expected, and they simply joined. Very few families in this study report this pathway.

The first two pathways are by far the most common, as the business, by the third generation, has become so large and complex that only those who can perform can find a place.

Entry may not be an all-or-nothing, one-time choice; it is an evolving conversation in the family. Working in the business is an opportunity whose end point is not necessarily business leadership. But it does carry responsibility:

> *I told my nephew, "Everything I'm teaching you will make you extremely marketable whether you stay with us or go elsewhere. There is going to come a time at some point in the future, where I'm going to come to you and say, 'time to sign in blood.' But until I do, you are free to come and go as you please, stay if you want to stay." Whether he stays in the business or not, he can be the person that carries on, that guy in the village. He doesn't have to work in the village to come back to the four meetings a year and know the village history. So I haven't asked him for a commitment to be chief of the village yet.*

Working in the business or family governance is not necessarily decided at an early career stage. Several families with well-developed family councils that oversee many households and complex family enterprises recruit leaders when they are older. A number of women who became family leaders mention that they first raised their own children, then slowly became involved in family leadership. They now are at a time in life where they can be "of service" to the family, and the family values their expertise. This family leader was called to service after a career in nonprofit management and after raising her family:

> *It's a full-time job. I work every day, but the family members approached me and were encouraging me to consider [the job of family council chair]. I worked as a legislative assistant for five years, and so I had this interesting mix of political background and a nonprofit background. My view of the family is you'd never want me to run the business, but I think the family is like a nonprofit organization. It's really more of a nonprofit entity. Once I started mulling over my own qualifications and having some cousins say, "Well, you'd be good at this, and you're well liked, and you've had leadership roles, and you're social," I kind of went down the list and had*

*that conversation with my family. It was good timing for me in my life. I was just about to be an empty nester. So that's how I ended up here.*

*Getting elected was a pretty grueling process. It wasn't just a phone call saying, "We think you're a great candidate; we'd like you to be family president." I had to do interviews; I had to take tests. It was pretty incredible. I'm kind of surprised I'm here actually. It's daunting at times because you want to be able to communicate. It's so important to communicate with the family, but it's a lot of people, personalities, and different groups.*

Preparing to be a family leader is different from being a business leader; it demands personal skills and capability, what is known as emotional intelligence or EQ. Because of the personal relationships and history, working for the family enterprise entails having the ability to communicate and positively engage divergent views of family owners. Such skills are less critical when the business one enters is not owned by one's family. Family leaders must learn traditional business skills as well as "EQ" skills to deal with family relationships.

Successful families all report that the bar for entry—the set of qualifications—becomes higher every generation, as the business becomes larger and more complex or as the family moves from being an operator of a business to a financial or family office model. If they wish to enter the family business, the members of the emerging generation learn that they have to become qualified professionals. Just showing up will not do.

A few families report a difficult transition when the family removes unqualified or underperforming family managers. The shift from a model where the business is available to anyone in the family to one where the family executive has to be qualified and accountable is painful for some families, causing conflict between family branches. One family member reports a deep conflict over the firing of a family leader and his replacement with a nonfamily CEO. Because the family leader was a valued family member and owner of a major share of the business, it took the active intervention of the next generation to help the family overcome the angry and hurt feelings.

The other shift is that while employment and business leadership is open to only a select few, many nonemployment leadership roles are open to family owners: to serve on the board, in family governance, or in philanthropy. By the third generation, young family members look to serve the family in all of these governance roles, rather than primarily as employees. Some of these roles are voluntary and unpaid while others have some compensation. Like employment roles, these positions require qualification and a level of skill.

One family decided not to have family members working in the business. The rising generation is expected to become involved in governance, common in families beyond the third generation:

*We don't allow the family to hold management positions in the company. So the majority of the seats are family seats in the board of the corporation, the family council, and the family foundation board, which are today occupied by members of G4 and a small minority by G3. Management is professional, with no family employees. We do offer family members internship opportunities and fixed-term job opportunities in the company. So we have an opportunity but also a challenge in the sense that it's not like we're always bumping into each other at the office and always together on business trips.*

Some families create a special role for family leaders working in the business. One fifth-generation US business that owns several companies, with twenty-four family members working in the business, has an extensive support network and career development process for family employees. They can advance, but the corporate culture makes it clear that nonfamily executives do not step aside for less-qualified family members. This family has an annual retreat for family employees and their spouses; the retreat focuses on bonding and also talking about the stress of combining family and business. There is a specific process for discipline, feedback, advancement, and difficulties for family members, all of which are designed so that family issues and conflicts do not get transferred into the business. *"The business is not designed to serve the family,"* the family "human capital" manager notes.

This chapter and others have described the breadth and depth of the shared family activities through which a generative family approaches the growth and development of its most important resource—the human capital of the rising generation—through family learning initiatives:

- Bringing family members together across generations to decide who they are as a family and what they want to do together
- Sharing information and teaching about the legacy and the family enterprise
- Creating education programs for the rising generation to learn and grow together
- Crafting skill and career development and mentoring programs for individuals

Together, these activities are a unique feature of a generative family. In addition to informal family gatherings and relationships, a long-term family enterprise must work actively to engage, develop, and incorporate members of each successive generation into the various family ventures. If not, the default is that they do not remain a legacy family much longer.

Employment in the business is not something generative family members can count on. Rather, the call is for people who are prepared, who have developed competency, who accept and live the values of the family, and who are deeply committed to serve the family for the long term in its education, social and service activities, governance, and family development roles.

## Taking Action in Your Own Family Enterprise
### *Defining Paths and Activities to Learn about the Family Enterprise*

The generative family, as we have seen, offers many paths to learn about the family enterprise in a direct and hands-on way. These opportunities are relevant at different times in your growth and development.

Here are some of the family activities that can be designed for rising generation family members as they grow up. It is important that they be clearly defined, with requirements and responsibilities clearly expressed. They should be arranged as opportunities that can be accessed at different times of life, progressing toward deeper involvement:

- **Visits to Family Enterprises:** Visits to see and feel what the family does, with meetings and talk with key employees, leaders, and advisors.
- **Internship:** An opportunity to work at one of the family ventures while pursuing one's education. It can be a summer job or part-time project during high school or college, or a longer and more formal learning experience. This is both an opportunity to determine if you want to work in the family enterprise and what that would entail, and a way to be aware so that you can pursue a role in governance.
- **Apprenticeship:** An intensive full-time introductory role, in which a family member works with the intention of learning a professional or skilled role, that offers a foundation for further development. The family enterprise often can provide such an opportunity for a young person, before he or she has to decide to pursue a career or role in one part of the family enterprise.
- **Mentoring:** A resource person, sometimes a leader from a family venture or an advisor, who offers a sounding board, advice, and support about a career and how to prepare and begin it. Sometimes this is a way of learning about and preparing for opportunities within the family enterprise, and sometimes in other places. The mentor is not assessing or evaluating performance but offering confidential support.

# 15

# Family Philanthropy

## Balancing Roots and Wings

*Cowritten with Isabelle Lescent-Giles, PhD,*
*and Jamie Traeger-Muney, PhD*

After leaving operational business leadership or selling the legacy business, members of each new generation have to find a reason for staying together. What creative purpose can be meaningful enough for them to take the trouble to attend meetings, align visions, and work together? Making more money is not much of a motivator; their concerns shift toward what can be done with the wealth their family has amassed, how the wealth can do more than just enrich their lives, how it can make a meaningful difference in the world.

This is enacted through the family's social mission, its commitment to wider community benefit. Family wealth allows them to undertake significant social transformation. By sharing concerns about social issues like access to sanitation, health care, education and work, and the future of our physical environment, young people are able to move beyond consumption and even guilt over having such wealth to become part of important social change efforts. While this has always been part of the responsibilities of wealth (*noblesse oblige*), the twenty-first century offers challenges that engage even the most apolitical families.

Family philanthropy and social commitment are central to every one of the global generative families in this study. It offers a pathway for meaning and engagement for young family members who may not identify with financial or business activities. As fewer people are needed to sustain the wealth, giving back is a path that sustains family connection and identity and serves as a reason for staying together in an otherwise dispersing extended family.

Generative families flourish by developing both roots and wings: they are firmly grounded by their values and their history while simultaneously remaining open to change and innovation in a way that allows them to soar. Through a mix of business and philanthropic activities, generations create social impact and build reputations for good citizenship. They embrace civic responsibilities and make public statements around the family's core values and purpose through how they share their wealth and energy as benefactors.

## Service to the Community

Young people are not only tied to the family by the wealth they expect to inherit and the things they own. Rather, they decide to dedicate time and energy to serve the family because of the opportunity to express their own personal values and aspirations to the collective actions of a great family. By the third generation, a generative family has come to focus much of its energy beyond creating wealth. The family has done wealth building quite well. Now "What is our wealth for?" takes on a new urgency. The family offers emerging generations opportunities to participate in family philanthropy and initiate new efforts that have both business and social value (e.g., social entrepreneurship). From the three boxes of the children's piggy bank, family members can now participate in adult giving that makes a difference in the community and the world.

Many young people today are dedicated to social innovation, sustainability, and service to the community. Of course, these values are often shared by previous generations, but the way these values are acted on differs in each generation. One generation gives to service programs in their local community; the next generation wants to help global refugees. Members of the rising generation expect that the family will listen to their ideas and commit to actions for social goals. They want to see the family wealth used responsibly to make a difference, and they have specific ideas for how to do that.

Young people are attracted to shared family philanthropy for several reasons:

- The family has resources and a network for making a difference, and family members can have more impact together than separately.
- The family is respected and visible, and family members can do service that is valued by their community, showing that they are not just "trust fund kids."
- Because of the family's wealth, family members are able to take on roles in nonprofits or jobs that do wonderful things but do not pay well.
- Members of the rising generation have personal bonds with others in their generation, and they like working together. They build generational community by doing something valuable, special, and concrete.

Expanding interest on *social capital* engages and inspires the living generation:

*I saw in [the rising generation] that there wasn't anything to really rally around. Initially, we started to engage family members at the family meeting in a discussion about philanthropy and shared plans. We asked, "What do you do, and why does that excite you, and what organizations do you find?" That morphed into people wanting to do collective philanthropy. At that meeting, we came up with parameters of how to do coordinated giving through our philanthropy division and appointed a chief philanthropy officer, a CPO, who's going to be a part-time employee with accountability and specific guidelines in place.*

Families like this one have found that by turning their focus to philanthropy and their social mission, they support the responsible stewardship of the family wealth in other areas.

Generative families view giving back as a critical element of raising members of a healthy next generation with strong roots and the ability to find their wings, adding value both in the family business and as global citizens looking to make a positive contribution in the world. As previous chapters showed, young people wrestle with the responsibility of wealth and the meaning and responsibility attached to their good fortune. They look to the family to help them find positive options to use their wealth and dedicate their lives.

A family leader who heads the family office echoes many of the families in this study by expressing the naturalness of this attitude:

> *Earlier generations made a lot of money, and they gave back a lot of money. So this has been a family value that has endured—we've always had a foundation; we've always contributed to the community. At all of our annual meetings, we reinforce this within our family by having a community service project.*

Neuroscientists and positive psychologists highlight the benefits of gratitude for individuals and families, linking gratitude to well-being, optimism, and better health. Brain research shows that the practice of gratitude leads to greater empathy and altruism as well as tangible benefits in terms of health and happiness. The researcher concludes, "Giving is better than receiving."[1] Families that practice gratitude and giving are more likely to nurture healthy businesses and happy families that last across generations.

Generative families remind us of the importance of small daily acts of charity. One family puts it in these terms: giving a new suit or work clothes anonymously to a young man from a poor background going for an interview is far from trivial as it may ensure the future of the whole family and be a decisive step out of poverty. Most of the families in this study remain grounded and embedded in their local community and are aware of the danger of looking at philanthropy through the sole lens of numbers. They remind us that individual impact may come from local knowledge and good timing and that returns cannot be directly measured by the size of the gift.

## The Moral Imperative of Philanthropy

Many generative families believe they have a moral and social responsibility to use a portion of their wealth toward doing good. One interviewee remarks, "*The philanthropic spirit is the key component of the whole thing to make sure that we never forget where we came from and that giving back is a key thing in the puzzle, and that's not only an opportunity to a certain degree—it's a family obligation.*" Many families express this sentiment more strongly by discussing the imperative of giving in their family. One leader of an Asian conglomerate notes, "*It's part of our DNA, part of our work.*" Another interviewee explains, "*It was basically taught to all of us that, to whom much is given, much is required, so it's expected to spend a certain percentage of your dividends helping the community, helping the world, doing some things, some small things to make the world a little bit of a better place.*" Or as a member of another family simply says, "*It's done because it is the right thing to do.*"

This is especially important to generative families that don't want their children to grow up entitled, living an unproductive life of excessive luxury. As older generations pass down the family values, they encourage members of the next generation to see philanthropy as a way to put their values into action and find a sense of purpose bigger than their own desires. One interviewee expresses this in the following way, "*One of the greatest antidotes to selfishness is philanthropy. If you're thinking what you can do for somebody else, you're not focused on what you're going to get.*" This family gives each member a copy of the founder's ethical will, outlining his philosophy and telling his descendants that if they want to be happy, they should think about what they can do for someone else, but if they want to be miserable, then they should focus on what they believe is owed to them.

A family charitable foundation allows the next generation to honor, capture, and put in practice values taught to them by earlier generations. "*It was a legacy we wanted to create for Mom and Dad, for all they've done for us and all they've done for the business and all they've done for the community,*" says one interviewee. Working together, this family chose a mission derived from the values of their parents and grandparents: "*We wanted to continue the spirit of what Mom and Dad started, a philanthropic spirit amongst our multiple generations, that allowed us to make a difference in these few areas.*" As generative families grow, philanthropic giving provides concrete opportunities to engage the next generation around social impact. Research shows that children with philanthropic parents are more likely to be philanthropic, demonstrating that this attitude does indeed get passed down from one generation to the next.[2]

Several US families in this study explain that philanthropy allows them to maintain a unified family after the business has been sold or is no longer run by the family. Non-US family business leaders express the wish and, for some, the non-negotiable expectation that their children will join and ultimately run one of the family businesses or the overall enterprise. In these families, where the next generation is expected to run the business or the family office, philanthropy can be a tool to develop stewardship and leadership skills without as much scrutiny and with more holistic performance reviews than in the business. As an educational opportunity, philanthropy provides a real forum in which members of the rising generation learn and practice through putting their values into action, fiduciary responsibility, and leadership skills.

Family philanthropy helps forge deeper connections and reinforce affinity within the family. When family members work together, values are passed on and reinforce families of affinity who stay together because they feel a strong sense of alignment and purpose. Giving provides opportunities to work together across generations and branches. The identity and meaning of family are about more than just creating wealth. It expresses values of giving and social responsibility to build a larger family identity beyond business. This gives family members greater opportunities to be involved with the family's endeavors as well as to get to know one another as the family grows exponentially. One interviewee observes, "*The foundation that my dad's parents established was a real bridge, not to my dad and his sister and brother but to my dad's niece and nephew from two families.*"

## Old Versus New Philanthropy: A More Strategic and Collaborative Approach

When one thinks of family foundations, the names of Carnegie, Rockefeller, and Ford and, more recently, Hewlett, Packard, Gates, and Buffett come to mind. US domination of the philanthropy narrative is partly due to a favorable legal and political environment, with policies that have long promoted private philanthropy through tax breaks. Another reason for this prominence is the early profession-alization of US foundations, which embraced business-savvy communication and marketing long before their non-US counterparts. Few non-US foundations make headlines, although that has begun to change. The group of global generative families in this study all share a deep philanthropic commitment.

Young philanthropists of the twenty-first century share traits with philanthropists of the early industrial age around scale, age, location, and degree of involvement. Most differences are in degree rather than in nature. Early nineteenth- and twentieth-century philanthropists were noted for creating powerful foundations to cement their legacy. About 120 years ago, Andrew Carnegie announced that he was giving away the bulk of his fortune and challenged other rich men to do the same, arguing it was their duty to do so. The Giving Pledge, founded in 2010, echoes Carnegie's example.

The impression that earlier philanthropists gave only in their old age whereas new philanthropists start giving early on needs a more nuanced understanding, as Ron Chernow points out in a 1988 biography of Bill Gates. Gates is now known at least as much for his philanthropy as for his founding of Microsoft. Yet back in 1998, Chernow reports that Gates said he'd "wait another 10 to 12 years to give away his fortune, because he [was] still consumed with business."[3] Chernow notes that, by contrast, when Rockefeller was in his forties, he helped create what is now Spelman College; in his fifties, he founded the University of Chicago; and in his sixties, he built what is now Rockefeller University. "I think that there's one kind of warning or perhaps inspiration for Gates," Chernow says. "Rockefeller was a devout Baptist who tithed from the time he was a teen-ager. He was not someone who postponed philanthropy until his later years."[4]

Families give to the communities where the business was founded through a sense of gratitude mixed with self-interest. They want to and are able to make their home communities better. They also want to thank the people who helped the family to thrive and establish its wealth.

New philanthropists, like the companies they found, are born into a far more global world with the problems of the greater world impacting them in ways like never before. They no longer live in a single community, and family members have spent time in many places. This is a major difference among generative families of this generation. In many cases, they turn to national and global causes as family wealth grows and business activities extend nationally and internationally. Today's new philanthropists, such as the finance and tech titans Warren Buffett and Bill Gates, are shaped by shrinking borders in a digital world and the familiarity with "born global businesses" (i.e., businesses that start trading across borders from the very beginning). These family foundations are attracted to global problems from the very beginning. Once it began, the Gates Foundation, for example, quickly focused on global "sticky" problems that governments had been unable to solve, such as health, education, and women's empowerment, both in developed and less-developed societies.

Today's mega-philanthropists hold specific, immediate, and detailed visions for their gifts and social impact. Older US foundations have long been professionalized. While older generations recruited staff with a background in professional donor engagement, marketing, and project management, the new generation of leaders includes social entrepreneurs and impact investors.

Another difference between first-generation mega-philanthropists and the generative families in this study concerns legacy and sustainability. Current philanthropists sometimes eschew creating perpetual foundations and allow donors to spend not just the earnings but also the capital of the foundation and don't mind their dissolution at the next generation. This allows them to focus their gifts for deeper and immediate impact without hindrance. Huge grants can change the face of a city, a community's energy use, the type of food we eat and how it is grown, or the morbidity level of a disease. However, the families in this study use philanthropy to further their legacy and want their foundations to be perpetual and sustainable. The families in this study also tend to have a more tightly controlled purse, with a shift away from recurring unconditional gifts. They want the ability to assess how their money is spent and to reaffirm control over grantees; as a result, there are more investments where families put up the seed money, but it's then up to the organization to sustain itself via internal revenue. New funding then goes to new initiatives on the condition of positive results from the earlier funding. The fourth and final difference between old and new philanthropy is in the more collaborative approach that this generation of philanthropists is embracing.

## Engaging the Next Generation Around Shared Purpose with Moral, Reputational, and Educational Goals

By the third generation, the entrepreneurial energy and the social commitment of new generations of the family shifts from the legacy company and investments to the creation of projects that extend the family values into the community. This is personal—it offers a meaningful life path for young people and a way for the family to share its wealth with the community it emerged from. As family members disperse to live in different places, they can remember and revisit their roots by developing new ventures with a triple bottom line—people, planet, and profit—or social enterprises as defined by law on a country-to-country basis. This is especially true as the family leaves direct involvement in or even sells its legacy business. The family's philanthropy is driven by a strong sense of purpose articulated around "who we are" and "why we are in business."

Passing core family values to the next generation through philanthropy is a recurring goal of generative families and a gauge of success:

> *I think success comes from passing on some formative values that [the younger generation has] grown up with, not necessarily tied to this family tradition but the value piece in terms of contributing to society in some meaningful way—being a good family person, being a good citizen. It doesn't matter what form that takes, but there's balance of family values; if you pass those on to your kids, that will help them out in life.*
>
> *If it gets them through school with a desire to learn, get joy in life and helping others, or just being productive members of society, that's success. It doesn't have to be premier business. As long as they are doing what they enjoy and drawing on the values we think have helped people and pass it on to their children, I think that's a good thing.*

Through the family foundation, wealth creators can educate, transmit values, and generate a sense of purpose in their children and grandchildren. In twenty-first century America, many creators of new wealth worry about the impact of wealth on their children and the weight of inheriting parents' expectations of what the family business should look like. Many tech billionaires have publicly stated that they want their children to inherit their entrepreneurial spirit, rather than the business they themselves created.

It is too early to know if they will walk the talk. But the children of many wealthy US givers are being groomed not to serve the business that created the family wealth but to run family foundations. For example, Warren Buffett decided not to leave large fortunes to his children, beyond a paid-for education and a home. Nonetheless, his three children run large foundations. The eldest two, Susan and Howard, run the family foundation, established in the name of their mother, and have their own foundations. And youngest son Peter, an award-winning musician, co-presides over the NoVo Foundation with his wife. Similarly, the children of 1980s tech billionaires are more likely to be part of the family philanthropies than to turn their parents' companies into family businesses.

Family foundations help the next generation embrace service to the family and its philanthropic mission. One interviewee states, "*A barrier for young people is they don't see themselves bringing much to the philanthropic effort when in fact it's the opposite—they have incredible skills that just need to be called out and named, and sometimes they don't see it themselves.*"

The following philanthropic family is committed to training its rising generation not only as a way to pass down its values from one generation to the next but also because the older generation recognizes how much new generations have to offer:

> *The next gen in our family, these twenty-somethings, have a different level of exposure to diversity, a different comfort and acceptance, growing up in more diverse societies. Our program itself has really illuminated and exposed them to those opportunities much earlier than I ever was. The way that young people can speak to this work, speak to justice principles and equity principles, I have found inspiring.*

*They have a different lived experience. They see technology in different ways to leverage social change. They come at it in a way that is inspiring and will continue to push us to change and evolve the way we do our own work. They're brave to do the work on themselves. They're much more willing to turn the mirror inwards, and this work requires that. I think older generations may have not had or maybe there's a little bit more discomfort in some cases or some families to do that, but the younger gens are saying if you want to do social justice, if you want to really practice authentic racial equity and embed that, we've got to unpack our own implicit bias, we have to understand the history that we weren't taught in school.*

*It speaks to the need for strategies in philanthropy, social change, or systems change work to be adaptive versus linear. This is the way we bring in new voices and engage others in our family in this journey. We have to be open to adapting, to new ideas, to diverse viewpoints we haven't had before. That adaptability, that iterative nature of this work and of the way we engage with each other, has to come together, has to be holistic.*

## Giving Circles and the Search for Individual Identity Through Philanthropy

Young people growing up in a family with great wealth often experience ambivalent feelings, including confusion, guilt, and even shame about having so much when others have so little.[5] In the 1970s, in addition to experiencing guilt and confusion about their wealth, scions of wealthy families also struggled with how vastly different their values were compared to those of their parents. In college, they began to reflect on the need for social justice and transformation. When their peers found out about their wealth, they were put on the spot or even accused of contributing to injustice and other social problems. Similarly, today's young people are often caught between parental values and their personal values and those of their peers.

In the seventies, several groups of young heirs began to organize groups of people who wanted to work out their relationship to their family wealth and how to contribute in a positive way to social change. On the West Coast of the United States, one such group organized the Vanguard Public Foundation. The East Coast soon followed with the Haymarket Foundation. A third group, the Threshold Foundation, was formed in Colorado in response to a letter inviting fifty young people who had "both personal wealth and a commitment to decreasing ecological destruction and human suffering."[6] These young people formed a public foundation and a supportive community around the value proposition that "everything is alive, everything is interrelated, and all life is sacred."[7] This foundation is both a place where people can talk about their values and goals for their personal wealth and a progressive grantmaking foundation to which they can contribute.

Threshold today continues to recruit members to its network and offers grants to many global organizations. The model of personal gatherings and exchange in a confidential and private environment as well as shared giving has been adopted by newer groups such as NEXUS, which works to bridge communities of wealth and social entrepreneurship. Currently, NEXUS has chapters in more than forty countries and has more than fifteen different task forces focusing on various areas of change-making.

These groups differ from family foundations in two ways. First, they work outside of the family fold, in groups of like-minded and age-related cohorts. Second, they offer a platform to share the dilemmas and challenges of growing up in a wealthy family as well as peer support to think positively and work out emotional ambivalence toward inheritance and personal worth.

Such groups have helped young people develop their own voices and forge a positive relationship with the family wealth they will inherit. The personal support, learning, and sense of community often empower members of the rising generation to return to their family, discuss social issues, and propose new ways and directions for the family philanthropy.

A related but slightly different network is the Global Philanthropists Circle (GPC).[8] GPC has roots going back to these pioneering networks and is similarly driven by the rising generations in large family businesses. GPC has gathered members from more than one hundred global families across thirty-three countries, all of whom give at least one million dollars per year. GPC reaches beyond family members through aiming to bring philanthropists, as well as leaders in business, civil society, and government, together at regular events. Cooperation, they believe, exponentially increases impact.

GPC's mission, like that of NEXUS, is to brainstorm, educate, share best practices, and forge partnerships around social transformation and social justice. It connects members with similar values, missions, and goals, encouraging them to form interest groups and develop joint programs. It also encourages sharing and learning. Families host group site visits to show what they are doing, share lessons learned, and receive feedback. A recent trip was hosted by a French family that has been working for more than thirty years in China; the trip showed participants their work firsthand and provided an opportunity for them all to discuss their own efforts while bonding with one another.

GPC's efforts often involve both impact investing and philanthropy, providing younger members the opportunity to view these things holistically, along a continuum, rather than as discrete activities. GPC members recognize that social change requires a mix of profit-making and nonprofit projects. What is important is to develop self-sustaining projects that multiply their efforts. Family foundations seed these projects with gifts, loans, and investments.

Meetings of GPC also offer young, college-age inheritors opportunities to develop a positive and complex identity as both family and individual donors. Jenna Liang, who is a senior advisor of the group, notes that in many of the group's conversations, next-generation family members remark that they can't talk about money in their family, even in terms of giving. These inheritors are trying to revision themselves from being privileged young people to agentic change-makers. GPC helps them explore personal goals, find ways to give their own money and personal time beyond the family, and make a difference as individuals. Liang says:

*The program for fourteen- to seventeen-year-olds is about the journey, understanding the history of systems, unpacking how systems don't work for everybody in our society. And so why is that? Where does that come from? And looking at race and racism in our country, historically, thinking about what it means to be in places or in positions of power and privilege, which young people, I mean in our family, they've had real challenge around coming to terms with this notion of being privileged. And privilege in our definition doesn't mean necessarily financial wealth, although certainly there is some level of privilege, but we don't have an inheritance that has continued for generations from the founder of this wealth and from the founder of the philanthropy. There were a series of trusts that were dispersed, but they stopped really at the fourth generation. So fifth generation, sixth generation, depending on how your family has navigated all of those finances, many of us don't have that level of inheritance or privilege. But there is privilege just by being white and by being a grant maker.*

*So what does that mean for young people to have those positions of power and privilege? And they don't love that. They don't love being known in that way. There's a lot of work on unpacking that and reconciling that and finding how they can leverage their privilege for impact and social good that's inclusive of all kinds of diverse perspectives.*

These future leaders then return to the family fold and feel empowered to share their learning journey with older generations and to apply their personal values within the business, the family office, or the foundation.

## Philanthropy as a Shared Family Activity

It is inspiring to discover what is most important to family members and come to consensus about how to strategically create the changes the family hopes to achieve. This provides family members with buy-in and makes it more likely that they are willing to invest both their time as well as their resources. In one of the families in this study, the annual giving is divided among the five branches. Even though each branch is free to make its own grant decisions, the family meets, and each branch discusses where it is giving and why. This allows family members to get to know what the other members value and where they are giving. Family members can get excited about where other members are giving, and pool their resources to support one family branch's choice.

The increased influence of the rising generation and of women making philanthropic decisions results in new thinking about how best to move the needle on the biggest social issues, instead of just simply writing checks or giving grants.[9] Giving time, not just money, is important for many of the generative families in this study. This not only serves as a way that families can live and pass down their values but also provides an opportunity for using philanthropy to create greater family closeness and connection, as these two families note:

1: *Working together as a family during Desert Storm, we pulled our money together to buy gifts for soldiers. Younger kids drew pictures and wrote letters. The whole family participated together.*

2: *When we have a meeting, we do something in the area that's a volunteer thing like go paint a shelter or do something that's not just handing somebody a check but actually making family members go, and they love it. It's wonderful.... That has been a huge value.*

These quotes express the experience of giving of time as well as money; such experiences bond the family together, creating lifelong memories.

Some families go on service vacations together, offering help in community projects around the world. One family recalls a trip to China with two generations, some of whom were as young as preteens. They saw the social challenges facing China in the early stages of its developmental journey. The trip became a touchstone learning for the family, helping them define a global focus for their philanthropy. One family member says, "*We try to get the family members involved in service projects in the community. We're helping somebody, and then you're also building relationships with other family members by working side by side.*"

Working together as a family to do good, particularly in one's community, becomes a powerful win-win, benefiting not only those to whom the service is directed but also the family as a whole, by deepening family relationships and the joy of making a positive difference in the world. For the families in this study that worked together, combining both financial giving with giving of their time, the impact of their philanthropy and their connections within the family increased exponentially. This is particularly impactful for members of the rising generation, giving them a sense of agency in their ability to effect positive change in the world and the ability to positively contribute to their family as well.

Generative families engage in philanthropy to have a positive impact in the world, build family relationships, and educate the next generation. All three of these motivations are admirable but can compete with one another for priority and focus. It is quite a challenge for the main purpose of a family foundation to serve *both* the mission and as a vehicle for family connection and education; ultimately, one purpose has to be primary and thus inform how the foundation is run. It is important for family members to be clear about the foundation's strategic mission and its primary purpose in order to effect sustainability across generations.

The chair of another family foundation expresses a similar level of responsibility that her family embraces through its philanthropy:

> *The fifth and the sixth generations are bringing another level of due diligence on ourselves and the work we have to do internally. And it's not a lot of families or a lot of foundations who can say, "Well, we did the racial equity training, check. And we did this. We looked at social justice and all the different principles, and we've done some DEI [diversity, equity, and inclusion] work, and we feel good about ourselves, so we're good." And that is not why we're doing this. So to get clear on the "why" is essential. Because the "why" is in service of our mission. The "why" is to build more just and sustainable communities in the United States. This is a public trust. I am not in a power privilege position that's just my luxury to give away money. This is a public trust that I mustered to the highest level. And I think our board and our family that are engaged in those ways take that very, very seriously that this is about service of advancing justice and equity and in our mission through different strategies.*

The next generation is adding a new layer to philanthropic governance, with regard to goals, practices, and diversity. As a recent article in the *Wall Street Journal* explains:

A clash of generations is taking place, as younger cohorts—mostly millennials and Generation Xers—are joining and changing their family's foundations. These younger board members bring with them new ideas about the way the foundations should be run. Many want to add more transparency and use new technology. They're interested in socially responsible investing and are often taking a more hands-on approach with their grantees than their elders have.[10]

Governance is critical to create sustainability with high levels of engagement and participation. Philanthropy is no exception. When families first begin a foundation, they seem to initially focus on one of two questions: What are we going to give to, or how do we want to invest our assets? While these are both critically important areas, one foundation director[11] suggests that one question, often ignored, needs to be attended to first:

*People rarely start with the governance, with the participation. Who's going to be involved? How are they going to be involved? What do we want to see in people who come to this table, whether it's by way of experiences, eligibility, or whatever? What do we expect of people who come to this table in terms of their commitment, their time, and how are we going to manage that participation? How do we make sure that governance is attended to?*

*Interestingly, my work tells me that if governance is attended to, the other two things tend to go well. If you're doing a good job of who's at the table, why they're at their table, and what they're expected to do, they're going to make good grantmaking choices, they're going to make sensible choices about their investments. Their investments are going to speak to what they're trying to accomplish programmatically, and their grantmaking choices are going to speak to that difference, their values, and their history as a family.*

*My experience with donors is that many of them are just so charmed by the notion of doing this work with their family, but they never actually tell their family why they're so charmed. So you may have people at the table out of a sense of responsibility or duty or respect for Mom and Dad. But you've never sat down with them and said this is why you're here.*

A seventh-generation family enterprise, with over four hundred family members, used its foundation as an opportunity to increase family participation:

*We have a lot of interest in participating [in the family company], but we only have so many places where people can participate. And clearly the board of directors is less and less attainable by family members because you really have to have some business qualifications to be there. There was a family member who wrote a proposal to actually create a family program within our foundation by creating four different focus areas that the family agreed on of where the funding would go. But then on each of those areas, there would be a board of family members volunteering.*

*They'd get their expenses paid to come to meetings, but their time was volunteered and each of the funded advisory committees have about ten people that meet three times a year. They have a bigger board of directors that oversees the funding choices.*

This proposal shifted the number of family members who could be in leadership positions within the family enterprise from ten to seventy people; they meet, stay connected, and get together every year:

*We've created this entity that's allowed a big family like ours to implement a value that's been very much a part of our family fabric and to engage a whole bunch of people that otherwise would just be coming to meetings and wouldn't have much of a role.*

Good governance requires knowledge and skills. One interviewee explains that increasing family connectivity through philanthropy backfired because of the time needed to come to a consensus:

> We've asked the next generation if they're interested in participating, but I think they're more reluctant to participate in it even though we've had things like this for a while where we would get like $500 to donate to the interest of your choice, but if you work with your sibling you would get $1,000 and if you work with your second cousin you get $1,500 each. It's a way we tried to get them to work collaboratively together. That turned out to be a lot of work, so it didn't actually work as well as it could have. It's hard to get people to engage across those things maybe because they feel they're not qualified or the issues are so big and daunting even though it can have a great impact on society and benefits.

Because there is already so much negotiation and joint fiscal responsibility, when there are differences around giving, some families don't want to have to negotiate more with relatives. They decide instead to divvy up their philanthropic resources and make individual giving choices:

> My uncle said, "I don't believe in more work for us. This is going to be a pain in the ass. I don't want to spend more time in doing anything like this." My parents said, "we are already very committed with our own charities. I'm not sure if this is worth doing something together." And the whole thing was killed. But unfortunately, my family was not able to see either the positive social family benefits that could be drawn from working together or the business benefits that could be drawn from having a smart philanthropic policy within the business.

Like developing a thriving business, creating a successful family foundation is no simple task. It requires leadership, strategic planning, and cooperation. One family member reports feeling that many people don't realize just how time-consuming it is to establish the infrastructure to do effective multigenerational giving:

> Philanthropy is by no means this magic bullet to get family members involved, whether it's just philanthropy and values or even to train them for responsibilities for later on, being on business boards and so on. There are so many other pieces that have to be properly in place for that to succeed. I just feel like it's too often put out there as, "You just do this; get them on the philanthropy board and give them some money to give away." There's a lot more that has to go into it before you even give that a shot. I think that's a bit of a misperception out there, that philanthropy is that way, the key way to get people involved. It certainly can be if it's done right, except it's more difficult than anyone realizes to do it right.

Without good governance structure and a willingness to understand the time limitations that members of the rising generation face, these goals can fail. One interviewee says,

> We expanded our philanthropy to include the next generation. We're starting to try to have people take on some of the responsibility. What we find is that they express a lot of interest and they think they want to take on the responsibility, but then when they get back to their real lives, it doesn't tend to happen.

Or as a member of another family reflects:

*Because there's a huge age range, it's difficult for some of the younger children to do it. So older members of the third generation, they're in for the adventures. Even though they think it's great work, getting the time together to meet is really hard because everyone is in school or they have a new job, they're employed, and they can't get the time off to come and meet.*

Because everyone is busy in our modern age, families that are able to successfully bring in the rising generation need to recognize the constraints of young members, starting their own families and career, to develop strategies for making participation more accessible. Some of these work-arounds include having virtual meetings and covering child care when in-person meetings are required.

## The Cynthia and George Mitchell Foundation: A Three-Generation Family Foundation Driven by the Founder's Imprint and Values

An example of how a family foundation has roots in the family values and teaches them to succeeding generations is the Cynthia and George Mitchell Foundation, a mission-driven, third-generation family foundation that seeks innovative, sustainable solutions for human and environmental problems in Texas, where the family originated.

*"His story was quintessentially American,"* a family statement said after George P. Mitchell's passing in 2013. He *"was raised as a child of meager means who, throughout his life, believed in giving back to the community that made his success possible and lending a hand to the less fortunate struggling to reach their potential. . . . He will be fondly remembered for flying in the face of convention—focusing on 'what could be,' with boundless determination—many times fighting through waves of skepticism and opposition to achieve his vision."*[12]

George Mitchell had a long history of supporting the economic revitalization of his hometown of Galveston and had a keen interest in science and sustainability. As their fortunes grew in the energy business, Mitchell and his wife, Cynthia, shared a vision with their family that the majority of the wealth they had created should be dedicated to making the world a more hospitable and sustainable place, signing the Giving Pledge in 2011. Since its incorporation in 1978, the Cynthia and George Mitchell Foundation has distributed or pledged more than $400 million in grants.

Currently, the board of directors of the foundation is made up of twelve members, including two generations of Mitchell family members.[13] The new generation preserves the values and interests George Mitchell espoused during his lifetime through the family foundation and offers grants in the fields of clean energy, land conservation, sustainability education, shale sustainability, and water.[14]

Katherine Lorenz, George and Cynthia's granddaughter and former deputy director of the Institute for Philanthropy, was elected president of the family foundation in 2011. She reflects on the foundation's history and purpose:

*My grandparents started the foundation. Only toward the later years of my grandparents' life did it start to become more of a true family foundation. My aunt was leading the foundation at that point and hired consultants who led us through a year-long strategic planning process where all family members over twenty-five, second- and third-generation direct descendants, were*

*(continued)*

*involved: ten children and twenty-seven grandchildren. That has been the most amazing aspect of the philanthropy we do together. It started when we voted on the issues we wanted to focus on first.*

*We then spent two different retreats with expert speakers on everything including: What are the issues? Opportunities? Challenges? Needs? What are other philanthropists doing? In that process, it went from having fifteen disparate voices on how we should address clean energy to a clear direction, based on the fact that we were learning and when you learn together then you're coming from the same perspective of how to move forward.*

*It was an amazing learning opportunity for all of us who weren't involved in clean energy issues, which most of us weren't. We might know something or be a little bit passionate, but we learned a lot together. It also then raised the game in terms of ways we can make an impact and think about moving forward in grantmaking in a way that we're all informed and able to make the decisions together. So we continued to learn together, and that has become one of the hallmarks of our foundation. We do that at least once a year.*

*Sustainability was important to my grandfather, so we had a learning experience on sustainability where we looked at what my grandfather felt about sustainability, what he cared about. We had videos of him, we talked to him, but we also said, what does that mean for us going forward? How do we want to focus the foundation? It was a lot about learning about them and their values. We also held a workshop in Galveston where we looked at where we have the most impact based on what my grandmother really cared about. The social issues. Then we talked about how we put their values into practice.*

*Those experiences are really amazing, especially for some of the younger people who didn't know my grandparents. It's a way to connect to what drove them and what they cared about and then putting those into practice in the world today. I think those are so powerful because it's connecting to the legacy, why we're even doing this, why they set up this foundation. It's helping us share values.*

*Many of the family don't live in Texas anymore, but we are all still very committed to doing the work there. Families run into the issue of differing passions, interests, and geographies. It's hard to keep families working together and excited about a geography that they're not connected to anymore. I think that will hit us one generation down, but even though many of the second-generation don't live in Texas, there's still a very clear sense of place and wanting to work there.*

*One other thing we've done that I highly recommend is we have a lot of documentation and videos and written information from my grandparents. We have an audio recording from both of my grandparents in 1993 about what they wanted with the foundation. My grandfather lived until 2013, so over 20 years we recorded videos that touched on what they wanted with the foundation, and they have come into play in helping guide the future.*

*It has been really critical because we've been able to revisit what they said they wanted. We bring those videos often into our learning journey, so we say we're going to look at this issue and here's what our grandparents thought about it and here's them talking about it, and that's how we've gotten to where we are today, and now we're looking at these issues going forward. I think that piece of bringing the history in is important to feel connected to it.*

*We don't always agree on what they would have wanted, but there is always a sense that we want to try and do what they would have wanted as opposed to "well, it's ours now, forget it." There's a strong feeling of it is their legacy—we are doing this how they would have wanted it.*

The Mitchell family highlights the importance of family retreats to reaffirm a sense of belonging together, build *familiness*, and share values. Generation families not only use family retreats to discuss business issues and wealth management but also as a way to communicate current goals and actions around social impact and invite the next generation to get involved and lead future initiatives. It is also an opportunity to identify pain points. Several of the families in this study, for example, want to introduce better measures of social impact but are struggling with the overly complex sets of metrics offered by finance.

## A Foundation for Community Development

As new generations arise, families become more involved in philanthropy. Some family members are excited to work together on huge projects that are only possible because of the family's company and the wealth it created. While they remain stewards involved in ownership, their energy is taken with philanthropic and community projects, which can lead to careers for several dedicated family members. Here is an example from a South American family:

*Our philanthropic foundation was started fifty years ago by my great-grandmother and her children. And today the focus and the strategy of the foundation has evolved. I recently stepped down from the board as I completed my sixth year or second three-year term. We have a maximum term limit on the foundation of six years. We recently reoriented our strategic focus to programs that promote education in order to have higher labor inclusion and to promote innovation and engage citizens.*

*It ranges from programs that are promoting and teaching skills to people with disabilities and also hoping to change the regulatory framework to create incentives for companies to employ people with disabilities and understand that someone with disabilities has other strengths that could be used very productively. That's one example of a program that we run with the Inter-American Development Bank. Other programs focus on teacher training in order to make some better teachers with the aim of generating, improving the quality of education. Other programs are on citizen engagement that help promote transparency in the way that local governments run the city by capturing and publishing indicators that are associated with the help of cities. Around security, around quality of air and water, around quality of education, mobility, the perception of the citizens of the cities of which direction is the city going. Is it improving or deteriorating?*

*Holding the local mayor's office accountable to those results and [holding] workshops and open forums where we present the data and initiate the discussion, construct an ideal discussion with elected officials around the trends that we've identified and would leave indicators. That's a program that we started over fifteen years ago, and we've replicated it to nine or ten cities in [our country] already. And in all the programs we seek to establish alliances. We don't do any one program by ourselves. We fund, we contribute funding but also contribute capable people from our team to help structure the program, to participate in the boards, to bring in other private and public funders and local and international donors to these programs. When experiments or programs are promising, we scale by replicating them in other regions of the country, or we use those lessons and learnings to influence public policy.*

*What we've tried to accomplish is far-reaching. We've tried to narrow it. Before we were more dispersed, we worked in health, education, in citizenship engagement, and promoting entrepreneurial development. Today we've tried to reduce it a bit, but it's still far-reaching with ambitious goals. I consider it as one of the more recognized foundations in our country not only because it's the oldest, but it's innovative in its approach and in the programs [we] partner in.*

*Our CEO organizes field trips to go visit the different programs. They're open to all family members. Not everybody makes use of them, but when people do participate, they rate the experience as highly rewarding.*

*In a rural area, [we] help farmers and members of these rural communities organize more efficiently whether it's for productive purposes in small companies or for social programs. The program is called "Focus." Our executive director organizes a visit with family members to go meet with the beneficiaries of this program and hear their experiences of why focus and support. The tools and resources that it provides these individuals have been life-changing for them and game-changing for them.*

*They went out for two days to visit these rural areas. It was so rewarding because it's an area that very few of the family members would've gone to visit on their own. Because we were able to witness firsthand the impact that the foundations in financial and human capital are having on*

*(continued)*

*the lives of individuals. We award prizes to the most innovative social initiatives in different cities. They can be for-profit or nonprofit and led by social entrepreneurs or generating well-being in their community.*

*In the annual event, we highlight the top prize winners, so that's another experience where the family sees firsthand examples of these contestants. For example, after one of those award cere- monies, we went to visit one of the winners, a garbage truck driver. He picked up garbage in the higher-income areas of the city and realized how many books were being thrown out and how scarce books were in his community. So he started picking up these books and putting them aside, and he opened up a public library inside his living room and created a public library that his neighborhood didn't have. We went to visit his house and the library in his living room, and he got computers, and there was a thriving community of kids going there to do homework and research and study after school. That was an example of one of the winners.*

*A similar situation happened in the foundation board where there is a restructuring further for professionalization of the board. As a result, several members of the third generation stepped aside and opened room for members of the fourth generation. All of the instances where there's been a significant outflow of third-generation members from the board have been a result of restructuring, of workshops that we've done to improve effectiveness of our governance in different boards. Open dialogue and structured discussions with the family have resulted in these changes.*

Over time, to sustain a family tribe of stewards of family wealth and resources, the family evolves by adopting an ever-widening circle of involvement. In order to encompass the size of their accumulated wealth and to use it wisely, generative fam- ilies develop a complex web of involvement and activities for each new generation. Only a few families decide to do this; the others, even if they have huge family for- tunes, take the path of fragmenting and dividing the wealth into smaller portions. Each household follows a different path, and the extended family wanes in signif- icance. In every generation, many generative families go their own ways. The ones that do not are able to amass a huge fortune and use it to have huge impact. Their social mission does great good in every corner of the globe.

## Taking Action in Your Own Family Enterprise

### Shared Family Engagement in Service and Philanthropy

Conversations, values, and goals may seem abstract. A generative family sees social impact as a shared, personal family activity. The family should not just think of giv- ing money to social impact and philanthropy but consider active ways that family members become engaged. There are things that the family can do together, and also impact-related activities that family members can pursue on their own and bring back and share with the family.

Here are some common ways the family does that:

**Shared Service Projects:** At a family assembly or family council meeting, the whole family can take some time to work in a service project and learn about it. After becoming involved, the family can contribute, and family members can decide to continue their service work on their own.

**Social Impact Travel:** On family vacations, the family can make sure to visit social impact projects to learn about human needs and how communities respond to them. They might visit an energy sustainability or community development project. This is an opportunity to learn and see how the family's wealth can provide impact to the world.

**Sharing Experiences:** Family members may be encouraged to be part of a service program or project as a volunteer. They can bring their experience to family meetings, and even suggest that the family contribute to them. They can also volunteer and visit projects the family supports, so that the family has direct understanding of how their efforts make a difference.

## Notes

1. Christina Karns, "When You're Grateful, Your Brain Becomes More Charitable," *The Conversation*, November 21, 2018, http://theconversation.com/when-youre-grateful-your-brain-becomes-more-charitable-105606.
2. "Women Give 2018: Transmitting Generosity to Daughters and Sons," Women's Philanthropy Institute, 2018, https://philanthropy.iupui.edu/institutes/womens-philanthropy-institute/research/women-give18.html.
3. Ron Chernow, quoted in Michael Fitzgerald, "A Tale of Two Titans: Gates and John D. Rockefeller," ZDNet, July 1, 1998, https://www.zdnet.com/article/a-tale-of-two-titans-gates-and-john-d-rockefeller/.
4. Chernow quoted in Fitzgerald.
5. In "Releasing the Potential of the Rising Generation: How Long-lasting Family Enterprises Prepare Their Successors," I talked about the challenges that members of the rising generation face in building a positive identity when coming from a family of wealth.
6. "Origin: Threshold Past and Present," Threshold Foundation, 2019, https://www.thresholdfoundation.org/origin.
7. Ibid.
8. The story of the Global Philanthropists Circle comes from Jenna Liang, a member of the staff. She is herself a member of a global philanthropic family with roots in China.
9. Sharna Goldseker and Michael Moody, *Generation Impact: How Next-Gen Donors Are Revolutionizing Giving* (Hoboken, NJ: John Wiley & Sons, 2017).
10. Veronica Dagher, "A Generational Divide at Family Foundations," *Wall Street Journal*, October 21, 2018, https://www.wsj.com/articles/a-generational-divide-at-family-foundations-1540174260?mg=prod/com-wsj.
11. Philanthropic consultant Virginia Esposito.
12. Devin Thorpe, "Businessman and Philanthropist George P. Mitchell Passes Away, Unlocked Shale Gas Revolution," MySocial Good News, July 26, 2013, https://mysocialgoodnews.com/businessman-and-philanthropist-george-p-mitchell/.
13. "Leadership," Cynthia and George Mitchell Foundation, 2019, https://cgmf.org/p/leadership.html.
14. "Programs," Cynthia and George Mitchell Foundation, 2019, https://cgmf.org/p/programs.html.

# 16

# Reflections on the Economic and Social Future of Family Enterprise

After reading a research report, the reader frequently steps back and asks, "So what?" The stories are interesting, and the commonalities are clearly drawn, but the reader, who may not own such an advanced enterprise or who advises mostly G1 and G2 families, may wonder what really can be done with the results.

I believe this project has great import to other families who want to develop and sustain their family enterprise and that it has much to offer these families' advisors. These stories also have something to say to nonfamily businesses, which also struggle to create alignment, serve social values, and adapt to continual change. This chapter shares some of these implications and also presents a review that any business family can take to heart.

## Global Context for the Future

This project began with a recognition that global family enterprise is a core social building block for civil society. In an impersonal world, the family enterprise is based on human relationships and values translated to fit the world of commerce, adding necessary humanity to the sterile landscape of the business world. Enduring family enterprises add strength, consistency, caring, and sustained productivity to the economies of every nation. Because of this, their experiences contribute a valuable alternative model to public, nonfamily enterprises.

The research documents the many contributions of these families beyond commercial success. These families have a deep impact on the community and on their loyal and long-term employees, suppliers, and customers. Business families form the economic foundation of many nations and are critical to their development. Their family nature leads them to stand for something enduring, excellent, and positive that is widely respected. They use their resources to develop and install future leaders who can continue the legacy. Business families are values-based, and their values are often as important as profits.

Generative, multigenerational families offer a model of wealth creation that diverges from the conventional model of pursuit of self-interest, focus on short-term profit, and aggressive competition. Business families play the game of private enterprise well. But they grow and remain profitable within a values-based legacy that links their success to the success of others. This model has a lot to teach to public, nonfamily businesses.

When we seek out long-lived businesses, the global terrain leads mostly to family enterprises. Public companies do not seem as resilient or adaptive. Their many unique and impactful qualities contrast favorably with those of nonfamily companies. With a family at the helm, the enterprise can sustain a vision and a set of values even as the enterprise continually takes new forms and develops new generations of leadership. A values-based enterprise can encompass not just profitability but also other social goals. Because such an enterprise looks to the long-term future and has the ability to reinvest resources, it is not uncommon for the family to consider the kind of future it desires in its community and even the world and to use the enterprise to help bring about this vision.

## Family Enterprise as a Safe Refuge from Global Instability and an Opportunity to Make a Difference

To succeed over multiple generations, a generative family enterprise must prepare, develop, and most of all, recruit members of the new generation to be responsible owner/stewards. The next generation can always decide not to continue or can continue without the capability to succeed. Generative families see their next generations deciding they want to continue (though a few family members always opt out and exit the family enterprise). What attracts members of the next generations?

Family members cite the parable of the bundle of sticks: one stick can be easily broken, but when combined into a bundle, they are almost impossible to break. This is how family members see their unified family. They decide that they can do something special together that they cannot do on their own. They see the value of the family legacy and opt to continue together. They take up the challenge.

Another reason they decide to continue, despite the many challenges they face, is that the family offers a safe haven, a refuge from global instability. Family members can be trusted because they are united by blood and have a common heritage and legacy. As nations and the global economy become unstable, the family enterprise offers a place where family members can feel comfortable, accepted, and capable of making a difference. The family develops governance and sustains its unity and alignment by retaining its unity in this global climate. The legacy, skills, and capabilities of the family make up a sustainable competitive advantage for the enterprise.

Much media attention has been focused on the dysfunctional effects of wealth on young people, who are seen as excessive consumers of luxury goods and entitled people not respecting the needs or values of others. In the interviews and observations, my research team and I saw more evidence of teaching, modeling, and passing on of values of responsibility, caring and respect for others, and contributing rather than consuming. Sustaining family wealth includes restraint in consumption as well as business growth. The ways that young family members add value, innovate, and become competent professionals in their families offer a positive view of inherited wealth.

Generative families, as this book has shown, are characterized not just as good businesses or smart portfolios of assets but as being strong avenues for investing in the development and preparation of the next, rising generation. From its resources, the family puts aside funding for many forms of education, mentoring, development, and shared learning. Family members form a community of learning, and with their intentions, they create an engine that can make it happen.

## Key Practices for Achieving Generativity

Following is a brief review of the goals and aspirations of generative family businesses and the means by which they accomplish these goals.

1. Maintain the family business as a successful enterprise:
   - Separate family from business concerns and work effectively in each area.
   - Hire professional, nonfamily leaders. This usually happens by the third generation.
   - Set strict conditions for family members who want to work in the company.
   - Reinvest in the company instead of taking short-term profits.
   - Consider the long-term future when making decisions.
   - Encourage leaders to let go and rethink what they are doing.
   - Maintain openness to new ideas and strategies.
2. Sustain the family vision and values in the business:
   - Hire professionals who understand and support the family values.
   - Form a family council or similar group to guide the leaders and maintain family values.
   - Instill the family's values in the rising generations.
   - Consider all stakeholders: family members, employees, shareholders, customers, and the community.
   - Include the business's impact on the nation and the world when making business decisions.
3. Maintain family interest in the business:
   - Maintain transparency in the operations of the business.
   - Offer opportunity and pathways to involvement for each new generation.
   - Create family camps and junior boards of directors to engage younger members.
   - Hold annual meetings where the members learn what the business has been doing and discuss issues for the future.

## Will There Be a Next Generation for Generative Families?

A family enterprise can't last forever. Though it can stem the tide of fragmentation, division, or dissolution over one or two generations, over time the extended family becomes too large to be sustained as a unified commercial entity. It then breaks up into smaller family or household units or distributes its wealth so that each individual can create his or her own future.

Do I expect that the generative families in the study will continue for further generations? My impression is that while they have been highly successful for three or more generations, many of the families in this study are not likely to survive as unified family entities for much longer than another generation. As they grow in numbers, the pressure for different paths and the sheer number of owners leads them to break down into smaller units. Individual households will exit, and businesses will be sold. There are many opportunities for the family to consider different directions, and I think the media have made a mistake to portray businesses that sell or separate as failures. A huge portfolio of businesses that offers hundreds of family descendants a legacy of values, support for personal development, a wonderful shared history, and an opportunity to make their own contribution and forge their own path cannot be seen as a failure in any way. The generative family enterprise is a choice made by some unique and dedicated families, but this choice is not right for many others.

After generations of success, each generative family has to ask itself in each generation, "Do we want to continue?" This depends on the will of the next generation to do what it takes and the strength and quality of various ventures of the family. But the key is the will of the next generation. Is there a group that has been prepared and has chosen to be ready, willing, and able to take up the reins? After several generations, it is neither a sin nor a failure to decide the answer is no.

The legacy of these families, even if it does not survive as a unified family tribe, will be seen in the values of the inheritors of these families, and their new ventures and the roles they take in the world. Beyond their family, we will see the family, before it ends as a formal entity, developing new generations of stewards and contributors. Its impact may last beyond its lifetime.

## Who Can Learn from This Research?

This research offers many insights to families in the early stages of their own businesses. The wisdom of the generative family can also be used by nonfamily businesses. While most businesses are not family-owned, it's possible to create a "family feeling" among managers and employees. This can occur when employees feel that they are treated fairly and included in the decision-making process. Family enterprises make a habit of getting input from as many family members—and other stakeholders—as possible. This custom can also be adopted by nonfamily businesses. While they may not have family members, they can get input from just as many other stakeholders.

The generative families studied here create and sustain extremely successful ventures, still profitable and growing over many generations. They have arrived at this success not by focusing on short-term profits but by maintaining a long-term outlook coupled with concern for all of the company's stakeholders. This stands in sharp contrast to the current emphasis on increasing profits and raising the price of a firm's stock by whatever means possible.

I hope that the business evolution and stories of these very rare, special, and unique family enterprises have enriched our understanding of how businesses can survive and thrive over many generations.

In conclusion, my research team and I want to thank the families that shared their experiences with us and wish them a wonderful future. They are our teachers, offering a picture of how business can be successful while also looking to the welfare of their stakeholders and the future of their communities and our planet. They help us understand how a business can take a broader view of its purpose than just financial gain. I hope that generative families can serve as a model not just for other families aspiring for longevity, but also for business in general, offering a model that challenges some of the more limited views that we see around us.

## Taking Action in Your Own Family Enterprise

In addition to reporting on the research, each chapter ended with a section applying the learnings to a developing family enterprise. The activities can be used by an advisor or family member to help the family look at how the insights of that chapter apply to their own activity.

### Family Self-Assessment

You can assess your own family enterprise (or if you are an advisor, the families you advise) and consider what you can do to lead your family down this path. Here are ten action steps that can be taken by any family that desires to thrive over generations as a generative, legacy family:

1. Your family has been successful in business and generated family wealth. Now you need to *decide as a family how you wish to use this wealth* for its highest and best purpose. You can choose to invest some of the wealth in the tasks described herein, thereby creating a generative family. This choice means that you will commit time, energy, and resources to this task and that you will involve the whole family.

2. *Become engaged, and ensure that this is not a task you outsource to others.* It is as simple as creating a family values statement or a financial literacy program for your children. These are important but only as part of a larger shared family project. This has to be done by you, working together with other family members to make it happen.

3. *Begin preparing the rising generation for the family's wealth through efforts in each individual household with their young children.* As a family, you can make it possible to talk about what it means to be privileged and how to use the special advantages that wealth brings to the family. Through your example, you can do things together that reinforce the family's values, such as providing service or living a modest lifestyle.

4. A major step forward is to *convene a cross-generational family meeting or meetings* to talk about the future path of the next generation. The first meeting should be well planned and last long enough for everyone to get to know one another, learn the history of the family and the family businesses, and talk about a vision for the future.[1]

5. Develop a *clear and explicit extended family values, vision, and mission statement.* This expresses what you want to achieve together as an extended family and sets out how you will do this. The values should be clear enough to guide behavior, and the vision and mission should be clear and concrete enough to guide decisions. The family may have values, a vision, and a mission for itself, as an extended family, as well as for its businesses and other ventures, such as the family foundation. But as each generation reaches adulthood, the values have to be reinterpreted and the vision and mission refined and updated.

6. *Inform and educate the rising generation, in stages as appropriate, about the history, nature, and structure of the various family enterprises.* Members of the rising generation should learn about the family trusts, businesses, philanthropic ventures, and most important, their obligations and responsibilities to the family, if they choose to participate actively.

7. *Support each individual to actively develop a life plan for personal and career development.* For a young person emerging from a wealthy family, this can be a difficult task. The family should recognize that this is not easy for some and offer support and resources when these young people are growing to adulthood to launch themselves and also to decide whether they want to become actively involved with the family in various roles.

8. *Convene the members of the rising generation and give them the opportunity to decide what they want for the future and in what way they want to be involved in the family enterprise.* They should get to know each other and make an active choice to be family partners and work together.

9. *Develop an active task force and organization to develop programs for the education and development of the next generation, with adequate family funding.* This task force or committee is usually integrated with a family council and other family governance activities.

10. *Set clear goals and criteria for the next generation, and assess annually whether they are being met.* Knowing what people think helps family members anticipate and talk about differences, rather than keeping those potential conflicts underground. It also helps you assess how you are moving toward shared goals.

## Note

1. Dennis Jaffe and Stacy Allred, *Talking It Through: A Guide to Conducting Effective Multi-generational Family Meetings About Business and Wealth* (New York: Merrill Lynch/Bank of America Corporation, 2014).

# Tools for Families (and Advisors)

Here are some practical tools that we have developed to help families as they enter the journey to become generative families. They each help a family to learn about itself and begin a conversation about becoming a generative family. They can be used by the family on its own, or with an advisor.

## Defining Personal, Family, and Business Values:

The Values Edge Process employs Values Cards as a tool to help an individual, couple, family, or team to define their Personal Values Pyramid, and then create together a Family or Team Values Statement. It utilizes a model of seven values categories—*Mastery, Self-Expression, Tradition, Relationship, Inner Development, Lifestyle,* and *Social*—to help individuals and families explore their values in relation to their personal motivations and life choices. The value categories are color coded to identify them easily. (See Figure A.1.)

Each kit includes decks of values cards, along with colored stickers for transferring values to a Display Card that preserves each person's Values Pyramid in a visible format that can be worn as a name card. By sharing personal values arranged in colorful pyramids, people in a family or a work team can easily experience their similarities and differences. It includes a Facilitators' Manual to guide a Values

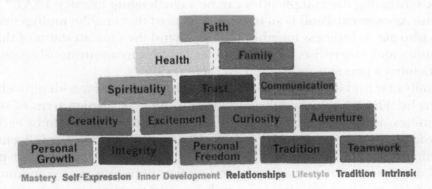

**Figure A.1  Sample Personal Values Pyramid.**

**Figure A.2   The full array.**

Discovery Session, which might include exploring personal values, and also defining team or family values.

The use of these cards adds concreteness and a well-grounded model to explore differences and similarities in their personal values and then integrate them into a shared team or family values statement. They can compare legacy and current values, or current and aspired future values, and develop an Action Plan as an individual, family, or work team. (See Figure A.2.) (For ordering information contact Dennis Jaffe, dfaffe@dennisjaffe.com.)

## Family Enterprise Assessment Tool (FEAT®)

For families that own a business or other shared investments across multiple generations, navigating the complexities can be a challenging journey. **FEAT® (Family Enterprise Assessment Tool)** is an online assessment that enables multigenerational families who are in business together to understand the current status of their family dynamics and enterprise. FEAT® enables families to anonymously gather each family member's perceptions with measurable results.

A family may find it difficult to talk about these issues, or even identify where the problems lie. FEAT® helps families understand their particular areas of strength, opportunities, and differences. FEAT® is a 50-question survey, taken by each member of a family, that provides feedback on 10 areas of successful family enterprise functioning, as a family and as a family enterprise. Each family report provides detailed information that can support families in productive communication, building trust, and creating strategies, policies, and practices to work effectively as a cross-generational team. (See Figure A.3.)

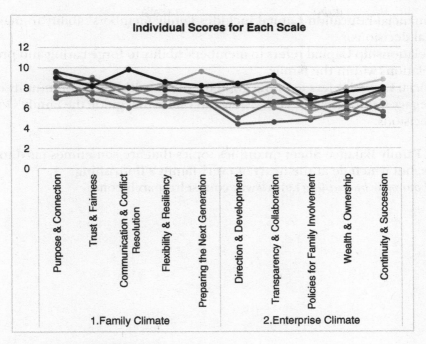

**Figure A.3   Sample of FEAT® in action.**

## KEY FEATURES

- User friendly, 24/7 online access for use on desktop or mobile devices
- 25 statements on family dynamics and 25 on family enterprise providing measurable results
- Compares perceptions of family members in 10 key areas of competency ranging from governance to preparing the next generation, to wealth and ownership
- Compares across family demographics such as gender, blood versus marriage, generation, ownership, and family branch
- Available for purchase by an independent family or a trusted family advisor

This tool was developed in partnership with Caroline Bailey of Premier Growth for more information, visit premiergrowth.com or email info@premiergrowth.com.

## Family Balance Sheet: Measuring Capital of the Family Enterprise

*The Family Balance Sheet*™ is an online tool to quantify a family's human, financial-educational, relationship, social, and legacy capitals. Most families focus on preserving and growing only financial capital. The failure to measure and grow the five qualitative capitals is the principal cause for the failure of family flourishing.

- Human Capital refers to family members' ability to develop character and skills.

- Financial-Education Capital includes family members' ability to make financial decisions.
- Relationship Capital refers to members' ability to forge caring and productive relations within the family.
- Social Capital refers to doing good for others within the community or world.
- Legacy Capital includes the vision and values that guide the family's long-term decisions.

The Family Balance Sheet quantifies topics that are sometimes hard to express in words, but which lie at the heart of every family's flourishing.

*Find out more by emailing* keith@wisecounselresearch.com.

# About the Author

For over 40 years, Dr. Dennis Jaffe has been one of the leading architects in the field of family enterprise consulting. As both an organizational consultant and clinical psychologist, he helps multigenerational families to develop governance practices that build the capability of next generation leadership and ensure ongoing capability of financial organizations and family offices to serve their family clients.

His work with families helps inform his training of financial advisors and wealth managers about the knowledge and skills needed to serve their client families. He is an acclaimed speaker and workshop leader in programs for business families and financial service firms.

Dennis lives in San Francisco with his wife, Cynthia Scott. He has three grown sons, and several grandchildren. His website is www.dennisjaffe.com, and he can be reached at djaffe@dennisjaffe.com.

Dennis is available to give talks and workshops based on this research.

## Publications and Tools

Dennis's books guide business families in working together to build a great family and a thriving set of family enterprises. They include:

- *Cross Cultures: How Global Families Negotiate Change Across Generations* (co-authored with James Grubman)
- *Stewardship of Your Family Enterprise: Developing Responsible Leadership Across Generations*
- *Working with the Ones You Love*

He is the creator of several widely used tools to help families learn about themselves and constructively grow across generations. The Values Edge uses a deck of cards to help individuals and families create personal and organizational values pyramids. The online Family Enterprise Assessment Tool (FEAT) enables multigenerational business families to understand the current status of their family dynamics and enterprise and explore their areas of difference.

## Current Activities

This book reports on a six-year project investigating successful, global hundred-year-old family enterprises. A member of Wise Counsel Research Associates, Dennis is also a Family Business Scholar at the Smith Family Business Program at Cornell University, a faculty advisor at the Ultra High New Worth Institute, a regular contributor to Forbes Leadership channel, reporting on family cross-generational family business and wealth, and a professional member of STEP (Society for Trust and Estate Planners).

He has been an active member of the Family Firm Institute since its inception, presenting at annual conferences, serving on the board, designing and delivering educational courses in their GEN program, and writing for the *Family Business Review*. In 2017 Dennis was recognized by the Family Firm Institute for his international work, and in 2004, received the prestigious Richard Beckhard Award for his contributions to professional practice.

## Previous Activities

For 35 years, Dennis was professor of Organizational Systems and Psychology at Saybrook University in San Francisco, where he is now professor emeritus. He received his BA in Philosophy, MA in Management, and PhD in Sociology from Yale University.

His global insights have led to teaching or consulting engagements at Hult University in Dubai, the Pacific Asia chapter of Family Business Network, and the Advisory Board of Chinese University of Hong Kong. He is part of the Polaris team working with the Family Business Network to create a roadmap for family and business sustainability.

He was Thinker in Residence in 2007 for South Australia, helping the region design a strategic plan for the future of Australian entrepreneurial and family businesses. He was the researcher for the JP Morgan 2005 study of best practices of multigenerational families, and a more recent study of succession in Asian families. In 2010 he was a visiting professor at the undergraduate family business program of Stetson University.

Dennis has been a frequent contributor to periodicals such as *Family Business* magazine, *Journal of Financial Planning, Private Wealth, Journal of Wealth Management,* and *Worth* magazine. His work has been featured in the *New York Times, Inc., NPR Marketplace, Entrepreneur, Time,* and the *Wall Street Journal,* and he was profiled in *People* magazine. In 2005 he received the Editor's Choice Award from the *Journal of Financial Planning* for his article on family business strategic planning.

Active in nonprofit governance, he served on the boards of the World Business Academy, Saybrook University, and the Center for Mind-Body Medicine.

## Pioneering Work in Values-Based Organizations and Holistic Health

As a founder and contributor to the field of organizational transformation and change leadership, Dennis co-authored a dozen influential management books, including *Getting Your Organization to Change, Rekindling Commitment,* and *Take this Job and Love It!* As founder of Changeworks Global, he guided organizations and family businesses to long-term change by unleashing the power of their employees. His research on the governance of start-up companies, After the Term Sheet, is an important contribution to the field of entrepreneurship. He is co-creator of

Mastering the Transition Curve, StressMap, and other tools that support personal and organizational success.

For three years, Dennis was co-editor of the *Inner Edge,* a magazine focused on spirituality in business. He was deputy director for research at the MacArthur Foundation–sponsored Healthy Companies Network from 1992 to 1995. As co-founder of the web firm MemeWorks, he pioneered online executive development tools. The video "Managing People through Change" was voted one of the Best Products of 1991 by Human Resource Executive. In the 1970s, his holistic health books, *From Burnout to Balance* (retitled and reissued as *Self-Renewal*) and *Healing from Within,* were each honored with the Medical Self-Care Book Award. He was co-author of the international bestseller *TM: Discovering Inner Energy and Overcoming Stress.*

# About the Research Team

**Peter Begalla** is conference chairman for *Family Business* magazine and *Directors & Boards* magazine; a consultant to multigenerational family enterprises; and a past lecturer in Family Business at Stetson University. As conference chairman, he brings together multigenerational family enterprises so they can share their stories, learn from one another, and develop practices that will sustain the family enterprise for generations. Other conferences include Private Company Governance Summit, Family Business Generational Wealth, and Character of the Corporation.

As a past lecturer in Family Business at Stetson University for over thirteen years, Peter helped hundreds of college-aged students establish a strong knowledge and skill set to successfully navigate the complex world of family enterprises. Classes included "Managerial Issues in Family Business: Harnessing the Strategic Value of Family" and "Personal and Professional Leadership Development in the Family Business." As a consultant Peter works directly with family enterprises on family governance, leadership succession, family dynamics, and next-gen development. Each engagement is tailored to the needs of the family and often includes multiple approaches such as strategic planning, meeting facilitation, multistep consultations, and custom workshops.

**Jane Flanagan** has spent her career working with and learning from family leaders and family office executives. She has interviewed hundreds of families to document best practices, ranging from family communication and strategies for engaging the rising generation to family office service delivery and compensation. She has helped families decide whether it makes sense to have a family office and has consulted with others to evaluate and streamline existing operations. As Director of Family Office Consulting at Northern Trust, she partners with an experienced team of subject matter experts to educate families about their options and help them find their best way forward. Prior to joining Northern Trust in 2019, Jane was a managing director with Family Office Exchange for 26 years.

**James Grubman, PhD,** is a consultant to multigenerational families and their advisors about the issues that arise around wealth. He helps families establish healthy patterns of communication, governance, estate planning, and parenting for succeeding generations. He is the author of the renowned book *Strangers in Paradise: How Families Adapt to Wealth Across Generations,* and co-author (with Dennis T. Jaffe) of *Cross Cultures: How Global Families Navigate Change Across Generations.* He has been published and quoted extensively by the *Wall Street Journal,* the *New York Times,* CNBC, and other media, including Malcolm Gladwell's 2013 book, *David and Goliath.* Jim holds Fellow status in the Family Firm Institute and the Purposeful Planning Institute, and he is one of only a handful of psychologists in the 20,000-member STEP organization. His global consulting practice, Family Wealth Consulting, is based in Massachusetts.

**Charlotte E. Lamp, PhD,** is a family business principal and consultant with Rockwood consulting. She is a third-generation shareholder of Port Blakely Companies and fellow of the Family Firm Institute. Presently, she is serving a fourth term on her family's council, providing expertise in governance and education. In addition, she consults with individual business families and provides captivating conference presentations.

**Isabelle Lescent-Giles, PhD,** is Professor of Strategy and Family Business at Hult International Business School, San Francisco campus. Her research, consulting practice, and teaching focus on helping current and future leaders of large family businesses adapt, innovate, and launch new business ventures, building upon their unique set of skills, values, history, and social capital.

She started her career in consulting at McKinsey. She continued to work closely with industry leaders, most notably as part of the IHEE think-tank on French competitiveness, and as a working group leader and researcher for the Conference Board in New York. Since 2005, she has worked as a senior consultant for the Winthrop Group, a boutique consulting firm that advises CEOs and top managers on transitions, change management, and strategic decision-making, using historical narratives to frame, define, and communicate change. She has taught at Oxford University, the Sorbonne, NYU's Stern School of Business, and the University of San Francisco. She has a PhD in economic history from the University of Paris–Sorbonne and is an alumni of France's Ecole Normale Supérieure (Ulm-Sèvres) and the Institut Universitaire de France. Isabelle lives in San Francisco with her tricultural family. You can contact her at isabelle.lescent.giles@faculty.hult.edu.

**Joshua Nacht, PhD,** is a consultant with the Family Business Consulting Group and works with multigenerational business families to leverage their strengths by focusing on effective governance, communication, and transitions. In 2015, Joshua earned a PhD in Organizational Systems, and his doctoral research, "The Role of the Family Champion," won the Best Dissertation Award from the Family Firm Institute in 2016. His co-authored book *Family Champions and Champion Families* explores the value of family leaders in creating enduring business family success. Joshua lives in Lyons, Colorado, where he enjoys cooking, listening to music, mountain biking, and nature excursions with his children. He can be contacted at nacht@thefbcg.com.

**Susan Massenzio, PhD,** is co-president of Wise Counsel Research. She is a psychologist with extensive experience consulting to senior executives and leadership teams of Fortune 500 financial services firms. Susan is co-author of *Cycle of the Gift, Voice of the Rising Generation,* and *Complete Family Wealth* (all published by Wiley). She formerly served as a senior vice president at Wells Fargo and at John Hancock, and a professor and program director at Northeastern University. Susan holds a BA in Sociology from Simmons College and a PhD in Clinical Psychology from Northwestern University.

**Jamie Traeger-Muney, PhD,** is the founder of the Wealth Legacy Group. She specializes in the emotional impact of wealth on inheritors, women, and multigenerational families. She works with her clients to concretize their values, develop a vision for their future, and create sound governance structures.

She has revolutionized the conversation of wealth and worth by providing an opportunity to openly discuss the roles money plays in their lives, enabling them to be passionately engaged in the world and to lead a rich life. Jamie's personal experience as a second-generation owner of a family business and board member of her family foundation, combined with her theoretical and practical expertise in wealth psychology, has given her a unique sensitivity to issues surrounding the intergenerational family dynamics of affluence.

**Keith Whitaker, PhD,** is co-president of Wise Counsel Research. He has consulted for many years with leaders of enterprising families and is co-author of *Cycle of the Gift, Voice of the Rising Generation, Family Trusts, Complete Family Wealth,* and *Wealth of Wisdom: The Top 50 Questions Wealthy Families Ask* (all published by Wiley), in addition to many articles and reviews. Keith formerly served as a managing director at Wells Fargo and an adjunct assistant professor of philosophy at Boston College. He holds a BA in Classics and Philosophy from Boston University and a PhD in Social Thought from the University of Chicago. *Family Wealth Report* named Keith the 2015 "outstanding contributor to wealth management thought-leadership."

# About Wise Counsel Research Associates

Wise Counsel Research Associates (WCRA) is a think-tank and consultancy devoted to helping leaders of families and businesses find trusted, strategic advice.

Our associates are leaders within the fields of family wealth and family business. They include James (Jay) Hughes, Dennis Jaffe, Susan Massenzio, Keith Whitaker, Hartley Goldstone, Christian Stewart, Mary Duke, Peter Evans, Mariann Mihialidis, and Scott McLennan.

We help families with wealth communicate about their planning, make decisions together, and develop the rising generation. With philanthropies, we consult on designing foundations, developing clear missions, and balancing family and philanthropic goals. We also consult with corporations on organizational design, leadership development, and team engagement.

Research is the foundation of our work. We study giving within families, the best practices of successful family businesses, the impact of wealth on women, and the role of advisors to enterprising families. We also regularly write, speak, and offer workshops on these and related topics.

Some of our featured books include:

- 100-Year Family Enterprise Research, six working papers (various years, Amazon)
- *Wealth of Wisdom: The Top 50 Questions that Wealthy Families Ask,* edited by McCullough and Whitaker (Wiley, 2018)
- *Complete Family Wealth,* Hughes, Massenzio, and Whitaker (Wiley, 2017)
- *Family Trusts: A Guide for Beneficiaries, Trustees, Trust Creators, and Trust Protectors,* Hughes, Goldstone, and Whitaker (Wiley, 2015)
- *Voice of the Rising Generation,* Hughes, Massenzio, and Whitaker (Wiley, 2014)
- *Cycle of the Gift,* Hughes, Massenzio, and Whitaker (Wiley, 2013)

Our associates have also developed and administer the Family Balance Sheet™, an online tool to quantify a family's qualitative capital—that is, its human, financial-educational, relationship, social, and legacy capitals. Most families focus on preserving and growing only financial capital. The failure to measure and grow the five qualitative capitals is the principal cause for the failure of family flourishing. We use the Family Balance Sheet to provide families with a sense of their existing strengths, their areas of opportunity for growth, and as a benchmark to measure that growth over time.

# Acknowledgments

This research project has drawn on the energy and thinking of so many people who have been so free in sharing and supporting this project.

First of all, I want to thank the research team, Peter Begalla, Jane Flanagan, James Grubman, Charlotte Lamp, Isabelle Lescent-Giles, Susan Massenzio, Joshua Nacht, Jamie Traeger-Muney, and Keith Whitaker. In addition to taking on a share of the interviewing, each of them has contributed ideas and help in so many ways.

- Keith is the steward of Wise Counsel Research, our group home, and editor and sounding board for many of the ideas developed here.
- Charlotte is the keeper of the demographic data, and, with the help of Jane Flanagan, prepared all the data charts, which meant going through all of the interviews.
- Isabelle and Jamie are partners and co-authors of the chapters on social impact and philanthropy, and also helped develop ideas in other parts of the project.
- Peter has been an incredible support in framing the issues and, through *Family Business* magazine and their Transitions conference, has helped me link to the community of families who are at or on their way to becoming generative families.
- Joshua did the first research into family champions and helped me learn how innovation could come as much from younger generations as older ones.
- Janet Schatzman did the vivid and kinetic graphic illustrations.
- Linda Tate served as editor.
- Susan Eckstrom provided administrative support throughout the project.

Second, thank you to the Merrill Center for Family Wealth, Merrill Family Offices Services, and the Bank of America Private Bank, for their support of the working papers that came from this research, and of the overall project. I would like to express particular gratitude to the Merrill Center for Family Wealth's leaders Stacy Allred, Matt Wesley, and Valerie Galinskaya, who provided not only financial capital, but every other kind of capital and support for the development of the values-based perspective that is the core of this research. They also served as co-authors of separate papers inspired by their research and their deep experience advising families of significant wealth.

Third, thank you to the small group of researchers and advisors who make up Wise Counsel Research. This is a think-tank in the deepest sense: colleagues who share a passion about families of wealth and a willingness to inquire and explore the environment to understand their needs. They offered a home for this project and a space where the ideas can be proposed, explored, and checked out.

Some special people have brightened many of my days, including:

- Jay Hughes is the spirit that underlies this project, an endless fountain of ideas and insights that form the cornerstone of this project.
- James Grubman is my alter-ego, my mentor, and friend, whose thinking has helped to shape and develop my ideas about the role of generative families, and my valued colleague and co-author for many of the ideas that emerge here.
- Christian Stewart has read, challenged, and helped to develop many of the concepts of governance and family stewardship.

Other important people to me who have influenced my thinking (I'm sure that I have left some out) include Laurent Roux, Jeremy Cheng, Kirby Rosplock, Mike Cole, Winnie Peng, Roger King, Kevin Au, Patricia Angus, Michael Preston, Richard and Lea Boyce, Babetta von Albertini, Annie Koh, David Bork, Joanie Bronnan Joe Field, Dirk Junge, and Fredda Herz Brown.

The first sponsors of this project included the Family Business Network, who gave me access to a group of generative families for the first phase of the research and welcomed me into the Polaris Initiative that helped me see up front the innovative and values-based work of global families.

FOX, the Family Office Exchange, and Sara Hamilton and Jane Flanagan, were the other initial sponsors, who provided access to families and much help in seeing how family businesses evolved over generations into family offices and other new ventures.

I have been a member of the Family Firm Institute since they began, and they offer a place to present and share ideas with others in this field, gathering old and new practitioners into a global community. The vision and continual leadership of Judy Green is much appreciated.

Also, the Purposeful Planning Institute, under John A. Warnick's leadership, has created a wonderful space online and in person for sharing ideas and learning. The Collaboration for Family Flourishing, and STEP, a global network of trust and estate professionals, also offered platforms to develop, write about, and present ideas. *The International Journal of Family Offices,* under the leadership of Barbara Hauser, also offered a learning group of editorial advisors and a platform to share important new ideas.

# Index